Pelican Books

Advisory Editor for Linguistics: David Crystal

Semantics

Geoffrey Leech was born in Gloucester in 1936 and educated
at Tewkesbury Grammar School and University College,
London, where he read English. From 1962 to 1969, when
he received his Ph.D., he was Assistant Lecturer, then Lecturer
in English at University College, London. Since 1969 he has
been at the University of Lancaster. He
studied linguistics at the Massachusetts Institute of
Technology in 1964–5 as a Harkness Fellow, and in 1972 was
Visiting Professor at Brown University, Providence, Rhode
Island. He has previously published *English in Advertising*
(1966), *A Linguistic Guide to English Poetry* (1969), *Meaning
and the English Verb* (1971), and has co-authored, with
Randolph Quirk, Sidney Greenbaum and Jan Svartvik, *A
Grammar of Contemporary English* (1972). He is now
Professor of Linguistics and Modern English Language at the
University of Lancaster. He is married, with two children.

Semantics

Geoffrey Leech

Penguin Books

Penguin Books Ltd, Harmondsworth,
Middlesex, England
Penguin Books Inc., 7110 Ambassador Road,
Baltimore, Maryland 21207, U.S.A.
Penguin Books Australia Ltd, Ringwood,
Victoria, Australia
Penguin Books Canada Ltd, 41 Steelcase Road West,
Markham, Ontario, Canada
Penguin Books (N.Z.) Ltd, 182–190 Wairau Road,
Auckland 10, New Zealand

First published 1974
Reprinted 1975

Copyright © Geoffrey Leech, 1974

Made and printed in Great Britain by
Hazell Watson & Viney Ltd.
Aylesbury, Bucks
Set in Monotype Times

Contents

Acknowledgements

As a writer on semantics has to try to play many parts (not only linguist, but philosopher, anthropologist, psychologist, even perhaps social reformer and literary critic), I am more than ordinarily grateful to those who have sustained me in these various adopted roles by their help, ideas, and specialist advice. They include Michael Breen (on language and concept formation), David Lightfoot (on 'anaphoric islands'), Floyd Lounsbury (on kinship semantics), Colin Lyas (on philosophy and linguistics), and Humphrey Prideaux (for a layman's point of view).

This book reached a final stage during a semester I spent as Visiting Professor at Brown University. It owes a great deal to my colleagues in the English language field at Lancaster for making the visit possible; to the Linguistics Department at Brown for giving me a pleasant and stimulating semester with free time for writing, and to Donald Freeman for deputizing for me at Lancaster.

David Crystal, the editor of the Penguin linguistics series, deserves my warm thanks for guidance, patience, and forbearance.

Symbols

The following symbolic conventions (mostly confined to the later chapters of the book) are listed for convenience:

* (asterisk) before an utterance, statement, etc. indicates that it is unacceptable or ill-formed

'boy' (etc.) – a cited expression in single quotation marks indicates a meaning rather than a form (p. 102)

boy (etc.) – a cited expression in italics indicates a form rather than a meaning

the (etc.) – a word in bold-face type indicates a formator, or 'logical' feature of meaning (pp. 161–4)

$\langle PN \rangle$ = downgraded predication (pp. 149–54)

(PN) = embedded predication (pp. 146–9)

A = argument (p. 128)

P = predicate (p. 128)

Introduction

Why study semantics? Semantics (as the study of meaning) is central to the study of communication; and as communication becomes more and more a crucial factor in social organization, the need to understand it becomes more and more pressing. Semantics is also at the centre of the study of the human mind – thought processes, cognition, conceptualization – all these are intricately bound up with the way in which we classify and convey our experience of the world through language.

Because it is, in these two ways, a focal point in man's study of man, semantics has been the meeting place of various crosscurrents of thinking, and various disciplines of study. Philosophy, psychology, and linguistics all claim a deep interest in the subject. But their interests are diverse because of their different starting points: psychology the understanding of the mind; linguistics the understanding of language and languages; philosophy the understanding of how we know what we know, of the rules of right thinking, and the evaluation of truth and falsehood. Semantics has often seemed baffling because there are many different approaches to it, and the ways in which they are related to one another are rarely clear, even to writers on the subject. It has also seemed baffling because it is 'cognition turning in upon itself': an activity which may seem to have much in common with a dog chasing its own tail.

For these reasons, or simply because it is a fascinating subject, semantics has provided material for many books. There have, indeed, been a number of other books with the same title as this present one. But this does not mean that each new book venturing on the subject is a waste of time, or a duplication of previous effort. Each new book is its author's unique attempt to shed new light on a subject which always threatens to return to primeval darkness, and such is the diversity of approaches that one may read two books on semantics, and find scarcely anything in common between them.

No one author can attempt an overall survey of the field of semantics – or at least, if he does, he will end up with a superficial compendium of 'what others have thought' about meaning. The only sensible course is to beat one's own path through the wilderness, and not to pay more heed than is prudent to what lies on either side. This is the spirit in which I write this book. I see semantics as one branch of linguistics, which is the study of language: as an area of study parallel to, and interacting with, those of syntax and phonology, which deal respectively with the formal patterns of language, and the way in which these are translated into sound. While syntax and phonology study the structure of expressive possibilities in language, semantics studies the meanings that can be expressed. It may convincingly be claimed that viewing semantics as a component discipline of linguistics is the most fruitful and exciting point of departure at the present time. Twenty years ago, linguistics, although a fast developing discipline in other directions, had all but abandoned semantics to the philosopher and the anthropologist. In the last ten years, however, there has been a swing away from a view of semantics as a messy, largely unstructured intellectual no-man's-land on the fringes of linguistics, and a tendency to accord to it a more and more central position in linguistic studies – a position which, at least in my view, it holds as of right. The concentration of intellectual effort in semantics has possibly by now reached its zenith; and it has already led to new illumination comparable to, if not greater than, that kindled by linguistic philosophers such as Wittgenstein and Carnap in the 1920s and 1930s.

Linguistics as the scientific study of language has brought to the subject of semantics a certain degree of analytic rigour combined with a view of the study of meaning as an integrated component within the total theory of how language works. To study the 'content' side of language without reference to the 'expression' side ultimately makes no more sense than to study the 'expression' side without the 'content' – something linguists have tried, and found barren.

The strength of the integrated view is that it makes possible a transfer to semantics of techniques of analysis which have proved successful with other aspects of language. But the extension of the horizon of semantics in one direction has limited it in another direction: the precise analytic methods developed in the study of grammar and phonology only apply to that part of meaning which is traditionally called 'conceptual' or 'cognitive'; other parts, which may be lumped together as 'connotative' or 'associative' meaning, have been somewhat neglected. One of my aims will be to correct this imbalance.

This book falls into two parts, between which Chapter 5 ('Is Semantics a Science?') acts as a bridge. The first four chapters form a 'pretheoretical' introduction in which I set out to give a general orientation to the subject, by trying to steer a careful course between the many misleading attitudes and approaches to which semantics is prone, and exploring the issues of communication and meaning which bring semantics into closest contact with the problems of modern life. Attention is given to questions such as the conceptual organization of the human mind (Chapter 3) and the 'strategic semantics' of advertising and propaganda (Chapter 4).

From Chapter 6 to the end, the book is devoted to the central, cognitive aspect of meaning, and presents a semantic theory on principles which have developed within modern linguistics. In this latter section of the book I consider the details of how the semantic structure of a language is organized, and inquire into such questions as 'How does one provide an exact definition of a given word?' 'How does one write rules to explain how such-and-such a sequence of phonetic symbols has such-and-such a meaning?' This theoretical study of meaning can be intellectually very exciting, but pursued to the extreme precision of mathematical formulation, it becomes highly complex and abstract. All I can do in an introductory book of this kind is to provide an idea of the types of analysis involved, and of the reasons which lead one to adopt one solution rather than another to problems of semantic description.

It is a considerable jump from the introductory discussion of human communication to the rarified field of theoretical semantics, and persevering readers who reach the later chapters will notice something of 'a change of gear' and an increase of difficulty, particularly in Chapters 7 and 11 to 14. There may well be some people who will blame me for trying to incorporate two such disparate types of investigation in the same book. But I believe this attempt can be justified: general issues of communication can only be fully appreciated in the context of a precise understanding of the conceptual/logical structure of language (there are many points in Chapters 1 to 4 at which I rely on more detailed explanations later in the book); conversely, theoretical semantics can easily lose contact with practical problems of communication, and so can suffer from a somewhat distorted, etiolated view of the subject it is meant to be studying (the formal logics of philosophers provide instances of this). In other words, I firmly believe that there is much to be gained from trying to bring 'pure' and 'applied' semantics together.

There is a school of thought – that which goes under the banner of 'general semantics' – that holds that the study of communicative processes can be a powerful force for good in the resolution of human conflict, whether on an individual, local, or international scale. Although I would hesitate to make such positive claims as this group (which tends, in my view, to take a rather naïve view of the causes of conflict), it must be true that the more we understand the cognitive and communicative structures of language, the better we are able to recognize and control the 'pathological' or destructive elements in communication, and the better we are able to appreciate and to foster the forces that make for concord.

This said, it has to be conceded that the primary appeal of semantics is an intellectual one, akin to that of mathematics or of any pure science. Only after seeking understanding for understanding's sake can one acquire the wisdom which consists in using that understanding for good ends.

1. Meanings of Meaning

Ogen Richards ←
Bloomfields

Ogen and Richards and After

The word 'meaning' and its corresponding verb 'to mean' are among the most eminently discussable terms in the English language, and semanticists have often seemed to spend an immoderate amount of time puzzling out the 'meanings of *meaning*' as a supposedly necessary preliminary to the study of their subject. Perhaps the best-known book ever written on semantics, that which C. K. Ogden and I. A. Richards published in 1923, had the very title *The Meaning of Meaning*, and contained, on pp. 186–7, a list of as many as twenty-two definitions of the word, taking different non-theoretical or theoretical starting points. Here, for interest's sake, is a selection of the meanings given:

> an intrinsic property
> the other words annexed to a word in the dictionary
> the connotation of a word
> the place of anything in a system
> the practical consequences of a thing in our future experience
> that to which the user of a symbol actually refers
> that to which the user of a symbol ought to be referring
> that to which the user of a symbol believes himself to be referring
> that to which the interpreter of a symbol
>   (a) refers
>   (b) believes himself to be referring
>   (c) believes the user to be referring.

Ogden and Richards, presenting this list, tried to show how confusion and misunderstanding come about because of lack of agreement about such basic terms as *meaning*. But they looked forward to a day when (as a result of the education of the public through their book and by other channels) 'the Influence of Language upon

Thought is understood, and the Phantoms due to linguistic mis-
conception have been removed'; from here, the way would be
open, they felt, 'to more fruitful methods of Interpretation and to
an Art of Conversation by which the communicants can enjoy
something more than the customary stones and scorpions'.

The fascinating glimpse of a utopia of pure, polite conversation
given us by Ogden and Richards is in part their own peculiar view of
things, but other semanticists (notably those of the General Semantics movement inaugurated by Korzybski's *Science and Sanity* in
1933) have also seen the solution of problems of meaning, thought,
and communication as a potential cure-all for the ills of modern
society. Other investigators have also, like Ogden and Richards,
looked towards science for the clarification of semantic concepts.
Ogden and Richards, in 1923, felt confident enough in the progress of science to assert:

> During the last few years advances in biology, and the psychological
> investigation of memory and heredity, have placed the 'meaning' of
> signs in general beyond doubt, and it is here shown that thought and
> language are to be treated in the same manner. (p. 249)

Ten years later, Bloomfield, in *Language* (1933), the most influential book on language to be published between the wars,
similarly hitched semantics to the onward march of science, but
with a slightly different emphasis. It was not the scientific study of
mental phenomena (thought and symbolization) that he saw as
providing the semanticist's answers, but the scientific definition of
everything to which language may refer:

> We can define the meaning of a speech-form accurately when this
> meaning has to do with some matter of which we possess scientific
> knowledge. We can define the names of minerals, for example, in terms
> of chemistry and mineralogy, as when we say that the ordinary meaning
> of the English word *salt* is 'sodium chloride (NaCl)', and we can define
> the names of plants or animals by means of the technical terms of botany
> or zoology, but we have no precise way of defining words like *love* or
> *hate*, which concern situations that have not been accurately classified –
> and these latter are in the great majority. (*Language*, p. 139)

Bloomfield, then, was less sanguine about the wonders of science
than Ogden and Richards. His conclusion, not surprisingly,

sounded a pessimistic note, which turned out to be the virtual death-knell of semantics in the U.S.A. for the next twenty years: 'The statement of meanings is therefore the weak point in language-study, and will remain so until human knowledge advances very far beyond its present state.' (p. 140).

Taken to its logical terminus, Bloomfield's argument implies a vision of an eventual period when everything would be capable of authoritative scientific definition, or in simpler words, when every-thing there was to be known would be known about everything – something even more illusory than Ogden's and Richards's idyll of a conversational paradise. Bloomfield was writing at a time when there was interest in the concept of 'unified science' – that is, in the idea that all sciences, from physics to psychology, could be cemented together into one vast monolith of knowledge – but even allowing for this, his picture of the semanticist waiting patiently for the accumulation and solidification of the totality of human knowledge relies on what in hindsight is a naïve view of the nature of science. Three flaws were latent in Bloomfield's approach.

Firstly, at any given time, there are usually competing scientific accounts of the same phenomenon. Which of them do we choose for our definition?

In the second place, science does not progress in the manner of a tub filling up with water – it progresses by a continuing process of revision and clarification, leading to greater clarity and depth of understanding. Since scientific statements are by nature provi-sional, it is difficult to foresee a time when everyone would be suf-ficiently confident that no further significant reformulations would be forthcoming to be able to start safely defining words like *love* and *hate*.

Thirdly, a definition in terms of a scientific formula, such as *salt* = NaCl, simply exchanges one set of linguistic symbols for another, and so postpones the task of semantic explication one step further. Assuming that scientific language, like everyday language, has meaning, we are faced with the problem of defining the meaning of 'NaCl'; and if we could replace this with a more precise or informative scientific formula, the same problem would arise with that, and so on *ad infinitum*. In other words, Bloomfield's recipe for discovering meaning leads into a path of infinite regression; it turns out to be a dead end not only on practical but on logical grounds.

The problems of Ogden's and Richards's and Bloomfield's approaches to meaning arise mainly from the determination to explain semantics in terms of other scientific disciplines. One may argue that much of the apparent ambiguity of the term *meaning*, which bothered Ogden and Richards, has the same source. Certainly most of the twenty-two definitions given by them (as the examples on p. 1 above show) are the authors' wording of technical definitions of philosophers, psychologists, philologists, literary critics, and other specialists; and much of the conflict between these definitions is explicable in terms of each specialist's need or desire to tailor the study of meaning to the requirements of his own field. So a philosopher may define meaning, for his purposes, in terms of truth and falsehood; a behaviourist psychologist in terms of stimulus and response; a literary critic in terms of the reader's response; and so on. Naturally enough, their definitions, springing from diverse frames of reference, will have little in common.

While admitting that study in related fields could provide insight for the student of semantics, many people will wonder why semantics need be considered dependent, in this way, on extrinsic considerations. In fact, as soon as we start to treat semantics as deserving its own frame of reference instead of having to borrow one from elsewhere, we dispel many of the difficulties that have beset its development in the past fifty years. An autonomous discipline begins not with answers, but with questions. We might say that the whole point of setting up a theory of semantics is to provide a 'definition' of *meaning* – that is, a systematic account of the nature of meaning. To demand a definition of *meaning* before we started discussing the subject would simply be to insist on treating certain other concepts, e.g. stimulus and response, as in some sense more basic and more important. A physicist does not have to define notions like 'time', 'heat', 'colour', 'atom' before he starts investigating their properties. Rather, definitions, if they are needed, emerge from the study itself.

Once this commonplace is accepted, the question of how to define *meaning*, which so preoccupied Ogden and Richards, is seen in its true colour as a red herring.

A Linguistic Starting Point for Semantics

So far I have been trying to clear the ground, by arguing that the study of meaning should be free from subservience to other disciplines. This leads naturally to the challenge: 'How then, should meaning be studied? What sort of questions should we be trying to answer in setting up a theory of meaning? What principles should form its foundations?'

One of the keynotes of a modern linguistic approach to semantics is that there is no escape from language: an equation such as *cent = hundredth of a dollar* or *salt = NaCl* is not a matching of a linguistic sign with something outside language; it is a correspondence between two linguistic expressions, supposedly having 'the same meaning'. The search for an explanation of linguistic phenomena in terms of what is not language is as vain as the search for an exit from a room which has no doors or windows, for the word 'explanation' itself implies a statement in language. Our remedy, then, is to be content with exploring what we have inside the room: to study relations *within* language, such as paraphrase or synonymy (both terms meaning roughly 'sameness of meaning'). Paraphrase, and some other relations of meaning capable of systematic study, are illustrated below. *Entailment* and *Presupposition* are types of semantic dependence holding between one utterance and another; *logical inconsistency* is a type of semantic *contrastiveness* between utterances.

1. *X*: The defects of the plan were obvious
   IS A PARAPHRASE OF *Y*: The demerits of the scheme were evident.
2. *X*: The earth goes round the sun
   ENTAILS *Y*: The earth moves.
3. *X*: John's son is called Marcus
   PRESUPPOSES *Y*: John has a son.
4. *X*: The earth goes round the sun
   IS INCONSISTENT WITH *Y*: The earth is stationary.

These are some of the relations of meaning between two utterances *X* and *Y* that a semantic theory may profitably try to explain; we shall look at these, and other, relations of meaning more carefully later on (pp. 84–7).

A second principle underlying present-day linguistic approaches to semantics is seeing the task of language study as the explication of the LINGUISTIC COMPETENCE of the native speaker of a language; that is, the provision of rules and structures which specify the mental apparatus a person must possess if he is to 'know' a given language. Applied to the semantic end of language, this leads to the question 'What is it to *know* the meaning of a word, a sentence, etc.? rather than just 'What is meaning?'. And among the evidence for such knowledge one may include recognizing semantic relations such as 1–4 above.

Another type of evidence that a person knows the semantics of a language is his recognition that certain utterances or expressions, although they obey the grammatical rules of the language concerned, are 'unsemantic' in the sense that they are aberrant or odd from the point of view of meaning. One such oddity is a TAUTOLOGY, or a statement which has to be true by virtue of its meaning alone, such as:

Monday came before the day which followed it.

We rarely have occasion to make such statements, because (except where we are explaining an unfamiliar linguistic usage) they tell a listener nothing that he did not know before, and so are communicatively empty. At the opposite side of acceptability are CONTRADICTIONS, or statements which are, by virtue of meaning, necessarily false:

Everything I like I dislike.
My brother had the toothache in his toe.

These are more decidedly deviant than tautologies: they are not just informationally vacuous, but are downright nonsensical. Modern linguistics has concentrated, in defining what a given language is, on specifying which sentences are acceptable within that language, and which are not – that is, on marking the boundaries between what is possible and impossible within the rules of the language. This has naturally brought into focus the native speaker's ability to discriminate between 'grammatical' and 'ungrammatical' sentences, and it is this ability in the area of meaning that we appeal to if we say that an ability to distinguish semantically odd sentences from meaningful sentences is a manifestation of his knowledge of rules of meaning in his language.

Semantically odd or deviant sentences are not restricted to contradictions and tautologies. There are, for example, questions which logically permit only one answer (*yes* or *no*), and so do not need to be asked: *Has your mother any sons or daughters?* There are also sentences which are unanswerable, because thay have absurd presuppositions: *Do you know how the man who killed his widow was punished?* This sort of whimsicality is a reminder of the 'tangle-talk' or nonsense rigmaroles which children indulge in as a kind of verbal sport:

> I went to the pictures tomorrow
> I took a front seat at the back
> I fell from the pit to the gallery
> And broke a front bone in my back.
> A lady she gave me some chocolate,
> I ate it and gave it her back;
> I phoned for a taxi and walked it,
> And that's why I never came back.

(Opie, *The Lore and Language of Schoolchildren*, p. 25)

The natural fascination children find in beating the bounds of meaningfulness might be counted among the symptoms of that 'intuitive grasp' of meaning, or SEMANTIC COMPETENCE as the linguist would call it, shared by the speakers of a language.

Language and the 'Real World'

But for the linguist, as for the philosopher, the main difficulty lies in drawing a boundary not simply between sense and nonsense, but between the kind of nonsense which arises from contradicting what we know about language and meaning, and the kind of nonsense which comes from contradicting what we know about the 'real world'. If a speaker of English is asked to comment on the utterance

(1) My uncle always sleeps standing on one toe   ←

he might exclaim: 'But that can't be true! No one can sleep like that!' His response would be similar to what he might say if faced with the contradiction

(2) My uncle always sleeps awake.   ←

But on reflection, he would probably explain the two absurdities differently. Sentence (1) would be unbelievable because of what he knows about the world we live in, more specifically about the posture in which sleep is possible. Sentence (2) would be more than unbelievable – it would point to the unimaginable, because of the contradiction between the two meanings of *sleep* and *awake*. But both statements would strike him as absurd in the same way, to the extent that they would both be necessarily false.

An analogy can be drawn here between the rules of a language and the rules of a game. Events within a football match, for instance, may be impossible (a) because they are against the rules of the game, or (b) because they violate natural laws regarding physical strength of human beings, the inability of footballs to defy ordinary laws of motion (e.g. by moving in the air like boomerangs), etc. Thus a football report that 'The centre-forward scored a goal by heading a ball from his own goal-line' would be disbelieved as physically impossible, while 'The centre-forward scored a goal by punching the ball into the goal-mouth' would be disbelieved on the grounds that if such a thing happened, the game could not have been football.

The difference felt between (1) and (2) above is brought out in the different strategies we adopt in trying to make sense of them. It seems to be an incontrovertible principle of semantics that the human mind abhors a vacuum of sense; so a speaker of English faced with absurd sentences will strain his interpretative faculty to the utmost to read them meaningfully. It is possible that readers of these pages have already found themselves exercising that faculty on these two sentences. For (1), *My uncle always sleeps standing on one toe*, two strategies of interpretation seem possible. The first is to assume a TRANSFER OF MEANING by which either *sleeps* or *standing on one toe* is understood in a new or unusual sense. *Standing on one toe*, for instance, might be taken as a hyperbole or exaggerated substitute for 'topsy-turvy', or 'in a weird posture'. The second strategy is to imagine some miraculous, unprecedented situation (e.g. the uncle's having subjected himself to training in a hitherto unpractised version of yoga) in which this statement might be true. For (2) *My uncle always sleeps awake*, however, only the first strategy of transfer of meaning can be applied: the solution here must be to resolve the semantic conflict between 'sleeping' and 'waking', by (for example) understanding *sleeps* in a metaphorical way as 'behaves as if asleep'. A factual absurdity can be made sensible by extending one's imagination to the conception of a possible world (perhaps a dream world or fictional world) in which it could be true. A logical contradiction is on the other hand a linguistic absurdity, which, if it is to be made meaningful, requires a linguistic remedy, a 'tampering with the rules of the language game', just as the impossible manoeuvre described under (b) above would require a rewriting of the rules of football.

The distinction between language (including 'logic') on the one hand, and fact or the 'real world' on the other, will be explored further in Chapter 2 (pp. 14–15), and in Chapter 10 we shall also investigate the notion of transfer of meaning, and see in what sense it amounts to a 'tampering with language'. At this stage, let us simply note that such a distinction is felt to exist, even though it is not easy for a linguist or a philosopher to justify it, or to prescribe how to draw the line in individual cases. Let us also note, by way of warning to the sceptic, that the price of ignoring this distinction between language and 'real world' is to enlarge the sphere of semantics (as Bloomfield by implication enlarged it) into the impossibly vast study of everything that is to be known about the universe in which we live.

Summary

In this chapter I have tried to make three main points about the study of meaning:

1. That it is mistaken to try to define meaning by reducing it to the terms of sciences other than the science of language: e.g. to the terms of psychology or chemistry.

2. That meaning can best be studied as a linguistic phenomenon in its own right, not as something 'outside language'. This means we investigate what it is to 'know a language' semantically, e.g. to know what is involved in recognizing relations of meaning between sentences, and in recognizing which sentences are meaningful and which are not.

3. That point (2) presupposes a distinction between 'knowledge of language' and 'knowledge of the "real world"'.

2. Seven Types of Meaning

Some people would like semantics to pursue the study of meaning in a wide sense of 'all that is communicated by language'; others (among them most modern writers within the framework of general linguistics) limit it in practice to the study of logical or conceptual meaning in the sense discussed in Chapter 1. It needs no great insight to see that semantics in the former, wider sense can lead us once again into the void from which Bloomfield retreated with understandable misgivings – the description of all that may be the object of human knowledge or belief. On the other hand, we can, by carefully distinguishing types of meaning, show how they all fit into the total composite effect of linguistic communication, and show how methods of study appropriate to one type may not be appropriate to another.

On this basis, I shall break down 'meaning' in its widest sense into seven different ingredients, giving primary importance to logical meaning or (as I shall prefer to call it) CONCEPTUAL MEANING, the type of meaning I was discussing earlier in connection with 'semantic competence'. The six other types I shall consider are connotative meaning, stylistic meaning, affective meaning, reflected meaning, collocative meaning, and thematic meaning.

Conceptual Meaning

CONCEPTUAL MEANING (sometimes called 'denotative' or 'cognitive' meaning) is widely assumed to be the central factor in linguistic communication, and I think it can be shown to be integral to the essential functioning of language in a way that other types of meaning are not (which is not to say that conceptual meaning is always the most important element of an act of linguistic communication). My chief reason for assigning priority to conceptual meaning is that it has a complex and sophisticated organization of a kind which may be compared with, and cross-related to, similar organization on the syntactic and phonological levels of language. In particular, I would like to point to two structural principles that seem to lie at the basis of all linguistic patterning: the principle of CONTRASTIVENESS and the principle of CONSTITUENT STRUCTURE. Contrastive features underlie the classification of sounds in phonology, for example, in that any label we apply to a sound defines it *positively*, by what features it possesses, and also by implication *negatively*, by what features it does not possess. Thus the phonetic symbol /b/ may be explicated as representing a bundle of contrastive features +bilabial, +voice, +stop, −nasal; the assumption being that the distinctive sounds or phonemes of a language are identifiable in terms of binary, or largely binary, contrasts. In a similar way, the conceptual meanings of a language seem to be organized largely in terms of contrastive features, so that (for example) the meaning of the word *woman* could be specified as +HUMAN, −MALE, +ADULT, as distinct from, say, *boy*, which could be 'defined' +HUMAN, +MALE, −ADULT (see p. 96).

The second principle, that of constituent structure, is the principle by which larger linguistic units are built up out of smaller units; or (looking at it from the opposite point of view) by which we are able to analyse a sentence syntactically into its constituent parts, moving from its *immediate constituents* through a hierarchy of sub-division to its *ultimate constituents* or smallest syntactic elements. This aspect of the organization of language is often given visual display in a tree-diagram:

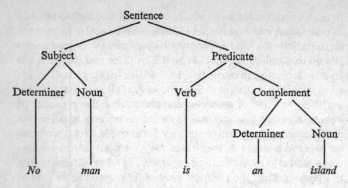

Or it can be represented by bracketing:

{(No) (man)}{[(is)] [(an) (island)]}

While it has long been understood that the syntax of a language is
to be handled in such terms, linguists have recently been coming
round to the view that the semantic level of natural languages has
its own constituent structure (see pp. 126–49), its own counterpart
of syntactic structure or (to use in many ways a closer analogy) of
the systems of symbolic logic set up by mathematicians and philosophers.

The two principles of contrastiveness and constituent structure
represent the way language is organized respectively on what
linguists have termed the PARADIGMATIC (or selectional) and
SYNTAGMATIC (or combinatory) axes of linguistic structure. It
will be my aim in the major part of this book (Chapters 6–14) to explore as fully as I can the application of these principles to semantic
analysis, and so to show how methods of study devised for other
levels of language can bring new precision and insight to conceptual semantics.

In this discussion, I have taken for granted a third generally
acknowledged principle of linguistic organization, which is that
any given piece of language is structured simultaneously on more
than one 'level'. At least the three following levels, in the pictured
order, seem to be necessary for a full account of the linguistic
competence by which we are able to generate or understand
linguistic utterances:

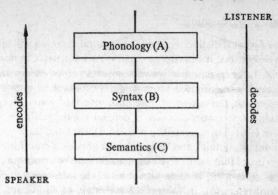

And this means that for the analysis of any sentence, we need to establish a 'phonological representation', a 'syntactic representation' and a 'semantic representation', and the stages by which one level of representation can be derived from another. The aim of conceptual semantics is to provide, for any given interpretation of a sentence, a configuration of abstract symbols which is its 'semantic representation', and which shows exactly what we need to know if we are to distinguish that meaning from all other possible sentence meanings in the language, and to match that meaning with the right syntactic and phonological expression. The ability to match levels operates in one direction (A → B → C on the diagram) if we are DECODING, i.e. listening to a sentence and interpreting it; and in the opposite direction (C → B → A) if we are ENCODING, i.e. composing and speaking a sentence. From this account it will be clear that conceptual meaning is an inextricable and essential part of what language is, such that one can scarcely define language without referring to it. A 'language' which communicated by other means than by conceptual meaning (e.g. a 'language' which communicated solely by means of expletive words like *Oh! Ah! Oho! Alas!* and *Tally ho!*) would not be a language at all in the sense in which we apply that term to the tongues of men.

Connotative Meaning

More of what is distinctive about conceptual meaning will appear
when we contrast it with CONNOTATIVE MEANING. Connotative
meaning is the communicative value an expression has by virtue of
what it *refers to*, over and above its purely conceptual content. To
a large extent, the notion of 'reference' overlaps with conceptual
meaning. If the word *woman* is defined conceptually by three
features (+HUMAN, −MALE, +ADULT), then the three properties 'human', 'adult', and 'female' must provide a criterion of the
correct use of that word. These contrastive features, translated into
'real world' terms, become attributes of the referent (that which
the word refers to). But there is a multitude of additional, non-
criterial properties that we have learnt to expect a referent of
woman to possess. They include not only physical characteristics
('biped', 'having a womb'), but also psychological and social properties ('gregarious', 'subject to maternal instinct'), and may extend to features which are merely *typical* rather than *invariable* con-
comitants of womanhood ('capable of speech', 'experienced in
cookery', 'skirt-or-dress-wearing'). Still further, connotative
meaning can embrace the 'putative properties' of the referent,
due to the viewpoint adopted by an individual, or a group of people
or a whole society. So in the past woman has been burdened with
such attributes ('frail', 'prone to tears', 'cowardly', 'emotional',
'irrational', 'inconstant') as the dominant male has been pleased
to impose on her, as well as with more becoming qualities such as
'gentle', 'compassionate', 'sensitive', 'hard-working'. Obviously,
connotations are apt to vary from age to age and from society to
society. A hundred years ago, 'non-trouser-wearing' must have
seemed a thoroughly definitive connotation of the word *woman*
and its translation equivalents in European languages, just as in
many non-western societies today womankind is associated with
attributes foreign to our own way of thinking. It is equally obvious
that connotations will vary, to some extent, from individual to
individual within the same speech community: to an English-
speaking misogynist *woman* will have many uncomplimentary
associations not present in the minds of speakers of a more feminist
persuasion.

It will be clear that in talking about connotation, I am in fact talking about the 'real world' experience one associates with an expression when one uses or hears it. Therefore the boundary between conceptual and connotative meaning is coincident with that nebulous but crucial boundary, discussed in Chapter 1, between 'language' and the 'real world'. In confirmation of the feeling that connotation is somehow incidental to language rather than an essential part of it, we may notice that connotative meaning is not specific to language, but is shared by other communicative systems, such as visual art and music. Whatever connotations the word *baby* has can be conjured up (more effectively, because the medium is directly representational) by a drawing of a baby, or an imitation of a baby's cry. The overlap between linguistic and visual connotations is particularly noticeable in advertising, where words are often the lesser partners of illustrations in the task of conferring on a product a halo of favourable associations.

A second fact which indicates that connotative meaning is peripheral compared with conceptual meaning is that connotations are relatively unstable: that is, they vary considerably, as we have seen, according to culture, historical period, and the experience of the individual. Although it is too simple to suggest that all speakers of a particular language speak exactly 'the same language', it can be assumed, as a principle without which communication through that language would not be possible, that on the whole they share the same conceptual framework, just as they share approximately the same syntax. In fact, many semanticists today assume that the same basic conceptual framework is common to all languages, and is a universal property of the human mind (see pp. 31–2).

Thirdly, connotative meaning is indeterminate and open-ended in a sense in which conceptual meaning is not. Connotative meaning is open-ended in the same way as our knowledge and beliefs about the universe are open-ended: any characteristic of the referent, identified subjectively or objectively, may contribute to the connotative meaning of the expression which denotes it. In contrast, it is taken as fundamental by anyone who studies conceptual meaning that the meaning of a word or sentence can be codified in terms of a limited set of symbols (e.g. in the form of a finite set of discrete features of meaning), and that the semantic representation of a sentence can be specified by means of a finite number of rules. This postulate of the finiteness and determinateness of conceptual content is not arbitrary, but is modelled on the assumptions that linguists generally make when analysing other aspects of linguistic structure. Without such assumptions, one can scarcely attempt to describe language as a coherent system at all.

Stylistic and Affective Meaning

We turn now to two aspects of communication which have to do with the situation in which an utterance takes place. STYLISTIC MEANING is that which a piece of language conveys about the social circumstances of its use. We 'decode' the stylistic meaning of a text through our recognition of different dimensions and levels of usage within the same language. We recognize some words or pronunciations as being dialectal, i.e. as telling us something of the geographical or social origin of the speaker; other features of language tell us something of the social relationship between the speaker and hearer: we have a scale of 'status' usage, for example, descending from formal and literary English at one end to colloquial, familiar, and eventually slang English at the other.

A recent account of English style (Crystal and Davy, *Investigating English Style*) has recognized the following main dimensions of stylistic variation (I have added examples of the categories of usage one might distinguish on each dimension):

A (Relatively permanent features of style)
INDIVIDUALITY (The language of Mr X, of Mrs Y, of Miss Z etc.)
DIALECT (The language of a geographical region or of a social class)
TIME (The language of the eighteenth century, etc.)
B
DISCOURSE avenues of commin
(a) MEDIUM (Speech, writing, etc.)
(b) PARTICIPATION (Monologue, dialogue, etc.)

C (*Relatively temporary features of style*)
PROVINCE (Language of law, of science, of advertising, etc.) *topic*
STATUS (Polite, colloquial, slang, etc, language)
MODALITY (Language of memoranda, lectures, jokes, etc.)
SINGULARITY (The style of Dickens, of Hemingway, etc.).

Although not exhaustive, this list indicates something of the range of style differentiation possible within a single language. It is not surprising, perhaps, that we rarely find words which have both the same conceptual meaning and the same stylistic meaning. This observation has frequently led people to declare that 'true synonyms do not exist'. If we understand synonymy as complete equivalence of communicative effect, it is indeed hard to find an example that will disprove this statement. But there is much convenience in restricting the term 'synonymy' to equivalence of conceptual meaning, so that we may then contrast conceptual synonyms with respect to their varying stylistic overtones:

$$
\left\{
\begin{array}{l}
\text{steed (poetic)} \\
\text{horse (general)} \\
\text{nag (slang)} \\
\text{gee-gee (baby language)}
\end{array}
\right.
\qquad
\left\{
\begin{array}{l}
\text{domicile (very formal, official)} \\
\text{residence (formal)} \\
\text{abode (poetic)} \\
\text{home (general)}
\end{array}
\right.
$$

$$
\left\{
\begin{array}{l}
\text{cast (literary, biblical)} \\
\text{throw (general)} \\
\text{chuck (casual, slang)}
\end{array}
\right.
\qquad
\left\{
\begin{array}{l}
\text{diminutive (very formal)} \\
\text{tiny (colloquial)} \\
\text{wee (colloquial, dialectal)}
\end{array}
\right.
$$

The style dimension of 'status' is particularly important in distinguishing synonymous expressions. Here is an example in which the difference of status is maintained through a whole sentence, and is reflected in syntax as well as in vocabulary:

(1) They chucked a stone at the cops, and then did a bunk with the loot.
(2) After casting a stone at the police, they absconded with the money.

Sentence (1) could be said by two criminals, talking casually about the crime afterwards; sentence (2) might be said by the chief inspector in making his official report. Both could be describing the same happening, and their common ground of conceptual meaning is evident in the difficulty anyone would have in assenting to the truth of one of these sentences, and denying the truth of the other (see p. 93).

If we extend the idea of linguistic situation a bit more we see that language can also reflect the personal feelings of the speaker, including his attitude to the listener, or his attitude to something he is talking about. AFFECTIVE MEANING, as this sort of meaning can be called, is often explicitly conveyed through the conceptual or connotative content of the words used. Someone who is addressed: 'You're a vicious tyrant and a villainous reprobate, and I hate you for it!' is left in little doubt as to the feelings of the speaker towards him. But there are less direct ways of disclosing our attitude than this: for example, by scaling our remarks according to politeness. With the object of getting people to be quiet, we might say either:

(3) I'm terribly sorry to interrupt, but I wonder if you would be so kind as to lower your voices a little.

or:

(4) Will you belt up.

Factors such as intonation and voice-timbre – what we often refer to as 'tone of voice' – are also important here. The impression of politeness in (3) can be reversed by a tone of biting sarcasm; sentence (4) can be turned into a playful remark between intimates if delivered with the intonation of a mild request.

Affective meaning is largely a parasitic category in the sense that to express our emotions we rely upon the mediation of other categories of meaning – conceptual, connotative, or stylistic. Emotional expression through style comes about, for instance, when we adopt an impolite tone to express displeasure (as in (4) above), or when we adopt a casual tone to express friendliness. On the other hand, there are elements of language (chiefly interjections, like *Aha!* and *Yippee!*) whose chief function is to express emotion. When we use these, we communicate feelings and attitudes without the mediation of any other kind of semantic function.

Reflected and Collocative Meaning

Two further, though less important types of meaning involve an interconnection on the lexical level of language.

First, REFLECTED MEANING is the meaning which arises in cases of multiple conceptual meaning, when one sense of a word forms part of our response to another sense. On hearing, in a church service, the synonymous expressions *The Comforter* and *The Holy Ghost*, both referring to the Third Person of the Trinity, I find my reactions to these terms conditioned by the everyday non-religious meanings of *comfort* and *ghost*. *The Comforter* sounds warm and 'comforting' (although in the religious context, it means 'the strengthener or supporter'), while *The Holy Ghost* sounds awesome.

One sense of a word seems to 'rub off' on another sense in this way only when it has a dominant suggestive power either through relative frequency and familiarity (as in the case of *The Holy Ghost*) or through the strength of its associations. Only in poetry, which invites a heightened sensitivity to language in all respects, do we find reflected meaning operating in less obviously favourable circumstances:

> Are limbs, so *dear*-achieved, are sides,
> Full-nerved – still warm – too hard to stir?

In these lines from *Futility*, a poem on a dead soldier, Wilfred Owen overtly uses the word *dear* in the sense 'expensive(ly)', but also alludes, one feels in the context of the poem, to the sense 'beloved'.

The case where reflected meaning intrudes through the sheer strength of emotive suggestion is most strikingly illustrated by words which have a taboo meaning. Since their popularization in senses connected with the physiology of sex, it has become increasingly difficult to use terms like *intercourse*, *ejaculation*, and *erection* in 'innocent' senses without conjuring up their sexual associations. This process of taboo contamination has accounted in the past for the dying-out of the non-taboo sense of a word: Bloomfield explained the replacement of *cock* in its farmyard sense by *rooster* as due to the influence of the taboo use of the former word, and one wonders if *intercourse* is now following a similar path.

COLLOCATIVE MEANING consists of the associations a word acquires on account of the meanings of words which tend to occur in its environment. *Pretty* and *handsome* share common ground in the meaning 'good-looking', but may be distinguished by the range of nouns with which they are likely to co-occur or (to use the linguist's term) collocate:

The ranges may well, of course, overlap: *handsome woman* and *pretty woman* are both acceptable, although they suggest a different kind of attractiveness because of the collocative associations of the two adjectives. Further examples are quasi-synonymous verbs such as *wander* and *stroll* (*cows* may *wander*, but may not *stroll*) or *tremble* and *quiver* (one *trembles* with *fear*, but *quivers* with *excitement*). Not all differences in potential co-occurrence need to be explained as collocative meaning: some may be due to stylistic differences, others to conceptual differences. It is the incongruity of combining unlike styles that makes 'He *mounted* his *gee-gee*' or 'He *got on* his *steed*' an improbable combination. On the other hand, the acceptability of 'The donkey *ate hay*', as opposed to 'The donkey *ate silence*', is a matter of compatibility on the level of conceptual semantics, (on such 'selection restrictions', see pp. 141–6). Only when explanation in terms of other categories of meaning does not apply do we need to invoke the special category of collocative meaning: on the other levels, generalizations can be made, while collocative meaning is simply an idiosyncratic property of individual words.

Associative Meaning: a Summary Term

Reflected meaning and collocative meaning, affective meaning and stylistic meaning: all these have more in common with connotative

meaning than with conceptual meaning; they all have the same
open-ended, indeterminate character, and lend themselves to
analysis in terms of scales or ranges, rather than in discrete either-
this-or-that terms. They can all be brought together under the
heading of ASSOCIATIVE MEANING, and to explain communication on these levels, we need employ nothing more sophisticated
than an elementary 'associationist' theory of mental connections
based upon contiguities of experience. We contrast them all with
conceptual meaning, because conceptual meaning seems to require the postulation of intricate mental structures which are
specific to language and to the human species.

Associative meaning contains so many imponderable factors
that it can be studied systematically only by approximative statistical techniques. In effect, Osgood, Suci and Tannenbaum proposed a method for a partial analysis of associative meaning when
they published their ambitiously titled book *The Measurement of
Meaning* in 1957. Osgood and his co-authors devised a technique
(involving a statistical measurement device, the Semantic Differential) for plotting meaning in terms of a multi-dimensional
semantic space, using as data speakers' judgements recorded in
terms of seven-point scales. The scales are labelled by contrasting
adjective pairs, such as *happy–sad*, *hard–soft*, *slow–fast*, so that a
person may, for example, record his impression of the word
bagpipe on a form in the following way:

	3	2	1	0	1	2	3	
good	___ : ___ : X : ___ : ___ : ___ : ___							bad
hard	___ : X : ___ : ___ : ___ : ___ : ___							soft
passive	___ : ___ : ___ : ___ : ___ : ___ : X							active

etc.

Statistically, the investigators found that particular significance
seemed to lie in three major dimensions, those of evaluation (*good–
bad*), potency (*hard–soft*), and activity (*active–passive*). It is clear,
even from this very brief sketch, that the method can provide no
more than a *partial* and *approximate* account of associative meaning: *partial* because it entails a selection from indefinitely many
possible scales, which in any case would only provide for associative meaning in so far as it is explicable in scalar terms; *approxi-*

mate because of the statistical sampling, and because a seven-point scale constitutes a cutting-up of a continuous scale into seven segments within which no differentiation is made – a process similar in its crudity to that of cutting up the spectrum into seven primary colours. This is not to disparage the Semantic Differential technique as a means of quantifying associative meaning: the lesson to be learned is, in fact, that it is only by such relatively insensitive tools as this that associative meaning can be systematically studied: it does not lend itself to determinate analyses involving yes–no choices and structures of uniquely segmentable elements.

Another important observation about the Semantic Differential is that it has been found useful in psychological fields such as personality studies, 'attitude measurement', and psychotherapy, where differences in the reactions of individuals are under scrutiny, rather than the common core of reactions that they share. This upholds what I said earlier in particular reference to connotative meaning: that whereas conceptual meaning is substantially part of the 'common system' of language shared by members of a speech community, associative meaning is less stable, and varies with the individual's experience.

Thematic Meaning

The final category of meaning I shall attempt to distinguish is THEMATIC MEANING, or what is communicated by the way in which a speaker or writer organizes the message, in terms of ordering, focus, and emphasis. It is often felt, for example, that an active sentence such as (1) has a different meaning from its passive equivalent (2), although in conceptual content they seem to be the same:

$\begin{cases} \text{(1) Mrs Bessie Smith donated the first prize.} \\ \text{(2) The first prize was donated by Mrs Bessie Smith.} \end{cases}$

Certainly these have different communicative values in that they suggest different contexts: the active sentence answers an implicit question 'What did Mrs Bessie Smith donate?', while the passive sentence answers an implicit question 'Who was the first prize donated by?' or (more simply) 'Who donated the first prize?'

That is, (1), in contrast to (2), suggests that we know who Mrs Bessie Smith is (perhaps through a previous mention). The same truth conditions, however, apply to each: it would be impossible to find a situation of which (1) was an accurate report while (2) was not, or vice versa.

Thematic meaning is mainly a matter of choice between alternative grammatical constructions, as in:

> (3) A man is waiting in the hall.
> (4) There's a man waiting in the hall.

> (5) They stopped at the end of the corridor.
> (6) At the end of the corridor, they stopped.

> (7) I like Danish cheese best.
> (8) Danish cheese I like best.
> (9) It's Danish cheese that I like best.

But the kind of contrast of ordering and emphasis illustrated by (1) and (2) can also be contrived by lexical means: by substituting (for example) *belongs to* for *owns*:

> (10) My brother owns the largest betting-shop in London.
> (11) The largest betting-shop in London belongs to my brother.

In other cases, it is stress and intonation rather than grammatical construction that highlights information in one part of a sentence. If the word *electric* is given contrastive stress in (12):

> (12) Bill uses an *electric* razor.
> (13) The kind of razor that Bill uses is an electric one.

the effect is to focus attention on that word as containing new information, against a background of what is already assumed to be known (viz. that Bill uses a razor). This kind of emphasis could have been equally achieved in English by the different syntactic construction of (13). The sentences bracketed together above obviously have, in a sense, 'the same meaning'; but all the same, we need to acknowledge that their communicative effect may be somewhat different; they will not each be equally appropriate within the same context.

Intended and Interpreted Meaning

I have now dealt with the seven types of meaning promised at the beginning of the chapter, but I do not wish to give the impression that this is a complete catalogue, accounting for all that a piece of language may communicate. These are, to my mind, the most important categories; but one might, for example, have added a category for the physiological information conveyed by an act of speech or writing: information about the sex of the speaker, his age, the state of his sinuses, and so on.

It may be wondered why I have avoided making a distinction between the INTENDED meaning, that which is in the mind of the speaker when he is framing his message, and the INTERPRETED meaning, or that which is conveyed to the mind of the listener when he receives the message. I have equated meaning in its broad sense with 'communicative effect', and 'communication' usually means transfer of information from a source (A) to a target (B). Further, one might argue, communication can only be judged to have taken place if we know that what was in mind (A) has been transferred to, or copied in, mind (B). All this is true, and yet a linguist may feel entitled to ignore the difference between the intention of a message and its effect, because he is interested in studying the communication system itself, rather than what use or misuse is made of it. He is interested in studying the semantic aspect of the language which we may assume to be common to the minds of (A) and (B), and this includes, incidentally, studying ambiguities and other aspects of language (e.g. variability of associative meaning) which give scope for miscommunication. But the important point is that meaning, for linguistics, is neutral between 'speaker's meaning' and 'hearer's meaning'; and this is surely justifiable, since only through knowing the neutral potentialities of the medium of communication itself can we investigate differences between what a person intends to convey and what he actually conveys.

Demarcation Problems

A further caveat about the seven types of meaning: there are always problems of 'demarcation', and more especially, problems of separating conceptual meaning from the more peripheral categories. The difficulty of delimiting conceptual from connotative meaning, noted earlier, is paralleled in other borderline areas, such as that between conceptual meaning and stylistic meaning:

(1) He *stuck* the key in his pocket.
(2) He *put* the key in his pocket.

We could argue that (1) and (2) are conceptually synonymous, and that the difference between the two is a matter of style (sentence (2) is neutral, while (1) is colloquial and casual). On the other hand, we could maintain that the shift in style is combined with a conceptual difference: that *stick* in a context such as (1) has a more precise denotation than (2) and could be roughly defined as 'to put carelessly and quickly'. There is support for the second explanation in the slight oddity of the following sentences:

?*He stuck the key slowly in his pocket.
?*He stuck the key carefully in his pocket.

[The preceding asterisk, according to a convention of linguistics, signals the unacceptability of a sentence.]

Often, in fact, the solution to a problem of delimitation is to conclude that quasi-synonyms differ on at least two planes of meaning.

As a second illustration, we may take a case on the border between conceptual and collocative meaning, that of the verbs *smile* and *grin*. Do these words have different conceptual meanings, or is it just that the range of expressions with which they habitually combine is different? Few would hesitate over which of the two words to insert in:

The duchess ——ed graciously as she shook hands with her guests.
Gargoyles ——ed hideously from the walls of the building.

But the question is whether such differences in collocation spring from different conceptual and connotative content: whether, for example, a *grin* can be defined as a broader, toothier and more potentially hostile expression than a *smile*, and is more likely to be found on the face of a gargoyle than that of a duchess for that very reason. This is a particularly complex case in that differences of stylistic and affective meaning are also clearly implicated. In fact, as already observed, affective meaning is a category which overlaps heavily with style, connotation, and conceptual content.

Summary

As this chapter has introduced quite a range of terms for types of meaning, it is fitting that it should end with a summary, and a suggestion or two for simplifying terminology:

→ SEVEN TYPES OF MEANING

1. CONCEPTUAL MEANING or *Sense*			Logical, cognitive, or denotative content.
ASSOCIATIVE MEANING		**2. CONNOTATIVE MEANING**	What is communicated by virtue of what language refers to.
		3. STYLISTIC MEANING	What is communicated of the social circumstances of language use.
		4. AFFECTIVE MEANING	What is communicated of the feelings and attitudes of the speaker/writer.
		5. REFLECTED MEANING	What is communicated through association with another sense of the same expression.
		6. COLLOCATIVE MEANING	What is communicated through association with words which tend to occur in the environment of another word.
7. THEMATIC MEANING			What is communicated by the way in which the message is organized in terms of order and emphasis.

I have here used SENSE as a briefer term for 'conceptual meaning', (or 'meaning' in the narrower sense), and will feel free to use it for clarity and convenience from now on. For 'meaning' in the wider sense which embraces all seven types listed, it is useful to have the alternative term COMMUNICATIVE VALUE.

3. 'Bony-Structured Concepts'

universality?

In the previous chapter I emphasized the role of language as an instrument of communication. But it is far more than this – it is the means by which we interpret our environment, by which we classify or 'conceptualize' our experiences, by which we are able to impose structure on reality, so as to use what we have observed for present and future learning and understanding. The extent to which, for example, the furthering of human knowledge through science is a *linguistic* activity has probably been underestimated. In this chapter I shall consider language, in its semantic aspect, as a conceptual system. Not as a closed, rigid, conceptual system which tyrannizes over the thought processes of its users, but as an *open-ended* conceptual system, one which 'leaks', in the sense that it allows us to transcend its limitations by various types of semantic creativity.

Language as a Conceptual System

The first question which arises is whether language is a *single* conceptual system, or whether there are as many conceptual systems as there are languages. Although much of present-day thinking has tended to hypothesize a universal conceptual framework which is common to all human language, common observation shows that languages differ in the way they classify experience. A classic instance of this is the semantics of colour words. We have, like many other creatures, the visual apparatus for discriminating colour differences, in terms of gradations of hue, brightness, and saturation. But in addition, unlike animals, we have the apparatus for categorizing these colours verbally, i.e. for placing a particular shade in one 'pigeon-hole' rather than another. For example, English (according to Berlin and Kay, *Basic Color Terms*, 1969) has a range of eleven primary colour terms ('black', 'white', 'red', 'green', 'yellow', 'blue', 'brown', 'purple', 'pink', 'orange', and 'grey'), whereas the Philippine language of Hanunóo (according to Conklin, 'Hanunóo Color Categories', 1955) makes do with four:

(*ma*)*biru* = black, dark tints of other colours
(*ma*)*lagti?* = white, light tints of other colours
(*ma*)*rara?* = maroon, red, orange
(*ma*)*latuy* = light green, yellow, and light brown.

The difference between the two colour terminologies can be diagrammed like this:

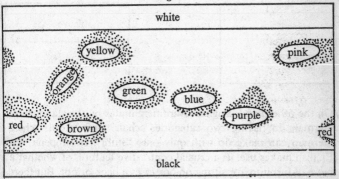

English

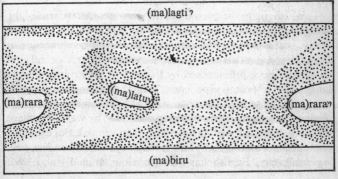

Hanunóo

These diagrams are reproductions of those in Berlin and Kay 1969 (pp. 22 and 29) in which the three-dimensional colour-solid is projected on to a two-dimensional rectangle, by the omission of degrees of saturation. The neutral colour grey is not represented.

Countless other examples of this kind of 'linguistic relativity' could be cited, even among languages such as French, German, and English, which are associated with closely interrelated cultures. Where English recognizes one category ('river'), French makes a distinction between a river flowing into the sea ('fleuve') and a tributary river ('rivière'). Or, in simplified visual terms:

English	*French*
'river'	'fleuve'
	'rivière'

On the other hand, English overdifferentiates by the standard of German, in having two categories 'chair' and 'stool' where German can make do with only one, 'Stuhl'. It happens that English makes use, as a crucial contrastive feature, of whether a piece of furniture for sitting on possesses a back or not. But there is no obvious reason why this feature should be made more of than, say, whether the article has three or four legs, whether it is made of wood, whether it has arms, etc.

This leads on to the question of the partial 'arbitrariness' of the categories language provides for us. By 'arbitrariness', I mean, firstly, that conceptual boundaries often vary from language to language in a way that defies principled explanation. A second kind of arbitrariness, presupposed by the first, is the arbitrariness of language in respect to experienced reality: languages have a tendency to 'impose structure upon the real world' by treating some distinctions as crucial, and ignoring others. The way a language classifies things is sometimes blatantly man-centred. For example, alongside more biologically motivated categories such as *dog*, *tree*, *vegetable*, etc., English has *pest* ('noxious animal') and *weed* ('noxious plant'). The same plant (e.g. a buttercup) may be classified as a 'weed' or a 'flower' according to whether it is found inside or outside the garden. It is instructive how such a classification may influence, or at least support, a person's response to the object. Although a countryman on an afternoon's walk may delight to see a field of buttercups, when he returns home, he views them as ugly weeds, to be ruthlessly eradicated from his garden. But we would be wrong to regard such distinctions of value as purely arbitrary: here the motivation is supplied by cultural norms, rather than by external reality.

'Relativist' and 'Universalist' Points of View

Enough has been said to illustrate the idea that each language imposes its own 'grid' on our experience, or (to change the metaphor) provides a set of 'pigeon-holes' by which we reduce our universe to order. This observation has led scholars in the past to suppose that the language one speaks profoundly affects one's thought processes and the way one interprets the world. Differences will be particularly far-reaching, for example, between the world-view of a native speaker of English, and that of a native speaker of an American Indian language in which not only classifications of natural phenomena, but abstract relations such as those of time and place, are represented in a very different manner. This relativistic view of the cognitive structure of languages has received the name 'the Sapir-Whorf hypothesis', after two American anthropological linguists who championed it in the 1920s and 1930s. Various arguments can be advanced against the Sapir-Whorf position. If we took up an extreme version of the view that each language forces us into its peculiar mental straitjacket, we would be at a loss to explain how in practice, it is possible to translate from one language to another. Also, a single language often has alternative conceptualizations of the same phenomenon: in English, for example, we can categorize human-beings by age into 'children', 'adolescents', and 'adults', or alternatively, into 'majors' and 'minors'. Furthermore, if we draw a distinction between meaning and reference (p. 14), we can say that even though there is no corresponding concept in one's own language for a concept in another language, one can nevertheless provide a description (if necessary a very detailed description) of its referent.

Nowadays, a more fashionable view is that language is basically an innate, or genetically inherited capability, which all human beings are 'programmed' from birth to develop. This implies a rejection of the Sapir-Whorf hypothesis (at least in its more extreme forms), and an adoption of the position that languages share the same basic conceptual framework. It can be argued, for example, that there is a universal set of semantic categories (animate/inanimate, human/non-human, concrete/abstract, etc.) from which each language draws its own subset of categories, and it is only in the choice from this subset, and in the permitted combinations in which they are expressed, that languages differ. One of the most striking instances of the 'universalist' trend is a recent persuasive attempt by B. Berlin and P. Kay (in *Basic Color Terms*, 1969), to show that primary colour terminology, an area of meaning seemingly so favourable to Sapir-Whorfism, is explicable in terms of a set of eleven universal colour categories, which may or may not be all present in a given language. There will be further discussion of Berlin and Kay, and more generally, of the universalist-relativist issue, in Chapter 11.

The Child's Acquisition of Conceptual Categories

How do we acquire conceptual categories in childhood? Here again, there are widely divergent points of view, extending from the dogged 'empiricism' of those who would argue that the cognitive system is learned entirely through experience from one's environment (which of course includes cultural conditioning), and the extreme rationalism of those who would claim that the cognitive framework does not have to be learned, as it is part of an inherited mental apparatus specific to the human species. This polarity of views is obviously the universalist-relativist controversy in a slightly different guise. The Sapir-Whorf position on language diversity is in alliance with the empiricist view of language acquisition, since the exposure of children to different cultural environments, in which they learn different languages, can explain how they come to learn different conceptualizations of experience.

Oppositely, a faith in linguistic universals leads one to postulate an inborn disposition in human beings to develop these universals: otherwise, how could the same features come to be distributed among all the languages of the world?

Just as the empiricist viewpoint was taken for granted by linguists of the generation of Sapir and Whorf, so today the wheel has turned full circle (largely due to the influence of Chomsky in such writings as *Cartesian Linguistics* (1966) and *Language and Mind* (1968)), and a modernized version of the old philosophical doctrine of 'innate ideas' has become respectable. Two *prima facie* arguments arising from modern linguistic research favour this point of view: as linguistics probes more deeply and precisely into the layers of linguistic structure, firstly it becomes more difficult to explain how a child learns so soon to manipulate the remarkable complexities of language, particularly on the semantic level, without having a 'head-start' in the form of some fairly specific language-learning capacity; and secondly, it becomes easier to see how in a multi-layered analysis of language, widely different structures in phonology and syntax can be reconciled with identical, or at least similar, structures on the semantic level.

On the other hand, that at least part of concept learning runs according to empiricist thinking is clear from the way we observe young children to acquire the conceptual categories of their language by a procedure of trial-and-error. It has long been noted that learning a concept such as 'cat' involves two complementary processes: (1) *generalization*, i.e. extending the name one has learned to apply to some referents (cat_1, cat_2, cat_3, etc.) to all objects sharing certain attributes of those referents ($cat_4, \ldots cat_n$); and (2) *differentiation*, i.e. restricting the reference of a word to objects sharing certain characteristics, but not others (e.g. *not* applying the word *cat* to dogs, tigers, etc.). These two processes go hand in hand in the learning of category boundaries, but a child cannot learn both aspects simultaneously, so he tends either to overgeneralize (e.g. identifying 'daddy' with all men) or to undergeneralize (e.g. identifying 'man' with all strange men wearing hats). These are some of the false generalizations my daughter was making at the age of two:

WORD USED	APPARENT RANGE OF REFERENCE
choo-choo (i.e. toy engine)	toys with wheels
ba-ba (i.e. sheep)	animals in fields (including cows)
book	books, leaflets, and newspapers
soo (i.e. *shoe*)	footwear generally, including boots and slippers
cup	vessels for drinking, including mugs, glasses, and the cat's bowl
Tom (her brother)	boys in general
on (i.e. *orange*)	yellow as well as orange

In some ways, her categories were less arbitrary than those instituted in the English language; for example, it takes a minute or so for us to sort out in our minds exactly what distinguishes a 'boot' from a 'shoe'. The 'shoe'/'boot'/'slipper' categories of English are difficult to justify logically, and in many ways it is more sensible to have one word for all articles of footwear.

That such trial-and-error methods are part and parcel of language learning suggests that the 'innate language capacity' in this respect takes the form of a general strategy whereby categories may be arrived at on the basis of experience, rather than a predisposition to select one set of categories rather than another. But as the 'empiricist' and the 'rationalist' points of view have at least some truth on their respective sides, it seems best, in such a speculative area as this, to adopt a rather cautious and unexciting compromise position. One such in-between position, which I find attractive, rests on a distinction between two types of semantic category (see Chapter 8, p. 161): DESIGNATORS, which refer to objects, qualities, goings on, etc. in the 'real' world (e.g. 'cat', 'red', 'run'), and FORMATORS or logical elements whose function and definition is internal to the language system (e.g. logical operators such as 'negation', 'all', and 'some'). We might then argue that only the logical components, or formators, are intrinsic to the universal language capability of man; designators are only *potentially* universal, in the sense that we regard them as language-neutral, and recognize their existence as common ground between two or more languages wherever there are grounds for doing so. Certain im-

portant designative categories ('animate'/'inanimate', 'concrete'/
'abstract', etc.) do indeed appear to be common to a large number
of languages, and are perhaps universal.

But the line between formators and designators is not easy to
draw, and certain concepts such as 'causation', which one would
expect to be universal, seem to lie somewhere between the two.
Evidence in favour of shared concepts in this sense comes from
translations: if we can explain how it is possible to translate
correctly from one language to another in terms of such a
commonalty of concepts, we have a case for hypothesizing their
existence.

Creativity (1): Lexical Innovation & anticreation

Discussion for and against semantic universals usually seems to
assume that a language forms a static, closed conceptual system,
and that once the fixed categories of the language have been acquired, our semantic equipment is complete. If this were true, it
would cause us to take very seriously the sinister idea that our
language is a mental straitjacket, which wholly determines our
thought processes and our assumptions about the universe.

But fortunately for the human race, language is only a mental
straitjacket if we allow it to become one: the semantic system, like
any other system relating to human society, is continually being
extended and revised. In a language like English, new concepts are
introduced in large numbers day by day and week by week, and in
very little time (owing to modern mass communications) become
familiar to many people. These new concepts are eventually not
felt to be strange, but are fully assimilated into the language, and
so become part of our standard mental equipment. The technique
by which the new concepts are introduced is lexical innovation,
which may take the form of NEOLOGISM (the invention of new
words, or more precisely lexical items – see Chapter 9, p. 179), or
TRANSFER OF MEANING (the derivation of new senses of established words). I shall confine my attention here to neologism, and
leave consideration of transfer of meaning until Chapter 10.

As an example of neologism, and the effect it has of extending
the conceptual system, I take the rather improbable case of the

word *defenestration*, which means 'a throwing out of the window', and occurs, to my knowledge, only in the phrase 'the defenestration of Prague', which denotes an incident at the outset of the Thirty Years' War, when a Bohemian Protestant assembly in Prague showed its antagonism to the Emperor by throwing his regents out of a window into a castle moat. However and whenever the word was invented (its first citation in the Oxford English Dictionary dates from 1620), one imagines it to have been fostered by generations of pedantic and tiny-minded history dons, who thought that 'the Defenestration of Prague' would make a fine resounding entry in a table of dates and events, or in a list of the causes of the Thirty Years' War. The fact that this word has gained some currency (though its usefulness is minimal) means that a new concept of 'throwing-out-of-the-windowness' has been acknowledged by the English language, and can be manipulated in the language just as if (say) it were the name of a previously undiscovered plant. As an abstract noun, it can in principle be used in a number of functions, as the following conceivable, though fictitious news items show:

... The troublemakers were threatened with summary *defenestration* ...

... the high incidence of wanton acts of *defenestration* is causing the British Railways authorities some disquiet ...

... the *antidefenestration* movement held a public meeting ...

... their behaviour became positively *defenestrational* ...

In this way, a new word not only provides us with an institutional piece of conceptual currency, but with a base from which still other words (like *antidefenestrational*) may be constructed.

It may seem that I have made an unjustified association between creating new words and creating new concepts; that the effect of neologism is merely to condense into a single word the same meaning that could otherwise be expressed by a whole phrase or sentence. My argument, however, is that combined with this abbreviatory function, the *word* as a syntactic element has a concept-defining role, as the following examples will help to show. Agent nouns such as *driver*, *copywriter*, *bed-maker* have in the first stages of their adoption a transparent equivalence to relative clauses, so that, for example, *driver* may be defined as 'a person who drives', *bed-maker* as 'one who makes beds' etc. But it would be false to claim that the single word and the syntactic construction have exactly the same meaning, for the word carries an additional message – namely, the calling into existence of a category. The word *bed-maker* asserts that there is a special institutional category of person, whose function or habit is to make beds. Notice the difference, for example, between asking the question *Is she a bed-maker?* and the question *Does she make beds?* A person questioned in this way could well reply 'Well, she does make beds, but she's not a bed-maker.' If an unlikely new word – let us say *rock-shredder* – were coined on this pattern, this would have a greater novelty value than the phrase (say) *a machine which shreds rocks*, because it would indicate that somewhere or sometime, someone had found it necessary to institute a class of object with this improbable role. This institutionalizing effect of neologism is observed in other types of word, such as abstract nouns and adjectives. We have *Powellism*, *McCarthyism*, and *Gaullism*, but no *Heathism*, *Nixonism* or *Kosyginism* (the asterisk is a way of marking non-existent or illegitimate expressions); but if the latter words were brought into use, they would impel us to search for some special *-ism* – a philosophy or way of life – that we could associate with these political figures. Advertisers are fond of coining new adjective compounds, such as '*ready-to-eat* cereal', '*top-of-the-stove* cookery', and part of the reason for this seems to be that the compound encapsulates a special, perhaps newly invented idea which the advertiser wants us to associate with his product: 'top-of-the-stove cookery' is a new concept of cooking, in which presumably the housewife does not have to bend down annoyingly to take things out of the oven; a 'ready-to-eat cereal' is an especially convenient sort of cereal that does not need to be prepared.

It is a symptom of the 'concept-forming' power of the word that once derived, a new word is launched on a semantic course of development independent of the meaning of the elements which compose it. When it was first used, *baby-sitter* no doubt had a meaning something like 'a person who *sits* with a *baby* (while the parents are out)'; but since then, the baby-sitting institution has broadened into something much more general than its name implies; it can apply to children beyond the age of infancy, and of course, a 'baby-sitter' can keep an eye on his or her charges without once taking up a sitting posture.

If neologism represents a type of linguistic creativity, it is the type of creativity that one finds supremely in the language of technology and of science, rather than in literature. Scientists are continually adapting and reordering their conceptual apparatus in order to give a precise explanation of what they observe; in order, we might say, to reduce the universe to order in new and improved ways. One has only to consider the vast influx of new terminology in a rapidly developing field such as computer science and technology (terms like *megabit, flip-flop, multiplexer, on-line*, and *Write Data Scoop Loop*), to realize how adaptable language has to be to meet the new demands man makes upon it.

The Anti-Creative Tendency in Language: 'Jargonization'

The metaphor which seems to characterize lexical innovation most usefully is that of a capsule or receptacle or package into which a particular semantic content is placed, so that it can henceforward be manipulated and shunted about as an indivisible unit of meaning. In fact, all categorization in language can be viewed as 'prepackaged experience' in this way, and it is important to see such 'prepackaging' as a mixed blessing. It is a good (and indeed necessary) thing from one point of view, for without it we could not have an ordered view of the universe at all; we could not build upon knowledge acquired at previous stages of our culture, or even communicate at all except by a rudimentary sign-system like those that some animal species have.

But on the other hand, the packaging has its bad side, (as suggested, indeed, by the phrase 'prepackaged experience'), in that we are always in danger of accepting the convenient packages as a substitute for the underlying reality. The packages (whose size and shape, as we have seen, are often arbitrarily fixed by the language) are like paper currency, which is simple and convenient to use, and works well so long as everyone accepts the benign fiction that such-and-such a piece of paper is worth such-and-such an amount of gold. It is both the great virtue and the great vice of linguistic categories that they simplify things for us, by disregarding many of the boundaries and gradations that could theoretically be distinguished. Whether simplification amounts to misleading oversimplification depends very much on individual cases.

One noted type of simplification arises with binary polar contrasts (see p. 108) such as *strong/weak*, *hard/soft*, *rich/poor*. In reality, there is a gradual transition, not a clear-cut boundary, between one category and another. But instead of saying (for example) that Mr Jones is 5′ 0″ and Mr Smith is 6′ 0″ tall against a national average of 5′ 8″, it is much simpler just to say that Mr Jones is *short* and Mr Smith is *tall*.

This polarizing tendency has been summed up (by Alfred Korzybski in *Science and Sanity*, 1933, and by S. I. Hayakawa, in *Language in Thought and Action*, 1964) in the phrase 'two-valued orientation', to be contrasted with a 'multi-valued orientation', which would give a more accurate account of the real circumstances. Two-valued thinking has its roots in the nature of language, for in all aspects of language, including semantics, it seems that binary contrasts are more common than other types of contrast. But as before, we must be careful not to overstate the extent to which man is the slave of language: language provides the means for multi-valued thinking as well as two-valued thinking, and all that can be said is that language strongly *predisposes* us to make binary distinctions, and so to impose a simplistic structure on our experiences.

A graphic account of the pressure towards two-valued thinking is given by Simone de Beauvoir in the part of her autobiography describing early childhood:

The world around me was harmoniously based on fixed coordinates and divided into clear-cut compartments. No neutral tints were allowed: everything was in black and white; there was no intermediate position between the traitor and the hero, the renegade and the martyr: all inedible fruits were poisonous; I was told I 'loved' every member of my family, including my most ill-favoured great-aunts. All my experience belied this essentialism. White was only rarely totally white, and the blackness of evil was relieved by lighter touches; I saw greys and halftones everywhere. Only as soon as I tried to define their muted shades, I had to use words, and I found myself in a world of bony-structured concepts. Whatever I beheld with my own eyes and every real experience had to be fitted somehow or other into a rigid category: the myths and the stereotyped ideas prevailed over the truth: unable to pin it down, I allowed truth to dwindle into insignificance.

Memoirs of a Dutiful Daughter, trans. J. Kirkup, Bk. I.

This view from within an alert and imaginative young mind gives an admirable picture of the inhibiting, anti-creative side of concept-formation.

The simplifying and stereotyping effect of conceptual categories, which is inherent in language anyway, can be exploited by lexical innovation in certain uses of the language, such as political journalism. This exploitation I call 'jargonization'. One of the functions of political journalism, we could say, is to interpret, to predigest, or to 'prepack' public events in a way that makes them easy to assimilate for a public that has neither the time nor the mental application to make an exact and detailed study of what is going on. For example, in reporting the struggle between communists and anti-communists in South-East Asia, terms such as *confrontation*, *escalation*, *de-escalation* and *Vietnamization* have been used as convenient counters standing for complex happenings in a confused political situation. American administrators and politicians have been stereotyped as either *hawks* or *doves* (can there be any more striking instance of two-valued thinking?). Such terms are familiar signposts, helping our minds to see a reassuring structure in what would otherwise be an incomprehensible state of flux.

Other terms have come into currency in connection with bargaining and negotiation. If one side in an industrial or international crisis makes a strategic (perhaps sensible) concession to the other, this is almost certain to be represented in some newspaper by the phrase *backing down* (i.e. coming to the verge of conflict and then yielding). A more drastic form of submission is a *climb-down*, or ignominious surrender, under pressure, of a claim one has strongly pressed for. *Sell-out* is the term inevitably used when one party to a dispute is seen to have betrayed his cause by yielding an important matter of principle. And so on. In one sense, such terms are now essential: they fulfil our need for means to structure and classify the complexity of conflicts falling short of war, or at least of total war, in a world where the pressures in the direction of solving disputes by peaceful means are immense. But we have to be continually on our guard against the artificial simplification and compartmentalization to which such jargon may habituate us, and also against an artificial dramatic heightening and polarization of attitude, by which fuzzy issues are made to appear clear-cut. The jargon becomes a substitute for independent judgement and thought.

Creativity (2): The Semantic 'Alertness' of Good Prose

I have mentioned the way in which the overexercise or exploitation of the prepackaging aspect of language can lead to a 'debasement of the linguistic currency'. Language therefore has within itself anti-creative pressures, and the function of the literary writer, in T. S. Eliot's words, is 'to purify the dialect of the tribe' – to restore the currency to its full value, and to resist the natural tendency to devaluation. Writers have always considered themselves the determined enemies of jargon and cliché, and a notable instance of this is the crusade George Orwell carried out against degenerate language, especially against those types of linguistic usage which have earned the disparaging titles 'journalese' and 'officialese'.

Orwell compared latter-day jargon with the simple concrete prose of the Bible, and in order to point a contrast, constructed a famous paraphrase of the following verse from Ecclesiastes:

I returned and saw under the sun, that the race is not to the swift, nor the battle to the strong, neither yet the bread to the wise, nor yet riches to men of understanding, nor yet favour to men of skill; but time and chance happeneth to all.

This becomes, in Orwell's parody of 'modern English':

Objective consideration of contemporary phenomena compels the conclusion that success or failure in competitive activities exhibits no tendency to be commensurate with innate capacity, but that a considerable element of the unpredictable must invariably be taken into account.

In his essay 'Politics and the English Language' from which this passage is taken, Orwell deplores the habit of what he calls 'gumming together long strips of words which have already been set in order by somebody else, and making the results presentable by sheer humbug'. Particular targets of his scorn were cliché phrases containing dying metaphors, like *toe the line*, *ride roughshod over*, *play a leading part in*, *militate against*, and *stand shoulder to shoulder with*; also vague grandiloquent phrases which can be replaced by a simple, more direct substitute, as *render inoperable* can be replaced by *spoil* or *ruin*, or *take into consideration* can be replaced by *consider*. The point about such phrases is that given one word, the other words follow almost as an automatic conditioned response: we no longer think about their individual meanings. The well-worn grooves of expression are an outward sign of the unadventurous, mindless thought-grooves that underlie them.

Orwell saw this trend not just as an invitation to slovenly thought, but as an insidious influence on the intellectual, aesthetic, and moral life of the community: 'Language becomes ugly and inaccurate because our thoughts are foolish, but the slovenliness of our language makes it easier for us to have vicious thoughts.' Other modern commentators have taken an even more dramatic view of the modern debasement of language. Hayakawa (in *Language in Thought and Action*) talks of the 'Niagara of words' to which we are subjected daily through the mass media of television, radio, and newsprint. Because of the Babel of competing linguistic stimuli, we stop our ears, like people standing in a market-place where every stall-keeper is shouting at the top of his voice. This in turn leads to a coarser and more undiscriminating use of language. In an age when the whiteness of a wash seems to be treated as a criterion for admission to heaven on the Day of Judgement, how on earth are we to devise a terminology for the things that really matter?

In the face of this trivialization of language, some poets have retreated towards incoherence, and according to the fears of George Steiner, in *Language and Silence*, they may eventually even give up the attempt to communicate altogether. We do not, however, have to take up such an apocalyptic view of the matter: we can see the artist in words, like all people of linguistic conscience, as waging his struggle against the irresponsible use of language that often goes with the stereotyping of linguistic responses. Resistance to these pressures can be equated with the ideal of prose writing: the ideal that has been summed up as the search for the *mot juste*, or, in Pope's definition of wit, as 'what oft was thought, but ne'er so well expressed'.

It might be argued that this goal scarcely merits the term 'creative': at best it is '*re*creative', restoring language to its full semantic value. But in fact it may be related to a purely mathematical sense of 'linguistic creativity' which is familiar in modern linguistics. Our linguistic competence (as Chomsky has pointed out) is such that with a finite number of rules, we can generate and interpret an infinite number of sentences. Day by day we encounter and produce sentences we have never met in our whole life before. In its semantic aspect, this creativity of linguistic resource may be demonstrated by our ability to make up and make sense of configurations (e.g. the statement 'I ate one hundred and seventy-nine alligators for breakfast last Tuesday') which have virtually a nil probability of occurring in day-to-day communication. But in performance, this creative or innovative power inherent in our language competence is eroded by our tendency to rely on well-worn paths through the theoretically infinite array of possible English utterances. Thus not merely individual concepts, but configurations of concepts, become stereotyped. The writer who resists this principle of least effort, by exploring new pathways and taking no meaning for granted, is in a real sense 'creative'.

Creativity (3): The 'Conceptual Fusion' of Poetry

Those types of creativity I have associated with the scientist and the prose-writer are by no means absent from poetry: poets have often aspired to the prose ideal, and have often extended their communicative resources by neologism. But there is a third and perhaps even more important notion of linguistic creativity which applies pre-eminently to poetry: one which amounts to actually breaking through the conceptual bonds with which language constrains us. If one of the major roles of language is to reduce experience to order, to 'prepackage' it for us, then the poet is the person who unties the string. It is in this context that the 'irrational' or 'counterlogical' character of poetry becomes explicable.

A very simple example of poetic irrationality is the Latin poet Catullus' famous paradox *Odi et amo*: 'I hate and I love'. The two-valued orientation of language makes us see love and hate as mutually exclusive categories: 'I love Lesbia' and 'I hate Lesbia' are looked upon as contradictory statements. But the poet, by presenting a seeming absurdity, shocks his reader into rearranging his categories; the stereotyped concept of love and hate as contrasting emotions is destroyed. A kind of 'conceptual fusion' takes place.

The quality just observed in poetic paradox is also present in metaphor – a more pervasive and important semantic feature of poetry. Again, the mechanism can be demonstrated by a very simple example. In an Anglo-Saxon poem, the expression *mere-hengest* ('sea-steed') is used as a metaphor for 'ship'. The connection between *steed* and *ship* lies in common connotations: both horses and ships convey men from one place to another; both are used (in the heroic context of the poem) for adventurous journeys and for warfare; both carry their riders with an up-and-down movement. By presenting the two concepts simultaneously, as superimposed images, the poet dissolves those linguistically crucial criteria which define their separateness: the fact that a horse is animate whereas a ship is not; and the fact that a horse moves over land, whereas a ship moves over water. The conceptual reorganization brought about in this metaphor may be diagrammed as follows (components in square brackets are regarded as connotative, or non-criterial features – see p. 14):

1. CATEGORIES IN THE LANGUAGE

Horse	*Ship*
1. animate	1. inanimate
2. on land	2. on sea
3. [for travelling on]	3. for travelling on
4. [with up-and-down movement]	4. [with up-and-down movement]
5. [for warfare, etc.]	5. [for warfare, etc.]

2. NEW CATEGORY BROUGHT ABOUT BY METAPHOR

Horse	Ship
1. animate 2. on land	1. inanimate 2. on sea
3.[for travelling on] 4.[with up-and-down movement] 5.[for warfare, etc.]	3. for travelling on 4.[with up-and-down movement] 5.[for warfare, etc.]

Through its power of realigning conceptual boundaries, metaphor can achieve a communicative effect which in a sense is 'beyond language'. It thus has a liberating effect, counteracting and reversing the child's progressive domination by the 'bony-structured' world of language as Simone de Beauvoir records it in her autobiography. As a chief instrument of the poet's imagination, metaphor is the means by which he takes his revenge on language for the 'stereotyped ideas' which have 'prevailed over the truth'. It is not surprising that children's language produces many instances of semantic 'mistakes' which strike the adult as poetic. Two cases in my own experience are a child's description of a viaduct as a *window-bridge*, and of the moon as *that shilling in the sky*, both based, significantly, on visual analogy. The *window-bridge* example is very similar to the *mere-hengest* of the Anglo-Saxon poet: the openings in a viaduct, when seen side on, are indeed very close in appearance and construction to the window-openings in the facade of a house. Using his generalizing ability, the child hits on physical appearance as a crucial criterion, at the expense of the criterion of function, which the language regards as more important. The difference between the two cases, of course, is that while the poet is familiar with the institutional categories and is aware of his departure from them, the child is not.

Summary

The points I have tried to make in this chapter are:

1. Conceptual meaning in a language can be described as a system of categories.

2. The categories vary from language to language, and are often arbitrary, in the sense that they impose an artificial structure on experience.

3. It is a matter for debate how far categories vary from language to language, and how far it is possible to postulate universal categories common to all human language.

4. The conceptual system of language predisposes us towards certain distinctions rather than others, but the extent to which man is the slave of his language in this respect should not be over-emphasized, as there are at least three senses in which he can be said to use the system creatively.

5. 'Semantic creativity' in the first sense is lexical innovation, which enables us to create new conceptual categories. This sense (at least in so far as lexical innovation is equated with neologism) applies pre-eminently to scientific and technical language.

6. The second type of semantic creativity is the 'semantic alertness' which resists the stereotyping tendency in linguistic use, and makes full inventive use of the infinity of possible configurations of meaning that can be expressed in the language. This sense applies particularly to literary prose.

7. The third type of creativity is 'conceptual fusion' brought about by 'counterlogical' devices such as metaphor and paradox. This is particularly associated with poetry.

4. Semantics and Society

In an ideal society of robots, each of whom had a preassigned role which he performed without demur, the only function of language would be to expound knowledge and pass information, so as to facilitate cooperation between members of society. We are only too aware that this is not the case in human society: all kinds of conflicts and pressures arise between one individual and another, or between one group and another, and language takes a major part in the way these interactions are played out. Although theoretically, and often in practice, conceptual meaning is the most important element in linguistic communication, its importance in some situations becomes reduced to almost nil; and more generally, the seven types of meaning listed on p. 26 vary a great deal in their contribution to the total communicative effect. My task in this chapter is to consider how our semantic competence is harnessed to various social needs, a task in which I cannot fail to take some note of the moral questions involved in the 'strategic semantics' of propaganda and loaded language generally.

Five Functions of Language

Before proceeding, let us look at the most important communicative functions of language.

Apart from the neutral *informational* function which everyone tends to assume is most important, language can have an *expressive* function; that is, it can be used to express its originator's feelings and attitudes – swear words and exclamations are the most obvious instances of this. Conceptual meaning is predominant in the informational use of language. But for the expressive function, affective meaning (what language communicates of the author's attitudes – see p. 18) is clearly all-important. A third function of language is the *directive* function whereby we aim to influence the behaviour or attitudes of others. The most straightforward instances of the directive function are commands and requests. This function of social control places emphasis on the receiver's end, rather than the originator's end of the message; but it resembles the expressive function in giving less importance, on the whole, to conceptual meaning than to other types of meaning, particularly affective and connotative meaning.

The expressive function has often been assumed to include the poetic use of language, but this view, I think, rests on an unacceptable, though popular, view of poetry as an effusion of the poet's emotions. Instead, I would prefer to recognize in poetry a separate *aesthetic* function, which can be defined as 'the use of language for the sake of the linguistic artefact itself, and for no ulterior purpose'. This aesthetic function, as we saw on pp. 41–5, can have at least as much to do with conceptual as with affective meaning. But the main semantic point about poetry is that it is language communicating 'at full stretch': all possible avenues of communication, all levels and types of meaning, are open to use. Both the poet and the reader bring a heightened sensitivity to meaning to bear on the act of communication.

Yet a further function of language, which the layman rarely takes seriously enough, is the so-called *phatic* function (after Malinowski's term 'phatic communion'), i.e. the function of keeping communication lines open, and keeping social relationships in good repair (in British culture, talking about the weather is a well-known example of this). The phatic function is at the furthest remove from the aesthetic function, in that here the communicative work done by language is at its lightest: it is not so much what one says, but the fact that one says it at all, that matters.

I do not claim that these five functions of language form an ideal classification: many other break-downs of function have been proposed, and (as we shall see) there is some difficulty particularly in separating the expressive and directive functions. In any case, allowance has to be made for the combined fulfilment of a number of different functions. Rarely is a piece of language *purely* informative, *purely* expressive, etc. Thus the remark 'I feel like a cup of coffee' may be read, in the right circumstances, as at once infor-

mational, expressive, and directive. But there is a particular interest
in the present classification (which is based roughly on Jakobson,
1960): it can be neatly correlated with five essential features in any
communicative situation, namely (1) *subject-matter*, (2) *originator*
(i.e. speaker or writer), (3) *receiver* (i.e. listener or reader), (4) *the
channel of communication* between them, and (5) the linguistic
message itself. Each of the five functions I have mentioned can be
identified with a special orientation of language to each of these
factors in turn:

FUNCTION	ORIENTATION TOWARDS
informational:	subject-matter
expressive:	speaker/writer
directive:	listener/reader
phatic:	channel of communication
aesthetic:	message

or in diagram form:

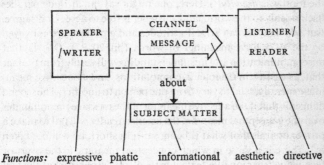

Functions: expressive   phatic   informational   aesthetic   directive

The functions which most directly involve the social roles of
language are the *expressive*, *directive*, and *phatic* functions; and it
is to these that I shall devote the rest of the chapter. It may be
wondered why the expressive function is included in this trio: after
all, one can use expressive language in a social vacuum (Robinson
Crusoe may have uttered an oath when he saw his clothes float
away on the tide). But when we are considering the public expression of opinions and attitudes, it is very difficult to recognize a
boundary between expressing one's own feelings, and influencing

those of others. There is no way of telling, from inspecting the text, whether the position adopted by a writer is actually an expression of his own convictions, or whether it is assumed solely for the purposes of argument. At least in ideological and religious discussion, the two things usually go together. This is why, in the discussion that follows, I shall treat the expressive and directive functions together.

Conceptual versus Affective Meaning

Whenever language is 'loaded' towards or against a given set of attitudes, there is a danger of confusion, unless the addressee is able to distinguish between the conceptual and affective content of the message. As we noted in Chapter 2, there is an overlap between conceptual and affective meaning, in that attitudes may be overtly expressed by words denoting emotion ('I *love* you') or words whose primary content is evaluative ('He made an *excellent* speech, but the food was *dreadful*'). Here, one might say, an attitude parades itself openly to the world, and a listener is free to agree or disagree. But two dangers can arise if attitudes and emotions are conveyed by the associative meanings of words (pp. 20–22). One is that miscommunication and misunderstanding will result from the fact that, as we saw in Chapter 2, connotations, and associative meanings generally, tend to vary from one person to another. The second danger is that if the affective meaning of the message predominates over the conceptual meaning, the listener/reader will fail to make a proper appraisal of what is being said; in short, he will be 'taken in'. There is a sense in which conceptual meaning is the overt or face-value meaning of a text: it is to all appearances what the text is 'about'. By the same token, there is something covert, implicit and potentially insidious about affective meaning: if a writer appeals to our emotions, we cannot confront his appeal with 'I disagree with what you say', or 'I do not share your feelings' in the same way as we could if he had made his feelings and values explicit. We only have a certain feeling that we are being called upon to respond emotionally, a feeling that may be difficult to put into words, and which may be even more difficult to counteract by argument.

The words which differ in associative meaning most notoriously are words referring to social groupings: nationality words, for example. We will all be fairly well agreed that an *American* is a person born or brought up in the U.S.A., and who has U.S. nationality. But affective connotations may differ according to our experiences or acquired prejudices about Americans: one set of associations might be 'Americans are brash, boastful, materialistic', another 'Americans are open-minded, generous, fair, business-like'. Terms referring to religious sects are equally likely to communicate different things. In Northern Ireland, the term *Catholic* is likely to have strong connotations (differing pointedly from one group to another) not generally felt by people living in England. For instance, it is possible that an Ulsterman would consider 'a loyal and patriotic Catholic' a contradiction in terms.

The danger seems to be greatest with words referring to political ideas or movements: *anarchism, communism, fascist, imperialism, Nazi, Powellite, racist, socialist,* etc. Here there seem to be such strong connotations on one side or the other that the dictionary sense of the word can be almost forgotten. A *liberal* according to the Concise Oxford Dictionary is one 'favourable to democratic reforms and [to the] abolition of privilege'. But in South Africa and quite widely in the U.S.A. *liberal* will have connotations of one who compromises with or encourages forces destructive to society – perhaps a dangerous political agitator. In contrast, someone on the left of the political spectrum in Great Britian will probably write off a liberal as an ineffectual moderate.

With a word like *democratic*, the connotative meaning seems to take over completely, so that supporters of two opposed political systems will claim that their own system is democratic and the other undemocratic. In such a state of affairs, it is doubtful whether 'The government of Liechtenstein is a democracy' tells us anything about the institution concerned, except that the speaker approves of it.

An unrestrained partisan user of language will tend to resort to what Hayakawa (in *Language in Thought and Action*) calls *snarl words* and *purr words*. Snarl words are words whose conceptual meaning becomes irrelevant because whoever is using them is simply capitalizing on their unfavourable connotations in order to give forceful expression to his own hostility. Terms for extreme or uncompromising political views, such as *communist* or *fascist*, are particularly prone to degenerate into snarl words. The opposite category of purr words has already been illustrated in the word *democratic*; other potential political purr words are *freedom, human rights, patriotic, fatherland, equality*.

Hayakawa gives a thought-provoking example of the kind of communicative disaster to which the variability of affective meaning can lead:

A distinguished Negro sociologist tells of an incident in his adolescence when he was hitchhiking far from home in regions where negroes are hardly ever seen. He was befriended by an extremely kindly white couple who fed him and gave him a place to sleep in their home. However, they kept calling him 'little nigger' – a fact which upset him profoundly even while he was grateful for their kindness. He finally got up courage to ask the man not to call him by that 'insulting term'.

'Who's insultin' you, son?' said the man.

'You are, sir – that name you're always calling me.'

'What name?'

'Uh . . . you know.'

'I ain't callin' you no names, son.'

'I mean your calling me "nigger".'

'Well, what's insultin' about that? You are a nigger, ain't you?'

Language in Thought and Action, pp. 90–91.

What was the cause of this breakdown of understanding on such a tender point? The white man was apparently using the word without being conscious of its affective meaning: he was using *nigger* simply as a familiar synonym for *negro*. But for the negro, the term had powerful affective connotations, as a snarl word used by whites as a term of contempt for blacks. Hence for him it was (what most people indeed recognize it to be nowadays) a symbol of racial hatred and oppression.

Nigger is a member of a class of denigratory racial, political, or nationality terms which have their own built-in affective bias: *Yank, Wops, Jap, red, pigs* are other examples. One may say that such terms (significantly, they usually occur in the plural) are ready-made for use as 'snarl words'.

The examples I have given suggest that the greatest dangers to intelligent communication come with cases where the affective meaning becomes a major part of, if not the whole of, the message. In the diagram below, if we let the large white circles represent the total meaning, and the smaller shaded areas the conceptual meaning, then the proportions of conceptual meaning might dwindle roughly as indicated, assuming a fairly typical use of the cited words:

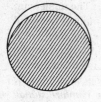 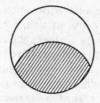 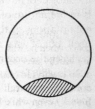

typewriter
(neutral, unemotive)

America
(somewhat emotive)

fascist
(snarl word)

'Associative Engineering': Euphemism and Image-Building

Words for which affective associations bulk large are by no means limited to areas such as race and politics. In private life, unpleasant associations are unavoidable in dealing with such subjects as death, disease, crime, and punishment, and it is on these subjects, as well as on the taboo-ridden subjects of sex and the excretive processes of the body, that *euphemism*, the linguistic equivalent of disinfectant, has an inevitable influence. Euphemism (Greek: 'wellspeaking') is the practice of referring to something offensive or delicate in terms that make it sound more pleasant or becoming than it really is. The technique consists of replacing a word which has offensive connotations with another expression, which makes no overt reference to the unpleasant side of the subject, and may even be a positive misnomer (as when a hostess asks a guest whether he would like to 'wash his hands'). By this means, people find it possible to live with, and talk about, things that would otherwise shock or disturb them. *Disease* and *indisposition*, now established words for illness, were originally euphemisms, meaning 'lack of ease' and 'lack of ability to do things'. *Concentration camp* was also originally a euphemism ('a place where the non-combatants of a district are accommodated') applied to a camp where political prisoners and prisoners of war are kept – a place no better, and in many cases much worse, than a prison. And there are many more well-known examples.

A euphemism is in a way the opposite of a snarl word: instead of maximizing the unpleasant associations of a term, one tries to purge the subject of its damaging affective associations. But a euphemism is in the nature of things a palliative, not a cure. The unpleasant connotations of the word are, after all, not the fault of the word itself, but of what it refers to. So the euphemistic expression which replaces the original term soon gets tarred with the same brush. This is why, for example, there are so many euphemisms in English for *lavatory* (itself originally a euphemism meaning 'wash-place'): *privy, water-closet, toilet, cloakroom, restroom, comfort station* (this last favoured on American campgrounds), not to mention the now ubiquitous *loo*. An example of a different kind, this time from the political field, is the multiplication of terms we use in referring to economically less favoured parts of the world: such areas are no longer referred to as *backward* or *undeveloped*, but as *developing countries, less developed countries, emergent nations*, etc.

It is to an example like this last, in which euphemism has a more conscious and persuasive character, that the expression 'associative engineering' seems appropriate. In a sense this is not euphemism at all. *Emergent nations* is not a nice label for something nasty: it is a label chosen with strategic tact, to pick out the optimistic and progressive aspect of the phenomenon labelled, and to play down the pessimistic aspect. The choice of term embodies a point of view, a political argument. A case where associations are more obviously chosen for political effect is *apartheid* ('separatehood'), considered as a euphemism for 'racial discrimination' or 'the colour bar'. It is an important point that the originators of the term would be unlikely to consider it a euphemism, or accept the offensiveness of what it refers to. 'Separatehood', they would say, does not have to involve racial inequality: and they would claim that the choice of a name involves not just a question of connotative meaning, but of conceptual meaning: to change 'apartheid' to 'racial discrimination' would be to talk about quite a different matter.

'Associative engineering' is not just a negative process of glossing over unwanted associations. Its positive side, the acquisition of pleasant associations, is equally important, and is well illustrated by the 'image-building' techniques of modern advertising. Manufacturers of men's cosmetics overcome the potential effeminate image of their product with aggressively masculine associations, in which the choice of product names like *Brut* play a part. A desirable image of affluence and exclusive high-living can be obtained by straightforward word-painting ('White tie, red sash, sunburnt ladies and steel bands – a real Caribbean affair . . .') or indirectly, by details of style:

From the most distinguished
tobacco house in the world
   (from an advertisement for Dunhills)

Cigarettes by John Player, England

In the first of these two extracts from cigarette advertisements, the choice of the word *house* is the detail to which I wish to point. *House* might be considered by the uninitiated an unremarkable alternative for *firm* or *manufacturers*; but its associations are with gentlemanly businesses carried on by long-established family firms – a far cry from the factory conveyor-belt. In the second phrase, it is not so much the choice of words as the syntactic construction (that of *by* connecting two noun phrases) that suggests exclusiveness. This construction usually indicates some kind of artistic activity: *Landscape gardening by X*; *Floral arrangements by Y*; *Costumes by Z*; so here again there is an effort to dignify the somewhat tarnished image of cigarette-makers and -marketers with overtones of quality and distinction.

Again, taking 'associative engineering' in the more general sense of 'strategic choice of label with regard to improving associations', we find cases which, like *emergent nations*, involve an issue of conceptual meaning, of how one 'conceptualizes' an institution. A B.B.C. programme on 11 February 1969 reported a proposal for establishing a new category of ordained priest, who

would do full-time work in a factory or office in addition to his
pastoral duties. When the question arose of what this new type of
cleric would be called, the B.B.C. interviewer made three sug-
gestions: *auxiliary priests, part-time priests,* and *worker priests.* For
reasons not difficult to appreciate, all of these were rejected:
'auxiliary priests' and 'part-time priests' sound too much like
second-rate assistants, whereas 'worker priests' seems to allege
that other priests do not work. Thus the arrival at a satisfactory
title (*self-supporting priests*) was a matter more of discarding titles
with unfortunate associations, and which would be likely to
offend, rather than of finding a positively suitable name for the
job. But I have given a strategic explanation: the church authorities, on the other hand, could give a conceptual explanation; e.g.,
that *part-time priest* is theologically inaccurate because a priest is a
priest all the time, even when working in a factory; that *worker
priest* is pleonastic in as much as all priests have work to do. Thus
an issue of associations, of 'the right image', can easily be turned
into an argument about dictionary meanings.

'Conceptual Engineering'

Examples like *apartheid* show that propaganda does not just take
the form of capitalizing on the affective meaning of a word at the
expense of its conceptual meaning; more importantly, it becomes a
matter of enlisting on one's own side the conceptual meaning of a
word, so that the favourable associations can be claimed for oneself, or the bad associations used to stigmatize one's opponent. If
the view is taken (as I have taken it here) that conceptual meaning
is a more fundamental part of linguistic communication than associative meaning, then this is a case of 'the tail wagging the dog' –
of language brought to a state where the associations of a word
determine its choice, and where the conceptual meaning is reduced to an ancillary consequence, which has to be 'squared' in
order for the use of the term to be legitimate. The situation re-
minds one of the principle of 'might is right': just as the first action
of a successful rebellion is to legitimize its rule and illegitimize that
of its predecessor in power, so many people turn to the dictionary
(or the private dictionary stored in themselves) as a guarantee of

verbal legality. Thus the principle of 'conceptual engineering' becomes part and parcel of 'associative engineering'.

Consider the word *violence*. Because of the irredeemably bad associations of *violence*, any public justification of political activities which lead to physical force or conflict must maintain the thesis that 'our actions are non-violent'. The *Guardian* reported on 2 September 1969 that a certain Mr O'Sullivan was arrested for trying to steal arms from a factory in Dagenham. When asked whether he was a 'militant', O'Sullivan replied that he did not know what the word meant, and went on: 'If it means using violence, I wouldn't agree. I would prefer to use the word *force*. Sometimes you must use force as a means to an end.' From this extract, it is difficult to tell whether O'Sullivan was purely indulging in associative engineering (using *force* roughly as a more pleasant synonym for *violence*, as one might prefer to call someone a *lady* rather than a *woman*); or whether he would have backed up his choice by dictionary arguments; e.g. that *violence* involves 'an extreme degree of force', 'aggressive force', or 'force which results in injury', etc., none of which applied to his actions. A more definite instance of the strategic definition of the word *violence* arises when militant bodies claim (as they have done in the past in Northern Ireland) that in breaking through police cordons with the weight of their bodies they are not being violent. Presumably in this case the argument runs that the police are themselves agents of force, and therefore any force applied against them is in the nature of passive resistance to force: the element of aggression is absent. This sort of semantic manipulation is possible because the conceptual meanings of most words, and especially of abstract words such as enter into political discussion, remain to some extent indeterminate (see p. 123). There is always room for disagreement on whether a given feature of meaning (such as the element of 'aggression' associated with *violence*) is a criterial feature, or simply a frequent connotation of the word.

Definition by partisan fiat can often go to the extent of reshaping the conceptual meaning of a word, so that it no longer matches the interpretation of most speakers of the language. After the kidnapping of a British diplomat by the Quebec Liberation Front, a spokesman for that organization referred to the kidnapping as a 'purely military action' against the 'British colonial government in Quebec'. The use of *colonial* here (in despite of the British North America Act of 1867) is one that I shall not speculate on; but *military* is a clearer case of conceptual engineering, in which the notion of open armed conflict is suppressed, but the moral implications of warfare are maintained: in a military situation, killing and the seizure of prisoners can be justified. The same communiqué referred to demands for the release of 'political prisoners', who in fact were members of the QLF jailed for such crimes as bomb-planting and blackmail. Here again, the valuable associations of *political prisoner* (overtones of secret police, imprisonment without trial, conviction merely for holding certain opinions, Amnesty International, etc.) were pressed into service against the Canadian authorities, at some cost to the normal understanding of what a political prisoner is. The QLF members in jail were probably 'political prisoners' in the nominal sense that they had done what they had done for political reasons: but what they had done was 'criminal' in a legal sense, independently of their political convictions. Reduced to a semantic argument, the question at issue was: Does *political prisoner* mean 'a person imprisoned for holding certain political views' (as I normally suppose it to mean) or 'a person imprisoned as a result of the illegal consequences of his political views'?

'Position'

Strategic semantics takes on a more elaborate form when it is a question not only of defining words, but of constructing a whole argument in favour of a given attitude. If one studies a piece of propaganda, one can usually find a structure analogous to a logical proof, except that the connections between one proposition and another, and even the underlying postulates, tend to be associative rather than conceptual. This quasi-logical network, which we may call the propagandist's *position*, is rather like a linguistic suit of armour protecting his attitudes. Polemics generally consists in trying to maintain one's own position intact whilst blasting holes in that of one's opponent.

For a simplified illustration of a position, we may return to the term *violence*, as considered earlier, and reconstruct the following 'proof' as the rationale underlying a person's linguistic behaviour:

(1) Being violent is bad.
(2) Being violent entails being aggressive.
(3) We are not aggressive.
(4) Therefore we are not violent.
(5) Therefore we are not bad.

A more extensive illustration will be provided by the following paragraph from a leaflet dropped on Czechoslovakia by the Warsaw Pact authorities at the time of their military take-over of the country, on 21 August 1968:

> Responding to the request for help received from leading Party and state leaders of Czechoslovakia who have remained faithful to *socialism,* we instructed our armed forces to go to the support of the *working class* and all the *people of Czechoslovakia* to defend their *socialist gains,* which are increasingly threatened by plots of domestic and foreign reactionary forces. [Italics added.]

The four expressions italicized in this extract are assumed, for the purpose of propaganda, to have strong favourable connotations. These expressions provide the 'associative postulates' which are the starting point for my analysis:

(1) Socialism***
(2) The working class***
(3) The people of Czechoslovakia***
(4) Socialist gains***

The three asterisks (***) are a mark of favourable affective meaning, and if one wishes, one may mentally translate them into conceptual terms by the phrase 'is/are good'. Thus 'Socialism***' can be rendered 'Socialism is good'. The object of the analysis is to arrive by deduction as many times as possible at the proposition 'We ***'. The number of times this can be done is an indication of the strength of affective bias in the passage. Here are two specimen 'proofs':

A. (1) Socialism ***   (given)
    (5) Therefore being faithful to socialism ***   (from 1)

    (6) Therefore the leading Party and state leaders of Czecho-
        slovakia who have remained faithful to socialism ***

                                       (from 5)

    (7) Therefore to give help to the leading Party and state
        leaders . . . ***   (from 6)

    (8) Therefore responding to a request for help from the lead-
        ing Party and state leaders . . . ***   (from 7)

    (9) We have responded to a request for help from the leading
        Party and state leaders . . .   (stated)

   (10) *Therefore we* ***   (from 8 and 9)

B.   (4) Socialist gains ***   (given)

   (11) Therefore to defend socialist gains ***   (from 4)

   (12) Our armed forces went to defend socialist gains   (stated)

   (13) Therefore, our armed forces ***   (from 11 and 12)

   (14) Therefore to instruct our armed forces to defend socialist
        gains ***   (from 11 and 13)

   (15) We instructed our armed forces to defend socialist gains

                                    (stated)

   (16) *Therefore we* ***   (from 14 and 15)

'Proofs' similar to B could also be constructed starting from postulates (2) and (3). The analysis is only fragmentary, and I would not
want to claim that it is anything more than a parody of a strict
logical proof: nevertheless, it shows how the logical and conceptual
content of language can be enlisted in support of the affective
content. This may be called euphemistic propaganda: its aim is to
show that what appears to be an invasion is actually nothing but a
friendly intervention. Hence many of the values are positive values
indirectly attached to the originator of the message. For propaganda which concentrates on the denigration of 'the enemy', a
similar analysis could be undertaken, but the values represented
by *** above would be 'bad' rather than 'good'.

In the Warsaw Pact example, there is a fairly direct relationship
between the 'position' and what is actually asserted by the text; in
other words, the argumentation is overt and undisguised. In other
circumstances, the 'position' is conveyed in a more subtle and
indirect manner, and one type of indirectness is exemplified in the
following, from a report published by the John Birch Society in the
U.S.A. in 1964:

How are we reacting to the realities of our world? What do we think of the steady gain of Communism – of the millions killed, tortured and enslaved by this criminal conspiracy? Do we still laugh at Krushchev's claim that our children will live under Communism? Do we shrug off Cuba? Will we shrug off Mexico? Are we concerned about the certain, documented, real influence Communism exercises in Washington? Do we watch with curiosity? Do we pull down the curtain on these disturbing thoughts? Do we draw down the warm covers of apathy around our necks?

What is interesting about this paragraph is that it overtly asserts nothing (it consists entirely of questions), and yet it presupposes or takes for granted a considerable number of propositions about Communism:

(1) Communism is gaining steadily.
(2) Communism is a criminal conspiracy.
(3) Millions have been killed by Communism.
(4) Millions have been tortured by Communism.
(5) Millions have been enslaved by Communism.
(6) Krushchev has claimed that our children will live under Communism.
(7) Communism exercises certain influence in Washington.
(8) Communism exercises documented influence in Washington.
(9) Communism exercises real influence in Washington.

These statements are part of the writer's 'position', but they are presented obliquely, in the form of presuppositions contained within noun phrases. Presupposition is a semantic relation which has been much studied in recent theoretical semantics, and will be considered more carefully later (see pp. 291ff). But for the present, we can simply note that as a propaganda tactic it not only has the advantage of indirectness, but is a way of presenting one's position to the reader as if it is a matter of common knowledge, which no one in his right mind would question.

I have presented 'conceptual engineering' and 'position building' chiefly from the directive point of view; but they could equally be considered from the expressive point of view, as ways in which a man's thought processes rationalize his attitudes. Like Orwell, we may well be worried as to whether bad habits of thinking and feeling and bad habits of language are part of the same vicious circle. Whether, for example, a tendency to argue from *ad hoc* definitions which suit one's case may not have causes and repercussions deeper down, in the degree to which people's feelings and prejudices are allowed to dominate intellectual processes. Similarly, looking at society as a whole, we may speculate that as more irresponsible propaganda gains currency, so it becomes more difficult to think clearly and in a disciplined way.

The Phatic Function

Having seen how the expressive and directive functions of language may reflect divisions and tensions between one social group and another, we turn now to the phatic function of language, the function of maintaining cohesion *within* social groups.

While phatic communion is important – perhaps far more important than we realize – for maintaining the equilibrium of society, it suffers from the major drawback of being, on the whole, dull and pedestrian. To show that our intentions are friendly, we indulge in 'small-talk', 'chit-chat', or 'sweet nothings'; for example, greetings, farewells, and routine polite questions such as 'How's the family?' and 'What happened to Spurs on Saturday then?'. The words are empty of meaning, in the sense that so long as a conversational hiatus is filled, what one says matters little. With strangers and casual acquaintances, it is advisable to have a repertoire of inoffensive remarks at your command, and on the whole, assertions must be uncontroversial. Hence the importance (in Great Britain) of remarks about the weather: if you say 'The nights are getting longer these days, aren't they', no one can possibly disagree with you. On the other hand, if you say as you pass a stranger 'Cold weather, isn't it', and he replies, 'No, actually the temperature today is higher than the seasonal average', you may well feel that he has mistaken the purpose of your remark, by treating it as *informational* rather than *phatic*.

Interesting explanations of phatic language have been put forward by experts in other fields than linguistics. The ethologist Desmond Morris, in *The Naked Ape*, notes that human small-talk has analogues in the animal world, notably in the mutual grooming customs of monkeys. He points out that this is one of the chief co-operative activities in which monkeys partake, and that whereas it has the practical effect of keeping the fur clean and clear of parasites, only an extension of this function to the social function of maintaining group cohesion can account for the inordinate amount of grooming in which monkeys indulge. Language in man is closely parallel to grooming in monkeys: it is an extremely important cooperative behaviour (it may have originated in the need for close cooperation in activities such as hunting); but the amount of talking that goes on can only be adequately explained by the secondary function of maintaining social contact.

A different account of phatic language as a substitute activity has been put forward by the social psychiatrist Eric Berne in *Games People Play* (1966). He argues that phatic communication (which he calls 'stroking') is an adult substitute for the unusual amount of handling and cuddling that a human baby requires, and normally receives, for his proper development. When he grows up, the human being does not lose this constant need for physical reassurance, but a great deal of the need is rechannelled towards reassurance administered by verbal rather than physical contact. Thus phatic language becomes characterized, in Berne's terms, as a mutual stroking ritual, in which a balance is maintained between the amount of pleasure administered and received.

Here is an example of what Berne calls 'an 8-stroke ritual' (the dialect is American English):

A: Hi!
B: Hi!
A: Warm enough forya?
B: Sure is. Looks like rain, though.
A: Well, take cara yourself.
B: I'll be seeing you.
A: So long.
B: So long.

This ritual is satisfactory, because each participant receives four strokes, and goes away well disposed to the other, having had the right amount of reassurance. When A and B first met, they may have had to partake in a more elaborate ritual; when they get to know one another well, they will probably make do with a more streamlined ritual of two strokes:

A: Hi!
B: Hi!

If B strokes too little or too much, the result is to upset the balance. An over-effusive reply will give A the feeling that B is looking for a way to take advantage of him; an under-effusive reply such as

A: Hi!
B: (no reply)

will leave A feeling anxious and unrewarded.

In a context such as this we can appreciate why silence can be so devastating to good social relations: it is not just a neutral response but can easily be interpreted as a hostile one. We might, indeed, equate the phatic function in general with the avoidance of un-looked-for silence. Particularly at social functions such as sherry parties, the conversational ball must be kept in the air at all costs, or else one seems to be breaking off diplomatic relations with one's interlocutor. This presents a problem: topics such as health and weather are soon exhausted, and further things to say must be invented. From this, it is easy to see how joke-telling, saying witty things, and general verbal foolery acquire importance quite out of proportion to their apparent merit.

Phatic language has its parallels in public affairs. Everyone is familiar with occasions when statesmen and politicians make public utterances which are elaborate ways of saying nothing. The cliché formula about 'full and frank talks on a wide range of subjects of mutual interest' has become almost *de rigueur* for announcing the outcome of political meetings whose confidentiality remains sacred. We might say such 'non-communiqués' are attempts to maintain communication channels (namely, to satisfy the expectation of the mass media and the public that *some* sort of statement should be made) in cases where the actual passing of information would bring to light differences which the negotiating parties are trying to pretend do not exist. This is in marked contrast to pro-paganda statements of a more militant kind, in which a political power is emphasizing the solidarity of its own group, and the struggle it is waging against hostile forces. In the one case there is reliance on neutral terms such as *problems*, *discussions*, and *mutual concern*, while in the other case there is a strong tendency towards two-valued thinking and a polarization of 'good' and 'bad' associations. Anyone who describes a political situation as a 'problem' is already seeing both sides of it.

On its most exalted and public level, the phatic function is found in ceremonial speeches by heads of state. The following is the opening of President Kennedy's inaugural address:

Mr Chief Justice, President Eisenhower, Vice President Nixon, President Truman, reverend clergy, fellow citizens, we observe today not a victory of party, but a celebration of freedom – symbolizing an end, as well as a beginning – signifying renewal, as well as change. For I have sworn before you and Almighty God the same solemn oath our forebears prescribed nearly a century and three quarters ago.

The world is very different now. For man holds in his mortal hands the power to abolish all forms of human poverty and all forms of human life. And yet the same revolutionary beliefs for which our forebears fought are still at issue around the globe – the belief that the rights of man come not from the generosity of the state, but from the hand of God.

We dare not forget today that we are the heirs of that first revolution. Let the word go forth from this time and place, to friend and foe alike, that the torch has been passed to a new generation of Americans – born in this century, tempered by war, disciplined by a hard and bitter peace, proud of our ancient heritage – and unwilling to witness or permit the slow undoing of those human rights to which this Nation has always been committed, and to which we are committed today at home and around the world.

In this speech – a masterpiece of its genre – the informational function of language is reduced to a minimum, and although one might say that here the expressive and directive functions coalesce with the phatic, it is the non-controversial as well as the non-informative nature of the speech that needs to be stressed. If we regard the main audience of the speech as that majority of 'average Americans' who are emotionally committed to the institutions of their country, there is scarcely anything that can be disagreed with in the speech. This significant similarity between President Kennedy's address and a remark about the weather should not, of course, blind us to the emotive power of the speech, and to the use of political affective words (*rights of man*, *human rights*) which shows its affinity with political propaganda. But the function of the speech is not so much to change attitudes, as to reinforce or intensify them.

Language as a Substitute for Action?

We have seen how phatic language can in some senses be regarded as a substitute for physical activity ('stroking' or 'grooming'), and the same point might be made, perhaps more forcibly, with reference to the expressive and directive functions of language. A verbal insult is like the shaking of a fist, in that it stands for (or is a ritual symbol for) physical assault. A verbal attempt to change behaviour is an alternative to brute coercion. The language of militancy (using that significant word in its widest sense) is inescapably marked by a strong preference for military metaphors: *fight*, *struggle*, *victory*, *never surrender*, *campaign*, *crusade*, *close our ranks*, *defend our rights*, *make a stand*. One is reminded of the famous judgement on the United Nations that 'Jaw, jaw, is better than war, war'. People would find the history of degrading and acrimonious dispute in the United Nations easier to bear if they realized that it is necessary, if human-beings are to live at peace and to survive, to have a substitute, in the form of verbal shakings of fists, for physical conflict.

The school of General Semantics (which has had continuing though moderate influence in the U.S.A. since Alfred Korzybski published *Science and Sanity* in 1933) is dedicated to the belief that misuse of language is a major cause of human conflict, and a major danger to the future of the human race. Hayakawa, the best-known popularizer of this school of thought, puts it as follows in the introduction to *Language in Thought and Action* (p. 18):

It will be a basic assumption of this book that widespread intraspecific cooperation through the use of language is the fundamental mechanism of human survival. A parallel assumption will be that when the use of language results, as it often does, in the creation or aggravation of disagreements and conflicts, there is something linguistically wrong with the speaker, the listener, or both. Human 'fitness to survive' means the ability to talk and write and listen and read in ways that increase the chances for you and fellow members of your species to survive together.

While I am in sympathy with Hayakawa's general drift, I believe that he, and other General Semanticists, make the mistake of assuming too readily that 'bad' language is a cause, rather than a symptom, of human conflict. This attitude can lead to an over-optimistic faith in the curative powers of semantics:

No full fledged science [of semantics] has yet appeared. but it is obviously on the way. When it does appear, God help the orators, the spell-binders, the soothsayers, the propagandists, the Hitlers, the orthodox Marxists, the dogmatists, philosophers and theologians. The Wonderland in which they perform their enchantments will then be clearly seen for what it is. (Stuart Chase, *The Tyranny of Words*, 1937, p. ix)

But if it were somehow found possible to ban the inflammatory use of language, one suspects that men would soon resort more readily to blows on the head; if the 'hidden persuaders' were suppressed, brute force would become the first rather than the last resort.

On the other hand, there does seem to be a sense in which an overemphasis on affective rather than conceptual meaning constitutes a perversion of language: the central and explicit aspect of meaning, that which man relies on to order and to convey to others his experience and understanding of the world, should not be irresponsibly pressed into the service of emotion and prejudice. The lesson to be learned is that only by educating ourselves and others to a 'semantic alertness', can we keep such dangers at bay.

Summary

According to the scheme presented at the outset of this chapter, language has at least five functions in society:

  (i) conveying information (*informational*)
 (ii) expressing the speaker's or writer's feelings or attitudes (*expressive*)
(iii) directing or influencing the behaviour or attitudes of others (*directive*)

(iv) creating an artistic effect (*aesthetic*)
 (v) maintaining social bonds (*phatic*)

and many abuses or mistakes in communication involve the confusion of these different functions.

I have concentrated here especially on the directive and phatic functions of language, since they most clearly show language in the service of, or in interaction with, other forces in society. Studying these functions is also instructive in disposing of the fallacy that the main purpose of language is always to convey information, and the related fallacy that conceptual meaning is the most important semantic ingredient of all messages.

Directive language (in propaganda and loaded language generally) capitalizes on the affective and associative power of words, often with the result that conceptual meaning is subordinated to associative meaning, and is manipulated in its interests.

The phatic function, again, robs conceptual meaning of its central position in the communicative process: what information is conveyed may well be an insignificant matter in comparison with the fact that communication is being kept up at all. Not *what* is said, but *the fact that* it is said becomes crucial.

In spite of the undoubted power that language can have over the attitudes and behaviour of men, it must surely be a mistake to assume that in the social sphere, any more than in the psychological sphere, man is the slave, and language the tyrant. The relation between language and social organization or social control is a complex one of reciprocal dependence. This means that for the health of humanity, we should train ourselves to the same kind of responsible and critical scrutiny of linguistic communications as of social and political institutions.

5. Is Semantics a Science?

The first four chapters of this book have been largely unscientific, or – as I would prefer to say – prescientific. In them I have reported and proposed various ideas and classifications, various structurings of semantic phenomena, but none of these has really added up to a scientific theory. An example of prescientific thinking is the classification of language functions (informational, expressive, etc.) given on pp. 67–8. This classification provides no criteria by which the proposed division of functions could be confirmed or shown to be false. How, for example, could I show, using objective evidence, which of the five functions are applicable to a given utterance? There is no experiment which will separate them out, like a chemical analysis separating the ingredients of a compound. The most I can claim for such an analysis is that as a method of reducing the phenomena in question to some sort of order, it seems to fit my remembered experience, and to give some sort of intuitive satisfaction. Or we might take, as another example, my explanation of metaphor as a 'conceptual fusion' on pp. 44–5. This explanation entirely begs the question of what is a concept, or of what experimental evidence we might bring to bear to show that the conceptual reordering postulated there actually takes place when one describes a ship as a 'sea-steed'. How on earth can one justify in scientific terms talking about a 'concept' – something which, if it exists, is locked up in the brain away from observation – as an element of a scientific description at all?

I do not intend to apologize for this prescientific thinking. It is useful to have rough-and-ready ways of charting an imperfectly explored terrain – which is what semantics is. We need tentative ways of looking at and rendering orderly a range of phenomena so vast and perplexing. But there is a difference between saying 'this is a useful way of looking at it', and saying 'this is *the* way of looking at it – because this is the way it is'. That goal of absolute certainty is the mark to which it is the aim of science to approximate more and more nearly; and the gap between relative lack of confidence, and relative confidence in the truth of one's claims, is the gap that has to be bridged if semantics is to be a science in any proper sense. One of the most important stages in bridging the gap is to devise strictly and explicitly formulated theories, so that anyone can see what is and what is not being claimed – this has been one of the major achievements of recent linguistic semantics in comparison with the efforts of earlier periods. Another important stage is to render such theories accountable to objective data – something which preoccupied linguists of the Bloomfield era, but about which linguists of the more recent Chomsky era have troubled little. Further stages towards a fully developed scientific method would be to be able to account for *all* the data at one's disposal, and to account for it in the *simplest* way possible. Spelling out these four requirements in order (although really they ought to be sought simultaneously) we may say that (a) a fair degree of *explicitness*, the *sine qua non* of scientific endeavour, has been attained; (b) but that *objectivity* has on the whole not even been sought recently, let alone attained; (c) that *simplicity* of explanation has been implicit in all argumentation in favour of one theory or solution rather than another, but that explicit talk of the measurement of simplicity, which was often on the lips of linguists in the mid-sixties, has not been prominent since linguists turned their attention seriously to semantics in the later sixties; (d) that *completeness* of description is likely to be out of the question for a long time ahead, since the complexity of linguistic data is such that the more *explicit* formulations become, the less *data* the investigator seems able to cover. No one has produced a complete account of language in general, or even of a single language, or even of the semantic aspect of a single language, or even of one major area of the semantics of a single language. All semantic theories are very tentative, and very partial.

So semantics is a would-be science rather than a science; but to be a would-be science is important: to have reached the stage of advancing towards the goals which ensure an increasing approximation to the truth is not to be despised. This is the ideal to which any sphere of knowledge progresses – not because there is a snob value, or guarantee of respectability, in being able to call one's studies 'scientific', but because the pursuit of goals of empirical investigation is a mark of one's seriousness in wanting to find out the truth.

The Contextual View of Meaning *empirical* } contrast ←
mentalism

If recent linguistics has emphasized the *theoretical* aspect of scientific investigation, the linguistics of the preceding era (roughly 1930 to 1960) gave pre-eminence to the EMPIRICAL or OBSERVATIONAL aspect: an approach which manifested itself in the attempt to base meaning on context. 'Contextualism', as I shall call this tendency, has shown itself to be a relative failure, but it is important to study it, and take note of the reasons for its failure, if one is to understand present-day thinking in semantics.

Contextualism has a superficial attractiveness for anyone who aspires to the ideal of scientific objectivity. If meaning is discussed in terms of ideas, concepts, or internal mental states, it remains beyond the scope of scientific observation; so instead, goes the argument, we should study meaning in terms of situation, use, context – outward and observable correlates of language behaviour. As J. R. Firth, the leading British linguist of the period, put it in 1930:

> If we regard language as 'expressive' or 'communicative' we imply that it is an instrument of inner mental states. And as we know so little of inner mental states, even by the most careful introspection, the language problem becomes more mysterious the more we try to explain it by referring it to inner mental happenings which are not observable. By regarding words as acts, events, habits, we limit our inquiry to what is objective in the group life of our fellows.
> *Speech*, repr. in *The Tongues of Men and Speech*, 1964, p. 173.

Firth had been influenced in this view by the great Polish-born anthropologist B. Malinowski, who, in his study of the part played by language in primitive societies, had found it appropriate to treat language as 'a mode of action, not an instrument of reflection'. 'Language in action' and 'Meaning as use' might be taken as twin slogans for this school of thought. Certainly at one time, not too long ago, the statement of the philosopher Wittgenstein, that

'For a large class of cases . . . the meaning of a word is its use in the language' was the most quoted, though perhaps not the most studied, of pronouncements on meaning. Similarly the simple 'language games' invented by Wittgenstein, to illustrate how in a limited context the meaning of a word can be understood simply from observing what is going on, seemed to linguists an object-lesson in how meaning should be studied.

Not only anthropology and philosophy, but a third discipline relating to semantics – psychology – appeared to support the contextualist viewpoint. Bloomfield drew on behaviourist psychology when he defined the meaning of a linguistic form as 'the situation in which the speaker utters it, and the response which it calls forth in the hearer'. By way of illustration (in Chapter 2 of *Language*) he described a simple situation in which that immortal couple, Jack and Jill, are walking down a lane:

> Jill is hungry. She sees an apple in a tree. She makes a noise with her larynx, tongue, and lips. Jack vaults the fence, climbs the tree, takes the apple, brings it to Jill, and places it in her hand. Jill eats the apple. *Language*, p. 22.

Of this situation Bloomfield distinguished three components:

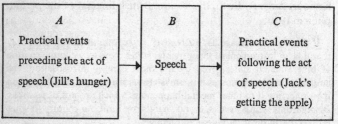

These he interpreted in stimulus-and-response terms as follows:

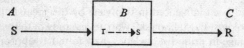

(where s and r stand for verbal stimulus/response, and S and R for external stimulus/response).

Thus, in Bloomfield's eyes, language came to be regarded as

basically a remote control system, by which a stimulus to one organism of the human species can result in a response in another organism.

Another behaviourist approach to meaning was that of the American philosopher Charles Morris, whose ideas gained some currency among linguists in the forties and fifties. Morris recognized five basic components in any communicative situation:

a *sign*
an *interpreter*: an organism for which something is a sign
an *interpretant*: the interpreter's reaction to the sign
a *denotatum*: the something else to which the interpretant is a partial response (or in other words, the *referent*)
a *significatum*: those properties which identify a denotatum as being a denotatum of the sign (or in other words the *meaning*).

These are my own simplified explanations of Morris's terminology: something of the forbiddingly technical flavour of his own explanations can be sampled from this definition of the *sign*:

Roughly: something that directs behavior with respect to something that is not at the moment a stimulus. More accurately: If A is a preparatory-stimulus that, in the absence of stimulus-objects initiating response-sequences of a certain behavior-family, causes in some organism a disposition to respond by response-sequences of this behavior-family, then A is a sign.

A simple sign situation of the kind that Morris deals with is the following. A dog is kept in a pen for the purpose of experiments. When food is placed for him in a certain place A, a buzzer sounds. After a while, the dog learns to associate the buzzer (which we may call S_1) with the food, so that when he hears it, he responds to some extent as if he had actually seen or smelt the food: that is, he moves over to A, where the food is placed. The buzzer sound S_1 is now a *sign*; the dog is the *interpreter*; movement towards A is the *interpretant*; the food placed at A (say a bone) is the *denotatum*; the set of conditions (e.g. the qualities of being edible, tasty, nourishing) which make the bone a denotatum of S_1 constitute the *significatum* of the sign. We can see that the buzzer, in this situation, is analogous to a simple linguistic message, such as 'Grub up!' or 'Dinner time!'.

It is noticeable that the situations to which Malinowski, Bloomfield, and Morris naturally turn when they want to illustrate the contextualist thesis are all 'primitive' in one sense or another. In fact, contextualism in its crudest form (which we may summarize in the formula 'MEANING = OBSERVABLE CONTEXT') is incapable of dealing with any but the simplest and most unsophisticated cases of language use. In most circumstances in which linguistic communication occurs (say, telling a story, giving a lecture, gossiping about the neighbours, reading a news bulletin) observing the situation in which speaker and listener find themselves will tell us little, if anything, about the meaning of the message. Manifest inadequacies of this simple-minded contextualism are that speech may take place in the absence of the objects being talked about (what Bloomfield calls 'displaced speech'), that anyway many linguistic forms, such as words referring to states of mind, have no observable correlate, and that some linguistic forms have no correlate in the contemporary real world at all (e.g. *dragon*, *gladiator*, A.D. *1990*).

In practice, therefore, linguists like Bloomfield espoused a weaker form of contextualism, in which the relation between context and meaning was more indirect, and which may be expressed in a formula like 'MEANING IS ULTIMATELY DERIVABLE FROM OBSERVABLE CONTEXT' or 'MEANING IS ULTIMATELY REDUCIBLE TO OBSERVABLE CONTEXT'. One way of modifying crude contextualism in this direction is to say that whereas meanings are *learned* by reference to context, their use may be free of context from then on. In effect, this means accepting the internal mental record of previous contexts as equivalent to those contexts themselves. More generally, the requirement that context should be observable may be relaxed, so that the attitudes of speaker and hearer, their previous mental histories, and so on, may be taken into account. Even broad abstractions such as 'British culture' have been accepted as part of the contextual description of an utterance. An additional extension of the contextualist thesis is to bring in *linguistic* context as well as (or instead of) non-linguistic context. Thus the probability of one word's co-occurrence or collocation with another (see p. 20) comes to be regarded as part of its 'meaning'.

Although this weaker form of contextualism has the advantage of approximating 'context' more nearly to what we usually understand by 'meaning', it has the corresponding disadvantage of rendering 'context' a much more abstract notion, so that it is more and more difficult to relate it to observation. Thus the goal of scientific objectivity, which provided the reason for adopting a contextualist position in the first place, recedes into oblivion. Worse, one may arrive at a kind of mongrel 'mentalist contextualism', by which the investigator claims to be correlating language with situation, but is in effect relating it to those 'inner mental states' reprehended by Firth.

An additional, purely logical, objection to contextualism is that it falls prey to the 'linguistic boot-straps fallacy' we met earlier in Chapter 1 (p. 5). By this I mean that the semanticist 'tries to lift himself by his own boot-straps' in the sense that he describes meaning in terms of language, thereby begging the question of how the meaning of the language he has used to describe meaning is itself to be described. An illustration of this fallacy may be taken from Morris's book *Signs, Language and Behavior* at a point (p. 156) where he is elaborating his dog-and-buzzer situation in order to account behaviourally for the meaning of formators, or logical elements of meaning such as 'and' and 'or':

Suppose that S_1, S_2, and S_3 are signals to the dog of food in three different places, so that the dog, when hungry, seeks food in the place signified by the stimulus presented to it. Now if a new stimulus, S_6, be combined always with two of these other stimuli (as in, say, S_1, S_6, S_2), and if the dog then, without preference, seeks food at one of the two places signified and at the other place if and only if food is not secured at the place first approached, then S_6 would be a stimulus which has much in common with the exclusive 'or' of English ('at least one but not both').

What stares us in the face is that Morris, in giving a behavioural explanation, provides a far more complicated communicative object for us to study and explain than the original sign-sequence. His description of what 'exclusive *or*' means presupposes that we already know the meaning of such logical elements as *if*, *if and only if*, and *not*. The whole exercise amounts to the same thing as equating two logical formulae:

X exclusive-*or* Y = (X if and only if *not*-Y) and (Y if and only if *not*-X).

The best that can be said for such contextualist explanations therefore is that they correlate two sets of linguistic expressions (in itself not a futile procedure – but a different procedure from that which is apparently aimed at). The only way out of this circularity would be to resort to non-verbal characterisations of context (e.g. pointing to objects instead of describing them in language); in which case semantics would attain the absurd status of the science of the ineffable.

In view of these defects, it is not surprising that in practice contextual semantics made little progress. Although there were many programmatic formulations and anecdotal illustrations of how the job might be done, virtually no systematic accounts of particular meanings in particular languages were produced. One achievement was to direct attention to the previously neglected areas of stylistic and collocative meaning (pp.16, 20). But in general contextualism had the opposite effect to that intended: it took the mind of the investigator away from, rather than towards, the exact study of data.

How do we deal with Context?

Recent work in semantics has returned to the 'mentalism' against which Firth, Bloomfield, and their contemporaries reacted. One might claim that this is simply a recognition of common-sense reality: meaning actually *is* a mental phenomenon, and it is useless to try to pretend otherwise. Later in the chapter we shall pursue this further, and consider in what sense there can be a 'science' of mental phenomena. But first, let us at least acknowledge that there is some degree of common sense on the side of the contextualists – that context is an undeniably important factor in communication; and let us consider how this semantic role of context can be allowed for within a theory based on conceptual meaning.

Ordinary observation supports the importance of context in a number of ways. We have all experienced the bewilderment which results from lack of contextual information: for example, when we tune in to the twelfth instalment of a twelve-part serial.

In addition, we may recall familiar examples where the contextual predictability of meaning enables us to understand such skeleton messages as:

(1) SPLASH! UPSIDE DOWN
(2) IT'S OFF!
(3) STICK IT ON FOULNESS
(4) JANET! DONKEYS!

Without the clues of the original context, the present reader will find it difficult to make any sense of any of these. They are (1) a news headline announcing the splash-down of Apollo 13 in October 1970; (2) another newspaper headline announcing the termination of the British Dock strike in July 1970; (3) a car sticker seen at the time of the controversy over the placing of London's third airport (1971) (Foulness, of course, is a place and not a state of filth); (4) a celebrated recurrent remark by the hero's aunt Betsey Trotwood in Dickens's *David Copperfield* (the remark was an order to her maid to carry out a routine task of driving donkeys off the grass). In each of the four cases, the originator of the message has assumed an unusual amount about what background knowledge is in the mind of the reader.

More widely, we may say that specification of context (whether linguistic or non-linguistic) has the effect of narrowing down the communicative possibilities of the message as it exists in abstraction from context. This particularization of meaning can take place in at least the following ways:

(A) Context eliminates certain ambiguities or multiple meanings in the message (e.g. lets us know that *page* in a given instance means a boy attendant rather than a piece of paper).
(B) Context indicates the referents of certain types of word we call DEICTIC (*this, that, here, there, now, then*, etc.), and of other expressions of definite meaning such as *John, I, you, he, it, the man*).
(C) Context supplies information which the speaker/writer has omitted through ellipsis (e.g. we are able to appreciate that

Janet! Donkeys! means something like 'Janet! Drive those donkeys away!' rather than 'Janet! Bring those donkeys here!', or any other of the indefinitely many theoretical possibilities).

The first of these roles, the so-called DISAMBIGUATING role of context, may be illustrated by the simple sentence *Shall I put this on*? It makes a great difference to the understanding of this sentence to know whether the speaker is holding up (1) a portable radio; (2) a sweater; or (3) a lump of wood. The difference does not simply lie in the changing referent of *this*, but in the sense one attaches to *put . . . on*:

(1) = 'switch X on'
(2) = 'don X', i.e. 'put X on oneself'
(3) = 'place X on top of (something else, such as a fire)'.

The same point could be made if we replaced *this* in the sentence by the noun phrases (1) *the portable radio*, (2) *the sweater*, or (3) *the lump of wood*, except that it would be made in a slightly different way: we would not be talking about the *non-linguistic* environment of the whole sentence, but about the *linguistic* environment of the phrase *put . . . on*:

(1a) Shall I put the portable radio on?
(2a) Shall I put the sweater on?
(3a) Shall I put the lump of wood on?

But the way in which context operates on meaning is not so straightforward as so far suggested. In fact, 'disambiguation' is not only an ungainly, but a misleading term, as the effect of context is to attach a certain *probability* to each sense (the complete ruling-out of a sense being the limiting case of *nil* probability). Sentence (2a), for example, allows not only the 'wearing' sense of *put . . . on* (sense 2), but the sense of 'placing on top of something else', such a pile of clothing (sense 3). The former alternative tends to occur to us because it is far more probable than the latter; but the latter is far from impossible. Once we attune ourselves to these things, we realize that there are far more potential ambiguities than appear at first glance. Thus sense (2) of *put . . . on* could apply in sentence

(1a) in the unlikely case of a radio being treated as something to wear (if, for instance, a person were to balance it on his head as a hat). What is more, sentence (2a) could have all three meanings: meaning (1) could be read into it if someone invented an electric sweater (on the analogy of an electric blanket). Contextualists are inclined to play down ambiguities of this kind, arguing that they would not arise if we were able to supply a more detailed specification of the context. But on the other hand, it is everybody's experience that ambiguities do occur and can cause mistakes of communication. A plausible example would be an instruction shouted to someone upstairs to *put the electric blanket on*; the intended meaning might be that he should place it on the bed; the actual interpretation could be that he should switch the current on.

Within a semantic approach based on conceptual meaning, all these observations suggest that meaning-in-context should be regarded as a narrowing down, or probabilistic weighting, of the list of potential meanings available to the user of the language. For example, if we suppose that the dictionary entry for *put ... on* provides us with just the three meanings already listed, then the dictionary senses, as represented in the top box of the following diagram, will be modified in context roughly as indicated in the three lower boxes:

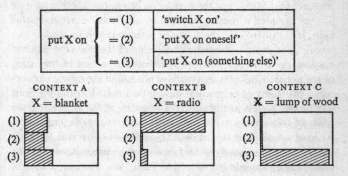

The shaded parts of each rectangle represent my rough estimate of the relative probabilities of the three meanings.

The contextualist position is thus reversed. Instead of seeing total meaning as an aggregate derived from contexts, we see the contextual meanings as dependent on a previously established set of potential meanings. This does not conflict with what we know about how context contributes to the learning of meaning. It means, rather, that learning meaning through context is seen as a process of inductive approximation to the semantic categories that the linguistic community operates with, as described on p. 78. Moreover, learning through context is seen as only part of the process of learning meaning: verbal explanation (definition, etc.), which in the later stages of language learning plays a role at least as important as context, can be given its full weight.

This view of context brings us back to the distinction between linguistic COMPETENCE and linguistic PERFORMANCE alluded to on p. 6. It is part of our COMPETENCE (the rules, categories, etc. that we know by virtue of being speakers of the English language) to know that *put . . . on* has at least the three dictionary meanings discussed above. But it is largely a matter of our linguistic PERFORMANCE (the practical use we make of those rules and categories) to know which meaning is most likely, given our background knowledge of the context. 'Background knowledge' can include here anything we happen to know about the state of the universe at the time that the linguistic expression under consideration was uttered. For example, it is relevant to interpretation (1) of sentence (2a) *Shall I put the sweater on*? to know whether anyone has yet invented a sweater warmed by an electric current. In this light, it is evident that the study of interpretation in context can involve that vast encyclopedic knowledge of the universe which it has already been suggested (pp. 9, 15) cannot be part of the study of semantics. Thus although we have not found the means to overcome problems of contextual description raised in the previous section, we have a justification for ignoring as far as possible the study of context where it interferes with the study of competence. At least we see that the study of meaning-in-context is logically subsequent to the study of semantic competence, rather than the other way around. In a sense, 'real world' knowledge is a kind of competence – part of a general 'communicative competence' – but insofar as they are kept apart in theory, linguistic knowledge and 'real world' knowledge mingle together only on the level of performance.

The solution of making semantics manageable by relegating context to performance is too harsh in some respects. Factors of situation can cause conceptual meanings to converge and diverge in a way which calls for systematic treatment. For example, although 'willingness' and 'ability' are in general distinct concepts, they converge *pragmatically* in the conventional reply to an invitation, as the following prepaid reply form shows:

> $$\frac{*I \text{ am willing}}{*I \text{ am unable}} \text{ to accept the invitation}$$
> *Delete as appropriate
> Date........   Signed...........

Normally *unwilling* would be treated as the antonym of *willing*, but in this context, a pragmatic opposition, cutting across conceptual boundaries, is set up for reasons of politeness (actually, in order to anticipate politeness on the part of the person replying). Such details cannot be handled in a conceptual theory limited to competence; but enough has been said to explain why recent semantic theories have tended to concentrate on the study of conceptual meaning in abstraction from the particularities of context. (We return to context in the more limited sense of 'situation of utterance' in Chapter 14).

Mentalism and 'Intuition'

This brings us to the question: 'What respectable alternatives are there to contextualism?' The reaction to this of most modern linguists, led by Chomsky, has been an unashamed return to the 'mentalism' from which the contextualists tried to escape. The notion that the primary function of language is 'the communication of ideas' has become acceptable again. What is more, it has been assumed, as a working basis for linguistic inquiry, that the data we need about language can be supplied by direct resort to intuition. How have modern linguists dared to take up this stance, which seems so utterly at variance with contextualist thinking, and indeed, so utterly in defiance of the whole empirical tradition of science? Chomsky's answer is a rhetorical shrug of the shoulders: in reply to the question 'How do we know that such-and-such a sentence is grammatical, that such-and-such an expression is synonymous with such-and-such another expression, etc.', he says: 'There is no very satisfying answer to this question; data of this sort are simply what constitute the subject matter of linguistic theory. We neglect such data at the cost of destroying the subject.' (*Current Issues in Linguistic Theory*, ·p. 79.) He even argues that the relation between competence and operationally derived data (e.g. results of tests in which speakers have to judge the acceptability of sentences) is so indirect that 'operational tests . . . must meet the condition of correspondence to introspective judgement' (p. 80). He justifies this apparently cavalier attitude by claiming (p. 81) that . . .

. . . at the present stage of the study of language, it seems rather obvious that the attempt to gain some insight into the range of data we now have is likely to be far more fruitful than the attempt to make this data more firm, e.g., by tests of synonymy, grammaticality, and the like. Operational criteria for these notions, were they available and correct, might soothe the scientific conscience; but how, in fact, would they advance our understanding of the nature of language . . . ?

In other words, the linguist has already plenty to do in explaining what is common knowledge about language. So far he has got nowhere near an adequate linguistic theory or an adequate description of this or that language. He is surrounded on all sides by a wealth of baffling data. So what business has he to worry about the impeccable pedigree of his data, any more than a primeval Linnæus, let loose in the garden of Eden, would worry about the epistemological reliability of his own senses? Thus what seems to be arrogance in Chomsky's rejection of the objectivity criterion can be regarded, more charitably, as a manifestation of extreme modesty: of a consciousness that linguistics is very far from achieving a scientific status comparable to physics, chemistry, or biology.

Chomsky's view on our intuitive access to the 'facts of language' has been widely espoused by semanticists, and it must be conceded that the liberation from guilt and worry about data has been accompanied by noteworthy advances, both through insight into

semantic structure and through the explicit formulation of semantic theory. To a surprising extent, argument in semantics does indeed seem to go forward on a generally agreed basis of common
data: investigators frequently agree as to which sentences are
synonymous, which sentences are ambiguous, which sentences are
ill-formed or absurd, and so on. Intuitions are consistent enough,
then, to form the basis of satisfactory argumentation. Differences
of intuition amongst speakers of a language are often treated as
relatively unimportant: they may indicate a certain difference of
'dialect' between one speaker and another, but are not likely to
affect crucially the argument for or against a particular theory or
descriptive account.

In the words of the philosopher W. V. Quine, the ultimate contextualist objection to mentalism was that it . . .

. . . engenders an illusion of having explained something. And the
illusion is increased by the fact that things wind up in a vague enough
state to insure a certain stability, or freedom from further progress.
('The Problem of Meaning in Linguistics', *From a Logical Point of
View*, p. 47)

But by an extraordinary irony the opposite seems to be the case:
mentalism has brought progress, or at least a remarkable state of
instability which is difficult to distinguish from progress, while
contextualism led precisely to the illusion described by Quine.

This does not mean that one can be happy with the indefinite
continuation of a science resting on *a priori* knowledge, and
governed by the principle 'Whatever I intuit to be the case, is the
case.' Taking this to its logical extreme, there would be nothing to
prevent a person claiming direct intuitive knowledge of all the
rules of English; in which case, it would be quite impossible to
conduct an argument which questioned the accuracy of his
description. But again, let us judge an approach by its fruits. While
the new acceptance of intuition has undoubtedly brought progress, as already mentioned, one cannot help detecting at the same
time the growth in some quarters of a nonchalant disregard of the
dangers of subjectivism. For example, Wallace Chafe, in a recent
very interesting book *Meaning and the Structure of Language*,
echoes as if it were unquestioned dogma Chomsky's assignment of

primacy to intuition: 'When introspection and surface evidence are contradictory, it is the former that is decisive' (p. 122). Elsewhere, however, Chafe complains that 'recent linguistic theory has suffered from an unsubtle view of meaning identity' (p. 87), which in practice means that he regards other people's intuitions on synonymy as less reliable than his own. When it reaches this stage of arguing from the superiority or finer discrimination of one's own introspections to that of others, is not linguistics moving too far in the direction of accepting intuitive response? Linguists have always been keen to disown subjectivity. Yet where is the dividing line between the linguist, with his introspective givens, and (say) the literary critic, with his individual response based on personal taste and discrimination?

Basic Statements: the Control of Intuition

What is needed, it seems to me, is firstly a control of the way in which intuition is resorted to, and secondly, an exploration of the means by which 'intuitive' analyses can be given support by objective evidence.

In practice, semanticists rarely 'misuse' intuition in the sense of claiming direct explicit knowledge of the rules of language. Instead, they argue from certain kinds of observation which they take to be self-evident, such as 'Sentence X is semantically deviant', matters on which, indeed, (despite Chafe's comment), linguists seem to find their intuitions considerably in agreement. Control of the use of intuition therefore amounts largely to codifying how intuition is in practice used. For example, linguists appeal to the synonymy of sentences, to the fact that one sentence entails or presupposes another, to various types of semantic abnormality. These may be incorporated in a list of types of statement about meaning, called here BASIC STATEMENTS, which I shall treat for practical purposes as 'given'. The task of semantics is then to explain such statements, by constructing theories and descriptive rules and categories from which they can be deduced. (A definition of each type will follow.)

Types of Basic Statement

(*X* and *Y* may be assumed for the present to stand for arbitrary sentences)

  1. *X* is synonymous with *Y*
    (e.g. 'I am an orphan' is synonymous with 'I am a child and have no father or mother')†

{

  2. *X* entails *Y*
    (e.g. 'I am an orphan' entails 'I have no father')
  3. *X* is inconsistent with *Y*
    (e.g. 'I am an orphan' is inconsistent with 'I have a father')

{

  4. *X* is a tautology
    (e.g. 'This orphan has no father')
  5. *X* is a contradiction
    (e.g. 'This orphan has a father')

{

  6. *X* (positively) presupposes *Y*
    (e.g. 'Is your father at home?' presupposes 'You have a father')
  7. *X* negatively presupposes *Y*
    (e.g. 'If he had a father, things would be different' negatively presupposes 'He has a father')
  8. *X* is semantically anomalous
    (e.g. 'The orphan's father drinks heavily')

This is not a complete list of types that might be considered as basic statements, but it is enough for the present purpose. The contrasting relationship between those types bracketed together will be clear from the examples given.

Why choose these as basic statements? Firstly, because they are statements at a level where investigators seem to find themselves intuitively in agreement. A second reason, no doubt connected with the first, is that they are statements easily translatable into terms of truth and falsehood. This in turn means that they lend themselves to tests of validity (of which more later).

† 'Orphan' is sometimes taken to mean a child missing just one parent (see O.E.D.), but, as this usage is unusual, the more common sense has been adopted.

The point about truth and falsehood can be demonstrated by the following partial definitions:

1. *X is synonymous with Y*
   X has the same truth value as *Y*,
   i.e. if *X* is true, *Y* is true and vice versa; also if *X* is false, *Y* is false and vice versa.

2. *X entails Y*
   If *X* is true, *Y* is true; also, if *Y* is false, *X* is false.

3. *X is inconsistent with Y*
   If *X* is true, *Y* is false; also, if *Y* is true, *X* is false.

4. *X is a tautology*
   X is invariably true.

5. *X is a contradiction*
   X is invariably false.

6. *X (positively) presupposes Y*
   Anyone who utters *X* takes the truth of *Y* for granted.

7. *X negatively presupposes Y*
   Anyone who utters *X* takes the falsehood of *Y* for granted.

8. *X is semantically anomalous*
   X is absurd in the sense that it presupposes a contradiction (therefore it makes no sense to ask whether *X* is true or false).

Why are these no more than partial definitions? Because if notions like synonymy were defined purely in terms of truth and falsehood, they would be wide enough to include cases which we recognize as belonging to that category on the basis of factual knowledge of the 'real world', rather than on the basis of conceptual meaning, and so we would be back once again to the original stumbling block of semantic theory (see pp. 9, 15), that it cannot hope to give an exhaustive account of our knowledge of the universe. For each 'semantic' (i.e. linguistic) category, there is a corresponding 'factual' category; for example:

1. 'Charlotte lives in Paris' is factually synonymous with 'Charlotte lives in the capital of France.'
2. 'It has been raining hard' factually entails 'The ground is wet.'
3. 'Jonathan has just eaten a seven course meal' is factually inconsistent with 'Jonathan is hungry.'

4. 'Houses are made of solid materials' is the factual equivalent of a tautology.

5. 'Mr Smith bit his own ear off' is the factual equivalent of a contradiction.

Since (for reasons already discussed) we do not require a semantic theory to be able to account for phenomena of this kind, we must add to the definitions of basic statement types the proviso that *the truth conditions hold' by virtue of conceptual meaning alone'*.

testability

To insist that the testability of semantic descriptions should depend on their consequences in terms of truth value is to place perhaps an unfortunate emphasis on assertions, at the expense of other types of speech acts, such as questions and commands. There is no doubt that questions and commands, not to speak of promises, warnings, and exclamations, have their own conditions of 'happiness' (see p. 343) or validity, parallel to the validity in terms of truth and falsehood that is applicable to assertions of fact. For example, one test of the validity or meaningfulness of a question is whether it allows the respondent a choice between the answers 'Yes' and 'No': in this sense the question 'Is your father a man?' is meaningless. Similarly, a command is only valid if it permits the person addressed to respond in the way directed: for this reason, 'Shut the window' would be a bizarre utterance if the window were already shut. If it were possible to measure accurately, say by electronic instruments, the 'bizarreness reaction' of a person addressed in these ways, there would be good grounds for augmenting our set of basic statements to include 'X is bizarre' or 'X is meaningless', where X is a question or command. But so long as we are restricted to testing by means of people's verbal responses, it is probably better to rely primarily on judgements of truth and falsehood – concepts which seem to have a fairly definite purport for all psychologically normal users of language.

But this still, of course, begs the question of how one decides whether a given case is 'semantic' or merely 'factual'. There are signs (p. 92) that testing will help to answer this question; but for the present, we may note that the investigator has to make this decision only in the implicit, pragmatic sense that the examples he will want and need to test will be semantic (logical) rather than factual. This distinction then becomes a question of how far a semantic theory can be extended. The more facts that can be explained the better; but there comes a point of diminishing returns, where the notion of a finite and exhaustive specification of meaning cannot cope with the open-ended vastness of human knowledge.

Let us take, as a particular case, the definition of the word *elephant*. There are indefinitely many properties of elephants (positive and negative) about which it is possible to construct absurd necessarily false assertions:

> The elephant had eighty legs.
> Elephants have horns.
> Some elephants talk sensibly.
> etc.

If we wanted our semantic theory to explain the absurdity of these statements, we should have to include such features as 'four-legged', 'hornless', and 'incapable of speech' in our definition of *elephant*. But if we included *all* such features, we should end up not with a dictionary entry, but with an encyclopedia entry of indefinite length. The two solutions must therefore be either (a) to include some features of this kind but not others; or (b) to exclude all such features. The first solution is unattractive because there are no obvious grounds for distinguishing properties which are criterial to the meaning of the word from those which are not. We arrive at an indefinite number of possible definitions, the choice between which is no less arbitrary than the toss of a coin. In other words, we find ourselves claiming that *elephant* has indefinitely many meanings, but that none of these meanings is more 'correct' than any other. The second solution, which has no obvious drawbacks of this kind, amounts to a refusal to anatomize the meaning of elephant any further than to define it as 'an animal of the species *elephant*'. The conclusion of this argument, which will be regrettable to some, is therefore that 'The elephant had eighty legs', and sentences of the same kind, are absurd in a way that semantic analysis cannot explain.

In this light, the borderline between 'semantic' and 'factual' ceases to be a crucial philosophical problem, and turns into the less crucial pragmatic problem of how to delimit the scope of a semantic theory; more precisely, of how far the atomization of meaning by linguistic methods can be pressed before we are confronted by an embarassment of choice between competing criteria. This way of attempting to 'draw the line' reflects an assumed difference between the finite systematic character of conceptual meaning, and the indefinite, open-ended nature of extralinguistic knowledge (see pp. 15–16).

Another question which arises here is whether ambiguity should be considered a basic datum of semantics; i.e. whether '*X* is ambiguous' should be classed amongst the types of 'basic statement'. It is true that linguists often assume the ambiguity of a sentence to be self-evident; but *the nature and extent* of ambiguity is often far from self-evident, and has to be explicated by resort to paraphrase, contextual clues, etc. It is arguable that ambiguity can always be reduced to a set of the types of basic statement we have already recognized. For example, to show why *Hugo is drawing a cart* is ambiguous, I can match it on the one hand with the synonymous sentence (a) *Hugo is drawing a picture of a cart*, and on the other with the synonymous sentence (b) *Hugo is pulling a cart*. The point is that (a) and (b) are not synonymous with each other. Since ambiguity can be reduced down in this way to more basic notions, and since it can only indirectly be translatable into terms of truth and falsehood, it is probably best excluded from the categories of basic statement. This is not to deny that informally, linguists may rely heavily on intuition of ambiguity as a clue to the formulation of analyses.

This issue of ambiguity leads incidentally to another observation: that it is misleading to regard *X* and *Y* in the formulae of basic statements as *sentences*. Sentences, as usually understood, are syntactic units; so that, for instance, it is natural to describe *Hugo is drawing a cart* as 'an ambiguous sentence' (i.e. a single sentence with more than one meaning) rather than 'two sentences sharing the same syntactic form'. So the *X* and *Y* which enter into relations such as entailment and synonymy are actually particular *meanings* of sentences, not the sentences themselves; they are semantic, not syntactic abstractions. We can recognize this difference and avoid confusion if we call *X* and *Y* 'assertions' or 'propositions', or (using a term of wider significance – see pp. 127–8) PREDICATIONS. Then we can say that an ambiguous sentence is one that expresses two or more predications. If a sentence (according to the traditional definition) 'expresses a complete thought', then a predication can be informally characterized as a 'complete thought' that a sentence expresses.

Semantic Testing

The notion of 'basic statement' not only codifies and controls the use of introspective evidence; it also shows the way towards objective testing procedures which enable the investigator to go beyond his own intuitions and to discover how far his own findings have general validity among the linguistic community at large. This is all the more necessary where the linguist is studying a language of which he is not a native speaker, so that his intuitions are likely to be second-hand or uncertain.

One way to provide objective support for an analysis would be to observe what sentences actually occur in a corpus of utterances; it might be predicted, for example, that contradictory and other nonsensical utterances just would not occur in everyday speech situations. Unfortunately, this sort of negative evidence is difficult to collect, and in any case all kinds of performance factors are liable to interfere. For example, tautologies and contradictions actually do occur in conversation, but usually with some special interpretation involving factors such as irony, metaphor, and hyperbole: *If you must go, you must go*; *He's his father's son*; *I literally died of laughter when I saw him*; etc.

A more promising alternative is to test basic statements by eliciting reactions from a sample of native speakers. If the results are to be truly representative of a linguistic community, such tests have to be presented in a way that can be understood by people with no technical knowledge of language. For example, it would be little use facing a representative collection of English speakers with the question 'Does sentence *X* entail sentence *Y*?', but it might well be worth while to ask them 'If sentence *X* is true, does sentence *Y* have to be true?' Hence the value of reducing questions of conceptual meaning to questions of truth and falsehood: notions which are familiar to everyone. Here are two examples of such tests, the first designed to test entailment and inconsistency, the second to test tautology and contradiction:

Entailment and Inconsistency Test

$\left\{\begin{array}{l} X: \textit{George is my half-brother} \\ Y: \textit{George is my brother} \end{array}\right.$

Instructions:

Assuming X is true, judge whether Y is true or not.

If you think Y must be true, write 'YES'.

If you think Y cannot be true, write 'NO'.

If you think Y may or may not be true, write 'YES/NO'.

If you don't know which answer to give, write '?'.

The responses 'YES' and 'NO' in this test are taken to be diagnostic of entailment and inconsistency respectively.

Tautology and Contradiction Test

My half-brother is my brother

Instructions:

If the statement would be true whatever the situation, write 'YES'.

If the statement would be false whatever the situation, write 'NO'.

If the statement could be true or false, write 'YES/NO'.

If you don't know which answer to give, write '?'.

Here again it is the first two responses ('YES' and 'NO') which are diagnostic: they indicate tautology and contradiction respectively.

From initial experiments I have conducted ('On the Theory and Practice of Semantic Testing', 1970) elicitation tests such as these promise to be reasonably reliable in producing clear-cut results. A 100 per cent confirmation is scarcely to be looked for, because all tests take place at the level of performance rather than competence, and so *ad hoc* metaphorical interpretations and other 'nuisance factors' are bound to interfere. (Such interference is inevitable seeing that the tests themselves operate at a PERFORMANCE level, whereas the phenomena being tested are factors of COMPETENCE.) Confirmation, in such a case, must be regarded as a probabilistic matter, and an 80 per cent predominance in one direction or the other is the most one can rely upon. Examples of what one may regard as definitive results for entailment and inconsistency are:

Entailment and Inconsistency Test

(Examples from Leech and Pepicello, 1972)

| | Percentages | | | |
Test Sentences	*Yes*	*No*	*Yes/No*	*?*
1. *X*: Someone killed the Madrid chief of police last night. *Y*: The Madrid chief of police died last night.	96	0	3	1
2. *X*: Every radio made by Stumpel carries a 12-month guarantee. *Y*: Some radios made by Stumpel do not carry a guarantee.	4	88	7	1

It is in line with normal scientific thinking that such tests should be seen as *confirming or disconfirming a hypothesis* rather than as *discovering* facts about meaning. Treated as discovery procedures, they fail because they cannot distinguish 'semantic' from 'factual' entailment, etc. But viewed as tests of hypotheses, they require neither the linguist nor the informant to make such discriminations: the 'factual' category is defined simply as that set of observations which the linguist is not interested in finding out about.

There is, however, an encouraging indication that elicitation tests such as these may provide an operational means of drawing the 'semantic'/'factual' boundary. Apparently people find it much easier to imagine exceptions to 'factual' than to 'semantic' laws, and such tests challenge them to exercise their imagination in this fashion. For example, the 88 per cent 'NO' response to Test 2 above contrasts with the much lower 50 per cent 'NO' response for *All of Mrs Jones's children are more than six feet tall* and *Some of Mrs Jones's children are less than five years old*, sentences which are inconsistent in terms of fact rather than of sense.

A second encouraging feature of such tests is the way in which informants, in making judgements about truth and falsehood, seem able to discount differences of associative meaning. In another test like Test 1 above the cognitive synonymy of the two sentences was reflected in a decisive 90 per cent 'YES' response, despite the very different stylistic meanings of the two sentences. The two sentences were:

X: He cast a stone at the policemen.
Y: He chucked a stone at the cops.

I find both this and the preceding observation encouraging, because they support the reality of that abstraction of 'conceptual meaning' on which the present semantic approach is founded.

But there are many problems to be overcome before these tests can acquire the degree of reliability which could challenge a linguist's certainty of his own intuitions. Ambiguity causes the greatest problem. While the purpose of semantic tests is to get at *meanings*, in practice meanings can only be pin-pointed by citing the *syntactic* forms in which they are embodied. These forms are often accompanied by alternative meanings, which are extraneous to the purpose of the test, and interfere with its result. But enough has been said to offer a glimpse of hope that eventually semantic testing will provide a firm objective basis for semantics.

Conclusion

In this chapter I have presented two opposed views of semantics as a science: the contextualist and the mentalist views. While the contextualist is unwilling to accept abstract entities (such as 'concepts') not accessible to operational tests, the 'neomentalist' takes a less stringent view of scientific truth, regarding an abstract theory of semantic competence as acceptable so long as it conforms to various standards – notably that of answerability to intuition, and ultimately (I have argued) to tests which 'objectify' intuition.

Mentalists vary in the degree of psychological reality they attribute to postulated rules of competence, and in the last resort, this must depend on the degree of confidence a semanticist has in his own analysis, which in turn must depend on how far he has attained such scientific goals as explicitness, completeness, simplicity, and conformity to data. A mentalist could scarcely argue that although his account of a given set of data is correct, it has nothing to do with what actually goes on in the brain of the native speaker.

As long as validation rests on intuition, however, it must be recognized that conceptual semantics requires a 'willing suspension of disbelief' from its students. In my experience, this is a sacrifice that quite a number of people of an empirical turn of mind find it difficult to make. However, from this chapter on I shall assume such an act of faith on the part of the reader, and hope that the intrinsic interest of the subject and of the way the 'rules of the game' operate will persuade him it is worth while to continue, and to set on one side any sceptical misgivings to which he may feel entitled.

6. Components and Contrasts of Meaning

In the remainder of this book I shall sketch a formal account of some important aspects of conceptual meaning, with particular reference to the English language. The approach I will follow is, in essentials, that which I developed more formally and in more detail in an earlier book (*Towards a Semantic Description of English*, 1969); but here I try to extend that approach to take in a range of topics of importance in contemporary semantic theory, including the relation of semantics to logic (Chapter 8), semantics in relation to the dictionary (Chapter 10), semantic universals (Chapter 11), and presuppositions (Chapter 13). On the way I shall refer to other approaches, and more generally the notes on Background Reading (pp. 360–70) will make clear the extent to which my ideas are paralleled by, or based upon, those of others working in the field. In general, there is much overlap between contemporary linguistic approaches to meaning, in spite of superficial differences of notation, and different theoretical starting points.

There are no standard notational conventions for linguistic semantics, and readers who compare this book with others in the same field will no doubt notice, and possibly be disturbed by, variations in the symbolization and diagrammatic representation of meaning. But once it is recognized that such conventions are simply devices for making structures and interrelationships of meaning clear, there is surprisingly little difficulty in adapting to variations of notational practice.

I shall concentrate in this chapter on the formal description of word meanings, and will leave till Chapter 7 the question of how such meanings are to be combined to make up the meanings of whole sentences.

Components of Meaning

The analysis of word meanings is often seen as a process of breaking down the sense of a word into its minimal distinctive features; that is, into components which contrast with other components. A very simple example of this is provided by the words *man*, *woman*, *boy*, *girl*, and other related words in English. These words all belong to the semantic field of 'the human race', and the relations between them may be appropriately represented by a two-dimensional 'field diagram':

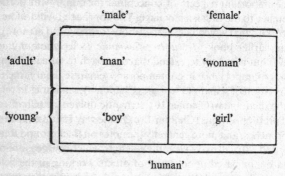

The diagram shows two dimensions of meaning: that of 'sex' and that of 'adulthood'; a third dimension is presupposed by the isolation of the field as a whole: that between 'human' and 'non-human' species.

Another, in many ways more convenient, way to represent these senses is to write formulae in which the dimensions of meaning are expressed by feature symbols like HUMAN and ADULT:

$$\begin{cases} +\text{HUMAN 'human'} \\ -\text{HUMAN 'animal, brute'} \end{cases} \begin{cases} +\text{ADULT 'adult'} \\ -\text{ADULT 'young'} \end{cases} \begin{cases} +\text{MALE 'male'} \\ -\text{MALE 'female'} \end{cases}$$

The meanings of the individual items can then be expressed by combinations of these features:

man: +HUMAN +ADULT +MALE
woman: +HUMAN +ADULT −MALE
boy: +HUMAN −ADULT +MALE
girl: +HUMAN −ADULT −MALE

These formulae are called the COMPONENTIAL DEFINITIONS of the items concerned: they can be regarded, in fact, as formalized dictionary definitions. The dimensions of meaning themselves will be termed semantic OPPOSITIONS.

I should point out that the features of an opposition are generally speaking of equal importance and mutually defining. It is an unfortunate side-effect of the labelling system that those features labelled ' + ' seem to be positive or marked, and those labelled ' − ' as negative or unmarked. In actual fact, for 'male', and 'female' one could just as easily use the reverse symbols −FEMALE and +FEMALE, or conventional symbols like ♂ or ♀. And as we shall see later, not all semantic contrasts are binary.

Using formulae like these, we can show the synonymy of two items by giving them both the same componential definition. For example, both *adult* (in its human sense) and *grown-up* can be given the same definition +HUMAN +ADULT, even though they clearly differ in stylistic meaning, the one being rather formal, the other colloquial. The opposite case to synonymy is multiple meaning or POLYSEMY, where one lexical item has more than one definition. *Man*, for example, has in addition to its definition +HUMAN +ADULT + MALE a broader definition consisting simply of the feature +HUMAN. (This is the meaning of *man* in a sentence like *Men have lived on this planet for over a million years.*) Another example of polysemy is *child*, which has one definition +HUMAN −ADULT, and another definition (see p. 248) as the opposite of 'parent'.

The definitions of *adult*, *child*, and *man* illustrate the further point that not all semantic oppositions relevant to a given semantic field need be operant in a given definition within that field: *child* and *adult* are not specified for sex, *man* (= 'human being') is unspecified for both sex and adulthood, and the adjective *female* (−MALE) is unspecified for both species and adulthood. We could, if we liked, represent this neutralization of oppositions by the symbol 'o'; the more fully expressed definitions would then be:

man:	+HUMAN (OMALE) (OADULT)
adult:	+HUMAN +ADULT (OMALE)
child:	+HUMAN −ADULT (OMALE)
female:	(OHUMAN) (OADULT) −MALE

In general, though, the 'neutral' dimensions may be omitted, and indeed it may be misleading to attempt to include them, as the number of semantic oppositions potentially available may be very large, and any attempt to list them exhaustively is likely to be incomplete.

The term COMPONENTIAL ANALYSIS has often been used for the method of analysis illustrated here, that of reducing a word's meaning to its ultimate contrastive elements. As a distinctive technique, componential analysis first evolved in anthropological linguistics as a means of studying relations between kinship terms, but it has since proved its usefulness in many spheres of meaning. It bears some resemblance to the mathematical process of factorizing a number, and a useful informal method of arriving at components of meaning is suggested by the analogy of arithmetical proportions. Just as we can pick out a common factor from a set of numbers by recognizing a proportionality in:

	4	is to	10
as	6	is to	15
as	8	is to	20
	$(2x)$		$(5x)$

so we can extract the features of sex and adulthood in:

	'man'	is to	'woman'
as	'boy'	is to	'girl'
as	'gander'	is to	'goose'
as	'ram'	is to	'ewe'
	(male x)		(female x)

	'man'	is to	'boy'
as	'woman'	is to	'girl'
as	'horse'	is to	'foal'
as	'cat'	is to	'kitten'
	(adult y)		(young y)

If componential analysis is a means of reducing meaning to its atomic parts, a question that obviously gets asked is 'Where does the atomization stop?' For example, why stop at the feature +HUMAN? Why not break this feature down into two further components, say 'FEATHERLESS' + 'BIPED' or 'HAIRLESS' + 'APE'? I have already answered this question in a general way on pp. 87-9; but a useful rule of thumb is to recognize an opposition of meaning wherever it proves its value by allowing us to make generalizations covering a range of lexical items. The feature +HUMAN, for example, is needed for a large number of words (*poacher, pacifist, priest, pugilist*, etc.) apart from those dealt with above, and −HUMAN is needed for a commensurately large number of words (*pussy, pelican, porker, panda*, etc.) referring to types of animal. In addition, the features +HUMAN and −HUMAN are important for explaining selection restrictions (pp. 141-6); for instance, for showing why *The panda confessed his mistake* is a deviant sentence while *The poacher confessed his mistake* is not. In contrast, the usefulness of having two separate dimensions of meaning ±FEATHERED and ±BIPED would be quite limited; it is true that we should be able to show the oddity of such sentences as *The poacher had three legs* and *The pugilist had feathers*, but this would be offset by the wastefulness of having to use two features instead of one on the very many occasions when it is necessary to draw a line between human and non-human species.

Meaning Relations

The only words for semantic relatedness in general use in our language are *synonym* (word of same meaning) and *antonym* (word of opposite meaning). But even the very simple illustration I have given shows up the inadequacies of this terminology, particularly in regard to contrasts of meaning. The proportions above show that there is no one answer to the question 'What is the antonym of *woman*?': *girl* and *man* are equally suitable candidates. The trouble is that the word 'antonym' encourages us to think that words contrast only on a single dimension; whereas in fact they may contrast with other words on a number of dimensions at once. Therefore a more general useful notion of 'semantic contrastingness' than antonymy is that of *incompatibility* (otherwise termed *meaning exclusion*). We may say that two componental formulae, or the meanings they express, are *incompatible* if the one contains at least one feature contrasting with a feature in the other. Thus the meaning of *woman* is incompatible with that of *child* because of the clash between +ADULT and −ADULT:

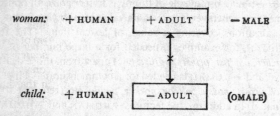

Other meanings incompatible with 'woman' are 'man', 'boy', 'girl', 'cow', not to speak of more remotely contrasted meanings such as 'tree' or 'screwdriver'.

Another relationship of meaning it is useful to distinguish is 'meaning inclusion' or *hyponymy*. This relationship exists between two meanings if one componental formula contains all the features present in the other formula. Thus 'woman' is hyponymous to 'grown-up', because the two features making up the definition 'grown-up' (+HUMAN +ADULT) are both present in the definition 'woman': +HUMAN +ADULT −MALE. 'Woman' is also hyponymous to 'female' and 'human being', as the following diagram shows (hyponymy is shown by the spatial inclusion of one formula, marked by an unbroken border, within the other, marked by a broken border):

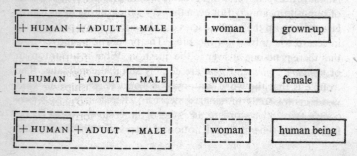

For a reason to appear later, identity of meaning is treated as a special case of hyponymy; therefore 'woman', like any other componential meaning, is hyponymous to itself:

One way to describe hyponymy is in terms of 'genus' and 'differentia'. The more specific term is called the *hyponym* of the more general, and the more general is called the *superordinate* term.

'Inclusion' is a confusing word to use in connection with meaning, because while in one respect (as we see from the diagram below) 'woman' includes 'grown-up', in another respect, the opposite is the case: 'grown-up' includes 'woman' in the sense that a general term might be said to include the meaning of the more specific term:

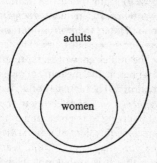

But in fact, in this latter sense of 'inclusion', we are really talking about the *reference* of a term (the set of individuals or objects it refers to), not the *meaning*. Because there is this inverse relationship between 'meaning inclusion' and 'referential inclusion', it is safer to avoid talking of inclusion altogether, and for this reason I follow John Lyons (1968: 453–4) in using the term *hyponymy*.

To recapitulate, the four componential relationships we have noted in the chapter so far may be separated into two pairs:

(1) Synonymy and polysemy are relations between form and meaning:

(a) *Synonymy*: more than one form having the same meaning.

(b) *Polysemy*: the same form having more than one meaning.

(II) Hyponymy and incompatibility are relations between two meanings:

(a) *Hyponymy* is the inclusion of one meaning in another.

(b) *Incompatibility* is the exclusion of one meaning from another. It is clearly necessary to regard hyponymy and incompatibility as relations between senses rather than between forms, for the reason applied to entailment and inconsistency, etc. in Chapter 5: in cases of ambiguity or multiple meaning, only *one* meaning of a form will generally enter into a semantic relationship. It would be wrong to say the word *child* is incompatible with the word *woman*, because it is for only one of the two main senses of *child* (that represented by +HUMAN +ADULT) that this statement is true. In the kinship sense of *child*, it is quite legitimate to say that a woman aged fifty is the *child* of someone in his seventies or eighties.

To avoid the loose thinking that arises from confusing form and meaning, I have written words in italics when discussing polysemy and synonymy, and written them in quotation marks when discussing hyponymy and incompatibility. This conforms to a convention whereby the italicized words represent forms, and the words in quotes represent the meanings corresponding to those forms. This convention will be regularly observed from now on.

For example, *child* is a way of referring to the noun *child*, while 'child' is a way of referring to the meaning of that noun, i.e. is an informal and imprecise equivalent of +HUMAN − ADULT (or any other meanings the word may have). 'Child' is an imprecise symbol for the very reason that it is ambiguous in the same way as the word *child* itself is: so we can only tell from context which definition is intended.

The Semantic Notation

Another vagueness, though this time not a particularly dangerous one, arises over the use of a semantic notation. In using a formula like +HUMAN +ADULT −MALE, I may be talking about it simply as a piece of notation (e.g. when I assert that +HUMAN +ADULT −MALE contains three features symbols), or I may be talking about it as the meaning represented by the formula (e.g. I may assert that +HUMAN +ADULT −MALE is incompatible with +HUMAN −ADULT). This ambivalence is relatively harmless, because the whole point about a notation is that it is meant to be completely unambiguous in pointing to one given meaning rather than another. Ideally, the notation, and the rules which are formulated for it, should reflect precisely the structure which, according to a linguistic description, exists in the language. But in practice a notation, by the very fact that it is a linear sequence of symbols expressing a multi-dimensional structure, may not be able to do this. To get it to mirror precisely the structure of meanings, we have to impose certain conventions on the notation, including the following:

(a) That the order in which components are placed is not significant in distinguishing meanings; thus +HUMAN +ADULT +MALE and +MALE +HUMAN +ADULT are simply notational variants of one another.

(b) That if there are two occurrences of the same feature in a formula, one of the occurrences is redundant; thus, +HUMAN +ADULT +MALE +ADULT is simply a notational variant of +HUMAN +ADULT +MALE.

(c) That the occurrence in the same formula of contrasting features (e.g. +MALE and −MALE) is a violation of the notational system. Thus the formula +HUMAN +ADULT +MALE −MALE is not a well-formed formula, and can have no reference to reality (no male women exist). If we met the phrase *male woman*, we would be forced to treat it as a play on words, and to try to find some special non-contradictory meaning for it – for example, by understanding it figuratively as 'a male person who behaves (in certain ways) like a woman'.

A notational system for meaning is important, because it is through such a system, and the conventions (such as those just given) we impose on it, that we specify the rules governing the structure of meaning. Although, as we have seen, two sets of symbols may be 'synonymous', in the sense of being variants standing for the same meaning, it is important to maintain the principle that no formula is ambiguous. Only in this way can we ensure that the notation precisely reflects the meanings it is designed to represent.

Justifying a Componential Analysis

Justifying a componential analysis means not only justifying the point at which one refuses to atomize further, but also showing that the contrasts and combinations of meaning one has recognized are necessary and sufficient to explain relevant data. The data of semantic analysis are regarded here (in line with the argument of Chapter 5) as a set of basic statements of entailment, etc. Thus the following relations of entailment are among the evidence I would produce in favour of the definitions I have given for words like *woman* and *man*:

> 'The secretary is a woman' entails 'The secretary is an adult.'
> 'I met two boys' entails 'I met two children.'

The link between componential analysis and basic statements is made through the mediation of such meaning relations as hyponymy and incompatibility: just as these have been defined in terms of componential analysis, so basic logical relationships such as entailment and inconsistency (or at least the most important types of entailment and inconsistency) can be defined in terms of hyponymy and incompatibility. A more precise understanding of these interconnections will emerge in Chapter 7; but for the present, we may observe from the examples above that if two assertions differ only in the substitution of a hyponym for a superordinate term, then one of the assertions entails the other. A similar sort of relation (though more restricted) holds between incompatibility and inconsistency:

> 'The secretary is a woman' is inconsistent with
> 　　　　'The secretary is a man.'
> 'Her best pupil is a boy' is inconsistent with
> 　　　　'Her best pupil is an adult.'

(Incidentally, in all such relations, we have to assume that expressions of definite meaning like *the secretary*, *she*, *John*, etc. have the same referent in both sentences.)

Some types of tautology and contradiction, too, can be defined in terms of hyponymy and incompatibility, as may be gathered from these examples:

'That man is an adult' is a tautology.

'That boy is a woman' is a contradiction.

Since the synonymy of truth value of two assertions is a special case of entailment (e.g. 'John is a grown-up' entails 'John is an adult'), it is simplest to define hyponymy (as we have already done) to include identity of componental meaning. Then there is a precise correspondence between entailment and hyponymy, and just as every assertion entails itself, so every componental concept is hyponymous to itself.

Some idea has now been given of how a componental analysis may be validated by following out its empirical consequences: that is, by using it to predict basic statements, which may then, in principle, be compared with judgements available to the analyst through introspection or informant testing. Yet another factor he has to take into account in the assessment is how economical his analysis is: for example, whether he fails to make a particular generalization, and so ends up stating the same rule in two different places, instead of stating it only once.

Justifying componental analysis by following out its logical consequences in terms of basic statements implies giving a certain priority to sentence meaning over word meaning; and this priority follows from my claim, in Chapter 5, that truth and falsehood, which are properties of sentence meanings but not of word meanings, are the surest basis for testing descriptions of meaning. Let us consider what this means as it applies to a concept like synonymy. The assumption is that an English-speaking informant will react with less confidence and consistency when asked, say, to judge the synonymy of *scared* and *frightened* as isolated words, than when asked to judge the synonymy of equivalent sentences containing them, such as (a) *John is scared of his father* and (b) *John is frightened of his father*. When asked to consider the equivalence of the words, he would probably be bothered by the more emotive and colloquial overtones of *scared* (factors of affective and stylistic meaning), whereas in judging the sentences in a frame of mind appropriate to truth value (i.e. whether they are true or false), he would be unlikely to let associative differences obscure the point at issue: namely, whether (a) could be false while (b) was true, or whether (b) could be false while (a) was true.

Taxonomic Oppositions

The three examples of semantic oppositions so far given are all of one type: there are two terms to the opposition, and the contrast between them is absolute, like a territorial boundary. This type of opposition may be called a *binary taxonomy* (the term 'taxonomy' indicating an arrangement of categories), and we might visualize it in the form of the accompanying diagram:

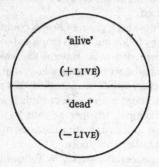

1. BINARY TAXONOMY

The absoluteness of the boundary needs explanation. It might be pointed out that in objective, physical terms, there is no clear-cut opposition between life and death; that there are even verbal strategies which allow us to point out the fuzziness of the borderline (e.g. we can say *In a technical sense he was alive, but for all practical purposes he was dead*). But the point is that in general, language behaves as if it were an absolute distinction. We observe, for example, in terms of logical consequences that

'The dead animal was still alive'
'John is both alive and dead'   } are contradictions
'John is neither alive nor dead'

'John is alive' is inconsistent with 'John is dead'
'John is dead' entails 'John is not alive'
'John is alive' entails 'John is not dead'.

(Again, it must be emphasized that the native speaker's instinct, in meeting sentences expressing the above contradictions, would be to force some sensible interpretation out of them by semantic transfer. But this does not affect the principle at issue.)

Not all oppositions are of this type; in particular, although languages seem to operate largely with binary contrasts, there are oppositions which involve more than two terms, and which may be called *multiple taxonomies*.

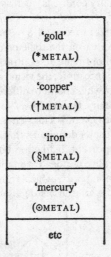

2. MULTIPLE TAXONOMY

Examples of this type are semantic classes dealing with types of metal, species of animal, or tree, or fruit, etc., primary colours, noises ('bang', 'crash', 'clatter', etc.) and types of vessel ('vase', 'mug', etc.). Here, as with binary taxonomies, the absoluteness of boundaries may be justified in logical terms, for example by the contradictoriness of a statement like 'This copper jug is made of silver'. But again, the language often has, at a more delicate stage, devices for indicating the shading off of one category into another. Thus despite the contradictoriness of 'This red book is brown', we have compound adjectives like *reddish-brown* and *brownish-red* to indicate transitional shades. In the diagram, the asterisk, dagger, and other symbols for distinguishing one component from another are purely arbitrary: all that is needed is some graphic cipher or other for marking the separateness of each.

Polar Oppositions

If semantic oppositions are not all binary, neither are they all taxonomic. Many binary contrasts, such as those expressed by the antonym pairs *rich/poor*, *old/young*, *deep/shallow*, *large/small*, etc., are best envisaged in terms of a scale running between two poles or extremes. Points on the scale can be roughly indicated, where required, by more delicate contrasts, e.g. between 'quite rich' and 'very rich'. Once more, the visual analogy is paralleled by logical characteristics, which point to differences between this type of opposition and binary taxonomies. Notice, for instance, that while the contradictoriness of *'This rich man is poor' and *'John is rich and poor' is just as definite as that of *'This dead man is alive', there is an important distinction between the deviance of *'This man is neither alive nor dead' and the acceptability of 'This man is neither rich nor poor', which shows that a polarity can accommodate a middle ground belonging neither to one pole nor to the other.

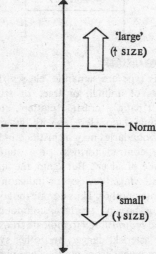

'large'
(↑ SIZE)

──────────────┼────────────── Norm

'small'
(↓ SIZE)

3. POLARITY

This middle ground implies the existence of a norm – and it is important to observe that the norm is *object-related* – that is, it can shift its position on the scale according to the object being categorized. For example, in terms of physical measurement, *young* does not mean the same in the phrase *young man* (aged seventeen to thirty?) and *young archbishop* (aged forty-five to sixty?). This relativity has curious logical consequences. With ordinary taxonomic features it is possible to make connections like the following, based on hyponymy:

'Xerxes is an alsatian' entails 'Xerxes is a dog.'
Therefore
'Xerxes is an adult alsatian' entails 'Xerxes is an adult dog.'
But the same inference cannot be made without hazard when the adjective expresses a feature of a polarity:

'Xerxes is a small alsatian' does not entail 'Xerxes is a small dog.'

Similarly, from the tautological character of 'An alsatian is a dog', one can draw the conclusion that 'An adult alsatian is an adult dog' is also a tautology; but not that 'A small alsatian is a small dog' is a tautology. The explanation is clearly that if the norm for a sub-species is different from that for the species as a whole, there is no guarantee that the hyponymic relationship is maintained. 'A small dog' means more fully 'A dog who is *small for a dog*', while 'A small alsatian' means 'an alsatian who is *small for an alsatian*'.

Some polar oppositions are basically evaluative, and for them there is not only an object-related norm, but a subjective, *speaker-related* norm as well. They include 'good'/'bad', 'beautiful'/'ugly' and 'kind'/'unkind'. These evaluative meanings are logically distinct from other polarities, because we cannot discuss their implications of truth value without distinguishing 'true for Mr X', 'true for Miss Y', etc. Hence they involve a relaxation of the rules of incompatibility: I cannot maintain that (a), 'London is beautiful' and (b), 'London is ugly' are necessarily inconsistent statements, because (a) could be true for one person, and (b) for another. But I can still hold that 'This beautiful city is ugly' is a contradiction, since 'beauty' and 'ugliness' (using the terms in their accepted senses) are mutually exclusive to the extent that they cannot be predicated of the same object at the same time by the same person.

Yet a third type of norm, a *role-related* norm, applies to some evaluative polarities, such as 'good'/'bad' and 'clever'/'stupid': thus a 'good boss' may mean not only 'a boss who is good as bosses go' and 'a boss who is good according to Mr X', but also 'a boss who is good *at being a boss*'. It is largely because of this three-fold variability of the norm that words such as *good* and *bad* are thought to be vague and shifting in their meanings.

Polar features of meaning are expressed not only through adjectives (*high*, *low*, etc.) but also through adverbs (*well*, *loudly*, *softly*, etc.), some nouns (*fool*, *pauper*, etc.), verbs (*love*, *hate*, *agree*, etc.), and determiners (*a few*, *many*, *a little*, etc.). In this book I shall symbolize the terms of a polar opposition by vertical arrows: ↑SIZE, ↓SIZE, etc.

Relative Oppositions

A further important type of binary opposition, a RELATION, involves a contrast of direction. Examples are: 'own'/'belong to', 'be in'/'contain', 'up'/'down', 'above'/'below', 'before'/'after', 'left'/'right', 'west'/'east', 'parent'/'child', 'teacher'/'pupil', etc. Relations cannot be considered apart from the two entities which they relate, which we may call, anticipating the next chapter, ARGUMENTS.* The contrast between two relative features consists in the fact that the two arguments (A_1 and A_2 in the diagram) may be related either in one order or in another. In form, the contrast may be expressed either by a different syntactic order, or by a different lexical item (with or without a change of syntactic construction). Thus the contrast between A_1 → PARENT A_2

and A_2 → PARENT A_1 can be realized *either* by keeping the same lexical item and reversing the syntactic positions of the arguments:

---

* Note that the term 'argument' is used here in a logical or mathematical sense which has little to do with the everyday sense of the term.

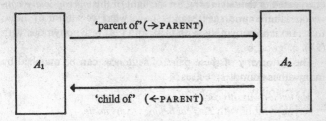

4. RELATION

    (1)   *John is the parent of James.*
    (2a) *James is the parent of John.*

or (often) by keeping the syntactic positions of the arguments constant, and changing the lexical form:

    (1)   *John is the parent of James.*
    (2b) *John is the child of James.*

Lexical pairs such as *parent* and *child* are called *converses*. Because of these alternative ways of expressing the same contrast, there arise cases of synonymy like:

    (1a) *John is the parent of James*
          is synonymous with (1b) *James is the child of John.*
    (2a) *James is the parent of John*
          is synonymous with (2b) *John is the child of James.*

If 'parent' is represented by →PARENT and 'child' by ←PARENT, it seems, then, that we have four different formulae representing only two different meanings:

(1a) 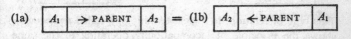

(2a) 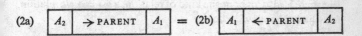

But it will be remembered that one of the conventions of our notation is that linear order of symbols is not distinctive. A natural extension of this principle is to say that in relational formulae such as those above, sequences which are mirror-images of one another represent the same meaning. In the light of this *mirror-image convention*, the notation as it stands shows what we want it to show: that (1a) is synonymous with (1b), and (2a) is synonymous with (2b).

The synonymy of these pairs of sentences can be matched by many other examples, such as:

> *My uncle owns this car*
> is synonymous with *This car belongs to my uncle.*
> *The green car was in front of the red bus*
> is synonymous with *The red bus was behind the green car.*
> *An oak chest contained all the family heirlooms*
> is synonymous with *All the family heirlooms were in an oak chest.*

But there are other relations for which no lexical converses exist. For example, there is no verb *to blep* (analogous to *contain* in the sentence above) such that *The fly was on the wall* means the same as *The wall blepped the fly.*

Relations, like polarities, vary in their logical characteristics. Many are like the 'parenthood' relation, where the directional contrast is mutually exclusive, so that it is impossible to maintain simultaneously that 'Alf is parent of George' and 'Alf is child of George' (assuming, as ever, that Alf and George are the same people in both assertions). Using $\rightarrow$R/$\leftarrow$R to represent any relative opposition, and A_1 and A_2, as before, to represent any pair of arguments, we may sum up this condition in the rule:

A_1	$\rightarrow$ R	A_2

is inconsistent with

A_1	$\leftarrow$ R	A_2

This type of relation, in logical terminology called *asymmetric*, shows the principle of incompatibility operating in the same absolute way for relative oppositions as for taxonomic oppositions. But there is also an opposite kind of relation, a *symmetric* relation, for which the following holds:

A_1	$\rightarrow$ R	A_2

entails

A_1	$\leftarrow$ R	A_2

e.g. 'John is married to Susan' entails 'Susan is married to John'. Here the contrast of meaning is effectively neutralized. Other relations are neither symmetric nor asymmetric. 'John loves Susan' neither entails nor is inconsistent with 'Susan loves John'; it is a matter of factual circumstance whether for a given pair of people, the relation of 'loving' is reciprocal. Hence only where a relative opposition is asymmetric does it define a relation of incompatibility.

Other logical attributes of relations are *transitivity* and *reflexivity* and their diametric opposites *intransitivity* and *irreflexivity*. *Transitivity*, in logical terms, is defined by the rule:

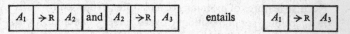

$$A_1 \;\rightarrow_R\; A_2 \quad \text{and} \quad A_2 \;\rightarrow_R\; A_3 \qquad \text{entails} \qquad A_1 \;\rightarrow_R\; A_3$$

For example, 'The king is in his counting house and his counting house is in his castle' entails 'The king is in his castle.' The relation expressed by *in* is thus transitive, as indeed most spatial relations are. *Intransitivity*, on the other hand, is defined by the rule:

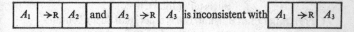

$$A_1 \;\rightarrow_R\; A_2 \quad \text{and} \quad A_2 \;\rightarrow_R\; A_3 \quad \text{is inconsistent with} \quad A_1 \;\rightarrow_R\; A_3$$

For example, 'Alf is the parent of George, and George is the parent of Ike' is inconsistent with 'Alf is the parent of Ike'. Again, many relations belong to neither category: the relation of 'loving' is neither transitive nor intransitive.

Relations which are invariably capable of linking an argument to itself are called *reflexive*. That is, for all reflexive relations, it is true to say ' $A_1 \;\rightarrow_R\; A_1$ is a tautology'. For example, 'Jack is *as old as* himself' is a tautology. If the opposite is the case, that is, if $A_1 \;\rightarrow_R\; A_1$ is a contradiction, then the relation is classified as *irreflexive*. For example, 'Jack is *in front of* himself' is a contradiction.

The particular combination of asymmetricity, transitivity, and irreflexivity is common to a large number of relations in natural language (e.g. 'above'/'below', 'before'/'after', 'ancestor'/ 'descendant'), and so it is worth while having a special name for it: we may call such oppositions *ordering* relations, because they place the arguments in an irreversible order in respect to the dimension of meaning concerned. Another important class is made up of those relations having the properties of symmetry and irreflexivity ('opposite', 'near to', 'be married to', 'similar to', etc.), which we may call *reciprocal* relations. As the directional contrast is in effect neutralized in reciprocal (and other symmetric) oppositions, it is useful to symbolize them by means of a double-headed arrow, to show that the relation operates in both directions at once: ↔MARRY, ↔NEAR, etc. Other relations can be symbolized by single-head arrows: →PARENT, ←PARENT.

Relative features of meaning are most often expressed by verbs ('own'/'belong') or prepositions ('over'/'under') or conjunctions ('before'/'after', 'while', 'because'/'so that'). But in comparative constructions, adjectives and adverbs, too, have relative meaning. Unequal comparisons (e.g. 'greater than'/'less than') have the character of ordering relations, as we notice from the following:

'Clive is taller than Bill' is inconsistent with
> 'Bill is taller than Clive.'

'Clive is taller than Bill, and Bill is taller than Susan' entails
> 'Clive is taller than Susan.'

'Clive is taller than himself' is a contradiction.

Also, the comparative forms of antonymous adjectives and adverbs are converses:

Clive is taller than Bill
is synonymous with *Bill is shorter than Clive.*

Other Types of Opposition

Other, less common types of semantic opposition include *hierarchic* oppositions (here symbolized by numerals, e.g. 1 LENGTH, 2 LENGTH, 3 LENGTH, etc.), which are like multiple taxonomies, except that they include an element of ordering.

5. HIERARCHY

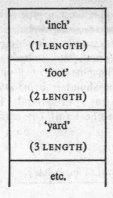

Examples are sets of units of measurement ('inch'/'foot'/'yard', etc.), and of calendar units such as months of the year ('January'/ 'February'/etc.), as well as the most fundamental hierarchy of all, that of number ('one'/'two'/'three'/etc.), which is open-ended, in that it has no 'highest' term. Terms of hierarchies are categorically exclusive like those of taxonomies, so that it is possible to derive from them contradictions and relations of inconsistency:

'Last Monday was a Tuesday' is a contradiction.
'Yesterday was a Sunday' is inconsistent with
            'Yesterday was a Monday.'

In other respects, hierarchies relate to polar relative oppositions; they obviously have to do with ordering and scalar positions, and this means that we can generate from them special classes of tautologies, contradictions, etc. such as:

'Monday was the day before last Tuesday' is a tautology.
'An inch is longer than a yard' is a contradiction.

The 'days of the week' opposition belongs to a special kind of hierarchy we may call *cyclic*, which has no first or last member, because for any two terms *a* and *b* of the hierarchy, it is possible to assert that *a* both precedes and follows *b*. 'Monday came before Friday' and 'Friday came before Monday' are both tautologous if we interpret 'before' in the more general sense, rather than in the narrow sense 'directly before'.

Last of all, there is an interesting type of binary semantic contrast, here called an *inverse opposition*, between such pairs as 'all'/'some', 'possible'/'necessary', 'allow'/'compel', 'be willing'/'insist', 'remain'/'become', 'still'/'already'. To visualise this relationship, we may imagine a football pitch bounded by two goal-lines, A and B. The whole terrain *in front of* goal-line A is one term of the opposition (say △ POSSIBLE), while the whole terrain *behind* goal-line B is the other term (▽ POSSIBLE):

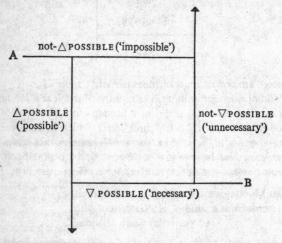

6. INVERSE OPPOSITION

The negations of the respective terms define complementary areas, as the diagram shows.

The main logical test for an inverse opposition is whether it obeys a special rule of synonymy which involves (a) substituting one inverse term for another, and (b) changing the position of a negative in relation to the inverse term. For example:

(1) *SOME countries have NO coastline* is synonymous with
                            NOT ALL countries have a coastline.

(2) *ALL of us are NON-smokers* is synonymous with
                            NOT ANY of us are smokers.

This illustration exemplifies the most important inverse opposition of all, that of *quantification*, which is represented by the positive terms 'all' and 'some', and the negative terms 'not all' and 'not any' (= 'none'). The semantic elements 'all' and 'some' are known respectively as the *universal* quantifier and the *existential* quantifier. (There is further discussion of quantification in Chapter 8, pp. 171–7). The following are further illustrations of the rule of synonymy which applies to inverse oppositions:

'We were *compelled* to be *non*-smokers' =
   'We were *not allowed* to be smokers'   ('allow'/'compel')
'It is *possibly not* true that Jack is a hippy' =
   'It is *not necessarily* true that Jack is a hippy'
                                 ('possible'/'necessary')
'The prisoners *insisted* on *not* eating their food' =
   'The prisoners were *not willing* to eat their food'
                            ('willingness'/'insistence')
'John did *not become* a smoker' =
   'John *stayed* a *non*-smoker'   ('become'/'stay')

Types of Opposition: Concluding Remarks

We have now seen that the phenomenon of 'semantic contrast' on which componential analysis is based is much richer and more varied than was apparent in the first simplified examples. While illustrating these various types of opposition, I have tried to show how their logical consequences (in terms of entailment, contradiction, etc.) differ from type to type, and therefore provide the motive for recognizing and defining the different types in the first place. By 'definition' here, indeed, I mean precisely stating the special conditions for entailment, inconsistency, etc. that apply to each type: the diagrams are no more than rough visual metaphors for these. Some of the special rules show interconnections between the different types; for instance, the tautology 'A tall man is taller than a short man' involves a connection between a polar opposition ('tall'/'short') and a relative opposition ('taller than'/'shorter than'). It might in fact be claimed that all types illustrated here could be ultimately reduced to one or two basic types – perhaps to just taxonomic and relative oppositions. For example, it has been argued (Bierwisch, 1970) that polar meanings should be explained in terms of relative meanings: e.g. that 'John is tall' should be analysed in comparative terms as 'John is taller than X, where X is the relevant norm'. Then the tautology 'A tall man is taller than a short man' could be derived directly from the transitivity of the 'taller than'/'shorter than' relation, without the need to introduce a special rule. The proof goes roughly like this:

$$\text{'}A_1 \text{ is tall'} = \text{'}A_1 \text{ is taller than X, where X is the relevant norm'.}$$

$$\text{'}A_2 \text{ is short'} = \text{'}A_2 \text{ is shorter than X, where X is the relevant norm'.}$$

$$= \text{'X is taller than } A_2, \text{ where X is the relevant norm'.}$$

Therefore 'A_1 is tall, and A_2 is short' =
    'A_1 is taller than X, and X is taller than A_2',
    which entails (by transitivity)
    'A_1 is taller than A_2'.

The difficulty is that the more one tries to reduce one sort of opposition to another in this way, the more complex and problematic becomes the task of relating semantic structure to syntactic structure – something which the linguist, because he sees semantics as only part of linguistic description, must take fully into account. My expectation is that the classification of different kinds of opposition on the present lines will prove to be a valid level of generalization, lending simplicity to the total account of how meaning works in relation to the structure of language as a whole. For this reason, as well as for ease of reading formulae, I have incorporated into the notation different feature symbols for each category of opposition, and it will be useful at this stage to list illustrations of these by way of summary:

1. BINARY TAXONOMY   2. MULTIPLE TAXONOMY

    + LIVE ('alive')   *METAL ('gold')
    — LIVE ('dead')   †METAL ('copper')
                                §METAL ('iron')
                                ⊙METAL ('mercury')
                                etc.

3. POLARITY

↑SIZE('large')
↓SIZE('small')

4. RELATION

→PARENT('parent')
←PARENT('child')

5. HIERARCHY

1LENGTH('inch')
2LENGTH('foot')
3LENGTH('yard')
etc.

6. INVERSE OPPOSITION

△POSSIBLE('possible')
▽POSSIBLE('necessary')

Relations of Dependence

Even with this more sophisticated picture of semantic contrastive-ness, we still have only a crude and incomplete view of how conceptual meanings are structured. The approximation can be improved if we turn now to the question of how the features of different semantic oppositions can be combined. The most elementary hypothesis to hold would be that every dimension of meaning is variable completely independently of all the other dimensions. But this view would be too simple. We have seen that the three dimensions ±HUMAN, ±ADULT, and ±MALE are independently variable in this way. But what about dimensions like ±ANIMATE and ±COUNTABLE? Plainly it makes no sense to combine either of the features +MALE or −MALE with −ANIMATE ('inanimate') or −COUNTABLE ('mass'). An 'inanimate male' object is just as much a contradiction in terms as a 'female male' object: or to look at the matter in a more positive light, both features +MALE and −MALE presuppose the presence of the feature +ANIMATE. We can symbolize this dependence through a tree diagram like (a), or through a field diagram like (b):

(a)   (b)

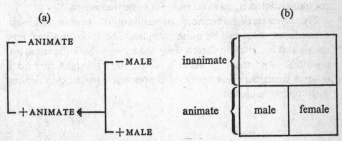

Or more explicitly we may formulate such a relationship through a *Rule of Dependence* which may be expressed as follows:

±MALE depends on +ANIMATE
(i.e. if +MALE or −MALE is present in a componential formula, then +ANIMATE is also).

The effect of this rule is to add the feature +ANIMATE automatically to any formula in which the feature +MALE or −MALE occurs. By this means we can account for the fact that a combination like 'female book' seems just as much a violation of semantic rule as 'female man':

−MALE −ANIMATE . . . [+ANIMATE]   'female book'
−MALE +HUMAN +ADULT +MALE   'female man'

Overtly, the componential meaning 'female book' does not contain a clash of features comparable to that of +MALE and −MALE in 'female man', but when we add the feature +ANIMATE (put in square brackets to show that it is supplied by a dependence rule), this brings to light a clash between −ANIMATE (implicit in the definition of *book*) and +ANIMATE. Rules of dependence are sometimes called 'redundancy rules', because they add features which are predictable from the presence of other features, and are therefore in a sense redundant to an economical semantic representation. Such rules are also found in phonology and syntax. Covert, indirect relations of incompatibility and hyponymy can also be established through rules of dependence: for example, the meanings 'man' and 'book' are indirectly incompatible, and hence 'X is a book' and 'X is a man' are inconsistent statements. In this way, dependence rules are important for extending the power of componential analysis to account for basic statements.

The interrelations between oppositions of meaning through dependence rules can be quite complex. The following is a very rough and incomplete sketch designed to show how the three oppositions ±HUMAN, ±ADULT, and ±MALE might fit into a general dependence network of taxonomic oppositions dealing with concrete objects:

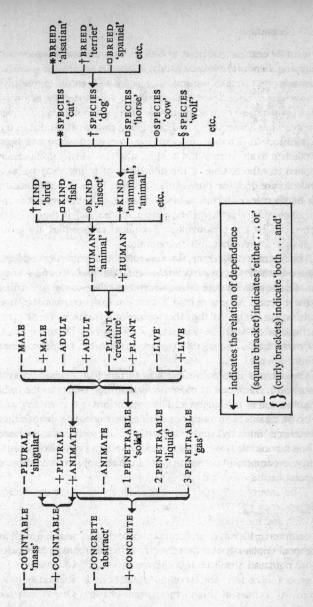

	indicates the relation of dependence
	(square bracket) indicates 'either...or'
	(curly brackets) indicate 'both...and'

* BREED 'alsatian'
† BREED 'terrier'
□ BREED 'spaniel'
etc.

* SPECIES 'cat'
† SPECIES 'dog'
□ SPECIES 'horse'
⊙ SPECIES 'cow'
§ SPECIES 'wolf'
etc.

† KIND 'bird'
□ KIND 'fish'
⊙ KIND 'insect'
* KIND 'mammal', 'animal'
etc.

− HUMAN 'animal'
+ HUMAN

− MALE
+ MALE

− ADULT
+ ADULT

− PLANT 'creature'
+ PLANT

− LIVE
+ LIVE

− PLURAL 'singular'
+ PLURAL

− ANIMATE
+ ANIMATE

1 PENETRABLE 'solid'
2 PENETRABLE 'liquid'
3 PENETRABLE 'gas'

− COUNTABLE 'mass'
+ COUNTABLE

− CONCRETE 'abstract'
+ CONCRETE

It must be emphasized here, as before, that the semantic oppositions and their interrelations need not reflect categories of scientific and technical thought: we are concerned with the 'folk taxonomy' or everyday classification of things that is reflected in the ordinary use of language. There are many instances where folk taxonomies involve what a scientist would consider a misclassification: in the past history of English, for example, the word *worm* has been applied to both worms and snakes, and the word *fish* has been applied to whales. One of the difficulties of trying to arrive at a 'folk taxonomy' for present-day English is the interference to varying degrees of technical taxonomies (e.g. the biological taxonomy in terms of classes, orders, genera, species, etc.) in the ordinary non-specialist use of language. Technical taxonomies are more highly structured than folk taxonomies.

The diagram shows how, through rules of semantic dependence, great economies can be made in the definition of words, and yet one can still show their interrelation with many other words. According to the diagram, for example, it is sufficient to define *spaniel* by one feature (□BREED). All the other feature of its meaning (†SPECIES, *KIND, −HUMAN, −PLANT, +ANIMATE, ¦PENETRABLE, +COUNTABLE, +CONCRETE) are predictable by dependence rules.

The diagram also points out how certain features and oppositions can be regarded as more important than others in the total organization of the language. The oppositions ±CONCRETE and ±COUNTABLE have many oppositions dependent on them (either directly or indirectly), and therefore have key positions at the head of the taxonomic 'tree'. The feature +ANIMATE is also important, as a component on which quite a number of semantic choices depend.

'Fuzzy Edges'

A common criticism of structural approaches to meaning such as componential analysis is that they try to make linguistic categories more rigid and absolute than they really are. There is certainly a degree of 'fuzziness' about componential boundaries, and we have seen two sources of this in the present chapter. One is that the language often provides at a more delicate level the means to break down the sharp categorical boundaries that we find at a cruder stage of analysis (so the notions 'hermaphrodite' and 'asexual' which are deviations in terms of the +MALE/−MALE dichotomy, are nevertheless capable of being expressed in the English language). Another is that there is often competition, even in the usage of a single speaker, between technical and 'folk' taxonomies.

'Fuzziness' is perhaps even more endemic to language than the above two cases suggest. There is often doubt in people's minds as to whether a given property is a criterial component of the word's meaning, or is simply a connotation. Let us take the definition of the verb *boast*: does it mean 'to praise oneself', or does it mean more than that, namely 'to praise oneself unjustifiably'? Many people will be uncertain, for example, as to whether a world champion boxer or chess-player is boasting if he claims 'I'm the greatest in the world'. No doubt he is indulging in self-exaltation, but then he is speaking no more than the truth.

A way out of this sort of quandary for the analyst is to give two or more overlapping definitions for the same word. For present-day English, for example, we may have to regard 'unjustifiability' as an optional feature in the definition of *boast*. Such coexisting overlapping meanings seem to be a common phenomenon, and presumably account for the way in which many words change their meanings in the course of history. Take *holiday*, for example: this has moved from the meaning of 'holy day' (viz., a Sunday or religious feast) to the present-day meaning of 'a period when one is not required to work'. The path it has taken from the one meaning to the other might be reconstructed as follows:

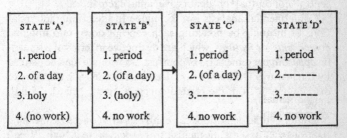

STATE 'A'	STATE 'B'	STATE 'C'	STATE 'D'
1. period	1. period	1. period	1. period
2. of a day	2. (of a day)	2. (of a day)	2. -------
3. holy	3. (holy)	3. ---------	3. -------
4. (no work)	4. no work	4. no work	4. no work

The items outside brackets are assumed to be criterial components, and those within brackets non-criterial, or connotative, properties. The change is here represented as a step-by-step progression, each step involving a change in a feature's status with regard to criteriality, or else the loss of a connotation altogether. The result, over a long period, is a complete shift in the reference of the expression so that the 'no work' aspect, originally no more than a connotation, is now a crucial feature of its meaning. But we cannot explain the change by saying that at given points in history, state 'X' was suddenly superseded by state 'Y': rather, at any historical period, the situation must have been similar to the present-day situation with *boast*: there would be two or more meanings, differing only in the criteriality or presence of one feature, and one of these alternatives would eventually win currency at the expense of the other.

Although considerations such as these complicate the task of componential analysis, a dedicated componentialist can still accommodate them in his system. Despite difficulties of imprecision and dangers of over-simplification it seems worthwhile to find out how far this quasi-mathematical approach can be taken, and to see what insights it can yield into the daunting complexities of conceptual structure.

Summary

In this chapter we began, with componential analysis, a quest for a precise model for describing the structure of meaning in that central 'conceptual' or 'denotative' area of semantics.

Componential analysis is a technique for describing interrelations of meaning by breaking each concept down into minimal *components*, or *features*, which are distinctive in terms of a semantic *opposition* or dimension of contrast. So 'woman' can be defined by the features +HUMAN +ADULT −MALE in such a way as to discriminate it from the related concepts 'girl', 'man', 'child', 'cow', etc.

Componential definitions can enable us to characterize meaning relations such as semantic inclusion or *hyponymy* (e.g. 'oak'/'tree') and semantic contrastiveness or *incompatibility* (e.g. 'tree'/

'animal'), as well as the more traditional notions of synonymy (sameness of meaning) and polysemy (multiple meaning). Componential oppositions are by no means always of the absolute 'yes'/ 'no' type (*binary taxonomy*), but may be gradable contrasts or *polarities* such as 'hard'/'soft', or *relational* contrasts such as 'over'/'under', as well as of a number of other types. These types of opposition may be distinguished by the differing logical consequences they have in sentences containing them; and more generally, particular componential analyses are to be justified by their ability to explain the logical characteristics of sentences, as shown in the native speaker's ability to recognize relations of entailment, tautologies, etc.

One further factor entering into the semantic structure of vocabulary is the network of dependence relations between semantic choices, such that a choice from one opposition is logically dependent on a choice from some other opposition (as the choice between +ANIMATE and −ANIMATE depends on the prior choice of +CONCRETE rather than −CONCRETE). Such dependence relations are accounted for by *dependence rules* (or *redundancy rules*).

Componential analysis does not answer all the problems of semantic structure and description. Its limitations, which have been widely commented on, should not lead one to abandon it, but to look for ways in which it may be fitted into a larger and more adequate model of conceptual semantics. This is the task to which I address myself in Chapter 7.

7. The Semantic Structure of Sentences

Componential analysis, the theme of the last chapter, has developed as a technique for analysing the meaning of words. But now we come to the question: 'How to describe the meanings of whole sentences?' The simplest and most naïve hypothesis is that the meaning of a sentence is the sum of the meanings of the words and other constituents which compose it. But the objections to this are manifest. Firstly, we could not, if this were the case, tell the difference of meaning between *My wife has a new dog*, *My new wife has a dog*, *My new dog has a wife*, etc.: all these would have to be regarded as synonymous. In the second place, if componential analysis applied to a sentence as a whole, then the occurrence of two contrastive features in different parts of a sentence would be a semantic violation (e.g. +ADULT in 'woman' and −ADULT in 'puppy' would clash in the sentence *The woman likes the puppy*). But as everyone can see, there is nothing objectionable about sentences of this kind. Some linguists have tried another solution, similar to this only more sophisticated, and that is to set up special rules ('combinatorial rules' or 'projection rules') which amalgamate the meanings of sentence constituents in special ways while converting them into the meanings of whole sentences.

But this whole approach, talking about semantics in terms of *words* and *sentences*, is a misleading one. Why should one attempt to describe meaning in terms of categories of syntax, any more than one would attempt to describe syntax in terms of phonological categories like stress and intonation? So far as I know, no one has ever managed to make the *syllable* a useful category for the syntactic parsing of sentence, although there are clear correlations between syllabic structure and units like words. In the same way, I suggest we stop trying to fit semantic analysis into the mould of syntactic units like nouns, verbs, etc., and instead look for units

and structures which operate on the semantic level. This is not to
ignore that such semantic categories will have correlations with
syntactic units and constructions: in fact, the simplicity of the statable relations between syntax and semantics (see Chapter 9) is an
important consideration in evaluating a semantic description as
part of the total description of a language.

Let us take componential analysis as a starting point. We have
noted that componential analysis, viewed as a description of meaning in terms of combinations of contrastive features, can be
applied to word meaning, but cannot be applied to whole sentence
meanings. Does this mean, then, that the word can be considered
the unit which is the upper limit of componential analysis? There
is evidence to the contrary. For example, English has a number of
words identifying the young of animal species, and these may be
defined componentially as follows (see the taxonomic diagram on
p. 121):

kitten: ∗SPECIES —ADULT
puppy: †SPECIES —ADULT
foal: □SPECIES —ADULT
etc.

It happens, though, that for some types of animal (e.g. monkeys)
we have no term for an ungrown member of the species. Does this
mean that we have no means of expressing the idea of 'young
monkey'? It certainly does not – I have just used the phrase *young
monkey* to express that very idea. What we can say, rather, is that
the combination of features #SPECIES —ADULT (where
#SPECIES = 'monkey') is expressed in English by a phrase, in-
stead of by a single word. The general conclusion this leads to is
that the semantic unit within which componential analysis applies,
though smaller than a sentence and not smaller than a word, has no
one-to-one correspondence with any one syntactic unit, such as the
word.

We may therefore think of semantic analysis in terms of a three-
tier system of units. At the top of the scale is the unit which corresponds roughly to a sentence, and to which questions concerning
truth and falsehood relate: this is the unit I earlier called a PRE-
DICATION. (Assertions, questions, and commands are kinds of

predication.) At the bottom of the analytic process are the minimal differentiating factors of meaning: semantic *features* (or components). Somewhere between the two there is a third entity – a unit which marks the upper limit of componential analysis, and which corresponds roughly to a word or a phrase in syntax. This unit I call, for lack of a better term, a *cluster*. The cluster is a unit which consists of features and which therefore enters into relations of hyponymy and incompatibility (pp. 100–1). And just as the relation of a predication to reality is discussed in terms of *truth conditions*, so the relation between a cluster and reality is that relation which is called *denotation* or *reference*: the cluster is the unit of language which has the property of *referring*.

Arguments and Predicates

What I have just said justifies an analysis in terms of *at least* three units of increasing magnitude. To show that *only* three units are required, I have to establish that the units I have called 'clusters' happen to correspond to elements into which predications are immediately divisible.

For this purpose, I return now to the discussion of relative oppositions in Chapter 6 (pp. 110–14), where I showed how an assertion like

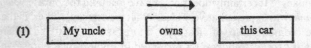

(1)   My uncle   owns   this car

could be broken down into two arguments (or 'logical participants'), 'my uncle' and 'this car', with a relational element linking them ('owns'). This linking element may be called (following logical rather than grammatical terminology) a PREDICATE. Just as subject, verb, object, adverb, etc. are constituents of sentences, so argument and predicate are constituents of the predications that sentences express. Arguments and predicates sometimes (as in (1)) match syntactic elements like subject, verb, and object, and sometimes do not. One has to avoid associating the 'predicate' in this sense with the 'predicate' of traditional grammar, and indeed, one must be wary of expecting these logico-semantic units to have any straightforward correspondence with syntactic units. In (2) below, for example, the predicate is expressed by *was in front of*, which is not a single unit at all in a syntactic sense:

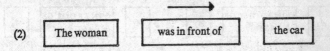

(2) | The woman | | was in front of | | the car |

Assuming that all predications can be divided up into units of this kind, the question we have to ask is whether arguments and predicates are identifiable as the 'clusters' within which componential analysis can be applied. The examples we have looked at encourage us to suppose that they are. Thus one of the arguments in (2), 'the woman', can be broken down exhaustively into a set of features:

the woman: +DEFINITE +HUMAN +ADULT −MALE
                      −PLURAL

and it is not difficult to imagine that a similar analysis could be carried out for 'the car'. What is perhaps less obvious is that predicates, too, can be broken down into sets of features, and can enter into relations of hyponymy and incompatibility. The predicate 'boiled' (in the sentence 'Adam boiled an egg') might, for example, be analysed provisionally into three components, →COOK, +IN WATER, and +PAST. The second of these components distinguishes 'boiling' from 'frying', and is dependent on the first component. The third component distinguishes past from present, and is expressed by the past tense *boiled* as contrasted with the present tense *boils*. The breaking down of 'boil' into two components is necessary in order to explain the entailment relation (which is not a relation of synonymy) between pairs of statements like the following:

'Adam boiled an egg' entails 'Adam cooked an egg.'

To illustrate the point further, here is a somewhat more complicated example of the componential analysis of predicates: an example taken from the semantics of spatial relations. Consider the predicate 'was in front of' in (2) above. A simple way to reduce this to contrastive components would be to separate the relative opposition between 'in front of' and 'behind' from the temporal opposition between 'past' and 'present'. We could then arrive at the following four-way contrast:

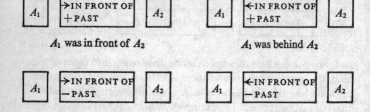

A_1 was in front of A_2 A_1 was behind A_2

A_1 is in front of A_2 A_1 is behind A_2

But this does not go far enough. Not only is the representation of the temporal meaning erroneous (for reasons we shall note shortly, on pp. 153–4), but also the analysis of 'in front of' fails to show its relation to other locative meanings, such as 'over', 'under', 'by', 'on the left of', etc. For this purpose, at least three semantic oppositions are needed:

$\left\{\begin{array}{l}\rightarrow\text{DIRECTION} \\ \leftarrow\text{DIRECTION}\end{array}\right.$ (directional contrast between 'in front of' and 'behind', 'over' and 'under', etc.)

$\left\{\begin{array}{l}+\text{VERTICAL} \quad \text{'vertical'} \\ -\text{VERTICAL} \quad \text{'horizontal'}\end{array}\right.$

$\left\{\begin{array}{l}+\text{PRIMARY} \quad \text{'primary horizontal axis' (front-to-back)} \\ -\text{PRIMARY} \quad \text{'secondary horizontal axis' (side-to-side)}\end{array}\right.$

We may add to these a reciprocal relation as a common ground to the whole analysis:

$\leftrightarrow$SPATIAL 'A_1 is in spatial relation to A_2'

And we also have to add the following dependence (redundancy) rules:

$\pm$VERTICAL depends on $\leftrightarrow$SPATIAL
$\pm$PRIMARY depends on $-$VERTICAL

The various prepositions *in front of*, *behind*, etc. may now be defined as:

(a) *over*   (b) *under*   (c) *in front of*   (d) *behind*
[↔SPATIAL]   [↔SPATIAL]   [↔SPATIAL]   [↔SPATIAL]
→DIRECTION   ←DIRECTION   →DIRECTION   ←DIRECTION
+VERTICAL   +VERTICAL   [−VERTICAL]   [−VERTICAL]
                                            +PRIMARY   +PRIMARY

(e) *on the left*   (f) *on the right*   (g) *beside*
[↔SPATIAL]   [↔SPATIAL]   [←SPATIAL]
→DIRECTION   ←DIRECTION   [−VERTICAL]
[−VERTICAL]   [−VERTICAL]   −PRIMARY
−PRIMARY   −PRIMARY

(Features in brackets are 'redundant' features predicted by dependence rules.) Because of the incompatibility of formulae (a) to (f), this analysis now shows the mutual inconsistency of all the following propositions:

'A_1 is in front of A_2'   'A_1 is behind A_2'
'A_1 is over A_2'   'A_1 is under A_2'
'A_1 is on the left of A_2'   'A_1 is on the right of A_2'

But the question might be asked: 'Does it have to be this complicated?' Why, for instance, should we not distinguish the three axes (vertical, primary, secondary) more economically by a single three-term opposition, instead of by two binary oppositions? Why, that is, do we have to make an initial cut between 'horizontal' and 'vertical' before separating out the two horizontal dimensions? One reason is precisely that otherwise the meaning of the word *horizontal* could not be explained (it could only be defined as a conjunction of two mutually contrasting features, 'primary' and 'secondary'). Another reason for making the dichotomy between 'vertical' and 'horizontal' involves consideration of the locative meaning of the preposition *by*. In fact, *by* has three locative meanings, on a scale of descending generality, and one of these meanings (the middle one) can only be defined by abstracting the feature of 'horizontality' (−VERTICAL). The three senses can be observed in:

(1) The shell exploded *by* the wing of the aeroplane.
(2) An oak tree stood *by* the farmhouse.
(3) The red car was parked *by* the green one.

Uppermost in (1) is the most general sense of *by*, that which may be paraphrased simply 'in spatial proximity to', without any restrictions as to spatial orientation. Here 'by' could include 'over' and 'under'. In (2), the sense is most likely to be 'near to on a horizontal plane', and therefore to contrast with 'over' and 'under'. In (3), the meaning of *by* is even more specific: it is equivalent to 'beside', and indicates proximity on the 'side-to-side' axis only. 'By' here contrasts not only with 'over' and 'under', but with 'in front of' and 'behind'. If in (1), *by* is defined as ↔SPATIAL +PROXIMATE, then for the second definition we need to add to this —VERTICAL, and for the third definition, the feature —PRIMARY:

by (1)	*by* (2)	*by* (3)
↔SPATIAL	[↔SPATIAL]	[↔SPATIAL]
+PROXIMATE	+PROXIMATE	+PROXIMATE
	—VERTICAL	[—VERTICAL]
		—PRIMARY

The point is that the second definition could not have been expressed componentially if the abstraction of 'horizontality' had not been isolated.

Yet a third reason for preferring this superficially more complex analysis is discovered if the field of data under consideration is widened to include the nouns *top, bottom, front, back*, and *side*. There is a clear parallel between these terms and the prepositions we have been considering: 'top' is to 'bottom' as 'over' is to 'under', etc. Therefore the same oppositions of ±VERTICAL, ±PRIMARY, etc. may be applied to them. But again, the necessity of distinguishing a feature —VERTICAL is demonstrated by the threefold ambiguity of the noun *side*, which is exactly analogous to the preposition *by*:

(1) the *side* of the balloon ('outer surface' in general sense)
(2) the *side* of the cake (as opposed to 'top' or 'bottom')
(3) the *side* of the car (as opposed to 'front' or 'back')

The second definition of *side*, like the second definition of *by*, requires the feature −VERTICAL 'horizontal axis'. Hence the more we try to extend the analysis to include a wider sweep of data, the more we discover the inadequacies of a solution which, in a limited context, seemed to be more economical.

Although the justification of this analysis, like the analysis itself, is incomplete, I hope that this discussion of spatial relations has sufficiently emphasized the point that predicates, like arguments, can be analysed componentially, and that considerations which enter into the evaluation of componential analyses can be applied equally to both. Therefore predicates, as much as arguments, can be identified as those intermediate units I have called 'clusters', and a more general applicability can be given to the following three-tier analysis of the meaning of sentences:

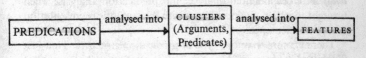

PREDICATIONS → analysed into → CLUSTERS (Arguments, Predicates) → analysed into → FEATURES

At this stage I shall venture a fairly complete semantic analysis of a simple utterance – fairly complete, that is, except for the justifiable omission of redundant features:

(A)

PREDICATION

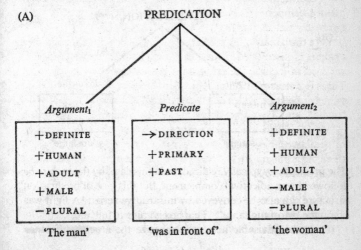

Argument₁	*Predicate*	*Argument₂*
+DEFINITE	→DIRECTION	+DEFINITE
+HUMAN	+PRIMARY	+HUMAN
+ADULT	+PAST	+ADULT
+MALE		−MALE
−PLURAL		−PLURAL
'The man'	'was in front of'	'the woman'

To assure oneself that all these contrastive features play a part in the meaning of the sentence, it is a useful exercise to vary the features one by one, noting what changes in the meaning of the whole result from this. For example, the substitution of ←DIRECTION for →DIRECTION would change the meaning to 'The man was behind the woman.'

Predication Analysis

We have arrived, by a process of argument and illustration, at a second kind of semantic analysis, which is interrelated with, and complementary to, componential analysis. This type of analysis consists in breaking down predications into their constituent 'clusters', and may therefore be not unfittingly called *predication analysis*. Componential analysis and predication analysis, when brought together, can provide us with the semantic representation of an entire sentence.

There is more than one type of predication structure. That just illustrated in diagram (A) is a *two-place predication*, because it has two arguments. Also very common are *one-place predications*, which contain only a single argument. Simple attributive sentences like *Alsatians are large* express such predications:

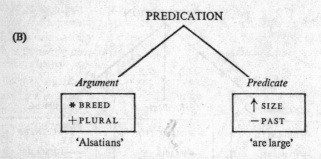

PREDICATION

(B)

Argument

* BREED
+ PLURAL

'Alsatians'

Predicate

↑ SIZE
− PAST

'are large'

The predicate is typically realized, as in this case, by the verb *to be* followed by an adjectival complement. But this type of predication structure can also be conveyed by intransitive verbs: 'A light was shining'; 'Morning came'; 'That box is going to fall' etc.

It may be advisable here to emphasize the crucial difference between the two similar terms 'predication' and 'predicate'. A 'predication' can be conveniently thought of as the semantic correlate of a *sentence*, and a 'predicate' (though with some danger of misrepresentation) as the semantic correlate of a *verb*. Just as each sentence pattern (e.g. Subject + Verb + Object) is associated with a particular kind of verb (e.g. transitive verb, intransitive verb), so each type of predication is associated with its own kind of predicate. Two-place predications contain a kind of predicate which may be called a *relative predicate*, since it contains at least one relative feature (e.g. →DIRECTION in diagram (A) above). The function of the relative feature is to determine the order of the arguments with respect to one another; therefore it is convenient (if there is one and only one relative feature in the predicate) to adopt a convention whereby the direction of the arrow determines which argument is called 'initial' and which 'final'. The initial argument, then, does not always correspond to the leftmost argument on the page:

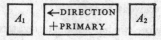

Here A_2 is the 'initial' argument, and A_1 the 'final' argument. This convention of terminology is not so perverse as it might seem, as it helps to underline the neutrality of semantic representations with respect to the left-to-right order on the page; and it is also useful when we come to plot the correspondence between semantic and syntactic structure (Chapter 9, pp. 195–7).

The predicates of one-place predications form a category I shall call 'attributive'. They do not contain relative features such as ←DIRECTION, because these require, for their ordering function to be satisfied, two arguments. But characteristic of attributive predicates are polar features, such as the feature ↑SIZE ('large') in diagram (B) above. Both relative and attributive predicates can contain features of tense, and in general, it may be taken that predicates (because there is no more and no less than one predicate per predication) contain those semantic features, such as tense and modality features, which are relevant to the predication as a whole, rather than to just part of it. That the predicate is the most central

and least dispensable part of every predication is reinforced by the
existence of 'no-place predications', i.e. predications containing
no argument at all. Examples are meteorological utterances like
It is raining and *It will be warm tomorrow*. We cannot consider the
element expressed by the subject *it* in these sentences to be an
argument, for *it* is semantically empty: notice, for example, that *it*
is so predictable that one cannot construct a question for which it is
an appropriate answer: **What was raining cats and dogs all last
night? *It*. The predicate of a no-place predication may be symbolized P^0.

It is doubtful whether further predication types apart from these
need be postulated, as what appear to be three-place and four-place
predications usually, if not always, prove to be reducible to com-
plexes of two-place and one-place predications. Thus 'John gave
the dog a bone' may be subdivided into two two-place predications
one inside another (see 'embedding', pp. 146–9):

'John caused X'
X = 'The dog received a bone'.

In summary, therefore, we have distinguished three types of predication, and three types of predicate:

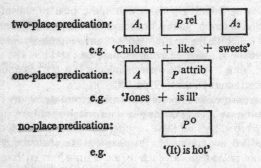

two-place predication: A_1 P^{rel} A_2

        e.g. 'Children + like + sweets'

one-place predication: A P^{attrib}

        e.g.   'Jones + is ill'

no-place predication: P^0

        e.g.   '(It) is hot'

Entailment and Inconsistency

In the last chapter we noted the close connection between hyponymy and entailment, incompatibility and inconsistency. But we are
now in a position to understand these connections more precisely,
and to state rough-and-ready rules to cover them.

Rule of Entailment: A relation of entailment arises between two assertions whenever (the assertions being otherwise identical) *an argument or predicate in one assertion is hyponymous to an argument or predicate in the other.*

For example:

(1) 'I saw $\boxed{\begin{array}{c} A_1 \\ \text{a boy} \end{array}}$' entails (2) 'I saw $\boxed{\begin{array}{c} A_2 \\ \text{a child} \end{array}}$',

(because the only difference between these statements is that one of the arguments of (1) is hyponymous to the corresponding argument of (2)). The variable element can also be a predicate:

(3) 'Turpin $\boxed{\begin{array}{c} P_1 \\ \text{stole} \end{array}}$ a horse' entails (4) 'Turpin $\boxed{\begin{array}{c} P_2 \\ \text{took} \end{array}}$ a horse'

(because 'stole' is a hyponym of 'took', just as 'boy' is of 'child'). Actually, entailment works in two different directions, according to whether the assertions are of 'general' or 'specific' meaning. For the specific assertions (5) and (6), the assertion containing the superordinate is entailed by the one containing the hyponym:

(5) 'The children were eating apples' i.e. '. . . some apples' entails
(6) 'The children were eating fruit' i.e. '. . . some fruit'

But for the general assertions (7) and (8) it is the other way round:

(7) 'Children are a nuisance' (i.e. 'All children . . .,
                Children in general . . . ') entails
(8) 'Boys are a nuisance' (i.e. 'Boys in general . . . ').

The latter type of entailment works only for hyponymy of arguments.

The rule connecting inconsistency of predications to incompatibility of clusters is similar to the rule of entailment, but more restricted, because it applies only to predicates:

Rule of Inconsistency: A relation of inconsistency arises between two assertions whenever (the assertions being otherwise identical) *the predicate of one assertion is incompatible with that of the other.*

For example:

(9) 'Mary [P_1 dislikes] work' is inconsistent with

(10) 'Mary [P_2 likes] work'

(11) 'Peter [P_1 is on the left of] his father' is inconsistent with

(12) 'Peter [P_2 is on the right of] his father.'

These rules of entailment and inconsistency may seem rather simple and trivial, but they are far wider and more powerful in their application than they appear from the examples given so far. To show this, I shall make four separate points:

1. These rules apply to all types of predications, not just to two-place predications. The following are examples of their application to one-place predications:

(13) 'This paint [P_1 is scarlet] ' entails

(14) 'This paint [P_2 is red] .' ('Scarlet' is a hyponym of 'red')

(15) 'This paint [P_1 is scarlet] ' is inconsistent with

(16) 'This paint [P_2 is blue] .' ('Scarlet' is incompatible with 'blue')

2. Because of the mirror-image convention (pp. 111–12), the rules apply no matter what the order the elements come in. So the en-

tailment of 'Presents please boys' by 'Children like presents'
follows from the fact that because *like* and *please* are converses, 'children' and 'boys' are corresponding arguments in
predications otherwise equivalent.

3. As we have seen, relations of hyponymy and incompatibility are
not limited to single words: they can hold between word and
phrase, or between phrase and phrase. So the entailment rule
covers cases like the following, where the difference between the
two statements is marked by the addition of one or more words,
rather than the substitution of one word for another:

(17) 'James is a lean, melancholy, poetry-loving brigadier' entails
     (18) 'James is a melancholy brigadier.'
(19) 'James is a brigadier' entails (20) 'James is an army officer.'
(21) 'His manner deeply offended me' entails (22) 'His manner
     offended me.'

4. The rules of entailment and inconsistency apply cumulatively, in
the following ways:

(A) If *X* entails *Y* and *Y* entails *Z*, then *X* entails *Z*
    (i.e. the entailment relation is *transitive* – see p. 113)
(B) If *X* entails *Y* and *Y* is inconsistent with *Z*, then *X* is incon-
    sistent with *Z*

These two supplementary rules may be illustrated by the following:

(A) *X*: 'Boys ran down the street' entails *Y*: 'Boys went down the
    street.'
    Y: 'Boys went down the street' entails *Z*: 'Children went down
    the street.'
    Therefore:
    X: 'Boys ran down the street' entails *Z*: 'Children went down
    the street.'
(B) *X*: 'John was singing drunkenly' entails *Y*: 'John was singing.'
    Y: 'John was singing' is incompatible with *Z*: 'John was silent.'
    Therefore:
    X: 'John was singing drunkenly' is inconsistent with
    Z: 'John was silent.'

Thus the rules of entailment and incompatibility I have given are far more wide-ranging than they seem at first sight, and provide strong support for the value of an analysis of predications into arguments and predicates.

Null Arguments

The term 'cluster' perhaps misleadingly suggests that arguments and predicates always contain a number of features. In actuality, some arguments and predicates contain only one feature; and some arguments even contain no features at all. These *null arguments* are void of content in the sense that they have the maximum generality of reference. They also have no syntactic realization, and their presence can only be detected negatively, for example, by the absence of an object from a verb which normally requires one:

John is eating (i.e. 'John is eating something-or-other')
(similarly *John is writing/reading/playing/driving/smoking*, etc.)
Other syntactic lacunae which mark null arguments are the absence of agent phrases with the passive, and the absence of argument-specifying determiners and prepositional phrases with abstract nouns:

The dinner was cooked (i.e. '. . . by someone-or-other')
The internment of extremists (i.e. '. . . by someone-or-other')
The internment (i.e. '. . . of someone-or-other by someone-or-other').

Because they contain no features, null arguments are by definition (see p.100) superordinate to all other sets of components. Hence we are able to explain (by the rule of entailment) why

(a) 'John is smoking cigars' entails 'John is smoking'
(b) 'John is eating nuts' entails 'John is eating' etc.

It is this explanatory power that in the main justifies the postulation of null arguments. There is thus an important difference, logically, between sentences like *John is eating* and *John is sleeping*. The latter contains a 'true intransitive' verb which is semantically equivalent to an adjectival complement (cf. *John is asleep*), and expresses a one-place predication. The former, on the other hand, expresses a two-place predication – but one in which the second argument is null, and therefore unexpressed.

Selection Restrictions

What I have said about null arguments begs an explanation of the fact that in some cases, the unexpressed argument does seem to have some content. In *The dinner was being cooked*, for example, no agent is specified, but at least we gather that the unspecified argument, the 'cooker', must be 'human'. By the same token, we would recognize the peculiarness of ** The dinner was cooked by a cockroach* or ** The dinner was cooked by a cup*, in the unlikely event of our encountering such utterances. At the root of both observations is the general principle that meaning seems to 'overflow sideways' from one part of a sentence to another: that certain features of meaning are predictable from environment, and that any contradiction of such features will result in an unacceptable utterance.

These phenomena are usually discussed, in linguistics, under the heading of *selection restrictions* (or 'co-occurrence restrictions'). Selection restrictions have been problematic for linguists, because although they require explanation in terms of semantic categories (such as 'human', 'animate', and 'concrete'), they have a superficial resemblance to the syntactic restrictions which go under the heading of 'agreement' or 'concord' (e.g., the rule that a singular subject must have a singular verb), and therefore invite treatment as an aspect of syntax. The following are examples of utterances which are unacceptable because they violate selection restrictions:

'Water is in love with my friend' ('Water' is inanimate, not animate)
'The girl assembled' ('Girl' is singular, not plural)
'Happiness is green' ('Happiness' is abstract, not concrete)
'The boys drank the cake' ('Cake' is solid, not liquid)
'The mouse neighed' ('Horse' is required, not 'mouse')

Chomsky in 1965 (*Aspects of the Theory of Syntax*) tried to deal with certain selection restrictions purely in terms of the co-occurrence of syntactic classes. For example, he indicated the acceptability of sentences like *John admires sincerity* beside the unacceptability of sentences like **Sincerity admires John* by making *admire* a member of the class of verbs which require an animate subject. This approach was mistaken in two ways. Firstly, it was an attempt to bring a semantic phenomenon within the realm of syntax; and secondly, it made the condition too strong, and so forbade the occurrence of sentences which are acceptable.

To take the first point first: there are various reasons why selection restrictions have to be treated as a semantic rather than as a syntactic aspect of language, and I have room to mention only two of these reasons here:

(1) If two words are synonymous, their selection restrictions are the same. Thus if we take *frighten* and *scare* to be conceptual synonyms (although they are stylistically different) both the sentences *The idea frightened the girl* and *The idea scared the girl* are acceptable, while **The girl frightened the idea* and **The girl scared the idea* are equally unacceptable.

(2) If two expressions are converses (e.g. *own* and *belong to*), they have the same selection restrictions, except that these restrictions apply in the reverse order. Thus *The man owned a fortune* and *A fortune belonged to the man* both make good sense, while **A fortune owned the man* and **The man belonged to a fortune* do not, unless inventively construed.

In both these cases, restrictions that would require two separate statements on the syntactic level can be brought together under one generalized statement on the semantic level. So the simpler account, in both cases, is that which deals with selection restrictions semantically.

The second objection to Chomsky's account is that it *compels* a verb to match positively the features of the subject and object, instead of allowing its co-occurrence *unless* there is an actual conflict of features. That is, Chomsky in effect says 'If feature X is in unit A, then feature Y must be in unit B.' This works fine in distinguishing cases like (1a) and (1b):

(1a) The horse neighed   (1b) *The horse miaowed

But it does not account for the acceptability of both the following:

(2a) The animal neighed   (2b) The animal miaowed

To account for the difference of acceptability between (1a) and (1b), in Chomsky's terms, we must suppose that there is a contextual restriction on the verb *neigh* which requires the presence of the feature 'horse' (□SPECIES) in its subject, while the verb *miaow* correspondingly requires the presence of the feature 'cat' (∗SPECIES). The latter condition is sufficient to show the 'ungrammaticality' of (1b). But according to *these* conditions, both (2a) and (2b) are wrongly regarded as unacceptable.

In fact, Chomsky restricted his analysis to a few prominent features such as those of 'animacy' and 'concreteness'; but another analysis of the same period by Katz and Fodor ('The Structure of a Semantic Theory'), which offered a more comprehensive approach to selection restrictions, has the same defect.

Weinreich, in his *Explorations in Semantic Theory* (1966), recognized that Chomsky's selection restrictions were too powerful, and proposed the idea of a 'transfer feature' which, through the operation of 'combinatorial rules' deriving the meaning of a sentence from the meanings of its constituents, would be transferred from one word to another word accompanying it. In Weinreich's system, selection conditions were only prohibitive where two contrasting features occurred within the same constituent. For example, the transfer of the feature 'cat' from the verb in (1b) to the noun would bring about a clash between opposing features 'horse' and 'cat'. But in (2a) and (2b) no such clash would occur – instead the transfer features would correctly mark the 'overflow' of meaning from verb to noun, by showing that the word *animal* would be understood, in (2a) and (2b), as referring to a horse and a cat respectively. Weinreich's theory therefore gave correct results where Chomsky's and Katz and Fodor's did not.

Weinreich, however, was working on the principle that meanings are described by reference to syntactic elements like words and sentences rather than by reference to semantic units like predicates and arguments. As soon as we put selection restrictions on a purely semantic footing, we see that they can be accounted for very simply, by a small addition to the framework of analysis so far proposed. This addition is to admit a type of dependence rule which connects features in neighbouring clusters. The dependence rules so far considered (pp. 119–20) relate features within the same cluster. For example, the rule

$\pm$MALE depends on +ANIMATE

tells us that if +MALE or —MALE is present in a componential formula, then +ANIMATE is also present (a componential formula, in predication analysis, being the content of a single argument or predicate). But selection restrictions can be easily accounted for by redundancy rules which may be called *contextual dependence rules*, and which require the presence of a given feature in an argument if another given feature is in the predicate of the same predication. For example, the selection restriction which forbids *'The horse owned the man' can be stated as follows:

→OWN in a predicate depends on +HUMAN in the initial argument (i.e. if →OWN is present in a predicate, then +HU-MAN is present in the initial argument of the same predication)

The whole predication *'The horse owned the man' can then be represented as follows:

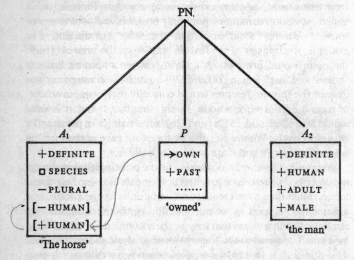

(I have omitted all redundant features except those necessary to the demonstration that the assertion involves a violation of semantic

rule.) The violation consists of the co-occurrence in A_1 of the feature [−HUMAN] (dependent on □SPECIES 'horse' in the same argument) and the feature [+HUMAN] (contextually dependent on →OWN in the predicate). It appears that all selection restrictions can be explained in this way as giving rise to a clash of contrasting features in the same cluster. In other words, a violation of a selection restriction is shown to be just a special case of a componential violation we have had to acknowledge elsewhere (pp. 103, 119) in explaining the oddity of, for example, 'male woman' or (by dependence rule) 'male house'.

This method of handling selection restrictions also accounts for the semantic 'overflow' in a sentence like *The animal neighed* or *The dinner was cooked*. In the former case, the feature □SPECIES is added to the argument 'the animal'; in the latter case, the feature +HUMAN is added to the null argument representing the 'cooker'.

Selection restrictions give rise to the problem of where to draw the line between 'linguistic knowledge' and 'real-world knowledge' that we have encountered in other aspects of semantic analysis (pp. 87–9). Does the feature →OWN, for example, attribute not only +HUMAN to its initial argument, but −HUMAN to its final argument? It is tempting to accept this analysis, and so to mark the sentence *'The horse owned the man' as a more extreme violation than (say) *'The horse owned the house.' But a moment's reflection would suggest that this would be overstepping the boundary of linguistic knowledge: ownership of people is acceptable in societies where slavery is an institution, and it is only through our knowledge that slavery does not survive in present-day human societies that we are able to regard 'X owned the man' as an aberrant statement.

Apart from accounting for an important class of semantically deviant sentences, contextual dependence rules can also help to explain some cases of entailment which cannot be straight-forwardly explained by the rule of entailment. Thus if it is assumed that 'galloping' is done by horses only, then the feature 'horse' may be added by dependence rule to 'The animal' in the former of these assertions:

X: 'The animal galloped quickly home' entails
Y: 'A horse went home'.

X is then shown to be logically equivalent to 'The horse galloped quickly home', and the rule of entailment does the rest.

Many metaphorical uses of language involve a violation of selection restrictions, and again contextual dependence rules help to explain why. Faced with an apparent clash of features such as +HUMAN and −HUMAN, we react by trying to find a way out of the semantic dilemma through transfer of meaning: often a metaphorical transfer.

(1) 'Time galloped by.'
(2) 'The railways are dying.'

In (1), the feature □SPECIES ('horse') is ascribed to the argument 'Time', and since 'horse' is ultimately dependent on +CONCRETE and 'Time' contains the feature −CONCRETE, a clash of features results. We make sense of this by interpreting *galloped* figuratively (roughly = 'passed by quickly *like* a horse galloping'). In (2), 'The railways' (−ANIMATE) clashes with the feature +ANIMATE added by the predicate 'dying'. Again a metaphorical interpretation is invited: roughly 'The railways are passing out of existence like an animate being dying.'

Subordinate Predications: Embedding

So far we have discovered the need to set up only a very simple structure for predications. In fact, the range of constituent structures for the predication can be summarized, it seems, in one simple rule:

Predication → (*Argument*)+*Predicate*+(*Argument*)

(The arrow means 'consists of', and the brackets indicate optionality.) The rule may be read 'A predication consists of a predicate, and either two arguments, one argument, or no argument.' In terms of diagrams, this gives us the following (PN = predication; A = argument; P = predicate):

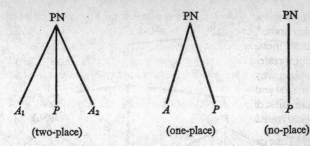

A_1 $\quad$ P $\quad$ A_2	A $\quad$ P	P
(two-place)	(one-place)	(no-place)

These tree diagrams are maximally simple in comparison with the sort of tree diagram one needs to explain the constituent structure of even the very simplest sentence (see p. 12), and it does, in fact seem to be true that while syntactic structure contains comparatively many types of constituent, and has varied rules for their combination, semantics has a basically extremely simple structural pattern. But the complexity comes, in semantics, in the number of times the same small repertoire of structures recurs within a single overall predication. To build this recursive principle into the picture of semantic structure so far given, we allow for the possibility that an argument may be not just a cluster of features, but a whole predication. The relation of this predication to the main predication of which it is a part is like that between a subordinate clause and a main clause. The introduction of this subordinate predication, or EMBEDDED PREDICATION, as I shall call it, now permits a great number of more complex structures such as the following:

(I)

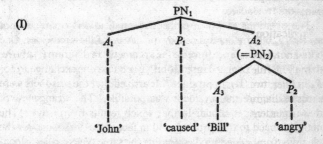

i.e. 'John made Bill angry'
or 'John angered Bill'
or 'John caused Bill's anger' etc.

(II)

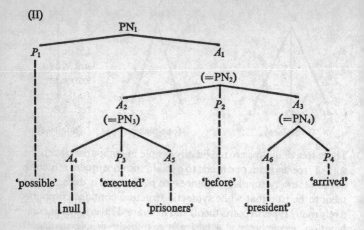

i.e. 'It is possible that the prisoners were executed before
the president arrived'

or 'The execution of the prisoners may have preceded the
president's arrival', etc.

It is not difficult to imagine how even very complex sentences may
be semantically analysed into smaller and simpler constituents
through this concept of embedding. But as we see from these
diagrams, the embedded predications (PN$_2$, PN$_3$, etc.) have many
varied syntactic realizations, and are not necessarily expressed by
subordinate clauses.

The positions at which embedded predications occur are not
arbitrary, but are determined by the nature of the predicates. One
could not, for instance, reverse the arguments in diagram (I) above,
to make *'Bill's anger caused John', nor could one exchange P_1 for
P_4 in Diagram (II), to produce *'It arrived that the prisoners were
executed before the president was possible.' The strangeness of
these assertions is similar to that which results from (say) *'The
man belonged to the fortune', and in fact we may account for the
placing of embedded predications by the same type of rule – a contextual dependence rule – as that required for selection restrictions.
But this type of contextual dependence rule imposes a rather

different kind of condition from that mentioned previously: instead of requiring that an argument should contain a given feature, it insists that an argument should take the form of an embedded predication. For example, of the two arguments connected by a relation of →CAUSE 'causation' (as in Diagram I), the final argument representing the 'result' or 'consequence' must be in the form of an embedded predication, while the initial argument representing the 'causer' can be either a set of features or an embedded predication. On these grounds we can eliminate an utterance such as *'God caused the world' or *'James caused the book', although we can allow 'God caused the world to exist' (i.e. 'God created the world') because it contains the embedded predication 'the world + exist'.

Downgraded or 'Featurized' Predications

There is a second way in which one predication may be included within another – and that is to reduce its position in the semantic hierarchy of analysis still further: to the status not of an argument, but of a *feature*. To see why this second type of subordination is necessary, consider the relation of entailment between:

(1) 'A man who was wearing a wig entered the room.'
(2) 'A man entered the room.'

It is clear that if the rule of entailment is to operate here, 'a man who was wearing a wig' has to be hyponymic to just 'a man'. This in turn means, in terms of componential analysis, that 'a man who was wearing a wig' has to be represented in the same way as 'a man' except that it may contain more features. But the element of meaning in terms of which (1) and (2) differ has itself the structure of a whole predication (roughly 'man'+'wear'+'wig'). That this is so is evident from the fact that it is subject to selection restrictions on its own account (*'. . . who was wearing a coefficient', for instance, would constitute a violation of selection restrictions). This means, then, that there is a semantic element which is equivalent to a feature in function, but which has the structure of a predication. This element I shall call a DOWNGRADED PREDICATION.

The most explicit way for a downgraded predication to be

expressed is by means of a relative clause; but usually shorter syntactic means of expression are also available:

A man who was wearing a wig
A man with a wig
A bewigged man

The most condensed form of expression of all, however, is to include the downgraded predication within the definition of a single word. Many nouns have such an element in their definitions: *butcher* 'a man who sells meat'; *cyclist* 'a person who rides a bicycle'; *seat* 'a place on which to sit'; etc. Adjectives, too, are sometimes to be defined by downgrading: *illiterate* 'who cannot read'; *rich* 'who has much property' etc. The downgraded predications may even contain further predications (either downgraded or embedded): for example, the proposition 'that God does not exist' is embedded in the definition of *atheist* ('a person who believes that God does not exist').

In the semantic notation and in diagrams, I shall indicate a downgraded predication by placing it in angle brackets: ⟨PN⟩. In the following diagrams, (A) represents an argument, and (B) and (C) are the expansions of the downgraded predications contained by that argument:

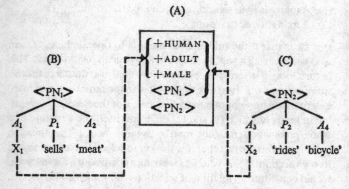

(A)

(B)   (C)

'a butcher who rides a bicycle'
or   'a butcher-cyclist'
or   'an adult male bicycle-riding seller of meat' etc.

The significance of 'X' as the expansion of the left-hand argument of both predications cannot be fully explained at this point (see further p. 169). It is sufficient to notice that a downgraded predication always shares part of the content of the argument in which it appears: one of the arguments *within* the predication (the one marked X in the diagram) always corefers to (i.e. has the same reference as) the remainder of the argument in which the downgraded predication itself occurs. This is marked in the diagram by the arrows with broken lines. If there are two downgraded predications within the same cluster, it is possible that the coreference of the one will include the other, but not vice versa. Thus in the diagram, the coreference of X_2 in $\langle PN_2 \rangle$ includes $\langle PN_1 \rangle$. (In this sense, an element of ordering, normally absent from componential formulae, is introduced.) The linking argument X is expressed, in relative clauses, by the relative pronoun *who, which*, etc.

We have now to distinguish two main types of downgraded predications:

1. a QUALIFYING PREDICATION occurs within an argument (like all examples considered so far) and underlies many of the adjectival functions of syntax: adjectives, relative clauses, qualifying prepositional phrases, etc.

    E.g. '*Rich* bachelors'
    'Bachelors *in London*'
    'Bachelors *who own fast cars*'

2. a MODIFYING PREDICATION occurs inside a predicate, and underlies many of the so-called 'adverbial' functions of syntax: adverbs, adverbial phrases, adverbial clauses.

    E.g. 'He got married *in church*'
    'He *soon* got married'
    'He got married *to please the family*'

An example of a modifying predication is $\langle PN_2 \rangle$ in the following:

(I)

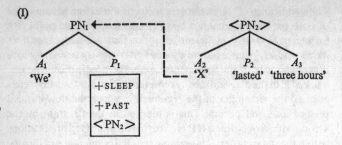

i.e. 'We slept, for three hours' or
'We slept, which lasted for three hours'

This account of 'adverbial' meaning correctly represents the entailment relation between the meanings of two sentences which differ only in the presence or absence of an adverbial construction:

'We slept for three hours' entails 'We slept.'
'John was singing drunkenly' entails 'John was singing.'

When the main predication has a second argument (i.e. is a two-place predication) the same principle applies, even though in syntax, the adverbial construction is typically separated from the verb phrase expressing the rest of the predicate:

(II)

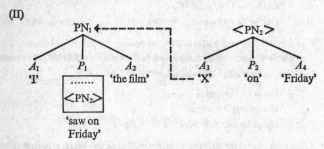

i.e. 'I saw on Friday the film' or 'I saw the film on Friday'

As diagrams (I) and (II) show, the coreferential link for a modifying predication usually equates one of its arguments with the whole of the main predication (with the exception of the modifying predication itself). Thus there is a very close relation between the statement represented by (I) above, and that represented by (Ia):

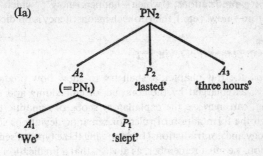

(Ia)

PN₂

A₂
(=PN₁)

P₂
'lasted'

A₃
'three hours'

A₁
'We'

P₁
'slept'

i.e. 'Our sleep lasted three hours'

The exact nature of the equivalence of the different structures depicted in Diagrams (I) and (Ia) must remain a mystery for the moment; we shall investigate it further in Chapter 12 (pp. 265–8).

As verbs (except *be*) are invariably predicate-expressing elements, the predicational status, semantically speaking, of adverbial elements is confirmed by paraphrases such as these, where the predication otherwise expressed by adverbial constructions is expressed by a clause with a main verb:

'We slept for three hours' = 'Our sleep lasted three hours.'
'John sliced the cake with a knife' =
    'John used a knife to slice the cake.'
'The food was stolen before the guests arrived' =
    'The theft of the food preceded the arrival of the guests.'

Such relationships do not exist in all cases, simply because English does not have verbs to express all the meanings which it can express adverbially.

Another function of modifying predications is in the definition of verb tenses. Up to now, I have indicated the meanings of tenses by features like +PAST, −PAST; but this can be seen, in retrospect, as an error. Such an analysis would cause us to predict inconsistency where none occurs; for example, according to the inconsistency rule, 'John was sleeping' should be inconsistent with

'John is sleeping', whereas we know in fact that both can be true at the same time. If on the other hand ~~tenses are taken to express modifying predications,~~ ('which+happen+now'; 'which+happen before+now'; etc.), then no such inconsistency is predicted.

More on Semantic Deviation

To conclude this chapter, I shall try to show how predication analysis, as enlarged by the concepts of embedding and downgrading, can increase the explanatory scope of semantic theory through the formulation of rules for semantic deviations such as tautology and contradiction. (In discussing these types of semantic deviation, we must remember, as always, that a predication represents only one possible interpretation of a sentence. If a predication is absurd, this does not necessarily imply that the sentence that expresses it can be given no meaningful interpretation. Even if no clear ambiguity is evident, one tries hard in ordinary communication to find a sensible meaning [e.g. an ironical one] for such an utterance.)

Tautology arises, roughly speaking, when the information contained in an argument of a predication includes the information contained in the remainder of the predication. In a one-place predication, this means when the argument is hyponymous to the predicate:

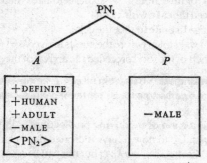

'The woman I love is female'

In a two-place predication, a tautology exists wherever a qualifying predication within one of its arguments entails the rest of the predication (for this purpose we assume that the linking argument 'X' in the downgraded predication is equivalent to the set of features to which it corefers; see further p. 170).

That is to say, [PN_1 minus PN_2] is entailed by PN_2.

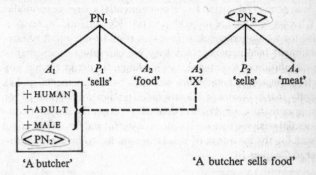

'A butcher'   'A butcher sells food'

The rule for contradiction is the opposite of that for tautology: for one-place predications, the rule is that the argument is incompatible with the predicate ('The woman I love is male'); and for two-place predications, that the qualifying predication PN_2 is inconsistent with the remainder of the main predication ('People who like tennis hate games').

The third type of semantic deviation, called semantic anomalousness, arises when one of the arguments or the predicate of a predication contains a clash of contrasting features, or contains two downgraded predications which are inconsistent:

'*Human horses* feed on oats'.
'This programme is for *the music-lover who hates music*'.

The argument in question has no conceivable reference to reality: there is no such thing, that is, as 'a human horse' or 'a music-lover who hates music'. Hence it is often said that such predications place the whole question of truth versus falsehood out of court. It makes no sense, according to this view, to inquire whether 'Human horses feed on oats' is a true or a false statement.

Violations of selection restrictions form an important category of semantic anomalousness.

Conclusion

The object of this chapter has been to show that predication analysis is a necessary addition to the componential analysis expounded in Chapter 6, if we are to be able to provide semantic representations for whole sentences. I have also tried to show that rules of entailment, inconsistency, tautology, etc. can validate the semantic representation of a sentence, by enabling us to derive from it predictions regarding entailment, etc. (i.e. basic statements, p. 84). Finally, in the concept of a downgraded predication, of predication acting as feature, predication analysis enlarges the scope of componential analysis, making it a more powerful and flexible means of describing the meanings of words: something to be explored further in Chapter 10.

8. Logic in Everyday Language

Logic, the study of the organization of rational thought (especially laws of valid inference), has always been regarded as the preserve of the philosopher. In the present century, this age-old study has evolved, through the development of symbolic logic, into a highly rigorous study allied to mathematics. Now, it seems, linguistics is invading the territory. After all, what has been the subject of Chapter 7, if it has not been a system designed to show logical relations both within and between sentences? A semantic representation is also a logical representation. Why, one might ask, has the linguist become involved in this way in a discipline which seems to be already managing without his help?

Logical Systems and Ordinary Language

Part of the answer lies in a difference of aim. The logician's aim, in devising a logical system, is very often normative rather than descriptive: that is, he is not so much interested in how people actually do organize their thoughts in language, as how they ought to do so if they are to avoid fallacious arguments which arise from ambiguity, structural confusion, etc.; in short, if they are to avoid the traps which everyday language sets for unwary thinkers. Historically, symbolic logic has in part arisen through philosophers' gradual discovery that the syntactic structures of a language reflect only imperfectly or indirectly the underlying structures of meaning. Logicians have therefore seen an advantage in abandoning ordinary language in favour of an artificial mathematical notation or 'calculus', which bears the same sort of relation to the 'natural logic' that people use in ordinary speech and thinking, as the language of arithmetic and algebra bears to ordinary English utterances about number. Once this step has been taken, neater and more abstract formulations are possible. Compare, for example, the following two statements:

(1) 'If you have ten cows and take six of them away, you are left with four'
(2) '10 − 6 = 4'

Liberated from ordinary language, such calculi tend to develop under their own momentum, the aim being to construct a strict deductive system, with no more primitives or axioms than are necessary, with adequate rules of inference, and so on. So developed, they become extraordinarily powerful systems of thought in their own right, in separation from their origin in ordinary language.

An example of the way in which natural language and mathematical logic have diverged is the method by which logicians have succeeded in reducing all the logical link-words and operators 'and' 'or', 'not', 'if', to a single primitive logical link 'neither . . . nor'. One of the steps in this exercise of reduction was the explanation of 'not-X' (where X is any statement) as an abbreviation for 'neither-X-nor-X'. Within this system, therefore, 'John is not a man' is treated as an abbreviation for 'John is neither a man, nor is he a man' (Quine, *Mathematical Logic*, pp. 45–6). Now, this may be highly satisfactory to the logician, because both statements have the same truth value; but for the linguist, this operation is totally illegitimate, because the sentence 'John is neither a man, nor is he a man' is not even a well-formed sentence within the terms of a natural language like English: there are virtually no circumstances, in ordinary speech, where one conjoins a sentence with itself. Hence the relation between the formalized artificial language of logicians and an ordinary natural language like English is somewhat problematic.

So far we have distinguished differences of aim; but the issue has, in addition, been compounded by misunderstandings between the practitioners of logic and the practitioners of linguistics. Some logicians have tended to assume that a grammarian is a logician who does logic rather badly, and some linguists have thought of logicians in a parallel light. But this sense of cross-purposes is now, hopefully, a thing of the past, dating from a time when linguists were concentrating their attention on the surface structures of linguistic expressions (phonology and syntax) rather than upon the logical structures underlying these. Since that time, the same sort of consideration that led philosophers to be dissatisfied with syntactic structure as a guide to logical relations has also led linguists to search for a deeper level of representation – a semantic or logical level of representation – to explain the meanings of a sentence, and their relation to its form.

To take an example: one of the most ancient philosophical problems is the puzzle of why *someone, anyone, everyone*, and similar expressions involving quantifiers (see p. 171) do not behave in the same way as words like *John, Bill,* and *Daphne*, though they can have the same grammatical function as nouns, and may act as subjects, objects, etc.:

(1) a Daphne is beautiful
    b You will marry Daphne
    _____
    c Therefore, you will marry someone beautiful

(2) a Someone is beautiful
    b You will marry someone
    _____
    c Therefore, you will marry someone beautiful

[Example adapted from George Lakoff, *Linguistics and Natural Logic*, 1970]

Why is the first of these syllogisms correct, while the second is not? It was logical problems of this kind that led philosophers to set up their artificial symbolic systems. In predicate calculus (the part of symbolic logic dealing with quantifiers such as 'all' and 'some') the problem is solved by expressing (2)a in quite a different way from (1)a. All statements which, like (2)a, contain quantifiers, are represented in a form which involves the use of variable symbols such as x and y. Thus while (1)a can be represented simply as 'Ba' (where B is a predicate 'beautiful' and a is a constant = 'Daphne') (2)a must be symbolized more elaborately as

$$(\exists x)\,(Px \;\&\; Bx)$$

(i.e. 'there exists an x, such that x is a person and x is beautiful'.) The symbol $\exists$ here is the so-called existential quantifier, which in the English language is often expressed by *some*.

This problem, which the logician has solved by a special notation, is now also a challenge to the semantically-inclined linguist, who has to construct a system of semantic representation which will reflect the same difference as is reflected in the logical calculus. But the linguist operates according to constraints different from those of the logician: he has to find not only the simplest rules for characterizing the logico-semantic representation of sentences, but also the simplest way of relating these semantic abstractions to the syntactic structure of sentences. It is evident that with quantification in particular, this is quite a problem as there is a considerable difference between the syntactic pattern of (2)a, for example, and its logical symbolization. Another constraint the linguist operates under is that he must not stray into any mathematically idealized or normalized system of logic, but must remain faithful to his semantic data – the semantic facts of usage, as reflected in the responses of native speakers of the language being investigated. These two constraints mean that the linguist is impinging on the logician's interest, without necessarily pursuing the same ends or arriving at the same conclusions.

Two final points: first, philosophers have never given up their interest in ordinary language, and indeed the formulation of many questions of philosophical inquiry often have their starting point in ordinary usage. The linguist's search for a 'natural logic' represents a convergence of his interest with two often conflicting preoccupations of philosophy: the clarification of how ordinary language works, and the schematization of logical laws. But as George Lakoff, a leading American linguist, rightly insists, 'natural logics are, of course, mythical beasts'. Such is the complexity of the field that present efforts at reducing it to rule can be regarded as at best a promising beginning.

Secondly and finally, there is yet another warning to be uttered: it is generally assumed that the principles of such a natural logic must be largely universal to all languages; but at the present stage of investigation, this is no more than an attractive conjecture, in tune with recent universalist tendencies in linguistic thought (see pp. 31–5).

Logical Features of Meaning: Formators

For present purposes, we may narrow down and clarify to some extent what the establishment of a 'natural logic' entails: it means characterizing the sentences of a natural language in such a way as to be able to show what relations exist between them, or between them and their parts, whereby we are able to draw inferences or conclusions about their truth, falsehood, meaningfulness, etc. This is, indeed, largely equivalent to the idea of a 'semantic representation' presented so far in this book, and especially in the last chapter. For example, the rules of entailment, contradiction, tautology, etc. in the last chapter are first approximations to rules which would be required for a 'natural logic' of English.

But only a part of the job has been attempted so far. Logicians themselves, when they discuss the rules of logic, spend a great deal of time explaining the use of a small number of common words, or their equivalents in a formal logical system: these are such 'logical words' as *not*, *if*, *all*, *or*, and *true*. To extend the predication analysis to be able to include the meanings of these terms would be to add a major component to the framework of semantic analysis that I have been constructing. All I can do in this chapter is to sketch very roughly their place in the total semantic system.

Sometimes a distinction (stemming from the work of the philosopher Charles Morris) is drawn between *designators* (roughly: features of meaning which involve reference to objects and situations outside language) and *formators* (roughly: features of meaning whose function is purely internal to the linguistic, i.e. logical, system). The latter type of feature may be regarded as a slightly more sophisticated version of the concept of 'logical words' mentioned above. More sophisticated because here as elsewhere, it is inviting unnecessary complexity to try to deal with meaning in terms of lexical or syntactic units. If we try to apply a distinction between 'logical' and 'designative' categories to words, for instance, we find it necessary to recognize the hybrid category of words which are partly logical and partly designative. There will be no problem in placing (say) *not* in the one category and (say) *cow* in the other. But in the following list of words, there is, as we see, a mixture of logical and designative functions:

	LOGICAL ELEMENT	DESIGNATIVE ELEMENT
never	negation	+ time
somewhere	quantification	+ place
who	interrogation	+ person
come	'thisness' (deictic meaning – see p. 168)	+ movement

It is for this reason, then, that the distinction between the logical and designative (referential) aspects of meaning is seen as applying to semantic rather than syntactic elements.

But why do we have to see these logical particles, or formators, as features on a level with components like +HUMAN rather than, say, as arguments or predicates, or even as types of semantic element which are extraneous to the type of semantic analysis we have been doing so far? The primary reason is that many of these formators are very closely parallel to designative features, in that they enter into semantic oppositions. There is a parallel, for example, between the contrast of +HUMAN and −HUMAN, and that of 'true' and 'false', so that we may be justified as treating the latter pair, just like the former pair, as two components of a binary taxonomy (page 106). Similarly, the quantifiers 'all' and 'some' contrast as terms of an inverse system (page 116), just as do the modal operators 'possible' and 'necessary', or the features which distinguish 'remain' from 'stay'. It is true that certain logical features (notably the definite feature expressed by *the*, and the feature of negation) do not seem to have any contrastive value: while it is possible to conceive of an opposition 'definite'/'indefinite' and 'positive'/'negative', there does not seem to be any good reason to recognize the unmarked categories by the presence of the feature 'positive' or 'indefinite', as this function can be better performed by simply omitting the features 'definite' or 'negative'. But until there are good reasons for thinking otherwise, we may still consider these to be semantic features, even though they seem to be exceptional in not having a contrastive value.

A further difficulty in the way of treating formators as features is that some formators (e.g. that of negation) appear to apply to the whole predication rather than to a single argument. We may circumvent this difficulty, as far as the present notational system is con‐ cerned, by assigning such formators to the predicate within the predication to which they apply: since one and only one predicate appears in each predication, the predicate may be regarded as the locus for all logical features whose effect cannot be seen to be re‐ stricted to one argument or to another, but appears to span the whole predication.

Many of these logical features are often thought of as operations (like addition and subtraction) rather than as static properties; and terms like negation, quantification, interrogation, etc., reinforce this impression. The quasi-operational character of formators is an important clue when we come to ask what their function is in human language. Why could not the human species manage per‐ fectly well with a semantic system including various types of op‐ position, rules of entailment, etc. of the type already described, without such elements as 'all', 'not' and 'if'? The answer seems to be that these elements greatly increase the power of human thinking, because they are instruments with which we can ex‐ plicitly manipulate the categories and relationships of meaning which exist on the level of semantic representation. For this reason, there are interesting correlations between logical features and the semantic categories we have dealt with in Chapters 6 and 7. 'If' for example correlates with the notion of *entailment*; 'not' with in‐ compatibility; 'and' and 'or' respectively with the combinatory and contrastive axes of componential analysis; 'true' with tauto‐ logy; 'false' with contradiction; and so on. It will be noticed, for example, that 'not' duplicates, in terms of conceptual meaning, the function of the binary taxonomy (+MALE/−MALE) in a pair of sentences like:

| 'My Cousin Leslie | *is not male* (not +MALE) | ' = 'My Cousin Leslie | *is female* (−MALE) |, |

But elsewhere, for example in colour terminology, the negative feature enables us if we wish to superimpose the model of +X and −X on an area of meaning which is not inherently structured in such terms:

'My car *is not red*' = 'My car *is blue or green or yellow or . . .*'

(As this shows, a longer way to express the idea of 'not red' would be by means of another logical feature, 'or', and exhaustive listing of all the 'non-red' colours.)

From the point of view of semantic description, logical features have to be viewed rather negatively, as features which are exceptional, in that if their behaviour is to be adequately explained, special rules have to be stated. To come down to earth still further, we may say that rules have to be stated for each logical feature, in order to explain the classes of basic statement (statements of entailment, inconsistency, contradiction, tautology, etc.) which result from its use. These special rules can indeed be equated with the meaning of these logical features; they have no reference to the world at large (except in combination with other features), and therefore their use has to be explicated entirely in terms of the semantic system of the language.

To do this exhaustively (as one would have to do if one wished to construct a complete 'natural logic') one would have to write a kind of 'dictionary' of logical features. All I can do in the remainder of this chapter is to give a rather sketchy sample of what that dictionary would have to contain. I shall do this by concentrating on a small number of logical features: 'not', 'and'/'or', 'the', 'some'/'all'. I shall represent these logical features, in the notation, by bold-face letters. Thus the names of the above features will be: **not**, **and**, **or**, **the**, **some**, and **all**. To avoid introducing further difficulties of comprehension, I shall not try to represent the contrastive values of these formators in the notation; thus I do not attempt to represent **some** and **all** by some such symbolism as $\triangle$SOME/∇SOME, although these formators in fact comprise an inverse opposition. On the other hand, I shall continue to use directional arrows for those formators which have a relative function: thus →**if** contrasts with ←**if**, etc.

1. *The negative formator* **not**

In natural language, there can normally be only one negative feature per predication (hence the sentence *John did not not open the door* is exceptional).

This is, incidentally, one of the differences between natural logic and formal logic – where negation signs (analogous to minus signs in arithmetic) can apply more than once to the same proposition. (What is often called a 'double negative' in uneducated speech is actually a double syntactic marking of a single negative: thus 'I don't want no dinner' = 'I don't want any dinner.') Since predicates, like negators, can occur only once per predication, the negator can best be located in the predicate, rather than in one of its arguments. But as far as symbolization goes, it is often convenient to indicate negation as a feature of the whole predication; hence the negative of a predication X can be written not-X.

Among the special rules that explain the use of **not** are the following:

(A) X is inconsistent with **not**-X

    e.g. 'These scissors are sharp' is inconsistent with
    'These scissors are not sharp.'

(B) If X is a tautology, **not**-X is a contradiction

    e.g. 'Apples are fruit' is a tautology, so
    'Apples are not fruit' is a contradiction.

(C) Conversely, if X is a contradiction, **not**-X is a tautology

    e.g. 'Apples are animals' is a contradiction, so
    'Apples are not animals' is a tautology.

2. *The coordinative features* **and** *and* **or**

An interesting type of opposition exists between the two coordinative features **and** and **or**: they are similar to inverse terms such as **possible** and **necessary**, except that not only one, but both of the arguments they link are predications (that is, they constitute predicates with two embedded predications as their arguments). It will be remembered (from p. 116) that the distinguishing mark of an inverse opposition is its adherence to a rule whereby the substitution of one feature for another is combined with a shift of the negative (actually a shift of the negative from the main to the embedded predication). We may now diagram the working of this rule (in terms of predication analysis) as follows:

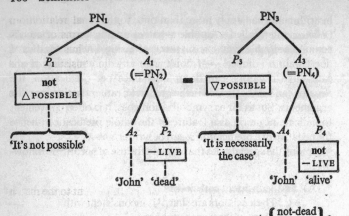

i.e. 'John can't be dead' = 'John has to be $\left\{\begin{array}{c} \text{not-dead} \\ \text{alive} \end{array}\right\}$,'

A similar rule operates for **and** and **or** but this time the negative is transferred to both embedded predications:

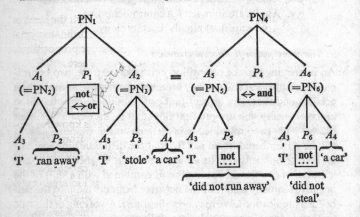

i.e. 'I did not run away or steal a car' = 'I did not run away and I did not steal a car.' Both figures only show half of the rule, which also applies in the reverse direction (e.g. 'It is **not** necessarily the case that X' = 'It is possible that **not**-X'; also '**not** (X and Y)' = '**not**-X or **not**-Y'). In this way we treat the logical connectives 'and'

and 'or' as predicates which contain a reciprocal relationship between two predications, and also contrast in terms of an opposition very similar to an inverse opposition. Thus 'and' and 'or' are in fact semantically complex elements consisting of one relative feature and one quasi-inverse feature.

Some additional rules connected with coordination are the ollowing:

$(X$ and $Y)$ entails (X)

 e.g. 'John went to the match and Mary went to the match' entails 'John went to the match.'

(X) entails $(X$ or $Y)$

 e.g. 'John went to the match' entails 'John went to the match or Mary went to the match.'

X and not-X is a contradiction

 e.g. 'John is married and (John) is not married.'

X or not-X is a tautology

 e.g. 'Either John is married or John is not married.'

There are many further complications connected with the semantics of coordination – notably the problem that coordinative propositions do not necessarily have only two member propositions. But there is no space to elaborate on such questions here.

3. *The feature of definiteness* **the**

All logical features dealt with so far have concerned predications as a whole, and have belonged to the sphere which is known as *propositional logic*. The feature of definiteness differs from these, in that definiteness belongs to the theory of reference rather than to the theory of truth and falsehood. In terms of predication analysis, this means that the definite feature is to be located in arguments, not in predicates. I have, indeed, marked a feature +DEFINITE in some of the diagrams in the previous chapter, but this was a makeshift device and must now be revised. In fact, the contrast between 'definiteness' and 'indefiniteness' is by no means a binary taxonomy: if it were, then 'the man' (+DEFINITE) and 'a man' (−DEFINITE) would be incompatible formulae. Yet actually the relationship between 'the man' and 'a man' is one of hyponymy:

We see this from the relationship of entailment in such cases as this:

'I saw the queen today' entails 'I saw a queen today.'

To account for these observations within the normal rules of componential analysis (see the definition of hyponymy, p. 100), it is best to mark the 'definite' feature by a single symbol (here the), and indefiniteness simply by the absence of that symbol. But componential analysis as it stands cannot deal with a further peculiarity of a definite feature: that any argument marked as 'definite' cannot be the superordinate term of a hyponymy relation. Thus it would be odd to claim that 'John entered the castle' entails 'John entered the building' (though 'castle' is hyponymic to 'building'), as the function of the is to indicate reference to a specimen of this category that everyone knows we are thinking about (i.e. which is uniquely determined by the context). Thus where *the castle* might be uniquely determined within a given context, *the building* might not. Within a given context 'John entered the building' might have no well-defined meaning at all, but would simply invite incomprehension, and the inevitable question '*what* building?'

In English, the presence of the definite feature the is marked by the definite article *the* in a noun phrase; it is also present in the meanings of the personal pronouns *he, she, you, they*, etc., and in deictic expressions (see p. 77) such as *this, here, now, that, there, then*. Proper names also contain the definite feature. Deictic words like *this* and *that* normally have reference to the situation outside language in which an utterance takes place: the reference is marked either as 'proximal' (as in *this*) or 'distal' (as in *that*), a distinction which can be represented by the features +THIS and −THIS. But also the definite feature the on its own (without deictic meaning) can point to the situation outside language, in a somewhat different way. If in a particular context the phrase *the X* is used, it will be understood that only one specimen or sample of the category X can be under discussion: for example, in a discussion taking place in the U.S.A., 'the President' will mean 'the President of the United States', while in a discussion taking place at a meeting of the Wigglesworth Women's Institute, it will mean 'the President of the Wigglesworth Women's Institute'. Other definite expressions which can have fairly obvious locally determined reference are *the*

*cat, the garden, the kitchen, the baby, the post office, the govern-
ment, the Queen.*

Often, though, the definite feature **the** (even when accompanied
by +THIS or −THIS) has its unique reference determined by the
linguistic context; that is, it COREFERS to an argument occurring
in the same or in a neighbouring predication. In (A) below, the
relation of coreference is shown by a broken arrow connecting *the*
with *a parrot*; in (B), the same sort of relationship is shown, except
that definiteness is expressed by the personal pronoun *it*.

(A) 'They have a cat and a parrot. The parrot is called Montague.'

(B) 'They have a parrot. It is called Montague.'

We have already met the concept of coreference in connection with
downgraded predications, the semantic correlates of relative
clauses. It may be noticed, in fact, that the two sentences at (A)
above have, when combined, the same meaning as (C), in which
the second sentence has been replaced by a relative clause:

(C) 'They have a cat and a parrot which is called Montague.'

When the feature of definiteness belongs to an argument which
has no designative content (i.e., when argument contains no features apart from **the**), the argument has 'zero expression', and is
marked syntactically, like a null argument, by the absence of a constituent where in other circumstances one would be present:

(D) 'They have a parrot ∧ called Montague'. (i.e. '... WHICH
    IS called ...').
    'He's calling ∧ next week'. (i.e. '... calling on THEM/US/
    YOU').
    'There's someone coming'. (i.e. '... coming HERE').

Again, as with null arguments, there may be an 'overflow' of
meaning to the unexpressed argument through contextual dependence rules (page 144): *He's winning!* means roughly 'He's
winning the race/game/etc.' and *Can I join?* means something like

'Can I join the club/society?'. We thus have two conditions in which a semantic element may be 'understood' or unexpressed in syntax: one is where the semantic element has complete generality of meaning (i.e. is a null argument). The other is where the semantic element has complete specificness of meaning, that is, where it contains only the definite formator **the**.

The definite formator's function of coreference can be roughly stated as follows:

Rule of Coreference: If there is an argument A_1 which contains the definite formator coreferring to an argument A_2, then the meaning of A_1 is equivalent to that of an argument A_3 containing the combined features of A_1 and A_2.

In simpler language, this means that coreference has the effect of adding the content of the argument coreferred to to that of the argument which corefers. A simple example of the working of the rule of coreference is as follows:

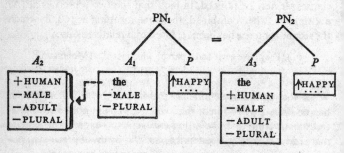

i.e. 'She is happy' = 'The girl is happy'
(where 'she' corefers to 'girl')

(Here I have not duplicated, in A_3, features which occur in both A_1 and A_2)

It is a fairly obvious condition of coreference that the rule cannot apply if it results in the co-occurrence within A_3 of two mutually contrasting features. Thus if A_1 were 'he' rather than 'she', it could not corefer to A_2 'a girl', since A_3 would then contain both features $+$MALE and $-$MALE.

4. *The quantifiers* some *and* all

The existential quantifier **some** and the universal quantifier **all** (to give them their usual names) enter, as noted earlier, into a type of semantic contrast called an inverse opposition. They are perhaps the most complex of all logical features in terms of their implications for 'natural logic', and all I can do here is to indicate briefly how they can be incorporated within the present framework. The important thing to notice is that although quantification is an operation which applies to arguments ('some fish', 'all wine', etc.), a quantifier has the character of a predicate rather than of a single feature. That is, while it may be satisfactory to represent the meaning of *the men* by the set of features (A), it would be an error to try to represent *some men* and *all men* in a similar manner, as in (B) and (C):

  (A) **the** +HUMAN +ADULT +MALE +PLURAL
  (B) **some** +HUMAN +ADULT +MALE +PLURAL
  (C) **all** +HUMAN +ADULT +MALE +PLURAL

One of the chief reasons for this is that quantifiers, like predicates, can be negated. Whereas a sentence like *The girls like pop-stars* can only be negated once (*The girls do not like pop-stars*), equivalent sentences with *some* and *all* have two negations:

  (1) 'Some girls like pop-stars.'
    (1a) 'No girls like pop-stars.'
    (1b) 'Some girls do not like pop-stars.'
  (2) 'All girls like pop-stars.'
    (2a) 'Not all girls like pop-stars.'
    (2b) 'All girls do not like pop-stars.'

Statements (1a) and (2a) are true negations of (1) and (2) respectively, as we see from the fact that (1a) is inconsistent with (1), and (2a) with (2). (The word *no* here may be interpreted semantically as 'not'+'some'.) This being the case, (1b) and (2b) cannot be negations of the main predication of (1) and (2) but of some subordinate predication within (1) and (2). These observations, therefore, point to an analysis of quantification in terms of the embedding of one predication inside another. Indeed, such an analysis is in any case required, to explain the negation-switching rule (p. 116) which applies to inverse oppositions, and which in the present case, explains the semantic equivalence of (1a) with (2b), and of (1b) with (2a).

For example:

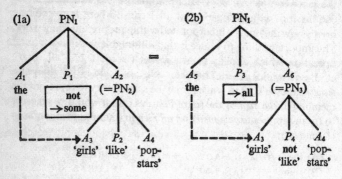

'No girls like pop-stars' = 'All girls do not like pop-stars'

(Incidentally, the sentence *All girls do not like pop-stars* is ambiguous, being equivalent on one reading to (2a) ('It is not true that every girl likes pop-stars'), and on another reading to (2b) ('For every girl it is true that she doesn't like pop-stars').

The above is only a rough semantic representation of (1a) and (2b). In actual fact, **some** and **all** are not logically simple, but are combinations (similar to **and** and **or**) of a relative feature with a feature from an inverse opposition. Therefore a fuller way to represent them would be in some such way as:

some $\boxed{\begin{array}{l} \rightarrow \text{QUANTIFY} \\ \triangle \text{SOME} \end{array}}$ **all** $\boxed{\begin{array}{l} \rightarrow \text{QUANTIFY} \\ \triangledown \text{SOME} \end{array}}$

We may indeed add further features to the former of these clusters, to define hyponymic terms like *many*, *a few*, and the numerals *one*, *two*, *three*, etc., as well as the negative quantifier *few* (= 'not many'):

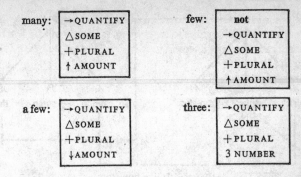

The diagrams for (1a) and (1b) indicate that quantification involves a relation of coreference between the main predication and the subordinate predication. If this relation did not obtain, it would be impossible to explain, in the notation, which of the arguments in the embedded predication is the object of quantification; that is, it would be impossible to show the difference (for example) between 'Girls like some pop-stars' and 'Some girls like pop-stars'. The relation of coreference has a further justification: assuming, according to the principle stated earlier, that the definite arguments (A_1 and A_5 in the figure) have zero expression, there is a remarkably direct relation between the semantic elements which have to be expressed, and the syntactic structure which expresses them. For (1a), for example:

$$A_1 \text{ (null)}; \; P_1 \text{ ('no')}; \; A_3 \text{ ('girls')}; \; P_2 \text{ ('like')}; \; A_4 \text{ ('pop-stars')}$$
$$\updownarrow \qquad \updownarrow \qquad \updownarrow \qquad \updownarrow$$
is rendered as: *No* + *girls* + *like* + *pop-stars*

In accordance with the point made earlier (pp. 152–3) about equivalent structures, another way of representing quantification is to treat the quantifier as a downgraded, modifying predication:

(3a)

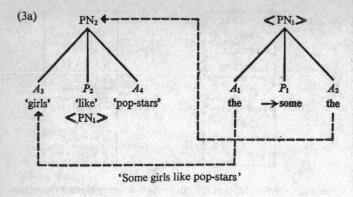

(3b)

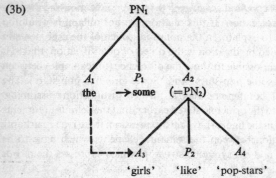

Figures 3a and 3b represent the same meaning ('Some girls like pop-stars'), but in the former version the quantifier is regarded as semantically rather like an adverb – and there is some syntactic support for this treatment in the fact that the word *all* can behave positionally like an adverb in English: *We were all at home*; *Our friends have all arrived.*

The reason for displaying the alternative structurings of Figure 3a and 3b here is that they help to explain one of the ambiguities that arise with quantification. When the existential and universal quantifiers occur together in the same sentence, two separate interpretations are possible; e.g.: *All girls like some pop-stars* can mean

(a) 'For every girl, it is true to say that there are some pop-stars that she likes.'
(b) 'There are some pop-stars such that they are liked by all girls.'

The second meaning is more prominent (and by some speakers is felt to be obligatory) in the equivalent passive sentence:

Some pop-stars are liked by all girls.

The difference between these meanings is usually explained in terms of the SCOPE of a quantifier. In meaning (a) **some** is included within the scope of **all**, while in meaning (b) **all** is included in the scope of **some**. In predication structure, the 'scope' of a quantifier can be interpreted as the embedded predication (PN_2 in Figure 3b) to which it is related through coreference. It is possible, then, to show the contrast in scope between (a) and (b) by combining within one predication the structural variants of quantification represented by Figures 3a and 3b:

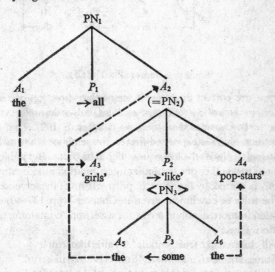

(Here I have departed from earlier practice, e.g. that of Figure 3a, by displaying the structure of the downgraded predication at the point where it occurs in the higher predication, i.e. in the predicate P_2.)

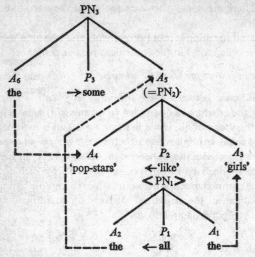

'Some pop-stars are liked by all girls'

If these are correct analyses, it seems that direction of subordination, in semantic structure, correlates with ordering in syntax (a topic to be considered in the next chapter, p. 199). That is, the quantifier which is expressed first in the sentence is normally the one which includes the later quantifier in its scope. But judgements differ as to whether one particular interpretation is necessitated, or merely favoured, by the active or passive form of the sentence.

The rules of entailment given in Chapter 7 (pp. 137–40) can be restated in more absolute terms for assertions containing quantification. Thus:

'All children like fruit' entails 'All girls like fruit';
'Some girls like fruit' entails 'Some children like fruit.'

In addition, the traditional syllogisms of Aristotelian logic can be regarded as rules of entailment involving the quantifiers, the coordinators, and the definite feature the. For example:

$\left\{\begin{array}{l}\text{(a) 'All teenagers like pop-stars'}\\[4pt]\qquad\qquad\text{and}\\[4pt]\text{(b) 'The girl next door is a teenager'}\end{array}\right.$

                 entails

    'The girl next door likes pop-stars.'

But it would be inappropriate here to enter into the precise formulation of these rules: enough has been said to indicate the importance and complexity of quantification as an aspect of 'natural logic'.

Conclusion

If linguistics is to approach nearer to the eventual goal of providing a characterization of the 'natural logic' that we ordinary language-users (as opposed to professional logicians) operate with, then one of the areas in which the challenge is greatest is that of exploring the implications of logical features such as have been considered in this chapter. I have provided no more than a glimpse of the way in which these features might be integrated within predication analysis, and of the sorts of special rules that have to be stated for them. There is much to be done before we have a formalized 'natural logic' to the degree of explicitness that has been achieved in axiomatic theories of formal logic, and perhaps it is too soon even to dream of this as the eventual outcome of current work in semantics. At least this discussion will have shown how some of the logical 'problems' which arise through a naïve equation of syntactic with semantic structure can be overcome through the elaboration of the notion of a 'semantic representation' in such a way as to accommodate such logical features as **all** and **not**. My next task will be to investigate the nature of the difference between 'semantic structure' and 'syntactic structure' which has been presupposed in this chapter.

9. Semantics and Syntax

Language can be described (as it is described by Wallace Chafe, in *Meaning and the Structure of Language*, p. 15) as 'a system which mediates, in a highly complex way, between the universe of meaning and the universe of sound'. The subject of preceding chapters has been the semantic 'end' of language, in particular, the conceptual semantic representation of sentences. But it is artificial to try and divorce semantics from language as a total system of communication. A semantic theory is in reality only a 'sub-theory' of a total linguistic theory, and an important factor in the study of meaning is being able to account for the relation of the semantic representation of an utterance to its representations at other levels, and particularly at the level of syntax. By this means alone are we able to show which semantic representations belong to which sentences, and therefore ultimately how language works as a conceptual communication system – as a means for transmitting configurations of ideas by means of noises or marks on paper.

Linguistic Levels

Linguists, of whatever theoretical persuasion, have always regarded the complexity of language to be such that it is necessary to set up more than one level of analysis. On the other hand, exactly which levels to recognize, and how they are to be interrelated, has been a matter of continuing debate. At present, for example, there is a controversy between the 'generative semanticists' and 'interpretive (or interpretative) semanticists' as to the relation between semantics and surface syntax (see pp. 326–33). Here, however, I shall adhere to the fairly traditional breakdown of language diagrammed in Chapter 2 (p. 13), where three main levels, semantics, syntax, and phonology are recognized. What I term 'syntax', by the way, corresponds to the traditional understanding of that term, except that it includes the grammatical ('inflexional') markings of words for such categories as 'singular' and 'plural', 'present' and 'past', etc. This level is often referred to in contemporary linguistic writing (for historical reasons discussed on pp. 327–8) as the 'surface structure' level.

But even the tripartite division of language into semantics, syntax, and phonology is a simplification in many ways. One of the factors ignored is another traditional division, cutting across the one already made, between the GRAMMAR and the DICTIONARY (or lexicon). The dictionary of a language has been often characterized as a list of all the *particular facts* about the language, i.e. those which cannot be generalized into rules. Thus it is a particular fact about English that the sequence of sounds /m/, /æ/, and /n/ conveys the meaning +HUMAN +ADULT +MALE. Particular facts also include irregularities, or cases which are exceptions to a given rule: for example, that *man* has a plural form *men* instead of *mans* is a fact for the dictionary. It happens that such particular facts can be stated with reference to certain elements (lexical items) generally commensurate with the grammatical units we know of as 'words'; but in some cases, the lexical item spans a piece of syntax larger than a word (as in *strike a bargain, under the weather, down and out*), in which case, we call it an 'idiom'; but in any case, a lexical item has to have its pronunciation and meaning (definition) specially stated, and therefore the dictionary impinges on all three levels of semantics, syntax, and phonology. The term 'grammar' has been frequently used in recent linguistics with an enlarged meaning, referring to the total system of a language, and its description. But I shall prefer to use it here in opposition to 'dictionary' (and in line with one of its traditional meanings) as that part of the system of a language which can be described in terms of generalizations, or rules. (This is a view of grammar and dictionary that must, however, be slightly revised in Chapter 10.)

The earlier diagram of language levels can now be presented in a rather less simplified way as follows:

Phonetic input/output

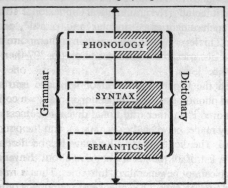

Levels of Linguistic structure

Obviously it is an advantage for the total simplicity of linguistic
description to put as much as one can into grammar; for example,
the dictionary definitions of terms like *man* and *woman* should be
minimal definitions (+HUMAN +ADULT +MALE, +HUMAN
+ADULT −MALE) since other features present in their meaning by
implication, (+ANIMATE, −PLANT, +CONCRETE, etc.) are
predictable by rule, namely by the dependence rules set out on p.
121. Nevertheless, it seems an inevitable part of the nature of language that idiosyncratic facts about particular lexical items should
constitute a large part of linguistic description.

In thinking of the relation between 'sound' and 'sense' in
language it is natural for us to imagine a directional model, which
may be either a speaker's model (converting semantic representation into phonetic output) or a hearer's model (converting
phonetic input into semantic representation). But clearly the same
relations hold between levels, in whatever direction the process of
communication is being operated. Therefore we should aim to
state rules which are valid both for the speaker and the hearer, so
that we do not have to state the same thing twice over, once for the
movement from sense to sound, and once for the movement from
sound to sense. This does not prevent some linguists from arguing
that it is inevitable, for the proper statement of the rules, that a
directional bias should be introduced. 'Generative semantics' (on

one interpretation of that term) means that the semantic representation is a 'base' from which syntactic (surface structure) representations are derived. 'Interpretive semantics', on the other hand, represents the view that semantic 'readings' are derived by interpretive rules from a syntactic 'base'. (See further, however, p. 331.) The view I present here is a neutral one: semantic representations and syntactic representations are regarded as having their own autonomous structures and their own conditions of well-formedness (i.e. grammaticality or meaningfulness); the function of rules relating them is then simply one of mapping one on to the other, an operation which can be applied indifferently in one direction or the other. Nevertheless, I shall find it convenient to call the rules relating semantics and syntax *expression rules*, and to think primarily in terms of a speaker's model (encoding) rather than a hearer's model (decoding). This is a matter of ease of exposition, and does not mean that I am adopting a unidirectional hypothesis that language is intrinsically organized in a sense-to-sound direction.

Semantic and Syntactic Well-formedness

Leaving open the question of whether the existence of any levels intermediate between semantics and syntax need be entertained, we may consider in the next few paragraphs some evidence in favour of the view that semantics and syntax have their own separate conditions of well-formedness. In the course of this, some of the types of expression rule relating semantics to syntax will be discussed and exemplified.

I have no room here to go into detail on the nature of English syntax, but will simply make use of syntactic elements and categories which will be more or less familiar to anyone who has 'done grammar' at school. Thus the main constituents of a simple English sentence to be considered are:

Noun phrases (NP); e.g. (1) *my best friends,* (2) *the beautiful girl in the corner,* (3) *some bitter disappointments,* (4) *he,* (5) *them,* (6) *Fred,* (7) *Fred's parents.*

Noun phrases consist of a head word (e.g. *friends* in (1))

preceded optionally by one or more pre-qualifiers (e.g. *my* and *best* in (1), *the* and *beautiful* in (3)) and followed optionally by one or more post-qualifiers (*e.g. in the corner* in (2)).

Verb phrases (VP); e.g. (8) *has caused*, (9) *have been visiting*, (10) *is making*, (11) *know*, (12) *is*, (13) *are*, (14) *working*, (15) *to try*. Verb phrases are either finite (i.e. contain a finite verb form such as *has* in (8) or *have* in (9)), or are non-finite, such as (14) and (15), which consist simply of non-finite forms (participles or infinitives).

Adjectives or *adjective phrases*; e.g. *unhappy*, *very ill*, *ready for a fight*, etc.

Adverbs or *adverbial phrases*; e.g. *here*, *quickly*, *in the morning*, *because of you*, etc.

In addition, embedded sentences (or subordinate clauses) can have syntactic roles similar to those of the constituents listed above. Adverbial and nominal clauses, for example, are embedded sentences which behave like adverbial phrases and noun phrases respectively:

what he said;   *because you are my friend*.

These constituents may have various functions within a sentence. Thus a noun phrase can be subject or object (the subject being the element which normally goes before the verb in declarative sentences, and has number concord with the verb):

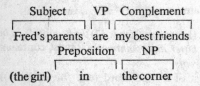

A noun phrase can also be a *complement* of an equative verb like *be*, or the object following a preposition:

The complement position can also be filled by an adjective or
adjective phrase:

Subject VP Complement
┌───┐ ┌─┐ ┌─────────┐
Fred   is   very ill

Both the ordering and the combination of the elements Subject (S),
Verb phrase (V), Object (O), and Complement (C), are strictly
limited in English. Thus the sequences SVO, SVC, SVOC, and
SVOO are acceptable:

(1) My best friends | have been visiting | Fred's parents. (SVO)
(2) Fred's parents | are | ready for a fight. (SVC)
(3) Fred | is making | them | unhappy. (SVOC)
(4) The beautiful girl in the corner | has caused | Fred | some
    bitter disappointments . (SVOC)

But other sequences are 'ungrammatical':

(5) *Fred's parents | ready for a fight | are. (SCV)
(6) *Some bitter disappointments | has caused | the beautiful
    girl in the corner | Fred. (OVSO)

In addition, each sentence pattern is associated with a particular
class of verb; thus

(7) *Fred is making very ill

is ungrammatical because *make* is not a member of the class of
verbs (equative verbs) which are capable of entering into the
SVC pattern.

Moreover, there are more general structural constraints, such
as that a sentence or finite verb clause (i.e. a clause containing a
finite verb like *is making* rather than a non-finite verb like *working*
or *to try*) must contain a subject:

(8) My best friends have been visiting Fred. (grammatical)
(9) *Have been visiting Fred. (ungrammatical)

Further, that generally speaking every sentence must contain a
verb phrase of some kind or other:

(10) *Fred very ill.

Examples (9) and (10) are clearly structurally defective, and cannot be considered well-formed English sentences. Such rules of syntactic structure have little to do with meaning. Thus sentences analogous to (5) and (10) would be perfectly normal in some languages other than English (e.g. Latin for (5), Russian for (10)); and sentence (10) in a way is a more direct reflection of the semantic structure of the sentence, which consists of Argument + Predicate, than is the corresponding SVC sentence *Fred is very ill*. It just happens that English sentences require a verb phrase, and where no content capable of being expressed by a verb is present, the 'dummy verb' *be* has to be introduced to fill out the structure of the sentence.

It will come as no surprise to someone who has followed this and the preceding two chapters carefully that there are some rather direct correlations between semantic elements such as arguments and predicates, and the syntactic constituents of a sentence. The more important of these interconnections are:

SYNTACTIC		SEMANTIC
Noun phrase	↔	Argument
Verb phrase	↔	Predicate
Adjective (phrase)	↔	Attributive predicate (p. 135)
Prepositional phrase	↔	Downgraded predication
Relative clause	↔	Downgraded qualifying predication (p. 151)
Adverb, adverbial phrase or clause	↔	Downgraded modifying predication *OR* Argument + Predicate (linked to an embedded predication)
Preposition	↔	Predicate
Conjunction	↔	Predicate (linking two predications as arguments)
Nominal clause (i.e. clause with the functions of a noun phrase)	↔	Embedded predication
'Nominalization' (i.e. noun phrase with an abstract a noun head derived from a verb or adjective)	↔	Embedded predication

This last correlation explains the fact that embedded predications are often rendered, in syntax, as noun phrases. Compare

She regrets *his failure to find a job*.

with

She regrets *that he failed to find a job*.

As we see in the table, the mappings are not one-to-one (if they were, there would be no need to recognize the distinctiveness of semantic and syntactic units), but are many-to-one in both directions. Which mappings apply to a given sentence depends a great deal on dictionary entries – an aspect of expression rules to be considered in the next chapter. It happens, for instance, that the English lexicon provides both an adjective and a verb to express the same predicate in *Two loaves suffice* and *Two loaves are sufficient*. But in the vast majority of cases, this choice of word class, and hence of clause type, is not available, and only one or the other can be used.

'Zero' Mappings

One of the more persuasive reasons for considering syntactic and semantic structural constraints as independent of one another comes from the existence of elements on one level which have a 'zero' mapping on the other level. We have already noted (p. 184) that the verb *be* can be regarded as a 'dummy element' in syntax, that is, as an element which exists on the syntactic level to fulfil certain conditions of syntactic well-formedness, but which has no semantic content. Another example of a dummy element is the empty subject *it* in sentences like *It is raining*. 'Rain', it was suggested earlier (p. 136), is a semantic predicate which is without arguments; however, syntax requires that a sentence should have a subject, and so the pronoun *it* is introduced to fill this grammatical function, even though it has no content to express.

The opposite situation arises with null arguments, and with arguments which contain no features other than the feature of definiteness. Both these types of argument, as I have already pointed out, have zero expression. However, the conditions under which there can be zero expression are also dictated by syntactic considerations. In an active sentence with a transitive verb like *enjoy*, neither of the arguments of a two-place predication can be unexpressed, even though the semantic conditions for zero expression may be present:

(1) The man in the street enjoys television plays.
(2) *The man in the street enjoys.
(3) *Enjoys television plays.
(4) *Enjoys.

Only (1) makes an acceptable English sentence. On the other hand, if the same predication is embedded, and is 'nominalized' as a noun phrase, either or both arguments can be unexpressed:

(1a) The man in the street's enjoyment of television plays (is on the increase).
(2a) The man in the street's enjoyment (is not to be despised).
(3a) Enjoyment of television plays (is on the increase).
(4a) Enjoyment (is the end of all art).

The reason for this difference is a syntactic reason: namely, that main clauses (which are finite-verb clauses) require a subject and (when the verb is transitive) also an object: while the rule that pre-qualifiers and post-qualifiers in a noun phrase are optional means that in nominalizations, the semantically analogous elements can be omitted. Hence the same rule which accounts for the omissibility of adjectives before a noun, and relative clauses after a noun, also accounts, incidentally, for the possibilities of zero expression in nominalizations.

There are a number of other circumstances in which zero expression is seen to occur only if it can be accommodated in syntactic rules. For example, if we were to turn sentence (1) into the passive it would be possible to omit the agent, the phrase which follows *by* and which corresponds to the subject in the active:

Television plays are enjoyed by the man in the street.
Television plays are enjoyed. (i.e. 'by people in general')

This can again be explained according to a very general rule of syntax – the rule (which has few exceptions) that adverbial elements of a sentence are optional. The agent phrase is a prepositional phrase which is directly part of a sentence, and so is classed syntactically speaking, as an adverbial, on a par with such phrases as *in the home* or *at weekends*. Once again, then, the independence of syntactic from semantic rules is emphasized: the same condition that accounts for the adverbial phrase's optionality in a sentence like *Television plays are enjoyed in the home* also accounts for the possibility of zero expression of the agent.

The following are further syntactic positions where optionality favours zero expression of one or both arguments:

(A) *Non-finite clauses* (where the subject is normally optional)
   To rob a child is a heinous crime.
   (Compare: *For a man to rob a child* is a heinous crime).

(B) *Agent nouns ending in -er*
   Fred's father is *a smoker*.
   (Compare: Fred's father is *a cigar-smoker*.)

(C) *Verbs capable of functioning as both transitive and intransitive verbs*
   The king *had been hunting*.
   (Compare: The king *had been hunting deer*.)

(D) *Prepositional adverbs corresponding in meaning and form to prepositions* (i.e. omissibility of the object of preposition)
   John fell *in*.
   (Compare: John fell *in the water*.)

Zero expression in this last case depends on whether there is a prepositional adverb of the same form as the preposition, and expressing the same meaning, except for the general indefinite or definite meaning of the associated argument. The double syntactic function of *in* in (D) may be contrasted with other prepositions for which there is no corresponding prepositional adverb in English: for instance, there is no **John came with* in English to correspond with *John came with us*, etc.

The lesson to be learned from these examples is that in determining the acceptability of an utterance we have to assess independently the well-formedness of the semantic and syntactic representations as linked by expression rules. To return to an earlier example: **John is making very ill* can be perfectly meaningful if we take it that the argument corresponding to the omitted object has zero expression (e.g. the meaning could be approximately 'John is making people-in-general very ill.') But meaningfulness does not guarantee syntactic well-formedness, and so the utterance of a perfectly sensible thought is 'blocked' by a rule of English syntax – namely, that the object is not omissible in an SVOC clause pattern.

Semantic Contrasts Compared with Syntactic Contrasts

The same point is reinforced when we turn from the consideration of syntactic and semantic constituent structure to a comparison of the two levels in respect of contrastive features. Syntax, like semantics, is organized in terms of contrastive oppositions (e.g. common noun versus proper noun; finite clause versus non-finite clause; past tense versus present tense). But firstly, syntax is much less rich in dimensions of contrast than semantics (because much of the contrastive structure of semantics is 'absorbed' by lexicalization – p. 191), and secondly, syntactic choices are obligatory where semantic choices are often optional.

This second difference can be illustrated from the oppositions of countability and plurality, which operate in relatively close correspondence on both levels of analysis, but are discrepant in one important respect. Both the similarity and the difference are highlighted in these diagrams, showing dependence relations:

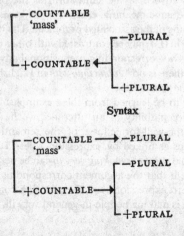

Semantics

```
┌─ —COUNTABLE
│    'mass'
│                        ┌─ —PLURAL
└─ +COUNTABLE ◄──────────┤
                         └─ +PLURAL
```

Syntax

```
┌─ —COUNTABLE ──────► —PLURAL
│    'mass'
│                        ┌─ —PLURAL
└─ +COUNTABLE ──────────►┤
                         └─ +PLURAL
```

The arrow pointing to the right in the syntactic diagram can be read 'has to be . . .', and symbolizes the essential difference between syntactic and semantic networks of contrastive features. In syntax the fact is that all noun phrases and finite verb phrases have to be classified as either singular or plural, even in cases (e.g. the case of mass nouns) where, in semantic terms, the choice is inappropriate. No contrast between 'one' and 'more than one' can be involved, for example, in the conceptualization of a substance like smoke; and yet syntax forces us to treat the mass noun *smoke* as singular rather than plural:

> *Smoke was billowing from the chimney*
> (not **Smokes were billowing from the chimney.*)

Thus although the categories of syntax are much fewer than those of semantics, they are given importance (sometimes inappropriate importance from the semantic point of view) through their obligatory status. These syntactic categories generally correspond with semantic features which are of particularly wide use either because they are formators (e.g. definiteness, negativity) or because they have a focal position in the taxonomic 'tree' of contrasts (p. 121; e.g. countable/mass, singular/plural.) The member of a syntactic opposition automatically selected when choice from the semantic opposition is inappropriate or neutralized is called the *unmarked* term, while the opposite term is called *marked*. Thus the choice of a singular noun phrase unless there are positive semantic reasons for choosing a plural one (as in the case of *smoke*) shows that 'singular' is the unmarked and 'plural' the marked member of the syntactic opposition of number. Similarly, in the syntactic choice in English between 'masculine' and 'feminine' (correlating with the semantic choice between 'male' and 'female'), the masculine term is the unmarked one. As evidence for this, note that if we had no specific sex in mind, we would say *Nobody in* HIS *senses would do that* rather than *Nobody in* HER *senses would do that*.

Before leaving the subject, let us consider two further cases where a choice that is irrelevant or inappropriate on the semantic level becomes compulsory on the syntactic level. Firstly, a distinction of tense (between present and past) is compulsory in the finite verb phrase. For example, in expressing a semantic relation 'John boy-friend of Patricia', we have to commit ourselves on whether this relation obtains in the present, or obtained in the past exclusive of the present:

John *is* Patricia's boy-friend.
John *was* Patricia's boy-friend.

That there is no *semantic* reason why tense should be specified in such cases is shown in our ability to evade time-specification in non-finite clauses, appositional constructions, and some other constructions expressing predications:

I went to school with *Patricia's boy-friend John.*

Here the question is left open as to whether John is Patricia's boy-friend now, or was so at some time in the past.

My final example is the contrast of definiteness (signalled by *the*) and indefiniteness (signalled by *a(n)* or 'zero article') in the noun phrase. This choice is obligatory, in the sense that all noun phrases must be either definite or indefinite. But definiteness, as I suggested in Chapter 8 (p.167), is on the semantic level a feature which belongs to arguments, not to predicates or predications as a whole. The question therefore arises what happens to the definite/indefinite contrast when the noun phrase expresses not an argument, but a whole predication (i.e. where the noun phrase is a 'nominaliza-tion')? One might suppose that the use of the definite article *the* in such cases becomes vacuous, since there is no concept of 'definite-ness' to be expressed. This is precisely what seems to be the case: as regards meaning there appears to be no difference between includ-ing and omitting the definite article in:

Robbery of old people is a heinous crime.
The robbery of old people is a heinous crime.

Here, in contrast to the choice between singular and plural, there is no marked or unmarked term: instead, the two possibilities seem to be in free variation.

Processes Involved in Expression Rules

Enough has been said to illustrate the idea that syntax and seman-tics are two levels with independent (though interrelated) sets of structures and contrasts, and with separate constraints of well-formedness. The conclusion to which this leads is that in accounting for the complex relation between the universe of sound and the universe of sense, a linguistic theory must specify for every language at least:

(a) the set of well-formed semantic representations
(b) the set of well-formed syntactic representations
(c) the rules (expression rules) for matching semantic representations with syntactic representations.

(We exclude from consideration here the phonological level.)

By this scheme we account for three types of linguistic oddity:

(1) Utterances which are semantically ill-formed but syntactically well-formed:
   (e.g. *John is bigger than himself.*)
(2) Utterances which are syntactically ill-formed but semantically well-formed:
   (e.g. *John are more big than his brother.*)
(3) Utterances which are both semantically and syntactically ill-formed:
   (e.g. *John are more big than himself.*)

It would be inappropriate to try to specify here the exact technical form of rules which relate the one level to the other (although much of recent linguistic research has been devoted to formulations in that area – see pp. 326 ff). Instead, I shall try to indicate in general terms what the functions of expression rules are. Up to now, the lack of 'fit' between syntax and semantics has seemed somewhat wayward and unprincipled. But certain general processes can be observed to operate, and these are relatable to observations about the difference between syntactic and semantic structures, and the apparent reasons for these differences. The four processes I shall identify (looking at language in terms of a speaker's model) are *lexicalization, structural compression, linearization,* and *thematization.*

'*Lexicalization*' is the process of 'finding words' for particular sets of semantic features, and has the psychological role (as I suggested on pp. 35–8) of 'packaging' a certain semantic content, so that it can be manipulated syntactically as an undivided unity. There is often a choice of lexicalizing a given content in more than one way (e.g. by selecting from a set of synonyms), or a choice of lexicalizing to different degrees (for example, selecting the term *philatelist* in preference to the phrase *person who collects stamps*). The decision to use a single word rather than a phrase, however, almost inevitably involves some change of conceptual meaning. For example, I observed in Chapter 3 that to use the single word like *bed-maker* rather than the phrase like *person who makes beds* involves the recognition of a category (here a category of person whose business or role it is to make beds).

The sense of a word (i.e. its dictionary definition) can in general be represented as a single set of semantic features, which may include downgraded predications. That is to say, on the whole, the content of a single word does not extend beyond the boundaries of a single argument or predicate. The main exceptions to this are the 'relating words' verbs, prepositions, and conjunctions, whose definitions may involve a 'merging' of predicates into a single syntactic element. For example, it has been suggested that the sense of the verb *kill* can be described in terms of the three predicates 'cause . . . become . . . dead'. The sentence *Florence killed the flea* can therefore be related to its semantic representation roughly as follows:

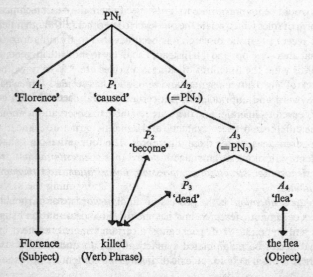

In any case, the restrictions of most lexical definitions to a single set of features does not prevent them from containing considerable structural complexity, since those features which are downgraded predications can themselves contain further subordinate predications. The meaning of the word *martyr*, for instance, if we define it as 'a person who dies because of his adherence to his religious faith' must contain two features +HUMAN and $\langle PN_1 \rangle$, where $\langle PN_1 \rangle$ is a downgraded predication with a structure at least as complex as the following diagram:

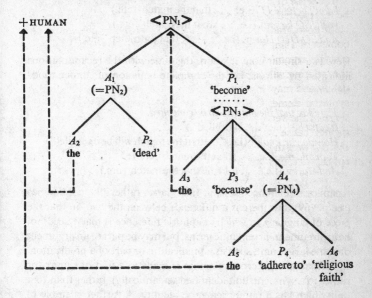

From this and the preceding diagram, it is easy to see that one of the effects of lexicalization is that of *structural compression*, that is, of reducing complexity of constituent structure, in terms of number of elements and depth of subordination: of cramming the same content into a smaller tree-diagram. This compression, which renders the message more manageable for linear presentation in the eventual form of a phonetic output, is brought about not only by lexicalization, but by zero expression and other devices of abbreviation.

One such device is the process of *anaphoric reference* by which repeated semantic content may be omitted altogether ('ellipsis') or may be recapitulated by a pronoun or some other 'proxy' form, such as the adverb *so* ('substitution'). In the following imaginary conversation, the 'proxy form' (whether a pronoun or another word) which substitutes for repeated content is printed in capitals:

> *They say that the match will be cancelled.*
> *Who said THAT?* (i.e. '. . . that the match will be cancelled')
> *Tom DID.* (i.e. '. . . said that the match will be cancelled')
> *I don't believe IT.* (i.e. '. . . that the match', etc.)
> *Well, SO he said.* (i.e. '. . . that the match', etc.)
> *And SO DID Harry.* (i.e. '. . . say that the match', etc.)

Here is a similar conversation, this time with the recapitulations indicated by ellipsis, i.e. the complete omission of 'understood' elements:

> *They say that the match will be cancelled.*
> *It can't be!* (i.e. '. . . cancelled'.)
> *How do you know?* (i.e. '. . . that the match will be cancelled')
> *Tom told me.* (i.e. '. . . that the match', etc.)
> *And Harry.* (i.e. '. . . told me that the match', etc.)

Anaphoric reference looks at first glance rather like coreference (see p. 169), but there is a difference between the two, in that the piece of language to which anaphoric reference is made need not be an argument, in semantic terms, but may be part of an argument or some larger unit, such as a predication or part of a predication. In fact, anaphoric cross-reference is made to a unit of syntax (or rather to a syntactic unit identified semantically), rather than to a unit which has a purely semantic identity. A further example of anaphoric reference makes this difference clearer:

> Which wine would you like, *the red* or *the white?*

The difficulty here is that the elements within which the omission takes place (*the red* [*wine*] and *the white* [*wine*]) express arguments which already contain the feature of definiteness (signalled by *the*). Therefore to explain this as coreference would be to suppose that these units contain two features of definiteness – one expressed by *the* and the other having zero expression, and having coreference to 'wine'. Moreover, the element to which reference would be made would be *part* of an argument, not a whole argument, as in the case of coreference. Hence on two counts it would be unsatisfactory to explain this as an instance of coreference. It seems, in fact, that anaphoric reference is a relation between syntactic units with their associated semantic content, rather than a relation between semantic units, as coreference is. We can say that for the above sentence, *the red or the white* (with ellipsis) and *the red wine or the white wine* (without ellipsis) are alternative textual realizations of the same semantic representation.

As the last example illustrates, ellipsis is a common accompaniment to certain types of syntactic structure, notably coordinative and comparative structures. Coordination is in semantic terms (p. 165) a joining of two or more predications, and so when in syntax the coordinators *and*, *or* and *but* link units smaller than a sentence, we can often postulate the ellipsis of elements corresponding to the rest of the clause in which the coordination occurs. For example:

> *The room contained a table and two chairs*

can be explained semantically as a combination of two assertions: 'The room contained a table' and 'The room contained two chairs'.

A third process performed by expression rules is (to use Wallace Chafe's term) that of *linearization*. This is the rendering of semantic representations (which as we have seen are indeterminate with regard to ordering in left-to-right or earlier-to-later sequence) into a fully sequential form appropriate to the unavoidably time-bound phonetic transmission of the message. The image of semantic structure used by Chafe is of a 'mobile' (*Meaning and the Structure of Language*, p. 5) of freely pivoting branches, as distinct from the two-dimensional tree diagrams which are appropriate for syntactic structures, and which (for lack of three-dimensional paper) I have had to use as a mode of display for semantic structures in this book. I have suggested that the only indicator of ordering, in semantic structure, is the arrow of directionality belonging to relational predicates. The consequence of this is that for any semantic representation of a sentence, there can be a number of different two-dimensional tree diagrams, arrived at by pivoting the branches connecting arguments and predicates to the nodes representing predications.

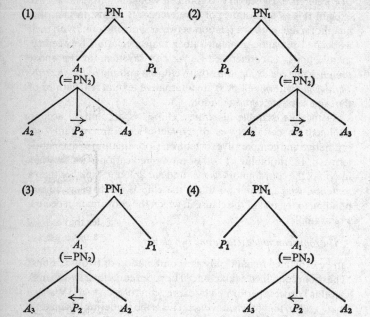

These four formulae are all visual variants of the same semantic representation. What happens in the course of linearization is that the definitions of verbs and other words expressing predicates specify which syntactic elements (subject, etc.) the arguments in these configurations are to be matched with. Thus one definition of the verb *remind* ('cause to remember') can be seen roughly as follows:

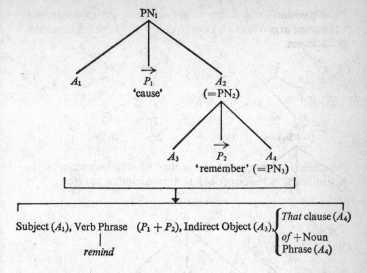

The brace at the end of the syntactic formula indicates that *remind* allows two kinds of objects: either a *that*-clause, or a noun phrase preceded by *of*, e.g.

Peter reminded me that I owed him a pound.
Peter reminded me of my promise.

As the order of subject, verb phrase, indirect object, etc. are determined by syntactic rules, no actual specification of order need be included in the definition.

There is a general tendency for the weight of syntactic structure to occur later rather than earlier in the sentence, so as to avoid strain on a person's short-term memory in the course of constructing and interpreting sentences. In syntactic tree diagrams, this is reflected in a tendency for right-hand branching to attain greater depth than left-hand branching. Thus (a) is more characteristic of syntactic structure than (b):

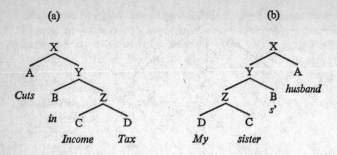

Even less characteristic of syntax than left-hand branching is the parenthetical inclusion of one structure in another, as in (c):

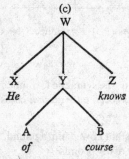

To the principle of avoiding structures like (b) and (c) in favour of structures like (a) can be added a second syntactic principle, which is that if an element of the sentence receives focal emphasis as 'new information', it should occur towards the end rather than the beginning of the sentence. In the light of this principle, we can explain why it is more natural to say *The box contained a bracelet* rather than *A bracelet was in the box*: 'a bracelet', being indefinite, is new information, in contrast to 'the box', which has presumably been mentioned before; therefore it is more natural to place 'the box' earlier in the sentence than 'a bracelet'.

These two principles of syntactic ordering obviously bring into play a further process, which I shall call *thematization*. This is the process of organizing the elements of a message so that weight and emphasis fall where is more natural in English – towards the end rather than the beginning of the sentence. To some extent, this thematizing function is performed by the normal process of matching semantic with syntactic elements. If, as has been suggested, adverbial elements of syntax (e.g. prepositional phrases of time) are matched with modifying downgraded predications, then the natural result of this matching rule is to turn a syntactically awkward configuration like (d) into a tree diagram like (e):

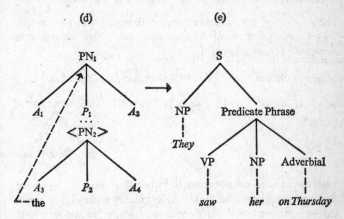

(d)   (e)

They saw-on-Thursday her

This is because there is a fairly general rule of English syntax that adverbials (especially those consisting of more than one word) most commonly occur in a final position, following the verb and (if any) its complements or objects.

But there is more to thematization than this. As we saw in Chapter 2 when considering 'thematic meaning', a language such as English contains a number of different syntactic devices or rules for varying the order of elements in a sentence. The most well-known of these is the rule converting active sentences into passive sentences:

Peter reminded me of my promise →
  I was reminded of my promise (by Peter).

Other instances are the rule which derives a sentence type with the introductory particle *There* from another sentence type with an indefinite subject:

A bracelet was in the box → There was a bracelet in the box

and the rule which postpones a clausal subject to the end of the sentence, substituting for it the dummy subject *it* in initial position:

That he has left surprises me → It surprises me that he has left.

These TRANSFORMATIONAL rules can be regarded as rules operating on syntactic structures together with their associated semantic elements, very roughly as follows:

Passive Rule: ... Subject [A_1] , Active Verb Phrase, (. . .) Object [A_2] ...

→   ... Subject [A_2] , Passive Verb Phrase, (. . .) (Adverbial Phrase)...

by   Noun Phrase [A_1

Such rules are essentially syntactic rather than semantic, however: they equate sentences having the same semantic representation, and can be compared with similar equative rules on the semantic level (rules of synonymy as considered in Chapter 7, for example, and the rules to be considered in Chapter 12, pp. 263–79).

In other theories (see pp. 327–8), transformation rules have a different and much wider role than has been assumed here; here I have regarded them purely as devices of linear organization on the syntactic level, as distinct from the rules of expression which map the semantic level on to the syntactic one.

Summary

If we view semantics as a part only of a total theory of language, then an important criterion for evaluating semantic theories and analyses is the simplicity of the rules mapping semantic on to syntactic representations. Hence the importance of studying the relation between semantics and syntax.

In this chapter I have presented a number of arguments for seeing semantics and syntax as distinct levels of representation, with distinct conditions of well-formedness or 'grammaticality'. I have also indicated a number of interrelated factors or processes which have to be dealt with in any semantic-syntactic mapping: 'lexicalization' (or the selection of lexical items to express a given content); 'structural compression' (or reduction of complexity of constituent structure through ellipsis and other means); 'linearization', or the rendering of the message in a linear sequence and 'thematization', or the arrangement of the message for the effective placing of weight and emphasis.

Although a precise formulation of the rules connecting semantics to syntax has not been attempted here, certain correlations between semantic elements (e.g. arguments) and syntactic elements (e.g. noun phrases) have been pointed out. How to formulate the relation between semantics and syntax is the subject of present controversy between advocates of 'interpretive' and 'generative' semantics within transformational grammar – a controversy to be briefly reviewed in the final chapter.

Meanwhile, in Chapter 10, we shall pursue the study of one aspect of the relation of semantics to syntax, by considering the way in which semantic and syntactic information is integrated within the dictionary of a language.

10. Semantics and the Dictionary

A language such as English contains a very large number of lexical items (i.e. words and idioms – see p. 179), and it is the function of a dictionary to list these items, and to give any necessary information (phonological, syntactic, semantic, stylistic, etc.) about the way they fit into the language system. The body of information given about one item may be called a 'lexical entry', and it is probably true that the most important part of a lexical entry, as far as the everyday user of dictionaries is concerned, is the semantic part of it, i.e. the definition. My purpose in this chapter is to investigate the nature of dictionary definitions, against the background of the dictionary as a whole, seen as a store of all the *particular* facts about a language (see p. 179). I shall also consider one important fact that is sometimes overlooked in the discussion of dictionaries: that dictionaries are open-ended, and are continually being adapted to new requirements by the addition of new lexical entries. This 'creative' or 'generative' principle of dictionaries can be accounted for by means of LEXICAL RULES, amongst which are rules of meaning transfer (e.g. rules which enable us to use words in new metaphorical senses). Yet such lexical rules are only *partially productive*, in the sense that they apply only to certain of the cases to which in theory they are applicable; hence the earlier characterization of the dictionary as the 'store of the particular (i.e. ungeneralizable) facts about a language' remains largely valid.

Practical and Theoretical Dictionaries

The preceding paragraph suffers from an unfortunate ambiguity which attends the use of the term *dictionary* as of the term *grammar*. In one sense, a dictionary is a reference book on the living-room or library shelf: in another sense, it is the 'inbuilt dictionary' which every one of us carries around as part of his mental equipment as a speaker of a language. As this book's central purpose is to explore the notion of 'semantic competence' (see p. 6 and elsewhere), it is the dictionary in this second sense (which we may distinguish by the term LEXICON) that is the present concern. The problem we shall shortly consider, then, is 'How do we provide a model, or theoretical system of representation, for what the native speaker of a language knows about its lexical items?' But first, some attention must be given to the differences between such theoretical diction-aries and the 'flesh-and-blood' dictionaries – practical dictionaries such as the Concise Oxford Dictionary – which lexicographers compile and which we all consult from time to time.

The first question that calls for explanation is why we need such practical dictionaries at all. If, as native speakers of English, we have our built-in English dictionary, why should we need to con-sult a dictionary to find out if we are using lexical items properly, any more than we need to consult an English grammar to find out (say) how to turn active sentences into passives? The reason is that the lexicon (as just observed) is open-ended in a way that a gram-mar is not. Whereas we have learned the grammatical rules of English in all essentials by the age of five, we continue the process of acquiring vocabulary and new uses of vocabulary right the way through our lives. The store of lexical information we carry with us is continually undergoing development and modification, through the written and spoken communications that we receive. Our lin-guistic education, in this respect, continues long past linguistic maturity in other respects; and to aid the process, culturally institutionalized languages such as English acquire what might be called a 'corporate lexical competence', greater than the lexical competence of any one of its users. This pool of lexical information is what is embodied in the printed dictionary.

This said, it must be recognized that like any 'living' social insti-tution, the dictionary as a reference book adapts to the various needs which society expects it to satisfy. We have learnt to go to 'the dictionary' for all manner of information on words (for ex-ample, their history and origin) apart from their form and be-haviour in the present-day language: and even for information that may more properly belong to an encyclopedia (such as how to recognize the national flags of the world) or to a book of etiquette (such as how to address an archbishop). Further, the dictionary comes to be looked on as a legislative organ, to which one turns for a standard of 'good' as opposed to 'bad' usage. This attitude is indeed encouraged by the phrase 'the dictionary', with its misleading similarity to 'the Bible'.

More important for our present concern is the tendency for a dictionary definition to go beyond the explanation of the mere sense of an item (see p. 88). Encyclopedic information about the referents of the item is often added for good measure, as in:

Wolf: Erect-eared straight-tailed harsh-furred tawny-grey wild gregarious carnivorous quadruped allied to dog preying on sheep etc. or combining in packs to hunt larger animals.

(Concise Oxford Dictionary)

This definition also exemplifies another unfortunate tendency: the tendency to substitute for the everyday meaning of a word a scientific or technical definition, thus pandering to the popular assumption (to which Bloomfield gave credence – see pp. 2–4) that the scientific explanation of a word is its 'real meaning', and hence that we ordinary users of the language are using the term 'vaguely' or 'inaccurately' if we do not know its scientific definition. To take this view is to deny the premise on which modern linguistic semantics, and the approach adopted in this book, is founded: that the meaning of a linguistic expression is precisely that knowledge which enables one to use it appropriately in linguistic communication, whether in everyday or specialist contexts.

On more practical grounds, such definitions as the above may be criticized because a number of words in the definition (*gregarious* and *carnivorous*, for instance) are far less familiar to the ordinary user of English than the word *wolf* itself. But we should not necessarily blame the lexicographer for embroidering on the bare stuff of meaning in this way. He might justifiably retort: 'How, then, would you define *wolf*?'; and certainly if the view of the meanings of such words on p. 88 is accepted, one could do little more, in a dictionary which aimed to present semantic realities, than define the word as 'an animal of the species "wolf"'. Perhaps a picture of the animal would come closest to the spirit of representing the single atomic feature §SPECIES. (One is in sympathy with the compiler of Chambers Dictionary of 1904, who defines *horse* 'the well-known quadruped'.)

But this quandary only arises because of two practical conditions of dictionary-writing. The first is the requirement, which lexicographers have taken upon themselves since the eighteenth century, to make dictionaries comprehensive even to the extent of defining easy words which anyone old enough to use a dictionary understands anyway. In a way, the definition of *wolf* is there 'just for the record', since whatever reason a person may have for looking up *wolf* in the dictionary, it can scarcely be in order to find out its meaning. The second practical condition is more important, because it arises from a basic unavoidable difference between 'practical' and 'theoretical' dictionaries: it is that a practical dictionary definition must consist of words. It has been argued that the lexical definition, as part of the native speaker's linguistic equipment, takes the form of a set of semantic features (some of which may be downgraded predications). Therefore the only completely satisfactory way to represent the meaning of a lexical item on paper must be by a set of feature symbols. But the practical lexicographer cannot use this method of explanation: if he did, he would convey nothing to the average dictionary-user. Instead, he has to resort to a circumlocution, i.e. a type of paraphrase. When he defines, he does not 'give the sense of' the headword (i.e. the word in bold type set against the margin), but provides another expression which *has the same sense as* the headword. If the definition is to be useful, the words it contains must be more widely used and understood than the headword; but as Dr Johnson noted in the preface to his dictionary as early as 1755, such words cannot always be found. Furthermore, there is no guarantee that the expression rules of the language furnish paraphrases for every word in the language. In Johnson's words:

Many words cannot be explained by synonimes, because the idea signified by them has not more than one appellation; nor by paraphrase, because simple ideas cannot be described.

In these circumstances, it is not surprising that lexicographers, even where their intention is to avoid doing so, frequently mingle the function of the dictionary with that of the encyclopedia or scientific handbook.

It is easy to criticize practical dictionaries from the lofty vantage-point of theory. These remarks are not intended as a critique of lexicographic practice, but rather as a warning as to the basic differences between a practical dictionary such as the *Concise Oxford Dictionary*, and a theoretical dictionary such as it is the aim of this chapter to investigate.

The Lexicon (or 'Theoretical' Dictionary)

In the remainder of this chapter, then, we shall consider a simplified model (or theoretical plan) of the lexicon of the English language, viewed as part of the competence of the native speaker of English. The lexicon will be considered as an unordered list or set of lexical entries. A lexical entry, in turn, will be considered as a combination of three specifications: a morphological specification (giving the form of the word in terms of stems and affixes); a syntactic specification (classifying the word in terms of its distributional potential within sentences); and a semantic specification (or definition).

The pronunciation and spelling of a word can be most economically shown indirectly, through the MORPHOLOGICAL SPECIFICATION, which breaks the word down into a structure of morphemes (stems and affixes). Such morphemes may obviously occur in a number of different words (as the stem *book*, for example, occurs in the words *book*, *bookish*, and *handbook*). This means that apart from the lexicon seen as a set of lexical entries, there must also be a *morpheme index*, which lists morphemes together with their pronunciation and spelling. Thus *book*, in our lexicon, is an indivisible unit and can be represented simply by means of an arbitrary subscript as (say) Stem$_{333}$, the assumption being that this stem is spelt and pronounced in the same way (subject to certain morpheme combination rules that we cannot go into) wherever it occurs. Affixes can similarly be given arbitrary subscripts. Thus specimen morphological specifications are:

book	Stem$_{333}$
bookish	Stem$_{333}$ + Suffix$_{15}$

| *handbook* | $Stem_{841} + Stem_{333}$ |
| *book-bindery* | $Stem_{333} + (Stem_{299} + Suffix_{65})$ |

From this last specification, it will be seen that the morphological structure of a word, like the syntactic structure of a sentence, may involve the bracketing together of two or more elements into a single compound constituent. Such complex elements (they always contain at least one stem) can be described as *bases* with respect to a larger combination of which they are a part. Single stems may also function as bases (as we shall see below, where the notion of *base* will be clarified).

The SYNTACTIC SPECIFICATION of an item consists in a set of features which classify it in terms of primary categories like 'Noun' 'Verb', 'Adjective' (i.e. parts of speech), and secondary categories within these categories, such as 'Countable' (Noun), 'Transitive' (Verb), 'Predicative' (Adjective), and so on. Like semantic features, these features are contrastive (e.g. 'Countable' contrasts with 'Mass'), but not necessarily in terms of binary oppositions.

The SEMANTIC SPECIFICATION (or definition) of a word is a set of semantic features of the kinds that will be familiar from Chapter 6: that is, contrastive features such as $+$HUMAN, $\rightarrow$CAUSE, $\uparrow$SIZE, etc., as well as downgraded predications, the semantic units which can be expressed syntactically in the form of relative clauses. Definitions which consist of a set of contrastive features (e.g. $+$HUMAN $+$ADULT $+$MALE) have already been sufficiently illustrated, but it may be appropriate to exemplify here something of the variety of definitions involving downgraded predications. For this purpose I shall represent downgraded predications not by tree diagrams as before, but by a sequence of symbols representing arguments and predicates (separated from one another by a full stop in the case of a two-place predication, and by a colon in the case of a one-place predication). The arguments and predicates will be indicated by italic letters (A, P) if no content is being specified, or otherwise by the feature symbols of the features they contain, or by makeshift glosses such as 'has', 'friend', etc. The symbol **the**, representing the feature of definiteness, will always occur in one of the arguments, since it is a general rule of downgraded predications (p. 169) that they are linked by coreference to the remainder of the predication or argument in which they occur, and this entails the presence of the feature of definiteness. (It may be helpful to read the feature **the** as if corresponding to a relative pronoun *who* or *which*.) The downgraded predication

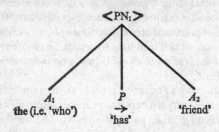

can thus be represented linearly as follows: ⟨**the**. →'has'. 'friend'⟩ (The directional arrow is only inserted where it is relevant to the distinction being made.) Further subordination within a downgraded predication can be shown linearly by additional bracketing, round brackets being used for embedded predications and angle brackets for downgraded predications. Thus the definition of *grandfather* ('male parent of [someone who is] parent of . . .') can be shown as:

+MALE⟨**the**. →PARENT.∅⟨**the**. →PARENT.∅⟩⟩

The null symbol ∅ represents a null set of features; arrows showing the relation of coreference are omitted.

(Remember that the arrow of →PARENT and of similar features signals the *direction* in which a relationship holds, *A*. →PARENT. *B* indicating that *A* is parent of *B*, and *A*. ←PARENT. *B* indicating that *B* is the parent of *A*. In general, I let the direction of the arrow lead from the *positive* or *active* member of a relative opposition. Thus 'parenthood' is positive where 'childhood' is passive; 'king' is positive where 'subject' is passive. This distinction is a rough, intuitive one, to which I shall not attempt to give any theoretical significance.)

With this preparation, a wide range of 'relational' definitions involving downgraded predications may be shown as follows (the ellipses (. . .) in these formulae indicate that additional features may sometimes be present, as *king*, for example, requires the feature $+$MALE):

- A. $+$HUMAN$(\ldots)\langle$the$.\rightarrow P.A\rangle$
  i.e. (roughly) 'a person who bears a certain active relationship (P) to someone/something (A)'
  OR $+$HUMAN$(\ldots)\langle$the$:P\rangle$
  i.e. (roughly) 'a person who has a certain attribute (P)'.
  bookseller, king, teacher, actor, coach, etc.
- B. $+$HUMAN$(\ldots)\langle$the$.\leftarrow P.A\rangle$
  pupil, subject, employee, etc.
- C. $-$ANIMATE$(\ldots)\langle$the$.P.$(PN)$\rangle$
  razor, seat, blackboard, path, vehicle, garment, etc.
- D. $\langle$the$.P.A\rangle$
  literate, legible, pitiful, wealthy, etc.
- E. $\langle$the$.$not-$P.A\rangle$
  illiterate, blind, deaf, dumb, etc.

Type A represents definitions of 'agent' nouns in a wide sense; that is, nouns denoting the person who engages in a certain activity (a bookseller is 'a person who sells books [for a living]' etc.). In this and in other types, the second argument of a two-place predication is very often null: $\langle$the$.\rightarrow P.\emptyset\rangle$.

Type B represents definitions of 'passive nouns' which fulfil an objective role in relation to the activity signified by the predicate P (as a pupil, for instance, is 'someone who is taught'). These terms sometimes form converse relations with agent nouns, as *pupil* is the converse of *teacher*, and *subject* of *king*.

Type C represents definitions of 'function nouns', that is nouns denoting objects (usually artefacts) which are identified by their functions: *seat* for instance, may be defined as 'an object for sitting on', and *razor* as 'an instrument with which to shave'. That words of this kind should be defined by *functional* criteria (rather than or in addition to concrete *physical* properties of the referent) is shown by the lack of any exhaustive characterisation in terms of appearance, shape, consistency, etc. There is little in common between safety razors and electric razors in terms of physical appearance: what is in common between them is the fact that they are both made and used for the same purpose. Similarly, it is difficult to think of what distinguishes a 'seat' from other objects, if it is not its use 'for sitting on': practically any object, whatever its size or shape, 'becomes' a seat if somebody decides to sit on it.

Type D shows the definition of adjectives in terms of a single downgraded predication: *literate* means 'who can read'; *wealthy* 'who has much money', etc. There seems to be a basic semantic difference between nouns and adjectives, in that adjectives are normally defined by a single feature (usually a polar feature such as ↑ SIZE, or a downgraded predication) while the definitions of nouns frequently consist of a combination of features. This difference helps to explain the traditional characterisation of an adjective as a word that expresses a 'quality', as opposed to nouns, which represent objects identifiable by a bundle of such 'qualities'.

Type E is similar to Type D except that the predicate is negative: *blind* means 'who cannot see', etc. For this type, as for Types B and D, the argument A seems to be almost invariably null.

Similar definitional types could be provided for other parts of speech, with the proviso (p. 192) that verbs, prepositions, and conjunctions sometimes involve more than one predicate.

Graded Acceptability

Lexical rules are rules accounting for the 'creative' or 'productive' aspect of the lexicon which allows us to form new words (for example, to coin the noun *uncrumplability* using as a stem the verb *crumple*) or to derive new meanings for existing words (for example, to use the word *gullible* in the phrase *gullible era* to mean 'an era in which people are gullible'). Obviously 'new' is a relative term in this connection: we cannot know whether a given use or coinage such as the above is unique in the history of the English language. But what can be said is that so far as the user is concerned, it could well be unique: it is an individual employment of a principle or rule which is available to users of the language as a means of extending their lexical repertoire.

Lexical rules not only explain how new lexical entries come into existence on the basis of old ones, but also explain the inter-relationships of derivation that we recognize between lexical entries already established in the language.

The examples of *uncrumplability* and *gullible* just given belong traditionally to two different aspects of linguistic study: word-formation, and transfer of meaning. In what follows, I shall suggest that these two processes, which have a great deal in common, are best subsumed under the single notion of 'lexical rule'.

What chiefly distinguishes lexical rules from grammatical rules is their limited productivity; that is, a lexical rule does not apply equally well to all the cases to which in theory it *may* apply. This can be clarified by an example:

We can trace new substances by various means
→(a) *New substances can be traced by various means*
→(b) *New substances are traceable by various means*.

From the initial sentence we may predict the acceptability of sentence (a), through the grammatical rule which relates active to passive sentences; likewise, for many cases, we can predict the acceptability of sentence (b), in which the passive meaning is conveyed by lexical means, through the suffix *-able*. But the difference lies in the fact that for many other cases, the application of the rule to produce (b) does not work: if the active verb had been *try*, *find*, or *get*, the (b) sentence would contain the adjectives **triable*, **findable*, and **gettable*, words absent from the regular English lexicon, although the verbs from which they are formed are very common. **Triable*, **findable*, and **gettable* are, we may say, *potential* English words, in the sense that they are well-formed according to rules of word-formation; but they happen not to have become established members of the English lexicon. (I am not saying that such words never occur, but that if they do occur, it will be with an air of strangeness, novelty, jocularity, etc.) To put the point more generally: we have to distinguish, with reference to lexical rules,

(1) The *ACTUAL* ACCEPTABILITY of lexical entries which have attained institutional acceptance.

(2) the *POTENTIAL* ACCEPTABILITY of any lexical entry that can be generated by a lexical rule.

(3) the *UNACCEPTABILITY* of a lexical entry not allowed for in the lexical rules at all. For example **sheepable* (where the deverbal suffix *-able* is added onto the noun stem *sheep*) is not a

possible English word at all – unless we imagine that *sheep* has been already converted into a verb.

It is in the realm of *actual* acceptability that we encounter the haphazard or idiosyncratic nature of the lexicon (that characteristic which makes it proper to describe the dictionary as 'the list of all the particular facts about a language'). And we may notice in passing that this same characteristic is seen in the arbitrariness of the phonological make-up of morphemes: *mat, met, bat, bet,* and *rat* are all English morphemes but **ret* is not. Nonsense syllables like **ret* are, we may say, 'potential morphemes', formed according to the rules of English phonology; they are therefore distinct from completely un-English combinations such as **shtrumpf,* in the same way as **gettable* is distinguishable from **sheepable.*

Actual acceptability is a graded concept. If, for example, we take a list of English nouns and add to them the suffix *-less*, it will be impossible to say exactly at what point unacceptability 'sets in':

—LESS: (a) *helpless*; (b) *friendless*; (c) *boyless*; (d) *houseless*; (e) *growthless*.

—SOME: (a) *troublesome*; (b) *fearsome*; (c) *scornsome*; (d) *joysome*; (e) *vanitysome*.

—EN: (a) *wooden*; (b) *silken*; (c) *larchen*; (d) *bronzen*; (e) *aluminiumen*.

The words in each of the three groups above are arranged roughly (according to my own judgement) in order of acceptability. No doubt if we heard any of the words labelled (c), (d), or (e) we would react to each of them with some feeling of surprise as to 'nonce formations', that is, as words made up on the spur of the moment for a temporary purpose. On the other hand, most English speakers would feel that, say, (e) in each group is less likely to be invented than (c).

A second notion of graded acceptability applies not to the individual instances, but to the rules themselves. Of the three suffixation processes illustrated above, the first (noun+*-less*) is more productive than the second (noun+*-some*), and the second is more productive than the third (noun+*-en*), which is indeed scarcely productive at all in present-day English.

The principle of partial productivity that we have seen to operate in suffixation can be observed equally clearly not only in other types of word-formation, such as prefixation and compounding, but in semantic transfer. If we take metaphor as one type of semantic transfer, then a 'dead metaphor' is one which has gone all the way towards complete assimilation as a separate definition of the word concerned (as *hit* in the sense 'successful pop song').

On the other hand, there are many metaphors which are 'moribund' rather than dead (e.g. *hawk* in the sense 'a person with warlike attitudes'). To illustrate degrees in the assimilation of a figurative meaning, let us examine the way in which animal words are applied metaphorically (and usually unflatteringly) to human beings:

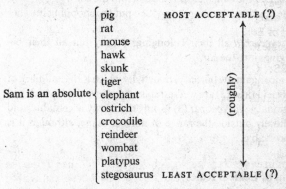

Sam is an absolute

pig	MOST ACCEPTABLE (?)
rat	
mouse	
hawk	
skunk	
tiger	
elephant	(roughly)
ostrich	
crocodile	
reindeer	
wombat	
platypus	
stegosaurus	LEAST ACCEPTABLE (?)

The parallel between this and affixation is seen to be extremely close if we compare such metaphorical extensions of meaning with the adjectives produced when the suffix -*y* is added to the nouns above: *piggy, ratty, mousy, hawky, skunky,* ... Although there are differences in the acceptability of corresponding items, we notice the same sort of scale of assimilation; and since the function of the suffix is quasi-metaphorical (e.g. *piggy* means 'like a pig'), there is also a close parallel of meaning.

Types of Lexical Rule

From what we have seen above, it is possible to think of semantic transfer, whether metaphorical or otherwise, in terms of a lexical rule in which the morphological and syntactic specifications of the item remain the same, and only the semantic specification changes. Both morphological derivation and semantic transfer, therefore, can be seen as instances of the same basic process of extending the repertoire of lexical entries. Yet a further type of lexical rule is that which usually goes under the name of *conversion*; that is, a change in the syntactic function (and usually the meaning) of an item without a corresponding change in morphological form. An example of a rule of conversion is that which enables us to form from nouns verbs with the meaning 'to put into . . .' or 'to put onto . . .':

(1) He *pocketed* the change. ('He put the change into his *pocket*.')
(2) He *netted* the ball. ('He put the ball into the *net*.')
(3) ?She *basketed* the shopping. ('She put the shopping into her *basket*.')
(4) *They *carred* all their belongings ('They put all their belongings into the *car*.')

We note once again the partial productivity which is the hallmark of lexical rules: (1) and (2) are well-established conversions which any good dictionary will record; (3) is only dubiously acceptable, and (4) is definitely outside the range of normal usage, although it is not inconceivable.

The Form of Lexical Rules

We are now in a position to state the general form that lexical rules take, in such a way as to include within the same formula morphological derivation, conversion, and semantic transfer.

The formula at its most general is a derivation of one lexical entry from another as follows:

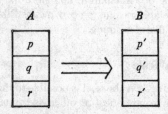

(where A and B are lexical entries; p is a morphological specification; q is a syntactic specification; and r is a semantic specification).

A rule of *morphological derivation* involves a change in the morphological specification; for example, the addition of an affix to the original morphological specification, which is called the *base*:

GENERAL FORM OF RULE: EXAMPLE:

$p_1 \Rightarrow p_2$ Base $\Rightarrow$ Base + Suffix$_{25}$

$q_1 \Rightarrow q_2$ Noun $\Rightarrow$ Adjective

$r_1 \Rightarrow r_2$ $A \Rightarrow \langle \textbf{the} . \textbf{not} \rightarrow \text{'has'} . A \rangle$

(e.g. *friend* $\Rightarrow$ *friendless*)

Usually, the morphological change is accompanied by a change of syntactic function and a change of meaning, as in the above example, which gives a skeleton lexical rule for the addition of *-less* to a noun. In some cases, however, there is no change of syntactic function: the addition of *-ie* to *aunt*, for example, does not affect the function of the word as a human countable noun. In fact, there is in this case probably no change of conceptual meaning either, since the difference between *aunt* and *auntie* appears to be a matter of stylistic meaning alone. For compound formation, the same general form of lexical rule operates, except that a base has attached to it, instead of an affix, a further base. A compounding rule is therefore a 'coalescence' of two lexical entries to form a third.

A rule of *conversion* is a lexical rule which involves a change of syntactic function without a change of morphological specification:

GENERAL FORM OF RULE: EXAMPLE:

$p_1 \Rightarrow p_1$ Base $\Rightarrow$ Base

$q_1 \Rightarrow q_2$ Verb, Transitive $\Rightarrow$ Noun, Concrete, Countable

$r_1 \Rightarrow r_2$ $\rightarrow P \Rightarrow \emptyset \langle \textbf{the} . \leftarrow P . \emptyset \rangle$

(e.g. *catch* [Verb] $\Rightarrow$ *catch* [Noun] (= 'that which is caught'))

This is an approximate statement of the rule which explains the existence of the noun *catch* as used in the sentence *The fishermen had a large catch*. Other nouns that can be used like this are *bet, hope, drink, find, bag, haul, bite, kill*. The change of syntactic specification is almost invariably accompanied by a change of semantic specification, as in this case. Conversion, as defined by this form of rule, does not necessarily involve a change of the major part of speech. There are many rules which bring about a change of secondary syntactic classification only; for example:

Mass noun $\Rightarrow$ count noun (e.g. *an embarrassment*; *two teas*; *how many sugars?*)

Count noun $\Rightarrow$ mass noun (e.g. *an area of table*; *half an inch of cigarette*)

A rule of *semantic transfer* is a lexical rule which brings about a change in the semantic specification only. The rule of metaphoric extension has already been mentioned as an example of this:

GENERAL FORM OF RULE:	EXAMPLE:
$p_1 \Rightarrow p_1$	Base $\Rightarrow$ Base
$q_1 \Rightarrow q_1$	Noun $\Rightarrow$ Noun
$r_1 \Rightarrow r_2$	$A \Rightarrow \emptyset \langle \text{the}.\leftrightarrow \text{SIMILAR}.A\rangle$

The rule as stated here goes only some way to an explanation of metaphor: it merely says that for a meaning 'A' we substitute the meaning 'something similar to A'. The ground or warranty for the comparison is something that has to be read into the formula. For example, *doughnut* in the phrase *a doughnut of mud* requires us to imaginatively fill in the details of the way in which a piece of mud may be seen as like a doughnut (e.g. being round, soft, and sticky). Additionally, the metaphoric rule is more general than most, because it can apply to various parts of speech, not just to nouns, as in the formulation above. A final limitation of this formula is that it does not fully explain the poetic use of metaphor as a means of 'conceptual fusion', as argued in Chapter 3. The everyday use of metaphor illustrated here keeps its feet firmly on the ground, in the sense that the literal meaning remains paramount: a doughnut of mud remains solidly and palpably a piece of mud, not a mysterious fusion of 'doughnutness' and 'muddiness' of the kind that, it has been suggested, characterizes poetic language.

Other types of semantic transfer are often designated *metonymy* in traditional terminology. Examples are:

1.
> The neighbourhood objected to his plans.
>   (*neighbourhood* = 'people in the neighbourhood')
> The whole town turned out to welcome us.
>   (*whole town* = 'all the people living in the town')

2.
> I enjoy Shakespeare immensely.
>   (*Shakespeare* = 'the works of Shakespeare')
> That sounds like early Beethoven.
>   (*early Beethoven* = 'the early works of Beethoven')

3.
> Nothing like it has happened since Napoleon.
>   (*Napoleon* = 'the time of Napoleon',
>   'the time when Napoleon lived')
> After the bomb, nothing could be the same again.
>   (*the bomb* = 'the invention of the bomb')

Each pair of examples illustrates a different rule, statable approximately as follows:

1. $A \Rightarrow$ +HUMAN $\langle$**the**. $\rightarrow$'is in/on'. $A\rangle$
   (where A contains the feature of 'place')
2. $A \Rightarrow \emptyset$ $\langle$**the**. $\leftarrow$'write'. $A\rangle$
   (where A contains the feature +HUMAN)
3. $A \Rightarrow$ 'time' $\langle$**the**. $\rightarrow$'at'. (PN)$\rangle$
   (where the embedded predication PN contains A)

This third rule, which might be read: 'the time at which something to do with A happened', exemplifies a type of metonymic rule which is like the metaphoric rule in that it introduces variable information (similar to the variable 'ground' of a metaphor). That is, we interpret the content of PN as 'the invention of A', 'the life of A', 'the founding of A', etc., according to context.

But whatever differences there may be between one rule and another, for all lexical rules the change of semantic specification is in essence the same, in that the new specification (r_2) includes the old specification (r_1). In most cases (as in the three metonymic rules above), the result is that the old specification is 'pushed down' into a subordinate position within r_2, usually the position of an argument in a downgraded predication. In this position it no longer governs the selection restrictions of the lexical item, so that (for instance) as a result of Rule 2 above it is possible to say

John knows his *great authors* off by heart.
I've been reading some *Dickens*.
Any *old master* is worth more than its weight in gold these days.

using nouns which are originally personal nouns in contexts appropriate to nouns of non-human reference. (Incidentally, these examples show that a proper noun can also become grammatically reclassified as a common noun – the transfer of meaning is often accompanied by a secondary syntactic conversion.) We might note that by a further metonymy, such proper names can be treated as concrete inanimate nouns:

John threw his *Shakespeare* at Peter's head.
His wife owns a gilt-framed *Rembrandt*, which she keeps in a secret room.

As the cases of metonymy so far considered apply primarily to nouns, it is as well to conclude this exemplification with a rule which applies to a different word class – specifically to adjectives which refer to emotional or other inner states, and apply in the first instance to animate (especially human) beings. Such adjectives as *sad, friendly, melancholy, gay, dismal, sincere* are 'on their home ground', we may suppose, when they are being used with a human noun (*sad child, friendly person*, etc.); but they are frequently used in a transferred sense of 'expressing or evincing X' (where X is the emotional or other inner state): *a sad face, a friendly greeting, gay clothes, a sincere answer*, etc. Yet a further transferred sense (sometimes not easily distinguished from the last) is that of 'causing or evoking inner state X', as in *a sad story, a melancholy landscape, a thirsty meeting, a dismal failure*.

From all these examples, it is easy to see how rules of transfer take on importance in the interpretation of sentences which are at face value absurd in one way or other, particularly through a violation of selection restrictions (see p. 141). Confronted with a combination such as

'The floor was more humane than the platform'

our first reaction is probably one of bafflement and surprise that the most obvious interpretations of the words are impeded by an absurdity (the absurdity of treating the inanimate floor and platform as if they were human). Our subsequent strategy is to find a rule of transfer which will render sensible what is apparently senseless (a strategy which is rather like directing traffic along a diversion when a main road is blocked). The most obvious solution here is to apply rule (1) above, and so to construe *floor* and *platform* as the 'people on the floor' and 'people on the platform', in the sense which is an established metonymy in discussions of public meetings. A second solution, less obvious, would be to apply the rule which interprets *humane* as 'expressing or evincing humaneness' – a meaning that might possibly be intended by someone who found the floor more comfortable to sit on than the platform, and thus regarded it as showing a greater degree of humaneness in the architect who designed it.

Further Observations about Lexical Rules

There are a number of further points I wish to make about lexical rules, in order to emphasize (a) that these rules are surprisingly powerful in their ability of generate new lexical entries; and (b) that the bringing together of morphological derivation, conversion, and semantic transfer as instances of the same general phenomenon is motivated by other common characteristics, apart from their partial productiveness. The five properties of lexical rules I shall dwell upon are (1) their diversity; (2) their semantic open-endedness; (3) their recursiveness; (4) their bi-directionality; and (5) their tendency to be distorted by the 'petrification' of lexical entries. The meanings of these various terms will be clear from what follows.

1. *Diversity*

The first point to notice is that the *diversity* of lexical rules is such as to allow the possibility of applying a large number of different rules to the same lexical entry. This is obvious enough in any case with regard to morphological affixation (consider the range of complex words derived from the noun *man* – *manly, manlike, mannish, manhood, unman, unmanly,* etc.). But it is less noticeable that rules of semantic transfer have a similar diversity, which can lead to many potential ambiguities in the meaning of a single item, such as the adjective *human*:

1. *human* offspring   'human' (+HUMAN)
2. *human* race   '(race) consisting of +HUMAN'
3. *human* voice   '(voice) of +HUMAN'
4. *human* elephant   '(elephant) like a +HUMAN'
5. *human* consumption   '(consumption) by +HUMAN'
6. *human* experimentation   '(experimentation) on +HUMAN'

Definitions 2–6 here can all be seen as derived from the basic definition +HUMAN, definition 1. One way to define a rule of semantic transfer, in fact, is as a 'rule which creates new instances of polysemy or multiple meaning'.

2. *Open-endedness*

The power of lexical rules to proliferate meanings lies not only in their variety, but in the fact that in some cases they are semantically open-ended, allowing the language-user freedom to read into a new lexical entry whatever information he finds necessary to the understanding of it. This element of imaginative 'reading-in' has already been noted in connection with the unspecified ground of comparison in a metaphor. But it can also be present in metonymic transfers, more especially in imaginative writing, in the sense that there may be not just a single path of semantic connection to be traced, but a whole range of possibilities, between which there seem to be no clear criteria of choice. When Frank Kermode in his book *Romantic Image* describes Henry James as 'the detached, ironical, adverbial James', we might wonder in what sense can a writer be *adverbial*? Could it be 'James, who likes adverbs', 'James, who uses many adverbs', 'James, who is given to modifying his remarks by adverbs'? The expression appears to communicate at a level which includes all these and many other possibilities, and any attempt to construct an explicit rule to link this use of *adverbial* to the dictionary definitions of that term would be a falsification. Instead, we must be content with the most general rule possible, producing the open-ended definition ⟨**the**.*P*.'adverbs'⟩ '(James) who has some-connection-or-other with adverbs'. It is up to the reader to fill in this unknown quantity P as best he may.

The semantic bridge can also be vague, and often extraordinarily indirect, with compounds, especially compounds formed by the joining together of two or more nouns. Although there are certain well-trodden paths of connection, sufficiently clear to be formulated as separate lexical rules, for many compounds X-Y it seems as if the most general rule 'X which-has-something-to-do-with Y' is the only one broad enough to include all the idiosyncratic readings that are possible. Consider the following three cases (in the latter two of which the first element X is itself a compound):

$X - Y$	
hunger strike	'strike in which hunger, rather than withdrawal of labour, is the weapon'
gunboat diplomacy	'diplomacy which relies on the use of gunboats or other demonstrations of force'
shotgun wedding	'wedding which results from the bride's father's threatening the prospective bridegroom with a shotgun'

The semantic connections are so idiosyncratic here that if one devised three specific transfer rules to account for them, they would have no use other than to account for a single example each. In any case, the circumlocutory explanation given on the right is only one of many possible verbalizations of the connection. Here as elsewhere, we must acknowledge the distinction between *ambiguity* (which results from diversity of specific rules) and *vagueness* (which results from general rules inviting the 'reading-in' of indefinitely variable specific information). One of the problems of lexicology must be to draw the line between these two phenomena, which can be similar in their effect, but which are totally different in theory.

3. *Recursiveness*

A third property which contributes to the power of lexical rules is their *recursiveness*, by which I mean the ability of a lexical entry which is the *output* of one lexical rule to be also the *input* to another lexical rule. If we remember that a lexical entry consists in a trio of specifications *p*, *q* and *r*, then the operation of this recursive principle may be represented by a sequence as follows:

$$\begin{Bmatrix} p \\ q \\ r \end{Bmatrix} \Rightarrow \begin{Bmatrix} p' \\ q' \\ r' \end{Bmatrix} \Rightarrow \begin{Bmatrix} p'' \\ q'' \\ r'' \end{Bmatrix} \Rightarrow \begin{Bmatrix} p''' \\ q''' \\ r''' \end{Bmatrix} \Rightarrow \dots$$

Again, on the morphological level, the results of the principle are not difficult to observe. From single stems, it is possible to build up stage by stage as follows a complex word like *drum-majorettishly*:

$$\left. \begin{matrix} \text{drum} \\ \text{major} \end{matrix} \right\} \Rightarrow \text{drum-major} \Rightarrow \text{(drum-major)-(ette)}$$
$$\Rightarrow \text{((drum-major)-(ette))-(ish)} \Rightarrow \text{(((drum-major)-(ette))-(ish))-(ly)}$$

The same principle is illustrated by complex noun-sequences such as *railway-station refreshment room*, composed by a multiple application of the noun + noun compounding process.

An example of recursiveness in rules of conversion is the noun *bag* (in the sense of 'a catch, that which is caught or bagged'). This is derivable from the verb *bag* (= 'to put in a bag, to catch'), which in turn is derived from the noun *bag* (= 'a limp receptacle'). Thus the three stages of the derivation process may be pictured as:

$$\begin{Bmatrix} \textit{bag} \\ \text{(noun)} \\ \text{'limp receptacle'} \end{Bmatrix} \Rightarrow$$

$$\begin{Bmatrix} \textit{bag} \\ \text{(verb)} \\ \text{'to put in a limp} \\ \text{receptacle'} \end{Bmatrix} \Rightarrow$$

$$\begin{Bmatrix} \textit{bag} \\ \text{(noun)} \\ \text{'that which is put in a} \\ \text{limp receptacle'} \end{Bmatrix}$$

Less noticeably, the same recursiveness of the derivation process can be observed in semantic transfer:

1. *topless dress*: '(dress) which has no top'
2. *topless dancer*: '(dancer) wearing a dress which has no top'
3. *topless bar-service*: '(bar-service) provided by girls wearing dresses with no top'

These three examples (the latter two from an issue of *Where to Go*, a magazine giving details of amusements in London) show the progressive 'pushing-down' of the basic literal meaning of the adjective. In a rough semantic notation, the three definitions can be represented as follows:

1. ⟨the. not → HAVE. 'top'⟩
2. ⟨the. → WEAR. 'dress' ⟨the. not → HAVE. 'top'⟩⟩
3. ⟨the. ← PROVIDE. 'girls' ⟨the. → WEAR. 'dresses' ⟨the. not → HAVE. 'top'⟩⟩⟩

An even more indirect interpretation of *topless* is evoked by the headline: TOPLESS BAN AT EARLS COURT which appeared in a Sunday newspaper in October 1969, when a model wearing a topless dress was forbidden to appear at the Earls Court Motor Show.

But illustrations of the recursiveness of semantic transfer need not be so exotic as this. Quite frequently, adjectives derived from proper-names have a similar development:

1. *Wagnerian opera*: '(opera) written by Wagner'
2. *Wagnerian heroine*: '(heroine) of an opera written by Wagner'
3. *Wagnerian heroine*: '(heroine) like a heroine of an opera written by Wagner'

The third step of this progression is an application of the rule of metaphoric transfer, common in adjectives of this kind: for example, *Homeric epic* may mean 'epic by Homer' or 'epic like that by Homer'; *Stygian gloom* may mean 'the gloom of the Styx' or 'gloom resembling (in its profundity) the gloom of the Styx'. This metaphoric step may also be observed, in retrospect, in the examples of multiple compounding mentioned earlier: *a shotgun wedding* is not necessarily a wedding at which the bride's father brandishes a shotgun; more generally, it is a wedding *resembling* such a wedding (in that the bridegroom is forced to marry the bride through parental pressure on account of the bride's pregnancy). Likewise, *gunboat diplomacy* does not necessarily involve the use of gunboats: it can be diplomacy relying on menaces of a different kind. From all these examples, we can see how semantic transfer leads to a 'telescoping' of semantic relations, so that much meaning comes to be compressed into a small space.

4. *Bi-directionality*

Up to this point I have represented the process of lexical derivation by a single-headed arrow ($\Rightarrow$), and have treated it as a unidirectional, or irreversible process. Now I wish to suggest that it might be better regarded as a two-directional process, and so more appropriately represented by a double-headed arrow ($\Leftrightarrow$).

First, however, let us consider what 'derivation' means. There are two senses in which a lexical entry L_2 can be regarded as unidirectionally derived from another entry L_1. One is the historical sense: L_1's occurrence in the language may predate the occurrence of L_2 and may be supposed, by historical causation, to have given rise to L_2. The other sense is a purely formal one, in which the lexical entry L_2 *includes* L_1 (in terms of its morphological form or semantic content). Thus whatever the historical facts of the case, it is natural to regard *kingly* as derived from *king*, because *king* is morphologically part of *kingly* and its meaning is presupposed by that of *kingly*. Historically, the simpler entry normally precedes the more complex one, and therefore the historical and formal notions of derivation coincide. But there are cases of 'back-formation' where the process has taken place in the opposite direction. In English, for example, the verb *peddle* (first recorded in 1532) appears to be historically derived from the noun *pedlar* (first recorded in 1377) by a reversal of the rule for deriving agent nouns from verbs. *Televise* (1927) is historically derived from *television* (1909). Other examples of back-formation are *reminisce* from *reminiscence*, *edit* from *editor*, and a growing class of verbs which have arisen by 'metanalysis' from compound nouns: *housekeep* from *housekeeper/housekeeping*, similarly *lip-read, vacuum-clean, brainwash*, etc.

Since historically the derivation can move in either direction, it is arguable that lexical rules should be formulated (for the purpose of representing linguistic competence) in a bi-directional form, the predominance of derivations from the simpler to the more complex form being regarded simply as a matter of historical probability.

One advantage of this position is that it helps the treatment of conversion: it disposes of the chicken-and-egg problem (often vexing to students of word-formation) as to which of two morphologically identical items is the base, and which is the derived form. For example, which is to be regarded as the base, and which as the derived form, *goad* as a noun or *goad* as a verb? If we relate this item to cases like the following:

wrap (verb) — *wrap* (noun = 'a garment with which to wrap oneself')
cover (verb) — *cover* (noun = 'a thing with which to cover something')

the temptation is to see this as a case of verb-to-noun conversion (*goad* = 'an implement with which to goad an animal'). But the inclination will swing in the opposite direction on consideration of a further set of parallel cases:

knife (noun) — *knife* (verb) (= 'to stab with a knife')
pin (noun) — *pin* (verb) (= 'to fasten with a pin')
whip (noun) — *whip* (verb) (= 'to beat with a whip')
glue (noun) — *glue* (verb) (= 'to fix with glue')

The New English Dictionary tells us that historically the verb *wrap* antedates the noun, while the noun *knife* antedates the verb; but all this shows is that there is reason to see the process of conversion as bi-directional, just as morphological derivation is seen to be bi-directional through instances of back-formation. Furthermore, there is a similar phenomenon in semantic transfer: we have assumed that with adjectives like *sad*, the basic meaning is that of 'being in an inner state X', and that from this may be derived the transferred meaning 'causing or evoking inner state X'; with *comfortable*, however, the historical movement seems to have been in the opposite direction: it may be that the meaning 'bringing ease or comfort' gave rise to a later meaning 'being in a state of ease or comfort'. Thus although the general tendency is for the simpler entry chronologically to precede the more complex one, we must allow, in all major types of lexical rule, for derivation to take place in either direction. This bi-directionality is yet another factor which adds to the power of lexical rules to produce new entries, and underlines the gap of unused 'capacity' between the theoretically enormous generative power of lexical rules, and the comparatively limited use that is made of them in practice.

5. '*Petrification*' of lexical meanings

As the discussion of lexical rules has already strayed into a historical dimension, it is worth observing that semantic transfer by metaphor or metonymy (together with the type of denotative shift described on p. 123) is among the most important mechanisms by which, in the history of a language like English, words extend and change their meanings. In fact, the study of the lexicon is at the crossroads of a historical and contemporary (*synchronic*) view of language; the lexicon is at once a storehouse of the results of applying lexical rules to the past, and a model for the present and future application of those rules. But on the semantic level, there is almost inevitably an uncomfortable lack of fit between the lexical entries that arise theoretically from the application of a lexical rule, and the actual lexical entries we find in the lexicon. This is partly because the effect of subsequent linguistic history is often to obscure an originally regular relation between different lexical definitions; and partly because even at the outset of its institutional existence in the language, a lexical entry usually denotes a more limited area of reference than is theoretically allowed for by the lexical rule. The whole process by which an institutionalized lexical meaning diverges from the 'theoretical' meaning specified in a lexical rule may be termed *petrification* (a term which, I hope, will suggest both the 'solidifying' in institutional form of a lexical entry, and the 'shrinkage' of denotation which often accompanies this process).

An example of the institutional narrowing of lexical meaning is provided by the two compound nouns *wheel-chair* and *push-chair*. The rules which originally gave rise to these compounds suggest definitions as follows:

wheel-chair 'chair which has wheels'
push-chair 'chair which one pushes'

but of course, a 'wheel-chair' is *more* than a chair with wheels, and a 'push-chair' is *more* than a chair which one pushes: to these partial definitions we must add the criteria which in practice narrow down the reference of the two terms: that *wheel-chairs* are 'for invalids' and that *push-chairs* are 'for infants'. The particular force of this illustration is, of course, that without the institutional factors which have limited the meanings of these compounds, one would feel free to use *wheel-chair* and *push-chair* interchangeably (since most wheel-chairs are pushed, and all push-chairs have wheels). A second illustration is the more recent compound *trouser-suit*, which in practice means not just 'suit with trousers' but 'suit with trousers *for women*'.

Further examples of 'petrification' have already been met in earlier sections of this chapter. Thus the verbs *bag* and *corner*, interpreted according to rule as 'to put into a bag' and 'to put into a corner', have in actual usage acquired the further elements of meaning italicized:

> *bag* (verb): 'to put X in a bag (*X being game or winnings*)'
> *corner* (verb): 'to put X into a corner *so that X cannot escape*'

Additional historical developments have included the denotative broadening of the meaning of *bag* (verb) to become almost equivalent to 'catch' (one can bag a criminal without using a bag); also the metaphorical extension of *corner* (verb) to refer to any situation in which a person is trapped by an adversary. Yet in spite of these changes, we still recognize these words as exemplifying the living rule of conversion given on p. 215, and therefore see them as parallel to *pocket, net*, etc. and other similar examples of nouns used as verbs.

A type of 'petrification' mentioned earlier in another connection is the process by which a metaphor becomes 'dead'. Various stages can be seen in this process: the first stage of 'petrification', almost inevitable in an institutionalized metaphor, is that the reference and ground of the comparison becomes limited by convention; in that, for example, *a fox* is '*a person* who is like a fox *in that he is cunning*' as opposed, say, to 'an animal which is like a fox in that it has a pointed nose'. A further stage is reached when the transferred definition loses its analogical feeling, so that *fox* is felt to be virtually synonymous with *a cunning man*. But even at this stage, a feeling of the link between the literal and transferred meanings may persist. The stage of absolute 'deadness' is reached only when the literal meaning has died out entirely (as it has, for instance, with *thrill*, derived from an Old English word meaning 'to bore or pierce'); or else, when the literal and transferred meanings have diverged psychologically to the extent that no connection is felt between them any more. Probable examples of this second circumstance are *crane* ('machine for lifting'), derived, presumably by a visual metaphor, from *crane* ('type of bird'); and *mess* ('dirty or untidy state of affairs'), derived from the now rare *mess* ('dish of food'). (For a survey of these and other examples, see R. Waldron, *Sense and Sense Development*, p. 173–85.)

Homonymy and Polysemy

The convergence of historical and synchronic approaches to the lexicon brings us finally to a problem which has been a long-standing matter of concern for students of semantics: how does one draw the line between *homonymy* (roughly 'two or more words having the same pronunciation and/or spelling') and *polysemy* ('one word having two or more senses')? The conventional rule-of-thumb answer to this is that we recognize a case of polysemy if the senses concerned are related. But when we ask what 'related' means, there are two answers, one historical and one psychological, which do not necessarily coincide. Two meanings are *historically* related if they can be traced back to the same source, or if the one meaning can be derived from the other; two meanings are *psychologically* related if present-day users of the language feel intuitively that they are related, and therefore tend to assume that they are 'different uses of the same word'. As we have seen with *mess* and *crane*, historically related meanings are not always psychologically related; oppositely, there are cases where historically unrelated forms are felt to be related psychologically. Examples cited for English (see S. Ullmann, *Semantics: An Introduction to the Science of Meaning*, p. 164) are *ear* ('organ of hearing' and 'ear of corn') and *weeds* ('wild, useless plants' and 'mourning garments worn by widow'). In both these cases the etymologies of the two meanings are quite different:

$\left\{\begin{array}{ll}\textit{ear} \text{ ('organ of hearing')} & \text{Old English } \overline{ea}re \\ & \text{(compare Latin } \textit{auris}, \text{ 'ear')} \\ \textit{ear} \text{ ('head of corn')} & \text{Old English } \overline{ea}r \\ & \text{(compare Latin } \textit{acus}, \textit{aceris}, \text{ 'husk')}\end{array}\right.$

$\left\{\begin{array}{ll}\textit{weed} \text{ ('wild useless plant')} & \text{Old English } w\overline{eo}d \text{ 'weed'} \\ \textit{weeds} \text{ ('mourning garments} & \text{Old English } w\overline{ae}d \text{ 'garment'} \\ \text{worn by widow')}\end{array}\right.$

Nevertheless, people often see a metaphorical connection between them, and adjust their understanding of the words accordingly. Thus what from a historical point of view is a homonymy resulting from an accidental convergence of forms, becomes reinterpreted in the context of present-day English as a case of polysemy.

If the account of the lexicon given in this chapter is accepted, then its contribution to the solution of the homonymy-polysemy problem is that it clarifies the meaning of 'psychologically related'. We may, in fact, say that two lexical meanings are 'psychologically related' if a user of the language is able to postulate a connection between them by lexical rules, e.g. by the rule of metaphoric transfer. This definition gains substance from the recognition that lexical rules have psychological reality, to the extent that they are part of the native-speaker's linguistic competence; also, from the recognition that the interpretation of existing lexical entries is as much a function of lexical rules as is the creation of new lexical entries.

An issue that this chapter has not so far clarified, however, is the definition of 'lexical item', i.e. the definition of what a 'word' is as far as the dictionary is concerned. One entity which *has* been precisely defined is the lexical entry, seen as a trio (p, q, r) of specifications morphological (p), syntactic (q), and semantic (r). Two useful ways to define 'lexical item' are:

(1) a bundle of lexical entries sharing the same morphological specification p_1
(2) a bundle of lexical entries sharing the same morphological specification p_1 and the same syntactic specification q_1.

The second definition makes us say that any two lexical entries related by conversion belong to different lexical items (e.g. *face* as noun and *face* as verb), while the first makes us regard these as variants of the same lexical item. Both definitions, on the other hand, bring together within a single lexical item cases of polysemy such as *face* (noun – 'front part of head') and *face* (noun – 'front part of clock'). In deciding where to begin a new headword some dictionary-compilers follow the first definition, and some the second.

The choice between definitions (1) and (2) is simply a matter of terminological convenience – to be pedantic, perhaps one should use a separate term for each (say *lexical item* for definition (1) and *lexeme* for definition (2)). Using either definition, we can explain polysemy happily enough as 'the existence of more than one semantic specification for the same lexical item'; and we can also define homonymy as the existence of more than one morphological specification sharing the same phonological or graphic form. Homonyms such as *mole* 'animal' and *mole* 'excrescence on skin' are then identified as different stems, $Stem_i$ and $Stem_j$, which happen to have the same pronunciation and/or spelling. In this way, some rather traditional ways of looking at words and dictionary entries can be accommodated in, and clarified by, a formal account of the lexicon.

Conclusion

We have seen in this chapter that the 'limited productivity' characteristic of lexical rules is found just as much in semantic transfer as in morphological derivation and syntactic conversion. Thus figurative meanings, far from being excluded from a formal theory of semantics, can be placed within a more general understanding of how lexical rules and lexical definitions operate.

This leads to the recognition of the important point (often overlooked in syntax as well as in semantics) that acceptability and deviation are gradable, not absolute yes-or-no concepts. This does not mean that the earlier accounts of contradictions and other violations of the semantic system (pp. 154–6) have to be revised. Rather, we point out that a sentence which is contradictory or otherwise absurd on one interpretation may *become* sensible through the operation of rules of transfer of meaning: acceptability therefore becomes a question of the ease with which a lexical rule may provide us with an alternative interpretation, if the face-value or literal interpretation is ruled out as a violation. An apparently ridiculous utterance such as *My uncle has recovered from his incurable disease* becomes sane through a semantic transfer which interprets 'incurable', for instance, not as 'that cannot be cured', but as 'that someone thought or claimed could not be cured'. Metaphor, irony, and similar effects cannot be legitimately separated from a formal account of the conceptual and logical structure of meaning.

11. Colour and Kinship: Two Case Studies in 'Universal Semantics'

What do We Mean by Semantic Universals?

One of the recurring speculations of linguistics is: how far is it possible to apply the same semantic analysis to all natural languages? How far, that is, are the rules and categories of meaning, such as we have considered in the past five chapters, characteristics of the human faculty of language, wherever it may manifest itself? It is commonly felt that the 'deeper' one gets into the substructure of language (i.e., the further one abstracts from the physical substance of language towards its conceptual content) the nearer one gets to a common core of linguistic universals.

But debate about universals can easily become confused unless certain distinctions are made. The first distinction is that made by Chomsky (1965: 27–30) between *formal* and *substantive* universals. Formal universals are, roughly, general characteristics or rules of language construction such as must be postulated by anyone who aims to construct a general linguistic theory; substantive universals, on the other hand, are universal characteristics of human language in terms of what units or elements or components a language contains. On the semantic level, we may associate formal universals with 'universal rules of logical structure' and substantive universals with 'universal categories of conceptual content'. Examples of statements postulating each type are:

(a) 'All lexical definitions in all languages are analysable as a set of components.' (*formal*)
(b) 'All languages have the contrast between "animate" and "inanimate".' (*substantive*)

The distinction between the two types of universality is not clear in all details, but it is easy enough to see why the first kind need not presuppose the second. Any serious linguistic theory must put forward some general hypotheses about the nature of human language, otherwise it ceases to have any interest except as an *ad hoc* procedure for analysing this language or that. (Thus, by aspiration at least, the bulk of the statements made in the past five chapters of this book have been statements about the universal character of human language: they would fail in generality if it were discovered that they were inapplicable to some languages.) Belief in formal universals, that is, is usually taken for granted by any theoretically inclined linguist.

On the other hand, a linguistic theory can get on quite well without substantive universals, and may in fact deny their existence. One can postulate some general principles of syntactic structure, for instance, and deny that there is some category 'noun' which is identical in all languages. Similarly for semantic analysis: one can believe in the applicability of componential analysis to all languages, without insisting that all languages make use of a contrast between +MALE and −MALE. Hence most of the discussion and disagreement on this subject centre round substantive universals.

A second distinction, within the category of substantive universals, should be made between a strong and weak interpretation of what 'universal' means. The strong version of a universal hypothesis would say 'all languages have a category x'. But common observation of variation between languages convinces us that in many cases at least, a claim of this strength is false. So with semantic features, as with phonological features, it is natural for a weaker version of a universal hypothesis to be proposed. This claims that 'There exists a universal set of semantic features, of which every language possesses a subset'. Pressed to its furthest extent, this hypothesis is so weak as to be vacuous: it could be satisfied by the limiting case of a purely 'Whorfian' world (p. 31) in which every language possessed its own set of unique features, and in which there was no degree of conceptual identity between languages at all. In practice, such a hypothesis becomes less weak to the extent that we are able to discover that the *same* semantic categories are operating in *different* languages. But the decision to espouse the weak universal hypothesis for semantic features and oppositions is a matter of principle rather than substance at the present stage of our knowledge: it means that categories of meaning can be regarded as 'language-neutral', i.e. as belonging to the common human faculty of language rather than to the ability to speak this language or that. 'Language-neutral hypothesis' might, indeed, be a better term to use for this case than 'universal hypothesis'. I shall nevertheless adhere to the usual practice of referring to both cases as 'universal', distinguishing where necessary between *strong* universality (= 'all languages contain x') and *weak* universality (= 'x is a member of a universal set').

One reason for the tentativeness of discussion of semantic universals is a scarcity of detailed research on the comparison of conceptual systems in different languages. But there are two notable exceptions to this generalization. Much attention has been given to the semantic fields of colour and kinship – two fields that have attracted the analyst's attention both because of their intrinsic interest to anthropologists and others, and because of their relative isolability, as conceptual spheres, from the rest of the language. Rather than give any speculations of my own on semantic universals, therefore, I shall give a brief and simplified account of semantics in these two areas, and from this draw what conclusions I can about the plausibility of a 'universalist' view of meaning.

Colour Terminology: The Hypothesis of Berlin and Kay

In the field of colour terminology, the study by Berlin and Kay *Basic Color Terms* (already discussed in Chapter 3, pp. 28, 32) is based on a comparison of almost a hundred languages. Berlin and Kay's book is remarkable not only for its coverage of data from a wide range of diverse languages, but also for the surprising support it gives to universalism on a terrain previously regarded as a happy hunting-ground for relativist semantics. It has, in the past, seemed almost too easy to show that the systems of colour terminology of different languages differ widely and unpredictably in the way they cut up the 'continuum of colour'. Contrasting colour-charts for such languages as Hanunóo and English (see p. 29) shows this clearly in diagrammatic form. Yet from the unpromising diversity of material from every major part of the world, Berlin and Kay arrive at the bold hypothesis that there is a universal set of exactly eleven colour categories, from which each language takes a subset.

The claim of Berlin and Kay is an unusually precise one: not only do they say there are eleven basic categories ('white', 'black', 'red', 'green', 'yellow', 'blue', 'brown', 'purple', 'pink', 'orange' and 'grey'), but that these categories are ordered (or in strict mathematical terms, partially ordered) as shown:

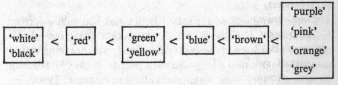

The ordering relation indicated by the symbol < represents 'conditional universality', and is explained as follows: for any two colour categories [x] and [y], [x] < [y] means that if a language contains y, it must also contain x. On this basis, it is possible to set up a small number of major types of colour vocabulary (Type 8 in the table is a category subsuming Berlin and Kay's Types 8–22):

Type	No. of terms	List of Terms	Example of language
1	two	'white', 'black'	Jalé (language of the New Guinea highlands)
2	three	'white', 'black', 'red'	Tiv (Nigeria)
3	four	'white', 'black', 'red', 'green'	Hanunóo (Philippines)
4	four	'white', 'black', 'red', 'yellow'	Ibo (Nigeria)
5	five	'white', 'black', 'red', 'green', 'yellow'	Tzeltal (Mexico)
6	six	'white', 'black', 'red', 'green', 'yellow', 'blue'	Plains Tamil (India)
7	seven	'white', 'black', 'red', 'green', 'yellow', 'blue', 'brown'	Nez Perce (North American Indian)
8	eight, nine, ten, or eleven	'white', 'black', 'red', 'green', 'yellow', 'blue', 'brown', 'purple' and/or 'pink' and/or 'orange' and/or 'grey'	English

The difference between Types 3 and 4, it will be seen, is not a question of the number of terms, but of whether 'green' or 'yellow' is the fourth term added: there is a possibility that either 'green' occurs without 'yellow' or that 'yellow' occurs without 'green', so that no ordering relation can be set up between these two categories. The four colours 'purple', 'pink', 'orange', and 'grey' are unordered for the same reason, and for convenience are placed together in the table.

To the hypothesis so far stated Berlin and Kay add a further 'evolutionary' hypothesis, which states that the types of vocabulary as ordered above represent a fixed sequence of historical stages through which a language must pass as its basic vocabulary increases. (Types 3 and 4 represent alternative stages; Type 8, on the other hand, can be regarded as representing a single final stage of development, as the last four terms 'purple', 'pink', 'orange' and 'grey' tend to get added quickly and in no fixed order.)

To anyone familiar with the apparent arbitrariness and diversity of colour terminologies, their comparative uniformity according to Berlin and Kay may look too good to be true. But Berlin and Kay make it clear that the neatness of this picture depends upon our acceptance of two important assumptions. The first assumption is that it is reasonable to draw a line between 'basic' colour terms and other colour terms of secondary importance. For example, *white*, *red* and *green* are judged basic colour terms in English on such criteria as:

(1) the fact that their range of reference is not included in that of any other colour term (as *scarlet* and *crimson* refer to types of *red*).
(2) the fact that they are not restricted in reference to a small number of objects (as *blonde* is largely restricted to hair).
(3) the fact that the meaning of the whole word is not predictable from the meaning of its parts (as it is in such cases as *blue-green*, *bluish*, *lemon-coloured*).

The second assumption is that since people are able to judge the focus or centre of a colour range more easily and consistently than they can judge its periphery, colour concepts should be identified by the foci rather than the boundaries of their range of reference. Accordingly, in a three-colour system, the terms 'white', 'black' and 'red' will obviously spread themselves over a wider range of hues and intensities of colour than they will within an eleven-term system; but because their foci correspond, it will still be possible to identify them as 'the same category'. One consequence of this interpretation of colour terms is, of course, that many objects that would be labelled by the 'red' term in one language would not be labelled by the 'red' term in another; still less, would the 'red' term in one language be infallibly translated by the 'red' term in another. Nevertheless, the important point is that within this system, colour semantics ceases to be completely arbitrary, and becomes predictable within quite narrow limits. As Berlin and Kay are keen to point out, there are, mathematically speaking, 2,048 possible combinations of eleven categories, whereas only twenty-two types actually occur in their data.

One or two problems arising from the data threaten the orderliness of Berlin and Kay's hypothesis: Russian and Hungarian, for instance, cause embarrassment by seeming to contain twelve basic colour categories. (In Russian, there is no general term for blue, but instead, two terms 'dark blue' and 'light blue'; in Hungarian, a similar situation arises with the category 'red'.) But on the whole, Berlin and Kay make a persuasive case for regarding colour categories as 'weak' universals; that is, for seeing them not as idiosyncrasies of individual languages, but as part of a general conceptual system common to the human race as a whole.

Kinship Semantics: Lounsbury and Goodenough

For those interested in the apparently contrasting semantic systems of different languages and cultures, kinship terminology, even more than colour terminology, has been a centre of interest. The most important contributions in this field have come from scholars with a primary interest in anthropology, such as F. G. Lounsbury and W. H. Goodenough, who were the first to develop the technique of componential analysis (see Chapter 6) to any degree of sophistication. (More recently, Lounsbury has developed a different method of analysis, which we shall not have occasion to discuss in this chapter, involving rules of reduction – see Lounsbury 1964a, 1964b, 1965.)

Like colour terminologies, kinship terminologies have traditionally provided linguistics with scope for the airing of 'relativist' ideas, since the categories of kinship manifestly differ radically from one language or culture to another. But there is also scope for the universalist – we see this from the fact that the 'data' for an analysis of kinship terminology is normally presented in terms of a universal or at least language-neutral set of symbols such as F = 'father', M = 'mother', B = 'brother', S = 'sister', s = 'son', d = 'daughter', H = 'husband', W = 'wife'.

Of course, talking of 'universal kinship categories' begs the question of whether there are *cultural* universals of kinship, that is, whether the cultural realities referred to by kinship terms remain constant from culture to culture. Some anthropologists would deny that they do. The situation is clearly different from that of colour terminology – where we assume a common human perceptual reality, shared by all races and cultures. If we propose semantic universals of kinship, we also, by implication, propose cultural universals. This extra assumption must be borne in mind in the discussion which follows.

The technique (see Goodenough 1956, 1965, 1970; Lounsbury 1956, 1964a) starts with identifying the range of reference of a term by a list of 'denotata', or specific relationships expressed in terms of the above symbols. Thus the range of the term *uncle* in English can be specified as:

FB ('father's brother'), MB ('mother's brother'), FSH ('father's sister's husband') or MSH ('mother's sister's husband').

The task of analysis is then to set up and justify the significant dimensions of contrast and the components of meaning which distinguish the use of one term from that of another. This entails finding common features in each of the denotata of a term (as 'male' 'collateral' and 'one generation above the person from whom the relation is being traced' are features common to the four denotata of *uncle* listed above); so that the disjunctive referential specification of a term (as 'x' OR 'y' OR 'z' . . .) is translated into a componential, *con*junctive listing of features ($a+b+c$).

In English, it is obvious that the dimension of sex (+MALE/ −MALE) is important as a distinguishing factor – it is the sole feature that separates 'uncle' from 'aunt', 'brother' from 'sister' etc. Another opposition of significance for English kinship usage is the distinction between *lineal* kin (related by vertical descent on the family tree) and *collateral* kin (whose connection involves a horizontal link between two siblings on the family tree). Brothers, aunts, nephews, cousins, etc. are all collateral, while fathers, daughters, grandparents, grandchildren, etc. are all lineal.

As an exemplification of the method, I have chosen part of Lounsbury's analysis of the kinship semantics of an American Indian (Iroquois) tribe, the Seneca (Lounsbury, 1964a). Table I gives a part of the data on which Lounsbury bases his analysis: the data given here covers only consanguineal (blood-related) kin within one generation of ego. (Incidentally, we use the terms *ego* and *alter*, according to anthropological convention, to refer respectively to the person from whom the relationship is traced, and the person who is actually referred to in the kinship term. Thus in the phrase *Charlie's aunt*, Charlie is ego, and his aunt is alter.)

It may reassure the reader later if I warn him now that kinship analyses have a mind-teasing quality of mathematical puzzles. The only cure for bafflement is to think hard and hope that the light will dawn!

TABLE I

1. *haʔnih* 'my father'	F; FB; FMSs, FFBs, FMBs, FFSs, FFFBss, etc.	A
2. *noʔyēh* 'my mother'	M; MS; MMSd; MFBd, MMBd, MFSd, MMSdd, etc.	A
3. *hakhnoʔsēh* 'my uncle'	MB; MMSs, MFBs, MMBs, MFSs, MMMSds, etc.	B
4. *ake:hak* 'my aunt'	FS; FMSd, FFBd, FMBd, FFSd; FFFBsd, etc.	B
5. *hahtsiʔ* 'my elder brother'	B; MSs, FBs; MMSds, FFBss, MFBds, FMSss, MMBds, etc. (when older than ego)	C
6. *heʔkē:ʔ* 'my younger brother'	(same, when younger than ego)	C
7. *ahtsiʔ* 'my elder sister'	S; MSd, FBd; MMSdd, FFBsd, MFBdd, FMSsd, MMBdd, etc. (when older than ego)	C
8. *kheʔkē:ʔ* 'my younger sister'	(same, when younger than ego)	C

9. *akyä:ʔseːʔ* 'my cousin'	MBs, FSs; MMSss, FFBds, MFBss, FMSds, MMBss, etc. *also*: MBd, FSd; MMSsd, FFBdd, MFBsd, FMSdd, MMBsd, etc.	}D

10. *heːawak* 'my son'	(a) s; Bs; MSss; FBss; MBss; FSss; MMSdss, etc. *for male ego* (b) s; Ss; MSds, FBds, MBds, FSds; MMSdds, etc. *for female ego*	
11. *kheːawak* 'my daughter'	(a) d; Bd; MSsd, FBsd, MBsd, FSsd; MMSdsd, etc. *for male ego* (b) d; Sd; MSdd, FBdd, MBdd, FSdd; MMSddd, etc. *for female ego*	}E

12. *heyẽːwõːtẽʔ* 'my nephew'	Ss; MSds, FBds, MBds, FSds, MMSdds, etc. *for male ego*	
13. *hehsõʔneh* 'my nephew'	Bs; MSss, FBss, MBss, FSss; MMSdss, etc. *for female ego*	
14. *kheyẽːwõːtẽʔ* 'my niece'	Sd; MSdd, FBdd, MBdd, FSdd, MMSddd, etc. *for male ego*	
15. *khehsõʔneh* 'my niece'	Bd; MSsd, FBsd, MBsd, FSsd, MMSdsd, etc. *for female ego*	}F

The glosses 'father', 'cousin', etc., are not to be mistaken for English translations of the Seneca words: they are no more than roughly corresponding labels, chosen on the grounds that the *nearest* kinsman denoted by the Seneca term would be denoted by that term in English. Like the labels 'black', 'white', etc., for colour categories, they represent merely a useful terminological convention. I shall follow the main steps of Lounsbury's argument, but shall change his presentation (including symbols) where necessary in order to make the analysis easier to follow within the context of this book. The data have already been prejudged by Table I, to the extent that certain groupings, A, B, C, D, E, F have been indicated. The solid horizontal lines, it will be seen, separate different generation groups:

Members of A, B are one generation senior to ego
Members of E, F are one generation junior to ego
Members of C, D are of the same generation as ego.

These features can be symbolized > GENERATION 'senior generation', < GENERATION 'junior generation', and = GENERATION
'same generation' respectively. For example: the definition of (1)
haʔnih 'my father' will contain the feature > GENERATION,
while that of (10) *heːawak* 'my son' will contain the feature
< GENERATION. The distinctions marked by the dotted lines will
be elucidated later: in fact, the main point of the argument that
follows is to show what these distinctions are, and why they are
crucial to the analysis.

If we take the opposition of 'generation' for granted, the next
step in the analysis is to take each generation group separately,
and to try to discover what other distinctions abstractable from
the data are criterial in defining the contrast between one term and
another.

For the separation of terms 1–4 so as to assign each a distinctive
definition, *two* binary contrasts are all that is required. Yet as
Lounsbury points out, at least *three* different possible criteria
present themselves:

(1) We can bracket together *haʔnih* 'father' and *hakhnoʔsēh*
'uncle' in opposition to *noʔyēh* 'mother' and *akeːhak* 'aunt'
on grounds of *sex*.
(2) We can bracket together *haʔnih* 'father' and *akeːhak* 'aunt' in
opposition to *noʔyeh* 'mother' and *hakhnoʔsēh* 'uncle' on
grounds of *side* (i.e. relatives on father's side versus relatives on
mother's side).
(3) We can bracket together *haʔnih* 'father' and *noʔyēh* 'mother'
in opposition to *hakhnoʔsēh* 'uncle' and *akeːhak* 'aunt' on
the grounds that the sex of alter is the same as the sex of the
linking parent of ego in the first two cases, but not in the
second two.

As this third criterion is more difficult to recognize than the other
two, it is worthwhile repeating some of the data from Table I,
italicizing the relevant kin, and showing whether they match or
do not match in sex:

1. *haʔnih* 'father'   F; F B; F M S *s*; F F B *s*; etc. ⎫
2. *noʔyēh* 'mother'   M; M S; M M S *d*; M F B *d*; etc. ⎬ match

3. *hakhno?sĕh* 'uncle' *M B*; *M* M S *s*; *M* F B *s*; etc. ⎫
4. *ake:hak* 'aunt' *F S*; *F* M S *d*; *F* F B *d*; etc. ⎭ do not match

In the case of the simple father and mother relations F and B, the equivalence-of-sex criterion is satisfied vacuously, by the fact that alter and the linking parent are one and the same person. It can be seen that for the first two terms, the sex of the italicized relations is the same, while for the second pair, it is different.

This last criterion, despite its unobviousness, will be shown to be a more significant one than that of side. But to discover this, we first have to consider in some detail the terms for kin of the first generation junior to ego (terms 10 to 15). One striking observation about this group is that terms are defined differently according to the sex of ego. Therefore, let us initially consider the definitions for a male ego (10a, 11a, 12 and 14) in isolation from the terms for a female ego.

Once again, at least three possibilities arise, and we are faced with the problem of which of these three oppositions is redundant. The three criteria pointed out by Lounsbury are:

(1) Distinction on grounds of sex of alter: 10a and 12 are *male*, while 11a and 14 are *female*.
(2) Distinction on grounds of sex of alter's parent: in 10a and 11a *male*, in 12 and 14 *female*.
(3) Distinction on grounds of equivalence or non-equivalence of sex between alter and alter's linking parent: in 10a and 14 they are equivalent, in 11a and 12 they are not.

To check on distinction (2), we examine the sex of the last symbol but one in each formula; to check distinction (3) we examine the sex of both the last symbol and the last symbol but one of each formula, and see whether they match or not.

These three putative oppositions therefore divide up the four terms under consideration as follows:

(1)			(2)			(3)	
10a	11a		10a	12		10a	11a
12	14		11a	14		14	12
'male'	'female'		'male parent'	'female parent'		'same sex'	'different sex'

When we consider the <GENERATION terms for a female ego, the same three possibilities arise, and by inspecting the data and applying these criteria we arrive at the following divisions:

(1)	
10b 13	11b 15
'male'	'female'

(2)	
13 15	10b 11b
'male parent'	'female parent'

(3)	
11b 13	10b 15
'same sex'	'different sex'

However, what is very disappointing about these diagrams is that in two of the three oppositions, the positions of the terms are reversed for the female ego. If we make use of oppositions (2) or (3), we find ourselves claiming that the term (10) *he:awak* 'my son', for example, has one meaning when used by a man, and a totally different, contrastive meaning when used by a woman. Clearly it would be a preferable solution, both for the elegance and the economy of the analysis, if oppositions (2) and (3) could be replaced by another opposition which assigned a single definition to the 'son' and 'daughter' terms (10 and 11) irrespective of the sex of ego. Lounsbury therefore discards these oppositions and proposes a further criterion:

(4) Distinction on grounds of sex equivalence or non-equivalence between ego and alter's linking parent.

To check this, in each formula we compare the sex of ego with the sex of the last symbol but one; in the case of the simple son and daughter relationships, equivalence of sex is satisfied vacuously by the fact that ego and the parent of alter are identical. This criterion provides a unitary definition for 10 and 11, and therefore is a more effective substitute for criteria (2) and (3):

(4)
For Male Ego

10a 11a	12 14
'sex equivalent'	'sex non- equivalent'

(4)
For Female Ego

10b 11b	13 15
'sex equivalent'	'sex non- equivalent'

If, as this analysis indicates, the concept of 'son' and 'daughter' rests on sex equivalence between ego and alter's linking parent, it is quite natural that the reference of these terms should vary according to the sex of ego. It is now possible to define the terms of the generation junior to ego:

10. *he:awak* 'son':   <GENERATION +MALE +EQUISEX
11. *khe:awak* 'daughter':   <GENERATION −MALE +EQUISEX
12. *heyẽ:wõ:tẽʔ* ⎱
13. *hehsõʔneh* ⎰ 'nephew': <GENERATION +MALE −EQUISEX
14. *kheyẽ:wõ:tẽʔ* ⎱
15. *khehsõʔneh* ⎰ 'niece': <GENERATION −MALE −EQUISEX

The dimension of sex equivalence, here symbolized by the features +EQUISEX/−EQUISEX, evidently has considerable similarity to one of the oppositions considered in the definition of >GENERATION terms. Moreover, when we look at the kin of ego's own generation (=GENERATION), we discover the possibility of a similar contrast there. It can be seen from Table I that the four brother-or-sister terms are distinguished from the 'cousin' term *akyä:ʔse:ʔ* by *an equivalence of sex between the linking parent of ego and the linking parent of alter*. For example, FBs is classed as a 'brother', while FSs is classed as a 'cousin'. (In the case of direct siblings, the symbols B and S can be expanded as Fs or Ms, Fd or Md, in which case the linking parent for both offspring is the same person, and so satisfies the criterion of sex equivalence vacuously.) In diagrammatic terms, the oppositions of these five terms can be represented as follows:

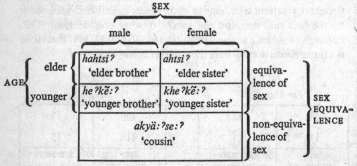

Notice that in the preceding analysis, we came across three contrasts which differ slightly but are all concerned with the equivalence of sex between relatives of the same generation. For senior generation kin, the question to be answered 'yes' or 'no' was: *Is there a sex equivalence between ego's linking parent and alter*? For junior generation kin, the question was the converse of this: *Is there a sex equivalence between ego and alter's linking parent*? And for kin of the same generation of ego, the question was: *Is there a sex equivalence between ego's linking parent and alter's linking parent*? In the conclusion of his analysis, Lounsbury says that these are all instances of the same semantic contrast, so that the analysis can be simplified by using a single componential opposition (which we may now symbolize ±PARALLEL) instead of all three. He justifies this simplification by reference to a principle less familiar to linguists in semantics than in fields such as phonology and morphology: the principle defined by structural linguists as *complementary distribution*. The essence of this principle is that if two or more linguistic elements are (a) similar in form and (b) non-contrastive with one another in function, then in fact they are not different elements at all, but variant instances of the same element. (On these grounds, for example, the phonologically distinct, though similar, endings of *want*ED (/ — id/), *ask*ED (/ — t/) and *amaz*ED (/ — d/) can be brought together as variants of the same morpheme – the point being that only one of these options can occur in a given context.) In the present instance, the criterion of *similarity* is obviously satisfied, in that all these oppositions involve equivalence and non-equivalence of sex; and the criterion of *non-contrastiveness* is satisfied in that the three oppositions apply respectively to >GENERATION, <GENERATION, and =GENERATION kinship terms. Accordingly we now have a single opposition, ±PARALLEL, which applies in all three generation categories, and which may be specified as follows:

+PARALLEL: 'There is equivalence of sex between the two kin of the generation above ego or alter (whichever of those is junior)'

−PARALLEL: (The negative of the above)

The ±PARALLEL opposition now replaces that of ±EQUISEX

used above for junior generation terms. (The choice of label reflects the anthropological distinction between 'parallel cousins' and 'cross cousins'.)

Referring back to Table I, we may now see that the broken horizontal lines separating classes A from B, C from D, and E from F, in fact correspond to the +PARALLEL/−PARALLEL distinction. For =GENERATION terms, there is a further opposition of seniority, which may be represented ±SENIOR; and to separate the field of kinship as a whole from other fields of meaning, the feature KIN may be included. With these additions, the componential definitions of terms 1–15 finally run as follows:

1. *haʔnih* 'my father'   KIN >GENERATION +PARALLEL +MALE

2. *noʔyěh* 'my mother'   KIN >GENERATION +PARALLEL −MALE

3. *hakhnoʔsěh* 'my uncle'   KIN >GENERATION −PARALLEL +MALE

4. *ake:hak* 'my aunt'   KIN >GENERATION −PARALLEL −MALE

5. *hahtsiʔ* 'my elder brother'   KIN =GENERATION +PARALLEL +MALE +SENIOR

6. *heʔkě:ʔ* 'my younger brother'   KIN =GENERATION +PARALLEL +MALE −SENIOR

7. *ahtsiʔ* 'my elder sister'   KIN =GENERATION +PARALLEL −MALE +SENIOR

8. *kheʔkě:*, 'my younger sister'   KIN =GENERATION +PARALLEL −MALE −SENIOR

9. *akyä:ʔse:ʔ* 'my cousin'   KIN =GENERATION −PARALLEL

10. *he:awak* 'my son'   KIN <GENERATION +PARALLEL +MALE

11. *khe:awak* 'my daughter'   KIN <GENERATION +PARALLEL −MALE

12. *heyě:wõ:těʔ* 'my nephew'   KIN <GENERATION −PARALLEL +MALE

13. *hehsõʔněh* 'my nephew'   KIN <GENERATION −PARALLEL +MALE

14. *kheyěwõ:těʔ* 'my niece'   KIN <GENERATION −PARALLEL −MALE

15. *khehsõ ʔneh* 'my niece'   KIN <GENERATION −PARALLEL −MALE

Further extensions and refinements of this analysis are discussed by Lounsbury; but this brief and simplified sketch has, I hope, illustrated the application of the technique of componential analysis to kinship sufficiently to show how the choice of significant components may be strictly governed by consideration of economy and the maximum generalization of contrasts.

Componential analysis, so considered, is a technique for analysing the kinship semantics of each language in its own terms, without any prior assumptions about a universal set of potential components of kinship. The only prior assumptions are to be found in the data of analysis, the so-called 'denotata'. The fact that the data for each language can be expressed in terms of the elemental family relationships of the 'nuclear family' (F, M, B, S, d, s, H, W) in itself suggests a universal or language-neutral conceptualization of basic kinship relations, even though anthropologists may disagree as to the precise significance of these universal categories, and even though the cultural interpretation of the categories varies from one language to another. Therefore kinship semantics seems to split into two levels – the universal level and the culturally relative level – and componential analysis may be seen as a mediation process between these two.

A Predicational-Componential Analysis of Kinship Semantics

By this time the reader may well be wondering what has happened to the system of predication analysis expounded in Chapter 7. One of the chief reasons for the postulation of predication analysis was the need to account for relational structures in meaning, as opposed to purely classificatory structure. That kinship terms involve relational structures is obvious: any expression like *Bill's mother* expresses a relation between two people, identified by the generalized labels *ego* and *alter*. Therefore why not try treating relationships *as* relationships, instead of reducing them to taxonomic classes? Predicational semantics should be well adapted to the analysis of kinship terms.

I propose to present now an analysis of English kinship semantics in terms of predicational as well as componential analysis, to show how the system outlined in Chapters 6 and 7 can be applied to this purpose. My goals will be (a) to show how certain advantages arise from using the predicational method, and (b) to explore, within a different framework of analysis, the need for analysing kinship meanings simultaneously on more than one level.

A fair amount of progress can be made towards a componential-predicational analysis of kinship by simply using the two oppositions of sex and parenthood:

$$\left\{ \begin{array}{l} +\text{MALE 'male'} \\ -\text{MALE 'female'} \end{array} \right. \qquad \left\{ \begin{array}{l} \rightarrow\text{PARENT 'is parent of'} \\ \leftarrow\text{PARENT 'is child of'} \end{array} \right.$$

We see that the second opposition is a relative opposition (p. 110) because of the converse relation between 'parent' and 'child':

John is a parent of Joe is synonymous with *Joe is a child of John.*

This converse relation of parenthood underlies all relations of reciprocality between sets of kinship terms (as *uncle* and *aunt*, for example, are reciprocal to *nephew* and *niece*).

On the predicational level, all kinship relations are represented as downgraded predications (pp. 149–54) within a single argument. Thus the meaning of the expression *The boy's mother* can be rendered by the left-hand diagram:

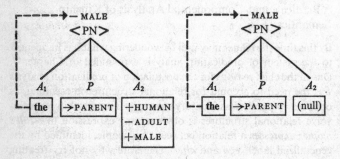

The definition of the word *mother* by itself can be represented in the same way, except that there the second argument (denoting ego) is null. This is indicated in the right-hand diagram above, or by the more concise notation of pp. 207–8 as:

mother: −MALE ⟨**the**. →PARENT.∅⟩
        'female (who is) parent of . . .'

As we noted in Chapter 10 (p. 208), a term like *grandfather*, the meaning of which includes a chain of two parental relationships, can be defined by means of one downgraded predication within another:

> *grandfather*: +MALE ⟨**the**. →PARENT.∅ ⟨**the**. →PARENT.∅⟩⟩
> 'male (who is) parent of (someone who is) parent of...'

As such downgrading structure is general to all kinship terms and therefore completely predictable for a given definition, we can adopt an even more simplified notation in which the brackets and the feature of definiteness are omitted. What is more, even the null feature symbol '∅' can be omitted as predictable, because no English kinship term contains any specification of the sex of ego or of linking kin. With all these omissions, the above definition of *grandfather* is reduced to a skeletal form as follows:

> +MALE. →PARENT.. →PARENT.

It is consequently possible to define a whole set of English kinship terms fairly simply as follows (*Note*: The two points '..' signal a null argument (except for the presence of the downgraded predication) – i.e. an unspecified linking kinsman):

father:	+MALE. →PARENT.
mother:	−MALE. →PARENT.
son:	+MALE. ←PARENT.
daughter:	−MALE. ←PARENT.
grandfather:	+MALE. →PARENT.. →PARENT.
grandmother:	−MALE. →PARENT.. →PARENT.
grandson:	+MALE. ←PARENT.. ←PARENT.
granddaughter:	−MALE. ←PARENT.. ←PARENT.
great grandfather:	+MALE. →PARENT.. →PARENT.. →PARENT.
(etc.)	

Having observed that the oppositions of 'sex' and 'parenthood' account without difficulty for the definition of lineal kin terms, let us now see if these two oppositions can provide definitions of collateral kin:

brother: +MALE.←PARENT..→PARENT.
sister: −MALE.←PARENT..→PARENT.
uncle: +MALE.←PARENT..→PARENT..→PARENT.
aunt: −MALE.←PARENT..→PARENT..→PARENT.
nephew: +MALE.←PARENT..←PARENT..→PARENT.
great niece: −MALE.←PARENT..←PARENT..←PARENT.
                                          .←PARENT.

On the face of it, these seem to be adequate definitions; for example, the definition of *brother* is spelt out as:

'male child of parent of . . .'

But the alert reader will notice that this definition errs in making the claim that every male person is his own brother. If President Nixon's brothers, for instance, are all those people who are male children of President Nixon's parents, then President Nixon must be his own brother. Putting it more technically, this definition wrongly makes out the 'sibling' ('brother-or-sister') relationship to be reflexive (p. 113). Notice, too, that all the other definitions of collateral kin above have a parallel flaw: according to the definitions of *uncle* and *aunt*, one's father is also one's uncle, and one's mother is also one's aunt.

Sadly, we must conclude that to account for collateral kin terms within a system of componential-plus-predicational analysis, it is necessary to bring into play a further semantic primitive, namely the relation of 'siblinghood'. This is represented with a double-headed arrow, because siblinghood, though irreflexive, is symmetric (p. 112); that is '*x* is a sibling of *y*' entails '*y* is a sibling of *x*'. Now *brother*, *sister*, etc. are redefined:

brother: +MALE.↔SIBLING.   'male sibling of . . .'

sister: −MALE.↔SIBLING.   'female sibling of . . .'

uncle: +MALE.↔SIBLING..→PARENT.   'male sibling of parent of . . .'

aunt: −MALE.↔SIBLING..→PARENT.   'female sibling of parent of . . .'

nephew: +MALE.← PARENT..↔SIBLING.　　　　'male child of
　　　　　　　　　　　　　　　　　　　　　sibling of . . .'
great niece:−MALE.← PARENT..← PARENT..↔SIBLING.'female child
　　　　　　　　　　　　　　　　　　　　　of child of
　　　　　　　　　　　　　　　　　　　　　sibling of . . .'

So long as the 'sibling' relation is defined as irreflexive, as well as
symmetric, this analysis gets round the problem of defining siblings
so as to exclude ego. But the relation ↔SIBLING is not really a
new semantic primitive at all, for its significance can be derived
from the already used opposition 'parenthood'. To explain what
sibling means, we need only say that 'siblings are two *different*
people who share the same parent(s)'. A formulaic version of this
statement is as follows:

Rule of implication (*A*)

'x.← PARENT..→ PARENT.y' entails 'x.↔ SIBLING.y' where $x \neq y$.

i.e. 'x is the child of the parent(s) of y' entails 'x is the sibling of y'
(so long as x is not identical to y).

   This special 'rule of implication' (a notion to be more fully explained in Chapter 12) defines the 'derived' relation of siblinghood in terms of the more basic relation of parenthood.

   As we have just seen, with the help of the 'sibling' relation,
more remote collateral relations, such as *uncle*, can also be represented. The same applies to relatives of more than one degree
of collaterality, that is to those who are denoted by the blanket term
cousin in its wide sense:

First cousin:　　　← PARENT..↔SIBLING..→ PARENT.
Second cousin:
　　　← PARENT..← PARENT..↔SIBLING..→ PARENT..→ PARENT
Third cousin: .← PARENT
..← PARENT..← PARENT..↔SIBLING..→ PARENT..→ PARENT
　　　　　　　　　　　　　　　　　　　　..→ PARENT

(etc.)

Although I do not wish to challenge the efficacy of a purely componential analysis on the lines of Lounsbury and Goodenough
for the limited purpose of analysing and classifying kinship terminologies, the analysis using both components and predication
structures has certain advantages which are not to be ignored, as

well as showing how kinship semantics can be integrated within a general theory of meaning.

Firstly, it correctly represents converse (p. 111) relations between kinship terms (e.g. between *parent* and *child*, between *grandparent* and *grandchild*, between *uncle-or-aunt* and *nephew-or-niece*, etc.). These converse relations are exhibited through the mirror-image relation of one formula to another. Thus, barring the feature of sex, which is variable, the formulae for *uncle* and *aunt* read from left to right are the same as the formulae for *nephew* and *niece* read from right to left.

Secondly, it correctly represents symmetric or mutual kinship relations, such as that between sibling and sibling, and that between cousin and cousin. These symmetric relations are shown by symmetrical formulae – i.e., formulae which read the same from left to right as from right to left.

Thirdly, it correctly indicates how more indirect kinship relations can be decomposed into a combination of more direct ones. For example, the following circumlocutions identify relations we would place in the category 'niece', and this is shown by the fact that the specifications of their meaning are subsumed in the definition of niece (i.e. are the same as the 'niece' formula except that they contain extra features):

brother's daughter: —MALE. ← PARENT . +MALE.↔SIBLING.
sister's daughter: —MALE. ← PARENT . —MALE.↔SIBLING.
niece: —MALE. ← PARENT. .↔SIBLING.

Similarly, one could show that all the following refer to first cousins of Malcolm:

Malcolm's uncle's son   *Malcolm's father's sister's daughter*
Malcolm's mother's nephew *Malcolm's mother's brother's daughter*
                etc.

It would not be difficult to show how this sort of analysis can be used to explain a large number of entailments, inconsistencies, tautologies, and contradictions – in short, a large number of basic statements (see p. 84) – which a semantic analysis, within the present conception, ought to be able to account for. (The ability to account for these basic statements is, indeed, what I mean when I

say above that the analysis 'correctly' represents certain facts.)
Here are examples of basic statements derivable from the
analysis, and illustrating the three advantages I itemized above:

'Bill is Jake's father' is synonymous with 'Jake is Bill's son'.
      (converseness of 'parent'/'child' relation)
'Bill is Kate's cousin' is synonymous with 'Kate is Bill's cousin.'
      (symmetry of 'cousin' relation)
'Susan is Mrs Brown's daughter's daughter' entails 'Susan is Mrs
Brown's granddaughter.'
      (decomposition of *granddaughter* into *daughter's daughter*)

But for a fuller analysis of English kinship usage, one would need
to grapple with further problems. Consider, for example, the above
definition of *uncle* as +MALE.↔SIBLING..→PARENT. This
deals only with blood-related uncles (FB, MB) and leaves out of
consideration uncles related through marriage (FSH, MSH). For
a fuller definition of *uncle*, therefore, one would have to
introduce an optional marriage link:

   uncle: +MALE[.↔MARRY.].↔SIBLING..→PARENT.

(the square brackets indicate optionality)
Even this is not an entirely adequate definition, since – as Goodenough points out in his study of Yankee kinship terminology
(Goodenough 1965) – not everyone who marries an aunt is regarded as an uncle.

   Consider also the terms *ancestor* and *descendant*. The system of
analysis given so far would not be able to yield unitary definitions
of these terms. Instead, the meaning of *descendant* would have to
be presented rather as an indefinitely large set of definitions like
this:

.←PARENT..←PARENT.   'grandchild' or
.←PARENT..←PARENT..←PARENT. 'great grandchild' or
.←PARENT..←PARENT..←PARENT. 'great great grandchild'
 (etc.)   ←PARENT. or . . . (etc.)

Ancestor would have to be defined similarly, as the converse of
descendant. But this multiple, open-ended specification of the
meaning of a single word runs counter to the principle, taken for

granted in the last chapter, that a definition should be a single specification consisting of a finite number of features (p. 192). We would like to show that 'grandchild', 'great grandchild', etc. are hyponyms of 'descendant', and yet avoid the recursive listing which was given above as a makeshift definition for *descendant*. One reason why this recursive definition is unsuitable is that it suggests that *descendant* is infinitely ambiguous, and that in one sense it is a synonym with *grandchild*, in another sense it is a synonym with *great grandchild*, and so on indefinitely. So to avoid making this absurd claim, let us formulate another rule of implication like that which introduced the 'sibling' relation:

Rule of implication (B):

(i) '$x. \rightarrow$ PARENT.y' entails '$x. \rightarrow$ LINEAL   .y'
                                        1 GENERATION
(ii) '$x. \rightarrow$ LINEAL   ..$\rightarrow$ PARENT.y' entails '$x. \rightarrow$ LINEAL   .y'
      i GENERATION $i+1$ GENERATION

i.e. (i) One's parent is one's first-generation ancestor, and
   (ii) One's parent's ith generation ancestor is one's own $i+1$th-generation ancestor
      (where i is any positive whole number)

The effect of this two-part rule is to derive from the relation of 'parenthood' two new semantic oppositions: the relative opposition of 'lineal descent' ($\rightarrow$LINEAL/$\leftarrow$LINEAL) and the hierarchic opposition of 'generation' (1 GENERATION/2 GENERATION/... etc.). One result of the rule is that for terms such as *father*, *grandfather*, etc. there are two different but (largely) equivalent definitions:

+MALE.$\rightarrow$ PARENT..$\rightarrow$ PARENT.$=$ +MALE.$\rightarrow$ LINEAL   'grand-
                                        2 GENERATION   father'
'male parent of parent of' $=$ 'male second-generation ancestor'

Such definitions do not represent an ambiguity, but rather alternative conceptualizations of the same content (see p. 257 below).

Another effect of this rule is the desired one of providing single definitions of *ancestor* and *descendant*, in such a way as to show 'grandfather', etc., to be hyponyms of 'ancestor', and to show 'grandson', etc., to be hyponyms of 'descendant'. In fact, the definition of *ancestor* seems to vary somewhat from speaker to speaker. Some people would feel that an ancestor should at least be of the male sex (and therefore distinct from an ancestress); others feel that a person must at least be dead, before he can qualify for this exalted station. So two possible definitions are:

$$ancestor: \begin{cases} +\text{MALE}. \rightarrow \text{LINEAL.} \\ -\text{LIVE}. \rightarrow \text{LINEAL.} \end{cases}$$

It goes without saying that Rule (B) can be read not only from left to right, but (according to the mirror-image convention) from right to left. Thus is also provides us with a unitary definition of *descendant*:. ←LINEAL.

If the sole purpose of Rule (B) were to permit unitary definitions of two relatively infrequent words of the English language, *ancestor* and *descendant*, its importance might not seem sufficient to merit the costliness of a special rule. But rule (B) is also necessary for the provision of a unitary definition of *cousin* (in its wider sense of any distant relation, viz. any relative remote by more than one degree of collaterality). All these, for example, are types of cousin:

(a) . ←PARENT..↔SIBLING..→PARENT   'first cousin'
     'child of sibling of parent of . . .'

(b) $\begin{cases} . \leftarrow \text{PARENT}..\leftarrow\text{PARENT}..\leftrightarrow\text{SIBLING}..\rightarrow\text{PARENT.} \\ . \leftarrow \text{PARENT}..\leftrightarrow\text{SIBLING}..\rightarrow\text{PARENT}..\rightarrow\text{PARENT.} \end{cases}$ 'first cousin once

                                                                     removed'

(c) . ←PARENT..←PARENT..↔SIBLING..→PARENT..→PARENT.
                                              'second cousin'

    (etc.)

But all these, and other types, can, thanks to Rule (B), be subsumed in the single formula: . ←LINEAL.↔SIBLING . →LINEAL.

But there is still one outstanding problem with cousins, and that is to explain the use of ordinal numbers like *second* and *third* when prefixed to cousin, and also to explain expressions like *once removed*, *twice removed*, etc. The former of these linguistic devices measures degrees of collaterality beyond two (i.e. the minimum number of generations one has to climb the family tree in order to reach a common ancestor). The latter device (of 'remove') counts the distance in generation between ego and alter – and here it might be noted that *cousin* is the only term that can apply equally to kinsmen senior and junior to ego in terms of generation. The difficulty is that even with the revised definition of *cousin*, using the →LINEAL/←LINEAL relationship, there is no unitary definition for (say) *cousin once removed* or *second cousin*: these terms represent intersecting variables which may range over a whole potentially infinite set of kinship relations. The only way to obtain unitary definitions of these terms is, it appears, to set up a further rule of implication:

Rule of implication (C):

'x. ← LINEAL   ..↔ SIBLING..← LINEAL   .y' entails
    i GENERATION j GENERATION

                                            'x. ↔ COUSIN   .y'
                                                m DISTANCE
                                                n REMOVE

(i.e. 'One's *i*th-generation ancestor's sibling's *j*th-generation descendant' is 'one's *m*th cousin *n*-times removed')
Conditions: *m* is the lesser of *i* and *j*; *n* is the difference between *i* and *j*.

Rule (C) introduces two further hierarchic oppositions, that of 'distance' (expressed by the ordinal number in phrases like *2nd cousin*, *3rd cousin*) and that of 'remove' (expressed by phrases like *once removed*, *twice removed*). By means of rule (C), the definitions of cousins (a), (b) and (c) above are reinterpreted as follows:

(a) .↔COUSIN.   (b) .↔COUSIN.   (c) .↔COUSIN.
   1DISTANCE   1DISTANCE   2DISTANCE
   0REMOVE   1REMOVE   0REMOVE

For (a) and (b), the difference between *i*GENERATION and *j*GENERATION is zero, and this means that although the feature 0REMOVE is recorded in the formula because of its contrastive value in opposition to 1REMOVE, etc., the dimension of remove does not get expressed: (a) and (c) are lexically realized simply as *first cousin* and *second cousin*.

Speakers of English tend to be vague nowadays about the precise meaning of such terms as *second cousin once removed*; but the definitions above accord with English dictionaries. The significant point is that we now are able to provide one single definition for an expression like *cousin once removed* $\left\{ \begin{array}{l} .\text{↔COUSIN.} \\ \text{1REMOVE} \end{array} \right\}$ where previously an indefinitely large set of definitions would have been necessary.

The final problem that arises is how to define the notion of 'kinship' itself. A first approximation to a specification of the general relation 'is kin to' would be: .←LINEAL..→LINEAL. (i.e. 'is a descendant of one's ancestor'). But this definition has the same kind of flaw as the definition of *sibling* as .←PARENT..→PARENT.: namely, it treats the irreflexive relation of kinship as if it were a reflexive relation, and so implies that I am my own kinsman. Therefore we require yet one further rule, parallel to Rule (A), to make clear that for *x* to be kin to *y*, *x* must be distinct from *y*:

Rule of implication (D):

'*x*.←LINEAL..→LINEAL.*y*' entails '*x*.↔KIN.*y*' (where *x* ≠ *y*) i.e. '*x* is a descendant of an ancestor of *y*' entails '*x* is kin to *y*' (where *x* ≠ *y*).

The rules just given (Rules of Implication (A) – (D)), bring a new dimension to semantic analysis, because they introduce the possibility of a *single meaning* (like 'first cousin') being specified in a variety of *different ways*.

(p) .←PARENT..↔SIBLING..→PARENT.
(q) .←LINEAL ..   ↔SIBLING..→LINEAL.
    1GENERATION   1GENERATION
(r) .↔COUSIN
    1DISTANCE
    0REMOVE

All these are definitions of (*first*) *cousin*.

Notice, however, that these definitions indicate not a triple ambiguity, but a single content which is capable of being conceptualized in three different ways. We can see a kinship bond either in terms of individual parent and sibling relations (the atomic relations which make up the 'nuclear' family unit), or we can see it in terms of mathematical coordinates on the broad expanses of a family tree – or we can see it from a combination of these points of view. Thus kinship may be regarded not as a single conceptual domain, but rather as a field in which different conceptual domains (different conceptualizations of the same content) overlap. Rules of implication such as Rules (A) – (D) seem to match up to psychological reality, in that the shortest formula (in terms of number of features) appears to represent the kind of conceptualization most appropriate to a given relationship. Thus the simplest definition of *nephew* (+MALE. ←PARENT.. ←SIBLING.) is also the one which accords best with one's intuitive feeling of what such a relationship is – manifested in contrast to the more cumbersome definition bringing in the question of ancestry:

+MALE.. ←LINEAL   ..←→SIBLING.
  1GENERATION

The concept of 'first cousin' can be represented equally simply in two ways (as we see from definitions (p) and (r) above), and this seems to reflect its ambivalence as a relationship which can either be regarded as the nearest representative of cousinship, or the remotest representative of that intermediate family orbit which includes grandparents, uncles, aunts, nephews and nieces. It is at the intersection of two major kinship fields.

Rules (A) to (D) above relate a detailed, atomic view of kinship by stages to a general, abstract view. The overlapping domains can be imagined as microscopes pointed at the same object, one focusing on a narrow-range with stronger magnification, another focusing on a wider range with weaker magnification.

Rules of implication

Rules of implication (or, as one might prefer to call them, 'semantic transformations') are needed for certain areas of meaning, such as kinship, where otherwise it would be impossible to provide a unitary, finite definition for a particular meaning. These rules are posited with reluctance, as they destroy the one-to-one relation of formulae to meanings which we should otherwise wish to preserve. But there seem to be many areas of lexical meaning where alternative conceptualizations are possible, and where therefore special rules of implication have to be set up. Apart from kinship, a simpler example of such semantic overlap is the relation between the two polarities 'warm'/'cool' and 'hot'/'cold'. Clearly the second opposition covers approximately the same area of meaning as the first, except that it represents a contrast of greater intensity. To convey this relationship between the two oppositions, special rules of implication would be required to explain such facts as the approximate synonymy of *The weather is hot* and *The weather is very warm*, also of *The weather is slightly hot* and *The weather is warm*. There is a similar overlap between the polarities 'like'/'dislike' and 'love'/'hate'.

Bi-directional rules of implication are, of course, rules of synonymy; and it might be asked whether Rules (A) – (D), and other rules of the same kind, would not best be formulated bi-directionally. My own mind is open on this matter, as I have yet to find enough convincing evidence in favour of one solution rather than another. There is one consideration which has led me to formulate these rules as unidirectional entailments in this chapter, but this consideration cannot be explained until we deal with the problem of the universality of kinship concepts – a subject to which we now return.

Kinship and semantic universals

The preceding componential-predicational analysis of English kinship semantics is like the purely componential analysis of Lounsbury's Senecan analysis in one respect: it can be seen as providing a bridge between the culturally very general, if not universal, categories of sex and parenthood involved in the 'nuclear family', and the culturally-relative factors of kinship classification which determine how generation seniority, collaterality, consanguinity, and other abstract variables of that kind are handled by a particular language. It is tempting to see the two oppositions of +MALE/−MALE and →PARENT/←PARENT with which we started the second analysis as strong universals, i.e. as semantic contrasts present in every language. But all such plausible generalizations seem to fall foul of counter-instances in anthropological literature.

Goodenough (1970: 4–38) reports a number of cultures (e.g. the Nayar castes of South India) in which the nuclear family of parents and children has no place: and Lounsbury (1969) rehearses cases of cultures where biologically one or the other parent is held to have an incidental part only in procreation. Therefore the abstraction 'parenthood' subsuming motherhood and fatherhood is at best only a near-universal (in the strong sense) of kinship semantics.

This brings us up against another anthropological debating point: how far should kinship relations be defined in terms of the biological primes of sex and procreation? How far, on the other hand, can they be regarded as purely social institutions? The analysis of English kinship usage given in this chapter provides for both 'biological' and 'social' views, if we identify the basic oppositions of 'sex' and 'parenthood' as biologically founded, and the derived relations of siblinghood, ancestry, and cousinship as definable in terms of rights, duties and other social rather than biological correlates. The rules of implication, then, have the effect of deriving the socially institutionalized superstructure of kinship from a core of biologically founded relations. It is appropriate that these rules should be formulated as uni-directional, rather than bidirectional entailments, to allow for cases where kinship relations exist in social terms (e.g. through adoption) without any underlying biological relation.

The rules of implication, so considered, become the means for stating differences between conceptualizations of kinship in different languages. For example, the 'parallel'/'cross' opposition in Seneca kinship terminology would have to be instituted through a rule roughly as follows:

Rule of implication (E):

(a) 'x .← LINEAL   ..→ LINEAL   . y'   entails
    α MALE γ GENERATION γ GENERATION α MALE
                                                                    'x.↔PEER   .y'
                                                                    +PARALLEL

(b) 'x .← LINEAL   ..→ LINEAL   . y'   entails
    α MALE γ GENERATION γ GENERATION β MALE
                                                                    'x.↔PEER   .y'
                                                                    −PARALLEL.

(where x may be identical to y)

Here use is made of a widely employed convention in linguistics: The Greek symbols α and β indicate variables ranging over the terms of an opposition. Thus αMALE ... αMALE represents matching features of sex; while αMALE ... βMALE indicates nonmatching features. γGENERATION ... γGENERATION symbolizes a matching number of generations. The rule defines the notion of 'generation-peer' which is as crucial to the Senecan system as 'sibling' is to the English system. Specimen definitions run as follows:

1. *haʔnih* 'my father'   +MALE.↔PEER   ..→PARENT.
                           +PARALLEL
5. *khehsõ͂ʔneh* 'my niece' −MALE.←PARENT..↔PEER   .−MALE
   (female ego)   −PARALLEL
9. *akyä:ʔse:ʔ* 'my cousin' .←PARENT..↔PEER   .→PARENT.
                             −PARALLEL

Two comments on the interpretation of these definitions:

(a) The ↔PEER relation is reflexive as well as symmetric, so *haʔnih* as defined above includes one's father in the narrow sense of 'male parent'.

(b) Recalling that the above, like all the preceding definitions of kinship terms, are simplified renderings of downgraded predications, we may define each 'elder sibling' or 'younger sibling' term by two separate downgraded predications: one relating ego to alter as regards kinship, and one relating them in terms of relative age. This overcomes what would be a problem if we tried to compress all of the meaning into one downgraded predication: how to get the 'older than'/'younger than' relation to stretch directly between ego and alter, while the 'sibling' relation links them only indirectly. Thus the meaning of *ahtsiʔ* 'elder sister' will be specified by three separate features, of which two are downgraded predications:

−MALE	(where X = 'who is child of parallel peer of
$\langle X \rangle$	parent of ego')
$\langle Y \rangle$	(where Y = 'who is older than ego')

We may assume that some of the derived relations introduced by implication rules (such as the 'sibling' rule Rule (A)) are widely applicable to different languages, and therefore that they can be treated as 'weak universals' in the sense of being language-neutral. Work by Lounsbury using his 'reduction rules' which are somewhat similar to the present rules of implication invites the conclusion that such rules are independent of given languages and cultures, and may form the basis for a general system of classification for kinship terminologies (Lounsbury 1964a, 1964b, 1965).

In comparison with colour-terminology, the cases for universals in kinship terminology is complicated by the cultural rather than physical or perceptual nature of the phenomenon studied. Relativists who are unconvinced by the analyses of anthropologists such as Lounsbury and Goodenough are unlikely to be any more convinced by the guardedly universalist speculations I have offered. There is room for disagreement even on so fundamental an issue as where the term 'kinship' refers to anything that can be characterized in a culturally neutral way. None the less, those that are philosophically inclined to the universalist position will find that an assumption of weak universals enables them to see a common basis in obviously similar conceptualizations of kinship that arise in geographically and linguistically diverse environments.

Conclusion

After observing Chomsky's distinction between formal and substantive universals, we have seen that the second of these categories demands a further subdivision into 'strong universals' (characteristics common to every language) and 'weak universals' (characteristics belonging to a universal set from which each language takes a subset).

An instance of a 'weak universal' hypothesis is Berlin and Kay's hypothesis that there are eleven basic colour categories, which are conditionally ordered such that the presence of one category depends on the presence of certain other categories. 'Weak' is, however, an unfortunate description of this hypothesis, since it makes strong predictions as to what is and what is not a possible set of basic colour categories for any human language. In kinship terminology, too, there are good (though not uncontested) arguments for taking up a weak universalist position.

The rules of implication introduced in this chapter form a bridge between the universal and culturally relative aspects of kinship semantics. But such rules have important applications outside the field of kinship, and it is to a more detailed study of them that we shall turn in Chapter 12.

12. Semantic Equivalence and 'Deep Semantics'

Much earlier we made the assumption (p. 97) that conceptual equivalence, or synonymy, could be shown directly by a system of semantic representation, such that whenever two or more expressions were synonymous, they could be shown to have the same semantic representation. But this assumption proved to be too strong when, in the last chapter, it was found necessary to set up special rules to account for the semantic equivalence of one semantic representation to another. The introduction of these rules at that point may have seemed somewhat arbitrary – an improvised *deus ex machina* to get the semanticist out of difficult analytic problems in connection with kinship semantics. It will now be my aim to say more explicitly why we need such rules. I shall give a number of instances of implication rules, and will then speculate upon whether these rules provide evidence for a level of 'deep semantics' (p. 280) – a level of linguistic organization even more remote from the phonetic substance of language than is the level of semantic representation as so far considered. This exploration will eventually lead me to reinterpret rules of implication as 'semantic transformations'.

To clarify matters, let us begin with one or two definitions:

1. *A Rule of Implication* is a rule which specifies that for a given semantic formula it is possible to substitute another semantic formula. This means in effect that for any rule of implication A → B, the logical consequences derivable from the formula B are also applicable to any sentence expressing formula A. As in the last chapter, we consider such rules to be in theory unidirectional substitutions, although in practice, most of the rules dealt with in this chapter are bi-directional, and can therefore be more fittingly formulated as 'A ↔ B' rather than 'A → B'. But this is an issue to which we return later.

2. *A Substantive Rule of Implication* is a rule of implication which makes mention of specific features (such as ←PARENT and ↔SIBLING).

3. *A Formal Rule of Implication* is one which makes no reference to specific semantic features, but rather states the equivalence of one generalized semantic tree-structure to another.

The distinction between substantive and formal rules of implication parallels Chomsky's distinction between substantive and formal universals (p. 232). Whereas the rules of the last chapter were substantive rules, dealing with particular concepts such as 'siblinghood' and 'ancestry', the rules to be dealt with in this chapter will chiefly be formal.

To conclude these introductory remarks, a word of caution: this chapter is highly tentative, dealing with a subject which to my knowledge is virtually unexplored territory as far as present-day linguistic semantics is concerned. The reader who finds the arguments to be given for 'deep semantics' unsatisfactory can, if he wishes, dismiss 'deep semantics' as a figment of my imagination.

Why Rules of Implication are Needed

The motives which lead us to establish rules of semantic equivalence are the same as those which lead us to any hypothesis in semantic analysis. These are:

> Firstly, the need to extend the semantic accountability of a theory, by showing how it is possible to deduce the logical consequences of an analysis (i.e. implications, inconsistencies, contradictions, tautologies, etc.) from the form of the semantic representation that that analysis assigns to utterances.
>
> Secondly, the need to preserve a general set of mapping procedures between semantic and syntactic structure (see pp. 184–8).

These principles may, of course, conflict; but in general, we try to preserve whatever generalizations can be made in both spheres.

It was the interaction of these two principles that led to the positing of Rules of Implication (A) to (D) in the last chapter: it was found that certain kinship meanings could be correctly represented (in terms of their logical consequences, as always) only at the cost of abandoning the key postulate that a definition of a word can be specified by a single finite set of semantic features. That is, there was seen to be a conflict between two postulates that had up to that time been treated as inviolable: the postulate of componential definition (pp. 11, 96) and the postulate of total accountability for basic statements (p. 84). In order to keep both of these intact, it was necessary to violate another postulate which had until then been tacitly adhered to: that there is a unique semantic representation for each meaning of a sentence. Why should this postulate have been considered more vulnerable than the other two? The answer must be that rules of implication are needed anyway: that far from being makeshift devices, they enable us to make generalizations about diverse phenomena which would otherwise have to be dealt with separately in an *ad hoc* way. The explanation of this answer, that is, is a positive demonstration that rules of implication are a valuable addition to semantic theory, and this is the task to which I now address myself.

The Rule of Subordination

The need for the *rule of subordination*, the first formal rule of implication to be considered, has already been anticipated in two previous chapters (pp. 153, 174). This is the rule that equates two semantic representations as follows:

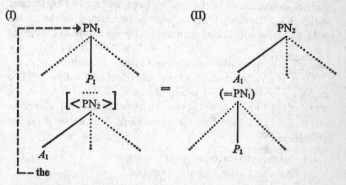

[*Note*: the dotted lines indicate optional unspecified elements of a predication.]

This rule, which inverts the relation of subordination between one predication and another, may be expressed in words as follows:

> If main predication PN_1 contains within itself a modifying predication (p. 151) PN_2, then an otherwise equivalent formula in which PN_1 is embedded as an argument in PN_2 may be substituted for it.

The previous occasions on which this rule has appeared have provided two motivations for it. The first motivation is that of explaining the synonymy of sentence pairs such as *We slept for three hours* and *Our sleep lasted three hours* (pp. 152–3). The second is that of explaining why sentences such as (1) and (2) are ambiguous in a way that sentences such as (3) and (4) are not:

> (1) All cats eat some bats.
> (2) Some bats are eaten by all cats.

> (3) Some cats eat some bats.
> (4) Some bats are eaten by some cats.

The point, as already observed in Chapter 8 (pp. 174–6), is that when quantifiers are mixed (i.e. when **some** and **all** appear in the same predication), the logical meaning varies according to whether the scope of **all** is included in the scope of **some** or vice versa. But when two identical quantifiers occur, whether two **some**s or two **all**s, there is a coalescence of the two readings, and scope of quantifier makes no difference. This coalescence (according to the earlier analysis of quantification) results from the operation of the rule of subordination; but the ambiguity of (1) and (2) shows that in the case of mixed quantification, the rule of subordination is blocked.

There is another case where the rule of subordination helps to explain a coalescence of interpretations, and this involves the scope of negation. Notice that the negative sentence (6) is ambiguous in a way that the corresponding positive sentence (5) is not ambiguous:

> (5) He listens to you on purpose.
> (6) He doesn't listen to you on purpose.

If the negative of (6) applies to the whole of the sentence including the adverbial *on purpose*, the meaning is:

(7) 'It is not true that he listens to you on purpose.'

and if, on the other hand, the adverbial is excluded from the scope of negation, the meaning is:

(8) 'On purpose, he doesn't listen to you.'

Other examples of the same kind of ambiguity are:

He hasn't been out of work for a long time.
I didn't marry Jane because she owned several oil wells.

The account of negation given earlier (p. 164) will not account for this ambiguity. Since every predication is capable of having one and only one negative formator, there should be a one-to-one correspondence between positive and negative readings. But notice that according to the rule of subordination, there are two ways of representing the meaning of an adverbial expression: it can either be a modifying (downgraded) predication, or a main predication in which the predication expressed by the main sentence elements of subject, verb phrase, etc., is embedded. That is, in sentence 5 above, the adverbial *on purpose* is a realization either of $P_2 + A_4$ in Diagram (III), or of $P_2 + A_4$ in Diagram (IV):

(III)   (IV)

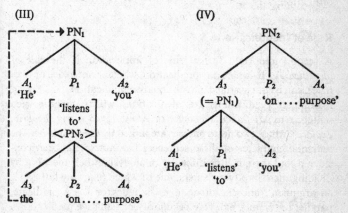

If, however, **not** is introduced into P_1 in diagrams (III) and (IV), the equivalence of (III) and (IV) no longer applies. As a general rule, the scope of **not** is restricted to the predication in which it occurs, so that in (III), where PN$_2$ is a part of PN$_1$, **not** includes PN$_2$ in its scope, while in (IV) it does not. Hence the negative counterparts of (III) and (IV) represent readings (7) and (8) respectively.

Hence our solution to the inequality of (5) and (6) is to argue that there are two semantic representations underlying each one; that in the case of (5) these two representations are shown to be equivalent by the rule of subordination; but that in the case of (6), the representations are non-equivalent, because of different scopes of the negative formator **not**.

The case of mixed quantification and the case of variable scope of negation are obviously not unconnected, as is argued, among other things, by the possibility of paraphrasing (1) and (2), through negation, as either:

No cat eats no bats.
Not all bats are not eaten by all cats.

In both mixed quantification and variable scope of negation, we explain an asymmetrical ambiguity as an exception to the rule of subordination; and in each case, the exception arises because the scope of a formator overrides the operation of the rule of subordination.

Rule of Identification

A second important formal rule of implication is the *rule of identification*, by which any predication, whether one-place or two-place, can be transformed into an equative predication.

Equative predications are predications which underlie such sentences as *My father is a doctor* or *Marco Polo is my favourite explorer*, where two noun phrases are linked by the verb *to be*. The semantic character of these sentences has not so far been considered, but there is little difficulty in analysing their meaning by dividing them into two clusters, one of which (e.g. 'my father') is an argument, and the other (e.g. 'is a doctor') is a predicate, parallel to 'is tall', etc. One peculiarity of equative predications, however, is that argument and predicate are minimally distinct, only the features of tense and aspect ('present', 'past', 'perfective', 'continuous', etc.), semantically, distinguishing one from the other. It is in fact possible for the two elements to switch roles, so that (9) and (10)

(9) My father is the doctor
(10) The doctor is my father

are logically interchangeable (though thematically different). The only difference between the analysis of (9) and (10) is that in (9) the feature of present tense is attached to 'doctor', while in (10) it is attached to 'my father'. If the tense feature were disregarded, then (9) and (10) would be truly interchangeable in terms of semantic representations, being mirror images of one another. Without the tense feature, then, an equative sentence can be considered a predication consisting of two equated arguments:

(V)

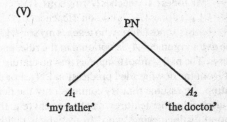

For the purpose of the rule of identification, we may safely disregard the feature of tense (which in practice makes little difference), and treat equative sentences as in the diagram above. The rule then says:

Any predication PN_1 containing an argument A_1 may be converted into an equative predication PN_2 in which one argument is A_1 and the other argument consists of a downgraded predication analysable as ⟨the+X⟩ (where **the** is a coreferential argument, and X is the set of constituents which together with A_1 make up PN_1).

This rather complex verbalization is clarified in the following diagrammatic version:

(VI)   (VII)

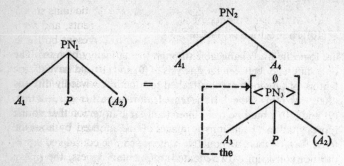

E.g. PN₁ = 'Mr Jones (A₁) teaches (P) my son (A₂)'

$$PN_2 = `\begin{cases} \text{Mr Jones } (A_1) \text{ is my son's teacher } (A_4)\text{'} \\ \text{Mr Jones } (A_1) \text{ is who teaches my son } (A_4)\text{'} \end{cases}$$

[*Notes*: The extra argument A_2 is optional in the rule, and is hence in parentheses. The null symbol $\emptyset$ signifies that no feature is present in A_4 apart from the downgraded predication PN_3. For simplicity of formulation, we assume that A_3 contains only the definite formator **the**, although other features may be present (e.g. the feature of personhood distinguishing 'who' from 'which') without substantially affecting the operation of the rule. Features of tense and aspect ('present', 'past', etc.) do not appear in the above formulation of the rule, and in general do not affect the equivalence of (VI) and (VII), since whatever tense features are present in (VI) will normally be matched in (VII).]

Among other things, the rule can be used to show semantic equivalence or quasi-equivalence of such sentence pairs as:

(11) *Englebert collects stamps* is synonymous with *Englebert is a philatelist.*

(12) *Jim is employed by General Motors* is synonymous with *Jim is an employee of General Motors.*

(13) *Mabel loves music* is synonymous with *Mabel is a music-lover.*

Why cannot we show these equivalences directly by showing each matching pair of sentences to have the same semantic representation? The answer is that this would violate the informal mapping rules laid down for relating semantic and syntactic structures. The first two correlations between syntactic and semantic units stated on p. 184 were that noun phrases express arguments, and verb phrases express predicates. But if we tried to represent both the right-hand and the left-hand sentences semantically by a straight forward two-place predication as in (VI), we should have a correlation between a predicate P 'love' and an awkwardly discontinuous syntactic sequence of constituents, viz. *is a . . . lover*. Moreover, we should have to abandon the assumption that nouns (such as *philatelist* and *music-lover*) can be defined by a set of features forming part of an argument (p. 209).

[*Note*: From now on I shall adopt, for conciseness, the linear bracketing method of semantic notation (p. 208) rather than the tree structure method. The rule of attribution, in terms of this more economical notation, is restated as follows:

(VIa)   (VIIa)
$$A_1 . P . (A_2) = A_1 : \emptyset \langle \text{the} . P . (A_2) \rangle$$

The rule of identification also shows the synonymy of sentences like:

(14) Bats cannot see.
(15) Bats are blind.

Accepting the approach to adjectival definition on page 210, we define *blind* by a formula of the generalized form $\emptyset \langle \text{the} . \text{not} P . A \rangle$. Thus sentence (15) has the semantic representation

$A_1 : \emptyset \langle \text{the} . \text{not} P . A_2 \rangle$ (roughly = 'Bats are which-cannot-see'),

while sentence (14) has the simpler representation $A_1 . \text{not} P . A_2$. By the rule of identification, these representations are equivalent.

More indirectly, the rule of identification, when combined with the mirror-image convention, shows the synonymy of:

(16) Mr Jones is William's teacher.
(17) William is Mr Jones' pupil.

The demonstration or 'proof' of this equivalence runs as follows [where $A_1 = $ 'Mr Jones'; $P = $ 'teach'; '$A_2 = $ 'William']:

(16) $= A_1 : \emptyset \; \langle \textbf{the} . \rightarrow P . A_2 \rangle$

   (i.e. 'Mr-Jones (A_1) is-who-teaches-William')

   $= A_1 . \rightarrow P . A_2$ (by rule of identification)

   (i.e. 'Mr-Jones (A_1) teaches ($\rightarrow P$) William (A_2)')

   $= A_2 . \leftarrow P . A_1$ (by mirror-image convention)

   (i.e. 'William (A_2) is-taught-by ($\leftarrow P$) Mr-Jones (A_1)')

   $= A_2 : \emptyset \; \langle \textbf{the} . \leftarrow P . A_1 \rangle$ (by rule of identification)

   (i.e. 'William (A_2) is-who-is-taught-by-Mr-Jones')

The rule of identification is used twice here: substituting first from right to left, then from left to right. Terms like *teacher* and *pupil*, whose directional semantic contrast can be shown in this way, may be called *indirectly converse*. More complicated cases of indirect converseness can be exhibited only by repeated applications of the rule of identification and the mirror-image convention. An example of this kind is the semantic relation between *grandparent* and *grandchild*, whose definitions (it will be remembered from p. 249) involve two stages of downgrading:

grandparent: $\emptyset \; \langle \textbf{the} . \rightarrow \text{PARENT} . \emptyset \; \langle \textbf{the} . \rightarrow \text{PARENT} . \emptyset \rangle \rangle$

grandchild: $\emptyset \; \langle \textbf{the} . \leftarrow \text{PARENT} . \emptyset \; \langle \textbf{the} . \leftarrow \text{PARENT} . \emptyset \rangle \rangle$

Suppose we wish to show the synonymy of sentences (17) and (18):

(17) Henry VII was Queen Elizabeth's grandparent.

(18) Queen Elizabeth was Henry VII's grandchild.

The proof runs as follows ['Henry VII' $= A_1$; 'Queen Elizabeth' $= A_2$]:

(17) $= A_1 : \emptyset \; \langle \textbf{the} . \rightarrow \text{PARENT} . \emptyset \; \langle \textbf{the} . \rightarrow \text{PARENT} . A_2 \rangle \rangle$

   (i.e. 'HVII (A_1) is-grandparent-of-Q.E.')

   $= A_1 . \rightarrow \text{PARENT} . \emptyset \; \langle \textbf{the} . \rightarrow \text{PARENT} . A_2 \rangle$ (by rule of identification)

   (i.e. 'HVII (A_1) is-parent-of parent-of-Q.E.')

   $= \emptyset \; \langle \textbf{the} . \rightarrow \text{PARENT} . A_2 \rangle . \leftarrow \text{PARENT} . A_1$ (by mirror-image convention)

   (i.e 'parent-of-Q.E. is-child-of HVII (A_1)')

   $= \emptyset \; \langle \textbf{the} . \rightarrow \text{PARENT} . A_2 \rangle : \emptyset \; \langle \textbf{the} . \leftarrow \text{PARENT} . A_1 \rangle$ (by rule of identification)

   (i.e. 'parent-of-Q.E. is-child-of-HVII')

$= \emptyset \langle \text{the.} \leftarrow \text{PARENT.} A_1 \rangle : \emptyset \langle \text{the.} \rightarrow \text{PARENT.} A_2 \rangle$ (by mirror-image convention)

(i.e. 'child-of-HVII is-parent-of-Q.E.')

$= \emptyset \langle \text{the.} \leftarrow \text{PARENT.} A_1 \rangle . \rightarrow \text{PARENT.} A_2$ (by rule of identification)

(i.e. 'child-of-HVII is-parent-of Q.E. (A_2)')

$= A_2 . \leftarrow \text{PARENT.} \emptyset \langle \text{the.} \leftarrow \text{PARENT.} A_1 \rangle$ (by mirror-image convention)

(i.e. 'Q.E. (A_2) is-child-of child-of-HVII')

$= A_2 : \emptyset \langle \text{the.} \leftarrow \text{PARENT.} \emptyset \langle \text{the.} \leftarrow \text{PARENT.} A_1 \rangle \rangle$ (by rule of identification)

(i.e. 'Q.E. (A_2) is-grandchild-of-HVII')

$= (18)$

Notice that wherever the mirror-image convention is applied here, it effects a reversal in the ordering of the main predication only. This limitation of the convention ensures greater clarity and explicitness in the presentation of the proof, though a shorter proof could be devised if the mirror-image convention were applied simultaneously to both main and downgraded predications.

Yet another use of the rule of identification is to show the near-synonymy of so-called 'pseudo-cleft' sentences such as (19), and corresponding sentences of simpler construction, such as (20):

(19) What the car hit was a lamp-post.

(20) The car hit a lamp-post.

The nominal relative clause *What the car hit* (19) is semantically represented by an argument containing a qualifying predication:

the $\langle \text{the.} \leftarrow P . A_1 \rangle$ 'that which the car hit'

Hence the following are semantic representations for (19) and (20):

(19) **the** $\langle \text{the.} \leftarrow P . A_1 \rangle : A_2$
(20) $A_1 . \rightarrow P . A_2$
$[A_1 = \text{'the car'}; A_2 = \text{'a lamp-post'}; P = \text{'hit'}]$

A slight difference of meaning between (19) and (20) comes from the presence of the initial feature of definiteness (**the**) in (19), telling us that the car hit some particular thing which is assumed to be known in the context. If we subtract this extra feature from (19), we end up with the formula

(19a) $\emptyset \langle \text{the.} \leftarrow P . A_1 \rangle : A_2$

which can then be shown to be equivalent to (20) by the following steps:

$$
\begin{aligned}
(19a) &= A_2 : \emptyset \, \langle \mathbf{the.} \leftarrow P.A_1 \rangle && \text{(by mirror-image convention)} \\
&= A_2 . \leftarrow P.A_1 && \text{(by rule of identification)} \\
&= A_1 . \rightarrow P.A_2 && \text{(by mirror-image convention)} \\
&= (20)
\end{aligned}
$$

There are other cases of semantic equivalence which require for their demonstration not only the rule of identification, but the rule of subordination as well. Consider the following pairs:

$\Big\{$ (21a) The Sultan's anger was great
(21b) The Sultan was very angry

$\Big\{$ (22a) Stonehenge's age is unbelievable
(22b) Stonehenge is unbelievably old

$\Big\{$ (23a) The boy's stupidity was unusual
(23b) The boy was unusually stupid

$\Big\{$ (24a) John's suffering was noticeable
(24b) John suffered noticeably

In each case we have the attribution of a quality to a person or object, and also an expression of the *extent* or *degree* to which that quality holds. In the second sentence of each pair, the extent is indicated adverbially (that is, in semantic terms, by a modifying predication). Thus an analysis of (21b) will be:

(21b) $A : \uparrow\text{ANGRY} \, \langle \mathbf{the.} \rightarrow \text{EXTENT.} \uparrow \text{AMOUNT} \rangle$
        'The Sultan was angry to a great extent' [A = 'the Sultan']

[*Note*: The polar feature $\uparrow$AMOUNT here I assume to be the same as that which occurs in the definitions of 'many' and 'much' as opposed to 'a few' and 'a little' (p.173). 'Very' ($= \langle \mathbf{the.} \rightarrow \text{EXTENT.}$ $\uparrow$AMOUNT$\rangle$) contrasts, in terms of this feature, with 'a little' or 'rather' ($= \langle \mathbf{the.} \rightarrow \text{EXTENT.} \downarrow$ AMOUNT$\rangle$).]

Notice that this analysis (by the rule of entailment on p. 137) shows, as it should do, that (21b) entails 'The Sultan was angry.' In the first sentence of each pair, e.g. (21a), the predication of extent is the main predication, while the attribution of anger, etc.

appears as a qualifying (downgraded) predication in its initial argument:

(21a) the $\langle$the. $\leftarrow$EXTENT.$(A:\uparrow$ ANGRY$)\rangle:\uparrow$ AMOUNT
'The extent to which the Sultan was angry was great.'

This analysis shows the abstract noun *anger* in (21a) to be an expression of extent, as in fact is indicated by the possibility of paraphrasing *the Sultan's anger* by *the extent to which the Sultan is/was angry* or *the extent of the Sultan's anger*.

Taking the above semantic representations of (21a) and (21b), we can show their near equivalence by a proof on the same lines as before. But first let us note that here again the synonymy is not quite exact, because of the initial feature of definiteness in (21a): (21a) assumes, where (21b) does not, that there is a given extent to which the Sultan was angry. We therefore subtract this feature, as in (19), and use (21ai) as our starting point:

(21ai) $\emptyset$ $\langle$the. $\leftarrow$ EXTENT.$(A:\uparrow$ANGRY$)\rangle:\uparrow$AMOUNT
$= \uparrow$AMOUNT:$\emptyset$ $\langle$the. $\leftarrow$ EXTENT.$(A:\uparrow$ANGRY$)\rangle$ (by mirror-image convention)
$= \uparrow$AMOUNT. $\leftarrow$ EXTENT.$(A:\uparrow$ANGRY$)$ (by rule of identification)
$= (A:\uparrow$ANGRY$).\rightarrow$ EXTENT. $\uparrow$AMOUNT (by mirror-image convention)
$= A:\uparrow$ANGRY $\langle$the.$\rightarrow$ EXTENT. $\uparrow$AMOUNT$\rangle$ (by rule of subordination)
$= $ (21b)

The proof works not only with adverbials of degree, as in (21–4), but also with some other types of adverbial expressions, e.g. manner adverbials:

(25) My uncle's walk was peculiar. (= 'The manner in which my uncle walked . . .')
(26) My uncle walked in a peculiar manner.

There is no difficulty in adapting the proof for (21) to account for the synonymy of (25) and (26), by substituting the adverbial relation $\rightarrow$MANNER/$\leftarrow$MANNER for that of $\rightarrow$EXTENT/$\leftarrow$EXTENT.

As a final example of the operation of the rules of identification and subordination, let us take the problem of demonstrating synonymy between comparative sentences such as:

(27) Paris is more beautiful than London.
(28) London is less beautiful than Paris.

The constructions *more . . . than X* and *less . . . than X* are parallel to intensifying adverbs like *very* in expressing degree or extent: consider, for example, the relatedness of (27) to *Paris is very beautiful, Paris is quite beautiful,* etc. Also, the relation between *more . . . than X* and *less . . . than X* is very similar to that between indirect converses like *grandparent* and *grandchild*. These two observations are incorporated into the semantic representation of comparative sentences as follows [A_1 = 'Paris'; A_2 = 'London']:

(27) A_1 : $\updownarrow$BEAUTIFUL $\langle$**the.** $\rightarrow$EXTENT. $\emptyset$ $\langle$**the.** $\rightarrow$GREATER . **the**[1]
$\langle$**the.** $\leftarrow$EXTENT. (A_2 : $\updownarrow$BEAUTIFUL)$\rangle\rangle\rangle$
('Paris is beautiful to an extent greater than the extent to which London is beautiful.')

(28) A_2 : $\updownarrow$BEAUTIFUL $\langle$**the.** $\rightarrow$EXTENT. $\emptyset$ $\langle$**the.** $\leftarrow$GREATER . **the**[1]
$\langle$**the.** $\leftarrow$EXTENT. (A_1 : $\updownarrow$BEAUTIFUL)$\rangle\rangle\rangle$
('London is beautiful to an extent less than the extent to which Paris is beautiful.')

Before we proceed, two points about these representations need to be explained: first, the symbol $\updownarrow$BEAUTIFUL indicates a neutralization of the polar opposition between $\uparrow$BEAUTIFUL 'beautiful' and $\downarrow$BEAUTIFUL 'ugly'. That is to say, in comparative constructions, as in 'How' questions and some other syntactic constructions, a polar dimension of meaning is specified without any indication of inclination towards one pole or the other. Notice, for example, that 'Welsh slag-heaps are more beautiful than English ones are' does not entail 'Welsh slag-heaps are beautiful'. Second, a feature of definiteness marked **the**[1] in both the formulae above once again mars the complete synonymy of the two sentences. The slight semantic difference between (27) and (28) resides in the assumption in (27) that the degree of beauty of London is known, and the opposite assumption in (28) that the degree of beauty of Paris is known. We therefore subtract these features from the formulae to make them completely synonymous before showing their equivalence:

(27) A_1 : $\updownarrow$ BEAUTIFUL $\langle$**the.** $\rightarrow$ EXTENT. $\emptyset$ $\langle$**the.** $\rightarrow$GREATER. $\emptyset$
$\langle$**the.** $\leftarrow$ EXTENT (A_2 : $\updownarrow$ BEAUTIFUL)$\rangle\rangle\rangle$ [1]
= (A_1 : $\updownarrow$ BEAUTIFUL). $\rightarrow$ EXTENT. $\emptyset$ $\langle$**the.** $\rightarrow$ GREATER. $\emptyset$ $\langle$**the.**
$\leftarrow$ EXTENT.(A_2 : $\updownarrow$BEAUTIFUL)$\rangle\rangle$ (by rule of subordination)   [2]

$= \emptyset \langle \text{the.} \rightarrow \text{GREATER.} \emptyset \langle \text{the.} \leftarrow \text{EXTENT.} (A_2 : \updownarrow \text{BEAUTIFUL}) \rangle \rangle.$
$\leftarrow \text{EXTENT} (A_1 : \updownarrow \text{BEAUTIFUL}) \rangle \rangle$ (by mirror-image convention) [3]

$= \emptyset \langle \text{the.} \rightarrow \text{GREATER.} \emptyset \langle \text{the.} \leftarrow \text{EXTENT.} (A_2 : \updownarrow \text{BEAUTIFUL}) \rangle \rangle :$
$\emptyset \langle \text{the.} \leftarrow \text{EXTENT.} (A_1 : \updownarrow \text{BEAUTIFUL}) \rangle$ (by rule of identification) [4]

$= \emptyset \langle \text{the.} \leftarrow \text{EXTENT.} (A_1 : \updownarrow \text{BEAUTIFUL}) \rangle : \emptyset \langle \text{the.} \rightarrow \text{GREATER.}$
$\emptyset \langle \text{the.} \leftarrow \text{EXTENT.} (A_2 : \updownarrow \text{BEAUTIFUL}) \rangle$ (by mirror-image
convention) [5]

$= \emptyset \langle \text{the.} \leftarrow \text{EXTENT.} (A_1 : \updownarrow \text{BEAUTIFUL}) \rangle. \rightarrow \text{GREATER.} \emptyset \langle \text{the.}$
$\leftarrow \text{EXTENT.} (A_2 : \updownarrow \text{BEAUTIFUL}) \rangle$ (by rule of identification) [6]

$= \emptyset \langle \text{the.} \leftarrow \text{EXTENT.} (A_2 : \updownarrow \text{BEAUTIFUL}) \rangle. \leftarrow \text{GREATER.} \emptyset \langle \text{the.}$
$\leftarrow \text{EXTENT.} (A_1 : \updownarrow \text{BEAUTIFUL}) \rangle$ (by mirror-image convention) [7]

$= \emptyset \langle \text{the.} \leftarrow \text{EXTENT.} (A_2 : \updownarrow \text{BEAUTIFUL}) \rangle : \emptyset \langle \text{the.} \leftarrow \text{GREATER.}$
$\emptyset \langle \text{the.} \leftarrow \text{EXTENT.} (A_1 : \updownarrow \text{BEAUTIFUL}) \rangle \rangle$ (by rule of identification) [8]

$= \emptyset \langle \text{the.} \leftarrow \text{GREATER.} 1 \langle \text{the.} \leftarrow \text{EXTENT.} (A_1 : \updownarrow \text{BEAUTIFUL}) \rangle \rangle :$
$\emptyset \langle \text{the.} \leftarrow \text{EXTENT.} (A_2 : \updownarrow \text{BEAUTIFUL}) \rangle$ (by mirror-image
convention) [9]

$= \emptyset \langle \text{the.} \leftarrow \text{GREATER.} \emptyset \langle \text{the.} \leftarrow \text{EXTENT.} (A_1 : \updownarrow \text{BEAUTIFUL}) \rangle \rangle.$
$\leftarrow \text{EXTENT} (. A_2 : \updownarrow \text{BEAUTIFUL}) \rangle$ (by rule of identification) [10]

$= (A_2 : \updownarrow \text{BEAUTIFUL}). \rightarrow \text{EXTENT.} \emptyset \langle \text{the.} \leftarrow \text{GREATER.} \emptyset \langle \text{the.}$
$\leftarrow \text{EXTENT.} (A_1 : \updownarrow \text{BEAUTIFUL}) \rangle \rangle$ (by mirror-image convention) [11]

$= A_2 : \updownarrow \text{BEAUTIFUL} \langle \text{the.} \rightarrow \text{EXTENT.} \emptyset \langle \text{the.} \leftarrow \text{GREATER.} \emptyset$
$\langle \text{the.} \leftarrow \text{EXTENT.} (A_2 : \updownarrow \text{BEAUTIFUL}) \rangle \rangle \rangle$ (by rule of
subordination) [12]

$= (28)$.

In the course of this proof we show in passing the near-synonymy
of (27) and (28) to both of the following:

(27a) The beauty of Paris is greater than the beauty of London
(i.e. 'The extent to which Paris is beautiful . . .')

(28a) The beauty of London is less than the beauty of Paris

These two sentences are respectively syntactic realizations (again
discounting extra features of definiteness) of formulae [5] and [8],
two midway stages of the proof.

Enough illustrations have been given of the different applications
of the rules of subordination and identification. These rules can
now be seen to be not merely *ad hoc* equations, but quite powerful
devices for accounting for varied and apparently unrelated cases of
synonymy.

Other Formal Rules of Implication

Of other formal rules of implication, I shall briefly mention two
which are somewhat different from the ones just dealt with, in that

they state an equivalence between two arguments A' and A'' rather than between two predications. (All the same, these rules may indirectly show equivalence between two predications PN' and PN'' which differ only in containing A' and A'' respectively.)

The first of these rules we have already met under the title of the *rule of coreference*. It was introduced when the feature of definiteness was being discussed (p. 170), but we can now see it as fitting into the category of formal rules of implication. It is this rule that states that if an argument A_1 contains the feature of definiteness (**the**) coreferring to another argument A_2, then the content of A_2 may be substituted for **the** in A_1 without change of meaning. Hence the equivalence of (29) to sentence (30b) in the two-sentence sequence (30):

(29) I met your sister at the concert last week.

(30a) I know your sister. (30b) I met her at the concert last week.

The second rule is the *rule of attribution*, which equates a component with a downgraded one-place predication in which that component constitutes the predicate. Thus for any argument A' containing a feature F^i, this rule permits the substitution of an argument A''^1 in every way identical to A', except that F^i is replaced by $\langle \text{the} : F^i \rangle$. For instance:

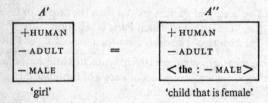

By reapplying the rule, we can of course end up with a set of features which are all downgraded predications:

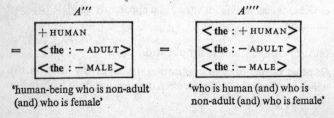

[*Note*: These formulae do not indicate the scope of coreference of **the**, which may be taken to be the whole of the argument except for the downgraded predication in which **the** occurs.]

If reapplied exhaustively, the rule of attribution will have the effect of reducing componential analysis to predicational analysis, at least, as far as arguments are concerned; and one might consider, in fact, whether the rule should not be extended to predicates also, in which case componential formulae as we have understood them up to now could come to be regarded simply as notational abbreviations for formulae consisting of downgraded predications. Although the implications of this are by no means trivial, for the present purpose I shall regard the rule of attribution as a formal rule of implication in the same sense as the other rules considered here, and will use it at this point simply as a means of pointing out the synonymy of expressions like:

man – male human being who is adult
stewardess – person who is female (and) who looks after passengers
sage – person who is old (and) who is wise.

Is There a 'Deep Semantic' Structure?

The question which arises now is whether the above formulation of these rules is the best, or whether some other formulation might be superior. We may want to ask, for instance, what it is in the nature of language that makes such rules as the rule of identification and the rule of subordination necessary. The question may also be prompted by an analogy with transformational rules at the syntactic level. In syntax, when sentences which closely correspond in meaning and in structural relations have superficially very different patterns (as in the case of matching active and passive sentences), the linguist has explained this relationship by reference to an 'underlying structure' which is all but identical for the two sentences. Thus both the sentences *Cats eat bats* and *Bats are eaten by cats* will be seen, within transformational grammar, as deriving from a 'deep structure' of approximately the same form. It is the role of the passive transformation to reorder the elements so as to produce the overt differences of order, verb form, etc., between the two.

A similar solution might be suggested for the correspondence between equivalent semantic representations on the semantic level. That is, if two semantic representations stand for the same meaning, then perhaps at a 'deeper' level these should be shown to have the same representation:

(VIII)

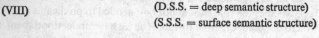

(D.S.S. = deep semantic structure)
(S.S.S. = surface semantic structure)

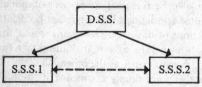

The broken horizontal arrow in this diagram represents the equating function of the rules we have been dealing with in this chapter; the diagonal arrows, which trace the unidirectional derivation of the two S.S.S.s from a single D.S.S., would be an alternative way of explaining equivalences between two different semantic representations.

At this stage I shall postpone discussion of the motivation for the 'deep semantic structure hypothesis', and shall briefly describe what deep semantic representations might be like. Let us think of 'deep semantics' not in constituent-structure terms at all, but in terms of networks consisting of branches with 'links' and 'termini'.

(1) Let us suppose that every two-place (relational) predication is symbolized on this deeper level by a branch consisting of two termini connected by a link (where a circle represents a terminus, and an arrow represents a link between them):

(IX)

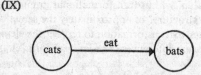

(2) Let us suppose that every one-place predication is represented
in the same way, except that the link has a terminus at one end
only:

(X)

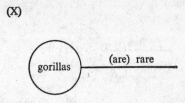

(3) Let us now say that if a predication is embedded in another, in
'deep' semantics this means that a branch is joined to another
branch in the shape of a 'T', thereby acting as a terminus to the
other branch:

(XI)

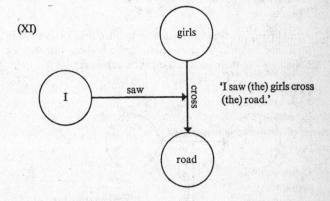

'I saw (the) girls cross
(the) road.'

In this system, it will be noted, arguments are interpreted as termini
(or ending-points of branches); predicates are interpreted as links
(= straight lines in the diagrams); and a branch is defined as a link
together with any terminus which is not itself a link (i.e. 'I saw' in
(XI) is one branch, and 'girls cross road' is another branch).

(4) Where there is a qualifying predication, i.e. a downgraded
predication within an argument of another predication, this

can in 'deep semantics' be interpreted as two branches sharing the same terminus:

(XII)

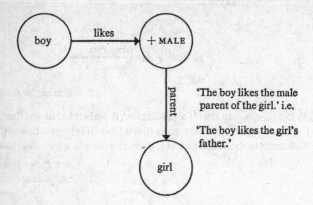

'The boy likes the male parent of the girl.' i.e.

'The boy likes the girl's father.'

(5) A modifying predication, i.e. a downgraded predication within predicate, becomes in 'deep semantics' a branch with another branch (= the main predication) as its terminus:

(XIII)

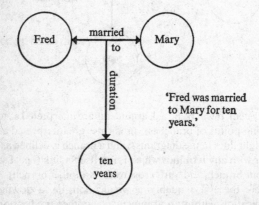

'Fred was married to Mary for ten years.'

(6) Coreference does not exist on this deepest level of semantics
– instead, the referential identity of two arguments is shown
directly in their having a single terminus as their source. Hence
it is possible, and in fact usual, for a deep semantic representation to form at some point a closed network:

(XIV)

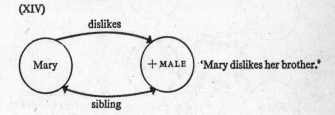

'Mary dislikes her brother.'

The simplest case of a closed network would be a reflexive relation, where one link begins and ends with the same terminus:

(XV)

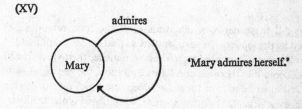

'Mary admires herself.'

More complicated networks are easily constructed by combinations of these principles:

(XVI)

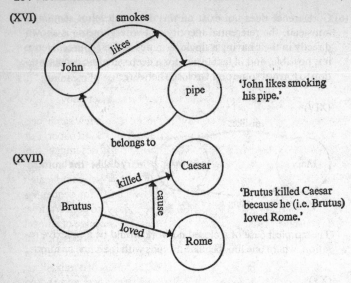

'John likes smoking his pipe.'

(XVII)

'Brutus killed Caesar because he (i.e. Brutus) loved Rome.'

[*Note*: All these network diagrams omit the time relations expressed by the tense of the verb, and are to that extent simplified.]

If coreference is excluded from deep semantics, then wherever in surface semantics there is a coreference relation, the two arguments involved must be part of the same 'deep semantic' network. This applies even when the two arguments are separated syntactically by a sentence boundary. For example, network (XVII) above could be converted on the surface level not only into a single sentence such as (31), but into a sequence of sentences such as (32) or (33):

(31) Brutus killed Caesar because he loved Rome.
(32) Brutus killed Caesar. This was because he loved Rome.
(33) Brutus loved Rome. For this reason he killed Caesar.

Thus deep semantics directly shows the synonymy of sentence-sequences to single sentences, or of sentence-sequences to sentence-sequences, in a way impossible in surface semantics, except through the operation of the rule of coreference. One of the implications of this is that the unit of deep semantics becomes a whole *discourse* rather than a single sentence. In fact a discourse might be defined as a stretch of language which can be represented on the deep semantic level as a single network. Such a definition would characterize (32) and (33) above as discourses, in contrast to (34), where one sentence arbitrarily follows another without any connection of meaning:

(34) Brutus killed Caesar. Martha's having another baby.

Naturally if a discourse has a length of more than a few sentences, it becomes exceedingly difficult to chart the network on paper. For a novel-length discourse, it is for all practical purposes impossible. In fact, one of the most important functions of the surface-semantic level of representation is surely to unravel complicated networks and cut them up into convenient units for sequential presentation and for syntactic expression; namely, to convert them into predications and hence into sentences. To conceive of a novel as a whole discourse representable by single network is not, of course, to suggest that the whole of that network must be in a writer's mind before he starts writing: the dynamics of composition is a separate consideration of semantic performance, and should not interfere with the theoretical conception of a network forming a total semantic unity.

We now have, then, a brief outline of a possible theory of deep semantics. The next question is: what motivation is there for postulating the existence of such a level of linguistic organization? One reason that *cannot* be given is the usual one of explaining basic statements of entailment, synonymy, etc.: deep semantics as just described must be on a level of 'pre-logical thought', for one can scarcely talk about the 'truth' or 'falsehood' of a network, nor can one easily subject it to logical operations such as negation. The arguments on behalf of deep semantics must rather be that it simplifies our total conception of language, and provides explanations for characteristics of language which would otherwise seem to be gratuitous.

For example, the single network of (XVII) can be shown, by suitable formulation of the rules of subordination and identification, to underlie all three of the following statements, which on the surface semantic level, as we have seen, would require three different constituent structures:

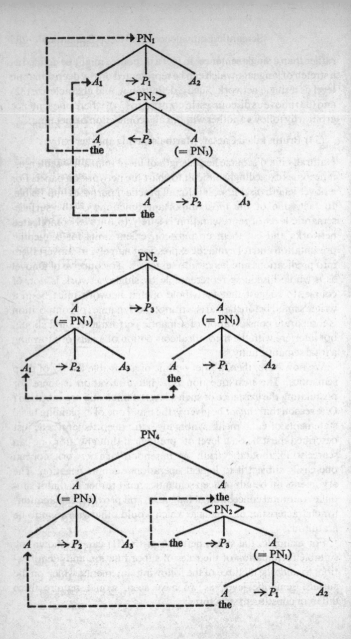

$[A_1 = \text{'Brutus'}; A_2 = \text{'Caesar'}; A_3 = \text{'Rome'}; \rightarrow P_1 = \text{'killed'}; \rightarrow P_2 = \text{'loved'}; \rightarrow P_3 = \text{'cause'}]$

(31a) Brutus killed Caesar because he loved Rome.

(31b) Brutus loved Rome, so he killed Caesar.

(31c) Brutus's love of Rome was the reason for his killing of
Caesar.

If we reformulate the rules of subordination, identification, and coreference so as to make them 'semantic transformations', or unidirectional rules of implication converting deep semantic representations into surface semantic representations, it then becomes possible to assign each of the rules a particular function. The function of the rule of coreference is to copy what is referentially the same argument in different places in the network, and so to convert closed networks into open networks. Network (XVII) can thus become either (XVIIa) or (XVIIb):

(XVIIa)   (XVIIb)

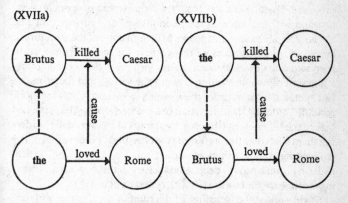

The rule of subordination's function is to pick a particular branch of the network to be the main predication, and so to assign a hierarchy of subordination (i.e. a 'vertical' ordering of inclusion) to two or more branches. Diagrams (XI) and (XIII) above show that whenever we have a 'T'-shaped junction in a network, this can be interpreted in constituent structure either (by laying the T on its side) as an embedding of the horizontal in the vertical, or (by standing the 'T' upright) as a downgrading of the vertical in the horizontal. These alternatives are the two formulae equated by the rule of subordination as stated earlier. Diagrams (XVIIa) and (XVIIb) are 'H'-shaped diagrams incorporating two 'T'-shaped junctions, therefore it is easy to see how they can be transformed in (31a) and (31b) respectively, according to which order of subordination is selected.

Here it must be noted that in deep semantic structure we take the mirror-image convention a stage further, and interpret it two-dimensionally: while in surface semantics left-to-right ordering is non-significant, in deep semantic networks top-to-bottom order is also non-significant, so that whichever way round a network is charted, so long as the same configuration of branches is retained, the network is unchanged. This abolition of ordering in deep semantics (except for distinctions of order intrinsic to relations and indicated by arrows) is not difficult to accept if we think of surface and deep semantics as stages of linguistic representation getting progressively further away from the requirement of sequential expression which conditions the phonological and surface syntactic levels of organization, and nearer to being a copy of the structure of events and circumstances we recognize in the reality around us. In deep semantics the sentence *I saw the girls cross the street* is simply a junction of two interacting events – the seeing, and the crossing. But syntax makes us order these events in two ways: (a) by 'horizontally' ordering them such that one event (the seeing) is expressed before the other event (the crossing); and (b) by 'vertically' ordering them such that the one event (the crossing) is subordinated (by embedding) to the other. In surface semantics, only the vertical ordering is retained; in deep semantics, even this concept of ordering disappears, and we are left with orderless networks.

Having noted the functions of the rules of coreference and subordination as respectively (a) breaking up closed networks and (b) assigning order of subordination to the branches of networks, we turn now to the rule of identification. In deep structure networks, there is nothing to prevent a chain of relations such as:

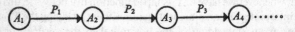

But in the surface structure, or constituent structure, conception of semantics such a recursive configuration has to be converted into a structure in which one relation is subordinate to another. Therefore, two alternative ways of representing this chain of relations are:

$$A_1. \rightarrow P.A_2 \langle \text{the.} \rightarrow P.A_3 \langle \text{the.} \rightarrow P.A_4 \rangle \rangle$$
$$A_4. \leftarrow P.A_3 \langle \text{the.} \leftarrow P.A_3 \langle \text{the.} \leftarrow P.A_1 \rangle \rangle$$

As we saw earlier, the effect of the rule of identification is to account for the equivalence of these formulae. Thus here again, a rule of implication turns out to make good sense as a rule for converting networks into a form suitable for constituent structure.

Apart from suggesting an explanation of why rules of implication are necessary to the functioning of language, the 'deep semantics hypothesis' accounts for another hitherto arbitrary-seeming characteristic of semantic representations. This is the principle that every downgraded predication is linked by coreference to the main predication of which it is a part. Now that we have seen the deep semantic configurations which underlie downgraded predications, we can understand why such a link of coreference is necessary: if downgrading is a constituent-structure reinterpreting of the junction between two branches of a network, then it can only represent that junction, or structural interlocking, by means of coreference, since there is no direct way in which a main predication can share the structure of a downgraded predication.

Finally, the 'deep semantics hypothesis' enables us to see a parallel between semantics and syntax: just as deep semantic networks are transformed into surface semantic tree-structure representations, so (it was suggested in Chapter 9) syntactic representations are converted into 'surface syntactic' structures for the linear presentation of the message so that emphasis and information focus may be effectively placed. In between the two sets of transformations we have rules (pp. 184–99) for mapping semantic representations onto syntactic representations. For each stratum of linguistic organization, there are certain functions which make that stratum an important stage in the overall mediating process which connects sound to meaning or meaning to sound.

All these arguments in favour of deep semantics are informal, and establish no more than a basis for looking with some degree of seriousness at what must remain a speculative hypothesis. The main attraction of this hypothesis is its ability to indicate why certain complexities of language are not arbitrary, but are an integral part of the way language has to operate as a multi-level coding device.

Conclusions

My main conclusions from this chapter are:

1. In natural language, semantic equivalence or synonymy cannot always be shown directly, by tracing two sentences back to the same underlying semantic representation. Instead, synonymy has to be shown indirectly by what I have called rules of implication.

2. Certain rules of implication (e.g. the rule of subordination and the rule of identification) can be shown to be highly motivated by their ability to account for apparently unrelated cases of synonymy which would otherwise have to be explained by separate statements.

3. Rules of implication can be speculatively reinterpreted as 'semantic transformations' mapping deep semantic representations on to surface semantic representations.

4. The deep semantic representations so postulated are viewed as relational networks, not as constituent-structure trees.

13. Presuppositions and Factuality

Three Semantic Relations: Entailment, Presupposition, Expectation

My main purpose in this chapter is to investigate the important concept of *presupposition*, but in order to do this effectually, I need to illustrate and distinguish three types of semantic truth-dependence:

X ENTAILS Y

> X: 'He married a blonde heiress.'
>
> Y: 'He married a blonde.'

X PRESUPPOSES Y

> X: 'The girl he married was an heiress.'
>
> Y: 'He married a girl.'

X EXPECTS Y

> X: 'Few men marry blonde heiresses.'
>
> Y: 'Some men marry blonde heiresses.'

All three of these relations are parallel to the extent that in each case we might say 'From X I conclude Y.' The first is the relation of *entailment*, which has been sufficiently discussed in earlier chapters; the second is the relation of *presupposition* which has been briefly mentioned in other chapters (p. 5, 8 ff); the third is a weaker relation which although it has often been discussed under the same heading as presupposition, is in my opinion best distinguished from it and given the separate name of *expectation*.

'Presupposition' has been a popular subject in semantics recently, and – as is often the case when a subject becomes the centre of attention – important distinctions have been blurred, with the result that 'presupposition' has become something of a 'catch-all' category. I hope that in this chapter I shall be able to clarify some lines of demarcation, and (more important) to show how it is possible to derive instances of presupposition, by rule, from the form of semantic representations. In this I shall try to give the same sort of treatment to presupposition as I gave to entailment in Chapter 7; and to the extent that I shall succeed, I shall have extended the scope of semantic theory to explain one further set of *basic statements* itemized in Chapter 5 (pp. 84–90). But presupposition is a complex subject, and many problems will remain unsolved.

1. *Presupposition versus Entailment.*

In terms of truth value, entailment was defined earlier (p. 86) as a relation between two assertions X and Y such that

(a) if X is true, Y has to be true
(b) if Y is false, X has to be false.

As always, of course, we are interested only in relations of entailment and presupposition which hold by virtue of conceptual or logical meaning, rather than by virtue of factual reality (pp. 86–7).

Presupposition (or more precisely *positive* presupposition) was characterized provisionally on p. 86 as a relation between X and Y such that 'anyone who utters X takes for granted the truth of Y'. This description as it stands is a vague makeshift, unless we can arrive at some reasonably precise understanding of what 'taking for granted' means. One way of making sense of this expression is to make appeal to the notion that an utterance or speech act may or may not have 'validity' or 'happiness' or 'appropriateness' (see Austin, 1962). Then the following definition (when compared with that of entailment above) will characterize both the difference and the similarity between entailment and presupposition:

Presupposition is a relation between X and Y such that
(a) if the uttering of X is valid, Y has to be true
(b) If Y is false, then the uttering of X is invalid or void.

The terms 'valid' and 'invalid' are used rather than 'meaningful' and 'meaningless', in order to try and make clear that the proper or successful use of X as a speech act, in pragmatic terms, is what is at issue, not its significance with regard to reference and truth value. Suppose a person is told 'Turn off the television' when the television is in fact already off. We would not say the utterance is false (since commands in any case cannot be true or false), but that it is in some way inappropriately spoken, just as the words 'I do' at a marriage ceremony would be void or inappropriate if spoken by a bigamist or by the bride's father.

While entailment is a relation restricted to assertions, the above example shows that presupposition can involve other types of predication as well. Thus although the *Y* of '*X* presupposes *Y*' has to be an assertion, *X* can be not only an assertion, but also a question or command or exclamation:

The book you stole from the library is interesting. (ASSERTION)
When did you steal the book from the library? (QUESTION)
See that you take back the book you stole from the library. (COMMAND)
What an interesting book you stole from the library! (EXCLAMATION)

All these carry the presupposition 'You stole a book from the library.'

As the force of 'validity' or 'appropriateness' has less clear outlines in popular usage than 'truth' and 'falsehood', it is not surprising that there has been much disagreement on how in practice to identify presuppositions. The cases in which there is most danger of confusion with entailment are those presuppositions for which the presupposing utterance (*X*), as well as the presupposed one (*Y*), is an assertion; but fortunately, in these cases, a clearer criterion of presupposition, formulated in terms of truth and falsehood, presents itself:

X ENTAILS *Y* means that
    If *X* is true, then *Y* has to be true
    (but if not-*X* is true, *Y* need not be true)

X PRESUPPOSES *Y* means that
    If *X* is true, then *Y* is true
    and also
    If not-*X* is true, then *Y* is true.

That is, if one negates the entailing sentence *X*, the entailment no longer obtains; but if one negates the presupposing sentence *X*, the presupposition relation still holds good:

> { 'He married a blonde heiress' entails 'He married a blonde.'
> 'He did not marry a blonde heiress' does not entail 'He married a blonde.'

> { 'The blonde he married was an heiress' presupposes 'He married a blonde.'
> 'The blonde he married was not an heiress' presupposes 'He married a blonde.'

This *negation test*, as it may be called, is a handy means of separating entailment and presupposition in cases where X is an assertion. But it cannot be applied to other types of utterance such as question and commands, for the obvious reason that only assertions can have the properties of truth and falsehood.

Now from the differences between entailment and presupposition, let us turn to what they have in common. They both satisfy the criterion of uncontradictability, by which I mean that if one conjoins X with the negation of its presupposition or entailment Y, the result is an absurdity:

*He didn't marry (a girl), but the girl he married was a blonde.
*He didn't marry (a girl), but was the girl he married a blonde?
*He didn't marry a blonde, but he married a blonde heiress.

All of these sentences are bizarre, but not all for the same reason: the first two result from the contradiction of a presupposition, and the third from the contradiction of an entailment.

2. *Presupposition versus Expectation*

Certain relations which I shall call 'expectations' are weaker than entailments and presuppositions, to the extent that they do not satisfy the criterion of uncontradictability. George Lakoff (1970: 32–4) gives the following examples:

'Few girls are coming.' → 'Some girls are coming.'
'If the F.B.I. were tapping my phone, I'd be paranoid.' →
> { 'The F.B.I. are not tapping my phone.'
> 'I am not paranoid.'

Lakoff refers to the relation symbolized by the arrow here as 'presupposition', although, as he himself points out, the 'presupposition' may be cancelled out by an appended qualifying statement:

> 'Few girls are coming, or maybe none at all are.'
> 'If the F.B.I. were tapping my phone, I'd be paranoid, but then I am anyway.'

It is for this reason that I class these as expectations, as distinct from presuppositions as so far considered.

The next task is to consider how to formalize presupposition and expectation within semantic theory – and I hope to show, in the course of what follows, that presupposition and expectation have two quite different semantic sources.

On the Predictability of Presuppositions

In treatments of presupposition I have seen, there seems to be no agreement as to how presuppositions are to be formally stated within semantic description. In one account, that of Lakoff (*Linguistics and Natural Logic*, 1970), it is tentatively suggested that presuppositions should be stated quite separately from the 'logical form' of a sentence; i.e. there should be no attempt to incorporate presuppositional descriptions into the type of tree-structure semantic representation we have been dealing with since Chapter 7. In this view, the semantic description of a sentence would contain a pair of specifications: Logical Form + Presuppositional Characterization.

But it would clearly be a great advantage if the presuppositions of an utterance could be predicted by rule from certain characteristics of its semantic representation; that is, if elements of a semantic description already assigned to a sentence for other reasons would also provide a characterization of presuppositions. It would further be an advantage if a single principle could account for – if not all – at least a significant proportion of instances of presupposition. If these two aims could be achieved, the treatment of presuppositions would parallel that already given to entailment in Chapter 7 (pp. 136–40).

My contention is that such a principle exists, and that it is the principle of downgrading. Accordingly, I suggest that a first approximation to a rule for presupposition is:

Rule of Presupposition: If a predication X contains within it (either directly or indirectly) a downgraded predication Y, then X presupposes Y' (where Y' is an independent assertion equivalent to Y).

This may be illustrated as follows:

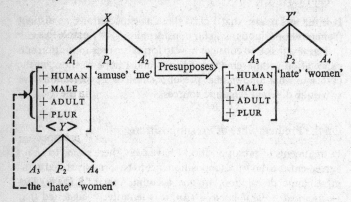

'Misogynists'
'Men who hate women' } amuse me' presupposes '(Some) men hate women'

The downgraded predication Y is identical to the main (presupposed) assertion Y' except that the rule of coreference has applied to A_3. This change is covered by the condition, in the rule, that Y and Y' are 'equivalent'.

Most of the examples of presupposition given so far have been of downgraded predications which find syntactic expression in relative clauses. But, as we have seen elsewhere, downgrading underlies many varied syntactic and lexical manifestations: relative clauses, reduced relative clauses, adjectives, prepositional phrases, adverbials, nouns, etc. Some of these variations are exemplified below:

(1) '*The Governor of Idaho* is currently in London' presupposes 'Idaho has a Governor.'

(2) '*Low-flying bicycles* can be dangerous' presupposes 'Some bicycles fly low.'

(3) 'My friend is *the mayor's son*' presupposes 'The mayor has a son.'

Less obviously, presuppositions can be expressed through other types of subordinate clause; e.g. nominal relative clauses:

(4) '*What annoyed me* was his hypocrisy' presupposes 'Something annoyed me.'

Indirect questions:

(5) 'I wonder *where he stole this car*' presupposes 'He stole this car (somewhere).'

Adverbial clauses:

(6) 'He was Arsenal's captain *when it was the best team in the country*' presupposes 'Arsenal was the best team in the country (at some time).'

Comparative clauses:

(7) 'Tom has a bigger stamp-collection *than I have*' presupposes 'I have a stamp-collection.'

Participial clauses:

(8) 'I don't regret *leaving London*' presupposes 'I (have) left London.'

Nominalizations (see p. 184):

(9) '*Lee's surrender to Grant* spelt the end of the Confederate cause' presupposes 'Lee surrendered to Grant.'

That-clauses:

(10) 'John knows *that we are helping him*' presupposes 'We are helping him.'

(Remember that the 'negation test' is a useful criterion of presupposition. If, for example, we wish to check the presuppositional relationship between the statements of (4) above, we make the first sentence negative ('What annoyed me wasn't his hypocrisy') and observe that the assumption of the truth of the second sentence remains unchanged. Similarly for the other cases.)

That downgraded predications underlie the majority, if not all of these cases, cannot be established without exhaustive analysis, so I must be content to point out just one or two details which support this claim. For example, in cases (4) and (6) paraphrases with relative clauses are possible: *What annoyed me* can be expanded as *That which annoyed me*, and *when it was the best team in the country* can be (stiltedly) elaborated as *at the time at which it was the best team in the country*. In any case, we have seen before (p. 151) that adverbial phrases and clauses are semantically representable as downgraded predications. In respect to (7), we noted in the last chapter that the semantic representation of comparative clauses involved downgrading (p. 276). More difficult cases are (8), (9), and (10), which on superficial grounds would appear to express not downgraded, but embedded predications. I shall return to *that*-clauses at a later stage (p. 310), and will merely point out here that participial and nominalized constructions can often be paraphrased with a *that*-clause; for example, (8) and (9) can be paraphrased:

(8a) 'I don't regret it *that I (have) left London*.'
(9a) 'The fact *that Lee surrendered to Grant* spelt the end of the Confederate cause.'

Enough has been said, I hope, to establish the plausibility of tracing a considerable range of presuppositions to the downgraded predication as a feature of semantic representations.

To increase our ability to derive presuppositions from properties of semantic representations, two further points may be noted:

(a) Presupposition, like entailment (p. 139), is a logically transitive relation (i.e. if X presupposes Y and Y presupposes Z, then X presupposes Z), as we can see from these examples:
   X: 'The inventor of the flying bicycle was a genius.'
   Y: 'Someone invented the flying bicycle.'
   Z: 'There is a bicycle which flies.'
(b) For any predication X, if X presupposes Y and Y entails Z, then X presupposes Z:
   X: 'Low-flying bicycles can be dangerous' presupposes
   Y: 'Some bicycles fly low', which entails
   Z: 'Some bicycles fly.'

With these cumulative rules, it is now easy to see how a single utterance can have a considerable number of presuppositions. But to press the point further, let us note that many other presuppositions can arise indirectly, through the operation of the rule of attribution mentioned in the last chapter. The effect of that rule was to convert a single componential feature such as —MALE into a downgraded predication ⟨**the**: —MALE⟩. This means that every single feature within an argument is potentially associated with a presupposition. Given an argument containing three features:

(a)

$$\begin{bmatrix} + \text{HUMAN} \\ + \text{ADULT} \\ - \text{MALE} \end{bmatrix} \quad \text{'woman'}$$

it is possible to change this, by the rule of attribution, into three different but equivalent representations as follows (remembering that the ordering of features is immaterial):

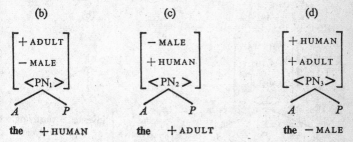

(b)   (c)   (d)

And each of these brings to light a separate presupposition:

(b) 'The/some adult female is/was human'
(c) 'The/some human female is/was adult'
(d) 'The/some human adult is/was female'

The fact that these presuppositions are too obvious to be noticeably communicative in most circumstances does not alter the validity of the observation that they are potentially present in any normal use of the word *woman*.

To digress briefly, it can now be seen that presupposition can be used in the definition of types of absurdity. Perhaps the most important type of contradiction (p. 86) is an assertion which is logically inconsistent with one of its presuppositions:

*'The illiterate boy was reading a newspaper' presupposes and is inconsistent with 'The boy could not read.'

A second type of absurdity already mentioned (p. 86) is a 'semantically anomalous' sentence, which presupposes a contradiction:

*'The orphan's father drinks heavily' presupposes *'The orphan has a father.'

Now to explain the relation between presupposition and downgrading more precisely, we need to call upon another rule of implication, the rule of coreference (p. 170). The effect of this rule, it will be recalled, is to substitute for any feature of definiteness **the** the set of features included in its domain of coreference. By this rule the qualifying predication X in (a) is shown to be equivalent to X' in (b):

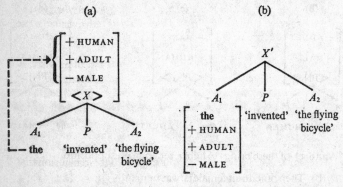

(a) 'The woman that invented the flying bicycle'

(b) 'The woman invented the flying bicycle'

And (b) in turn entails (see p. 168) the predication identical with itself except for the subtraction of the feature of definiteness: (c) 'A woman invented the flying bicycle.' Hence a presupposition within a definite argument can be given in the form of a definite statement like (b), or a more general indefinite statement like (c).

But having pressed the connection between presupposition and downgrading thus far, I shall now have to consider in what ways this connection fails. It is at this point that the concept of *factuality* becomes indispensable.

Factuality, Non-factuality, and Counterfactuality

It is necessary to restrict the rule of presupposition as so far given, so that it applies only to downgraded predications which are *factual*, i.e., which amount to assumptions of fact. Of the relative clauses of the following sentences, only the first carries the property of factuality:

(11) 'They'll send us postcards of the interesting places they visit' presupposes 'They will visit (some) interesting places.'
(12) 'Please send us postcards of any interesting places you visit' does *not* presuppose 'You will visit (some) interesting places.'
(13) 'If you enjoy history, Rome is the European city for you to visit' does *not* presuppose 'You will visit/have visited some European city.'

As these examples indicate, syntactic construction plays a role in signalling factuality or its absence: it is the occurrence of *any* that neutralizes the factuality of the relative clause in (12), and the infinitive clause that has a comparable effect in (13). Such a contrast may be observed not only in downgraded but in embedded predications:

'He forced me to attend the meeting' leads to the conclusion that 'I attended the meeting.'
'He wanted me to attend the meeting' does not lead to the conclusion that 'I attended the meeting.'

The contrast here is between commitment and non-commitment to the truth of what is said in the subordinate clause. There is still a further possibility, which is that there is a commitment to the falsehood of what is contained in the subordinate clause:

'It would be a pity if he attended the meeting' presupposes (or rather expects, see p. 294) 'He does not/will not attend the meeting.'

These three kinds of imputation may be termed *factuality*, *non-factuality*, and *counterfactuality*.

Although factuality corresponds to some extent with the choice of syntactic construction, in many cases it seems to be determined rather by the meaning of the lexical verb or adjective with which it is associated. Lakoff (in *Linguistics and Natural Logic*, 1970: pp. 30–43) suggests rules by which positive, neutral, and negative presuppositions are 'activated' by a given predicate – so that 'realize', for example, imposes factuality on the adjacent embedded sentence while 'want' does not. Within the framework of this book, no special apparatus is required for these rules, as they fall quite naturally into the category of contextual redundancy rules (pp. 141 ff) which, for a given predicate, assign semantic features or conditions to the preceding or following argument. 'Factuality', that is, can be treated as a kind of selection restriction.

A predicate (or more precisely, a feature in a predicate) may be classified as *factive*, *non-factive*, and *counterfactive* according to whether it ascribes factuality, non-factuality, or counterfactuality to the associated subordinate predication. Thus 'realize', 'suspect' and 'pretend' are instances of factive, non-factive and counterfactive predicates respectively.

'Marion realized that her sister was a witch' presupposes 'Marion's sister was a witch.'

'Marion suspected that her sister was a witch' does not presuppose 'Marion's sister was a witch', nor 'Marion's sister was not a witch.'

'Marion pretended that her sister was a witch' presupposes 'Marion's sister was not a witch.'

The form of the rules which specify these conditions might be written as follows:

REALIZE $\rightarrow$ (PN$^+$) [factive]
SUSPECT $\rightarrow$ (PN^0) [non-factive]
PRETEND $\rightarrow$ (PN$^-$) [counterfactive]

The raised '+', '0' and '−' are used here, and will be so used from now on, as symbols for the factuality, non-factuality, and counterfactuality of predications. (In a more precise analysis they would be represented as components of the predicate of the embedded predication.)

'Factive', 'non-factive' and 'counterfactive' are not totally distinct categories, since some predicates can belong to more than one of them: 'nice', for instance, can be both factive and non-factive:

'It's nice that John has many friends.'   [factive]
'It's nice to have many friends.'   [non-factive]

It is arguable that the relative opposition of *volition* can belong to all three categories:

'John insists on reading Mary's letters.'   [factive]
'John wants/wishes to read Mary's letters.'   [non-factive]
'John wishes he could read Mary's letters.'   [counterfactive]

Presumably, all three verbs *insist*, *want*, and *wish* have underlying them the same feature of 'volition' but differ in their factuality conditions (see Leech 1969b: pp. 214–6).

I think there is good reason to suppose that every predication is marked by a factuality feature of one kind or another. We have already seen the need for factuality contrasts in embedded and downgraded predications; it only remains to observe that in main predications, too, there is a contrast between factual utterances like 'My shoes are wet' and utterances which do not make claims of fact, like 'May they never forget your kindness', 'If only I hadn't eaten those oysters':

'My shoes are wet' entails 'My shoes are wet' (since every factual assertion entails itself).
'May they never forget your kindness' does not entail or presuppose 'They will never forget your kindness.'

(Notice that 'factuality' contrasts are independent of the contrast between statements and questions. 'Did you commit the theft?' is a *factual* question, in that it requires a factual answer, even though in itself it leaves the listener's guilt undecided. Compare this with the questions 'Why worry?' [non-factual] and 'Would you marry me if I asked you?' [counterfactual].)

Assuming, therefore, that every predication is marked for

factuality, non-factuality, or counterfactuality, let us turn to a distinction to be drawn between two kinds of factive predicates.

Pure Factives and Conditional Factives

Pure factives are predicates such as 'make sense', 'realize', 'be sorry', 'know', 'amuse', 'regret', 'bear in mind', 'appreciate', etc., which are in the main associated with *that*-clauses. *Conditional factives* (*cf* Karttunen, [1971], 'Implicative Verbs') are predicates such as 'cause', 'become', 'have to', 'force', 'see', 'hear', etc., mainly associated with infinitive constructions and nominalizations. When the factive predicate is positive, both these types behave in the same way, attributing factual reality to the following predication:

PURE FACTIVES:

(14) 'I'm *sorry* that he lost his job' → 'He lost his job.'
(15) 'The politicians *appreciate* that the result of the election will depend on the war' → 'The result of the election will depend on the war.'

CONDITIONAL FACTIVES:

(16) 'Airport police *forced* the hijacker to surrender his gun' → 'The hijacker surrendered his gun.'
(17) 'I *saw* Aunt Agnes down three whiskies' → 'Aunt Agnes downed three whiskies.'

But when each assertion containing a factive predicate is negated, the factuality of the embedded predication is maintained only in the case of pure factives:

PURE FACTIVES:

(14a) '*I'm not sorry* that he lost his job' → 'He lost his job.'
(15a) 'The politicians *do not appreciate* that the result of the election will depend on the war' → 'The result of the election will depend on the war.'

CONDITIONAL FACTIVES:

(16a) 'Airport police *did not force* the hijacker to surrender his gun' ↛ 'The hijacker surrendered his gun.'

(17a) 'I *didn't see* Aunt Agnes down three whiskies' ↛ 'Aunt Agnes downed three whiskies.'

The arrow → here may be read 'from . . . we conclude the truth of . . .', and its negation ↛, naturally enough, is to be interpreted 'from . . . we do *not* conclude the truth of . . . .' I have avoided using the term 'presupposition' here, since the difference between pure and conditional factives precisely coincides with the distinction between presupposition and entailment as explained earlier (p. 294): the criterion of the negation test illustrated earlier has just been used again to show that the subordinate predications of (14) and (15) are presupposed, while those of (16) and (17) are entailed.

It happens that the relation of entailment between a main predication and a predication directly embedded inside it, as in (16) and (17), has already been predicted by two rules: the rule of entailment and the rule of subordination (pp. 265 ff). The semantic representation for (17) in outline is as follows:

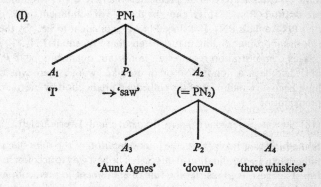

And this, by the rule of subordination, is equivalent to:

(II)

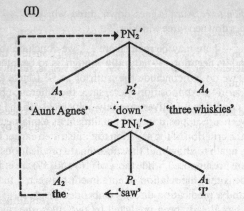

Now if PN$_2$ is taken out in (I) and treated as a separate independent assertion, then it is identical to PN$_2'$ in (II), except that PN$_2'$ contains an extra feature in its predicate – namely the downgraded predication $\langle$PN$_1'\rangle$. This means, by the rule of entailment (p.137), that PN$_2'$ entails PN$_2$. But since PN$_2'$ is equivalent to PN$_1$ by the rule of subordination, this in turn means that PN$_1$ entails PN$_2$.

This demonstration requires an important qualification. If P_1 in (I) had been a non-factive predicate like 'want', there would have been no entailment of the embedded predication by the main predication:

(18) 'I wanted everyone to leave' does not entail 'Everyone left.'

Something clearly obstructs the joint operation of the rules of entailment and subordination in this case. The best way to account for this, I suggest, is to restrict the rule of entailment to predications which are marked as 'factual'. In (18), the main predication 'I wanted X' is factual, but the embedded predication 'everyone to leave' is not. Therefore an entailment relation cannot hold between them. This restriction, that the two assertions in an entailment relation are 'factual', is a retrospective revision of the rule of entailment (p. 137), which now reads as follows:

Rule of Entailment (revised): A relation of entailment arises between two *factual assertions* whenever (the assertions being otherwise identical) an argument or predicate in one assertion is hyponymous to an argument or predicate in the other.

The revision is easy enough to accept, when we consider that the marker 'factual' means, when applied to assertions, no more nor less than 'judged to be true'. There seems to be no sense in which a non-factual or counter-factual utterance such as 'May your troubles be little ones!' or 'If only I hadn't eaten that cheesecake, I'd feel fine' can be considered to entail or be entailed by some other assertion.

The 'Chain of Factuality'

The account just given of the interrelation between entailment and embedding provides an explanation of the behaviour of conditional factives like 'see' when they are themselves embedded in a higher predication:

(19) 'The owner of the Lotus compelled Laetitia to let him drive her home.'

If we analyse this assertion in terms of a hierarchy of embedding, with one predication acting as an argument in another, we notice that the factivity of each predicate ensures that entailment relations are preserved right down the chain (the superscript ' + ', as before, signifies factuality):

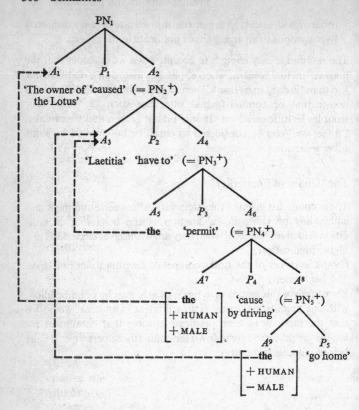

We assume here that 'cause', 'have to' and 'permit' are all conditional factive predicates. Thus the whole assertion PN_1 entails PN_2 ('Laetitia had to let him drive her home'); and this in turn entails PN_3 ('Laetitia let him drive her home'), which in turn entails PN_4 ('He drove her home'), which in turn entails PN_5 ('She went home'). Moreover, each PN_x entails each PN_y (where $x \leqslant y$) cumulatively, because of the transitivity of the entailment relation.

But as soon as we negate the main predication, all these entailments disappear by a kind of chain reaction. The negation of PN_1 means that PN_2 becomes $PN_2{}^0$ (i.e. takes on neutral factuality);

PN_2 now no longer provides the condition of factuality in PN_3, which therefore becomes PN_3^0, and so forth. The same chain reaction is brought about if we embed PN_1 in a higher predication with a non-factive predicate like 'want':

(20) 'The owner of the Lotus wanted to compel Laetitia to let him drive her home.'

From (20), we cannot conclude that Laetitia did actually let him drive her home. The chain of factuality can also be broken at some intermediate point by the introduction of a non-factive predicate somewhere in the hierarchy of embedding:

(21) 'The owner of the Lotus compelled Laetitia to let him try to drive her home.'

From this we gather that Laetitia was compelled to let the Lotus-owner *try* his driving exploit, but whether they ever got home is left unrecorded.

Factuality and Presuppositions

As we have already noted in examples (11) to (13), factuality contrast is a property of downgraded, as well as embedded predications; consequently, it affects presuppositions, as well as entailments. A parallel can be drawn in this respect between the quantifier 'any' and a non-factive predicate: just as a verb-meaning like 'try' or 'want' neutralizes the factuality of embedded predications, so 'any' neutralizes the factuality of downgraded predications, and thus erases a presupposition. Compare:

(22) 'Please forgive the inaccuracies in the report I sent you yesterday.'
(23) 'Please forgive any inaccuracies in the report I sent you yesterday.'

The utterance of (22) presupposes that the report has some inaccuracies, while that of (23) does not.

But downgrading differs from embedding in that the nonfactual chain-reaction just noted does not take place. Just as presuppositions are uninfluenced by the negation of a higher predication, so they are resistent to the influence of neutral factuality. For example, (22) above has these two presuppositions:

(24) 'The report I sent you yesterday has inaccuracies in it.'
(25) 'I sent you a report yesterday.'

These are hierarchically ordered, as in the 'chain of factuality' for embedded predications; (22) presupposes (24), which in turn presupposes (25). But the significant point is that even when presupposition (24) is neutralized by 'any', as it is in (23), presupposition (25) remains in force.

Another point to notice is that the main predication in (22) and (23) is imperative, and has neutral factuality (i.e. we do not know whether the request for forgiveness will be granted or not). But this does not prevent it from having factual presuppositions.

The conclusions that may be drawn are that (a) for any relation 'X presupposes Y', Y has to be factual, but X does not; (b) to the negation test (p. 294) for distinguishing presupposition from entailment may be added a 'factuality' test as follows:

'For any truth-dependence relation "X entails/presupposes Y", the neutralization of factuality in X nullifies an entailment, whereas it does not nullify a presupposition.'

How to Analyse Pure Factives?

We have already noted that pure factive predicates, such as 'know', 'be odd', 'realize', etc., confer the status of a presupposition on whatever assertion precedes or follows them in the form of a *that*-clause:

'It's odd that cigarettes cost more than cigars' presupposes
'Cigarettes cost more than cigars.'

This conclusion is reinforced by the observation that such assertions are unaffected by neutral factuality in a higher predication.

(26) Jim knows that it is lucky that the car skidded.
(27) Jim thinks that it is lucky that the car skidded.

Although in (27) the non-factive predicate 'think' replaces the factive predicate 'know' of (26), this has no effect on the presupposition that 'the car skidded'.

The dilemma we face with pure factives is that (a) the maintaining of expression rules relating semantics to syntax (p. 184) and (b) the maintaining of rules of presupposition and entailment call for two different solutions. The *that*-clauses in (26) and (27) function syntactically as objects and Noun Clauses, and therefore semantically one would like to analyse them as embedded predications (see p. 184). On the other hand, they function semantically (because of their status as presuppositions) like downgraded predications. Very tentatively, I suggest that we uphold the semantic generalization at the expense of semantic-syntactic one, and analyse factual *that*-clauses as having the semantic structure of downgraded predications. Evidence in favour of this decision is provided by the following:

(28) That girls are cleverer than boys is a fact.

(29) The fact is that girls are cleverer than boys.

(30) *Question*: Don't you understand that girls are cleverer than boys? *Answer*: I recognize that fact.

(31) Teachers recognize the fact that girls are cleverer than boys.

(32) Teachers recognize that girls are cleverer than boys.

In very many cases, as in (31) and (32), the expression *the fact* can be inserted into sentences with pure factives without any change of meaning. This encourages us to think of *the fact* as an optionally deletable element (for a syntactic analysis on these lines, see Kiparsky and Kiparsky, 1970). There are, of course, exceptions: for some reason unknown, one cannot insert *the fact* following the verb *know* (**I know* THE FACT *that you are lying*), although one may say *I know* AS A FACT *that you are lying*.

The question is, what semantic representation of the word *fact* should be given? When occurring as a noun phrase in an equative construction as in (28) and (29), it invites analysis (see p. 269) as an argument twinned with another argument which is an embedded predication:

(III)

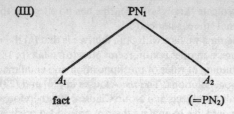

$$PN_1$$

$$A_1 \qquad\qquad A_2$$

fact $\qquad\qquad$ (=PN₂)

In sentences like (30), however, it operates in a two-place predication with the same set of verbs, adjectives, etc. that express factive predicates: *I realize/know/resent/etc. that fact*:

(IV)

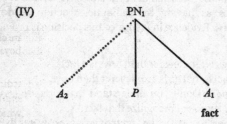

$$PN_1$$

$$A_2 \qquad P \qquad A_1$$

$\qquad\qquad\qquad$ **fact**

[A_2 in (IV) is an optional constituent of the formula]. Incidentally, I have represented the feature **fact** in bold type as a formator (p. 164), because there are special logical conditions for its use: namely that 'X is a fact' is logically synonymous with 'X' itself. In this respect, **fact** bears a resemblance to the formator **true**.

The semantic structure of (31) and (32) can then be seen, without the addition of further predication types, as the downgrading of a predication such as (III) in a predication such as (IV):

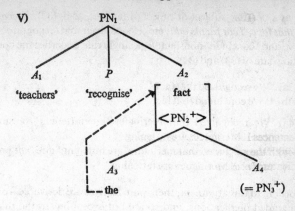

V)

PN₁

A₁   P   A₂

'teachers'   'recognise'   **fact**

$\langle PN_2{}^+ \rangle$

A₃   A₄

the $(= PN_3{}^+)$

'girls are cleverer
than boys'

In syntactic terms, this treatment amounts to regarding *the fact that X* as an appositional construction like *my friend the builder* (= 'my friend who is the builder') – an analysis which accords with many of the accounts in traditional grammars.

Taking diagram (V) to represent 'Teachers recognize (the fact) that girls are cleverer than boys', we derive from it, by the rule of presupposition, 'That girls are cleverer than boys is a fact' (= PN_2). This in turn entails (since **fact** attributes factuality to the predication which is its argument) 'Girls are cleverer than boys' (= PN_3). Consequently, whether or not PN_1 in diagram (V) is positively factual, PN_2 and PN_3 are. The conditions under which **fact** can occur as an argument can be specified by contextual redundancy rules (p. 144) which add **fact** to an argument conditional on the presence of a particular feature in the predicate. Pure factive predicates, then, are defined simply as those predicates which have a contextual redundancy rule of this kind.

An independent syntactic argument in favour of this analysis is the following. If all pure factive predicates add **fact** to an associated argument (which is an embedded predication), this will explain not only the occurrence (as in (31) and (32)) of factual *that*-clauses as objects or subjects, but also the occurrence of the word *fact* on its own as a possible subject or object of factives, as in (30): *I recognize that fact*; *That fact is odd*; etc. Hence given that 'recognize' is factive and 'conclude' non-factive, a single rule underlies the contrasting data of (33) and (34).

> (33a) 'We recognized that fact.'
> (33b) *'We concluded that fact.'

> (34a) 'We recognized that meringues are fattening' presupposes 'Meringues are fattening.'
> (34b) 'We concluded that meringues are fattening' does *not* presuppose 'Meringues are fattening.'

According to this argument, then, pure factives are derivable from downgraded predications, and so are not exceptions to the rules already given which link entailments with embedding, and presuppositions with downgrading.

A Problem of Scope of Negation

A further problem we have to deal with in matching these rules with the data is how to deal with the effect which syntactic ordering seems to have on the boundary between entailment and presupposition:

> (35a) The earthquake caused the collapse of the bridge.
> (35b) The earthquake did not cause the collapse of the bridge.

> (36a) The collapse of the bridge was caused by the earthquake.
> (36b) The collapse of the bridge was not caused by the earthquake.

Many people will feel that although (35a) and (36a) seem to mean the same thing (in that they could in no circumstances have different truth values), their negations (35b) and (36b) have a slight difference of logical meaning, namely that whereas from (35a), (36a), and (36b) we infer that the bridge collapsed, from (35b) we do not. This means, according to our negation criterion, that (35a) *entails* 'The bridge collapsed', while (36a) *presupposes* it. But this difference cannot easily be explained by the assignment of different semantic representations to (35) and (36), since the only difference between them is that the latter has been converted to the passive – a syntactic process which in general has no effect on conceptual meaning.

Here we have to look back to the distinction between conceptual meaning and thematic meaning, as discussed in Chapter 2 (pp. 22–3). Thematic meaning, that which is conveyed by the way the content of a message is presented in terms of order, emphasis, and focus, is a product of the surface syntactic form of sentences. I have argued that this thematic meaning is independent of the conceptual meaning embodied by semantic representations: indeed, that it belongs to a different level of linguistic organization entirely. But we have to observe now that thematic focus can have not only a *positive* effect of adding emphasis etc. to some aspects of the conceptual message, but also a *negative* effect of suppressing certain possibilities of interpretation which are implicit in the conceptual meaning as reflected in the semantic representation. An instance of this has already been noted in connection with quantifiers (p. 175): sentences expressing mixed quantification, such as

(37) All girls like some pop-stars.
(38) Some pop-stars are liked by all girls.

are in theory ambiguous, but ordering and intonation focus in practice disambiguate them, so that typically (37) and (38) have different conceptual meanings. We have also noted a case (p. 267) where surface structure ordering has a bearing on the interpretation of adverbials in relation to negation:

'I deliberately didn't hit him' ≠ 'I didn't hit him deliberately.'

In the last chapter, the term *scope of negation* was introduced to refer to the stretch of language over which the negative has its effect and it was noted that in conceptual meaning, this scope is bounded by the predication in which the negative formator **not** occurs. But in terms of thematic meaning, the scope of negation is normally limited still further to the part of the underlying predication which is expressed by elements following the negative word. This is a natural result of the tendency, in the informational organization of the message, to assign the first position in the sentence or clause to *old* (or 'given') information (i.e. that part of the message which has been previously mentioned, or can be otherwise assumed from context), and to place *new* information towards the end. One sign that the scope of negation is so restricted is that it is normal to use non-factual forms such as *any* and *yet* in place of *some*, *already*, etc. in a post-negative position, but not (except, conceivably, with quite a different meaning) in a pre-negative position:

Joe doesn't trust anybody   *Anybody doesn't trust Joe.

[Scope of negation is indicated here by the horizontal bracket.] Sentence (39) is to this extent atypical; it shows *somebody* occurring outside the scope of negation, although it is the object of a negative verb phrase:

(39) Joe doesn't trust somebody.

All the same, this oddity can be accounted for if, by the rule of subordination (p. 265), *somebody* is assumed to express a quantifier outside of the predication containing **not** (that is, if the negative is within the scope of the quantifier, not vice versa). In this instance, the conceptual rule for limiting the scope of negation restricts still further the thematic limitation.

With this preparation, we may return to (35b) and (36b), and see that the difference between them is a difference of scope of negation. Because *the collapse of the bridge* in (36b) precedes the negative it has the status of 'given information', and is outside the scope of **not**; but in the transition from (35a) to (35b), the *collapse of the bridge* falls under the scope of negation. The typical meaning for (35b) is therefore:

'The earthquake did something or other, but it didn't cause the bridge to collapse.'

In contrast, the typical meaning of (36b) is:

'Something caused the collapse of the bridge but it wasn't the earthquake.'

Although 'cause', as noted earlier, is a conditional factive predicate, we may argue that (36b) 'The collapse of the bridge was not caused by the earthquake' is not a true counterexample of the rule

that such predicates give rise to an entailment. The interpretation
of (36b) so as to allow for the possibility that 'The bridge did not
collapse' is acceptable according to conceptual semantics, but is
'filtered out' by the thematic rule which defines the scope of
negation. On the level of semantic representation (35b) and (36b)
are synonymous; it is only on the surface syntactic level that 'informational structure' filters out one of the possibilities of interpretation, and so turns 'the bridge collapsed' technically, by the
negation test, into a presupposition.

Other Presuppositions

In spite of superficially conflicting evidence, one can plausibly
maintain, as I hope I have shown, that a large central class of presuppositions is derivable by a single rule from the form of semantic
representations, given that those representations contain downgraded predications and markers of factuality. Many other cases,
which I have not had time to discuss, could be dealt with in this
way. It would not be difficult to show, for example, how presuppositions arising from selection restrictions are basically of the
same kind as those already considered. Examples of such presuppositions are:

'Brendon ate the pizza' presupposes 'Brendon is an animate
being.'
'Is the treasurer pregnant?' presupposes 'The treasurer is
female.'

The selection restriction is formalized (p. 144) as a contextual
dependence rule by which a feature such as +ANIMATE, −MALE,
etc., is added to the argument affected. Since by the rule of
attribution (p. 278) such features can be expanded into downgraded predications ⟨the: +ANIMATE⟩, ⟨the: −MALE⟩, etc., these
presuppositions can be indirectly derived within the same framework as the others.

Of course, I have not been able to show that the downgrading of
factual predications is the source of *all* positive presuppositions.
There are many cases which, so far as I can tell, defy analysis in this

manner. Examples are certain presuppositions associated with the adverbs *only* and *even* (see Horn 1969, Fraser 1969, 1971):

> 'Only the old people listened' presupposes 'The old people listened.'

I have also not been able to do justice, in this treatment, to negative presuppositions and their connection with counterfactuality:

> 'I wish you had signed the petition' presupposes 'You did not sign the petition.'

However, I hope this investigation has done enough to suggest how statements about presuppositions may be included amongst the 'basic statements' (p. 84) which a semantic theory is capable of explaining in a systematic way, and that such presuppositions can be accounted for without going beyond the notion of 'semantic representation' that has become familiar from earlier chapters.

Expectation

Earlier on I proposed the existence of *expectation* as a third relation of truth-dependence, weaker than entailment and presupposition in that it can be cancelled out by an appended 'qualifying' sentence:

(40a) 'Few old-age pensioners play football.'
(40b) 'Few old-age pensioners play football – *in fact, none at all do.*'

The first of these two examples, (40a), conveys the assumption or expectation that 'Some old-age pensioners play football' – but this expectation is cancelled out by the afterthought added in (40b). On the other hand, expectations are strong enough to impose conditions of well-formedness: sentence (41) is bizarre, because it has an expectation which is a contradiction:

(41) *'Few bachelors are married' expects *'Some bachelors are married.'

Evidently expectations cannot be ignored in a semantic theory which is committed to the explanation of conditions of semantic acceptability. But how are they to be explained?

My claim is that just as a central set of presuppositions can be explained by reference to the single structural principal of downgrading, so can most cases of expectation be explained by reference to the single semantic operation of *negation*. In (40), for instance, *few* means the same as *not many*, and *many* is a hyponym of *some* (see p. 173), so to get from 'few' to 'some' we subtract (a) the negative feature **not** and (b) at least one other feature. This seems to be a general procedure for deriving an expectation from the 'expecting' sentence. Another example of expectation connected with negation is:

(42) 'No one other than Peter came' expects 'Peter came.'

The interesting thing here is that (42) differs from (43) by a single linguistically significant property – namely that (42) *expects* 'Peter came', while (43) *presupposes* it:

(43) 'Only Peter came' presupposes 'Peter came.'

To (42), but not to (43), one could add '. . . and for that matter, Peter didn't come either'. In linguistic terminology, (42) and (43) may be said to constitute a 'minimal pair'.

The connection between expectation and negation is in fact twofold. Negative assertions have:

 (i) *a cancelled expectation* (which is the corresponding positive assertion, with **not** omitted).
(ii) *an actual expectation* (which is that part of the positive content of the assertion that remains after the negated content has been 'subtracted' from it).

For example, 'Few people died in the flood' has the *cancelled* expectation that 'Many people died in the flood', and the *actual* expectation that 'Some people died in the flood'. These two expectations seem to have their respective sources in two very general psychological principles governing the use of negation in ordinary discourse:

PRINCIPLE I: One doesn't bother to negate an assertion unless someone has or might have a reason to imagine it is true (CANCELLED EXPECTATION).

PRINCIPLE II: When one negates an assertion, it is assumed in most contexts that part of the content under the scope of negation remains positive (ACTUAL EXPECTATION).

It is intriguing that negative questions (which are often considered not to be negative in the strict logical sense, and therefore to be semantically unrelated to negative assertions) are like negative assertions in having both a cancelled expectation and an actual expectation. The negative question 'Can't you drive a car?' differs from the positive question 'Can you drive a car?' in conveying the following dual assumption on the speaker's part: 'I thought you could drive a car, but now it appears that you can't.' That is, there is a cancelled expectation ('You can drive a car') and an actual expectation ('You can't drive a car').

Because actual expectation, not cancelled expectation, is the relation that most concerns us, I shall now concentrate on Principle II above, and see whether it can be given a more precise formulation.

It has sometimes been pointed out (see, e.g., Katz 1964b) that most cases of negation are in a sense multiply ambiguous (or, as I should prefer to say, multivalent) because the condition of negation can be satisfied independently by the negation of any feature or combination of features within the scope of the negation. Thus (assuming a literal interpretation of *man*) 'Joe is not a man' can be interpreted according to context 'Joe is a human adult who is not male', 'Joe is a human male who is not adult', 'Joe is an adult male who is not human', 'Joe is a human-being who is not male and not adult', etc. Or, to take a slightly more complicated example: let us take for granted that *bachelor* is defined by the four features +HUMAN, +ADULT, +MALE, ⟨'never-married'⟩ (where ⟨'never married'⟩ is a downgraded predication); then some of the various readings that negation might theoretically have in a sentence like (44) are the following:

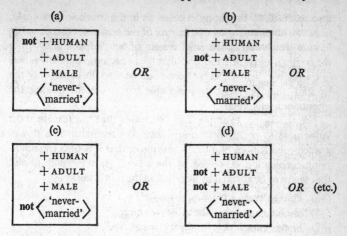

(44) 'My neighbour upstairs is not a bachelor.'

Fillmore (1969: 123) argues that in practice, interpretation (c) is chosen, so that (44) in effect means 'My neighbour upstairs is a married man'. This indicates, he suggests, a difference between *presupposed elements* of meaning (here 'man') and *directly asserted* elements of meaning ('never-married') in the semantic make-up of *bachelor*. I would point out, however, that the relation between (44) and 'My neighbour upstairs is a married man' is at best an expectation rather than a presupposition. We see this from the possibility of its being outweighed by a contradictory qualification:

'My neighbour upstairs isn't a bachelor – in fact he/she's not

even $\left\{ \begin{array}{l} \text{male'} \\ \text{human'} \\ \text{adult'} \end{array} \right\}$.

Fillmore's observation, assuming it is substantially correct, may be explained by the postulate that features of a definition can be ordered hierarchically according to their likelihood of being affected by negation. Such a hierarchic ordering no doubt closely parallels the ordering of features by dependence rules (p. 120). It also seems likely that in most cases, as in the 'bachelor' example, negation eliminates only one feature of the positive sentence – that feature which carries the chief weight of new information within the context, and is thus more vulnerable to negation than any other. 'Few people died' expects 'Some people died' because only the 'multal' feature ↑AMOUNT is liable to be erased, leaving the quantifier itself intact.

The 'bachelor' example also illustrates that the feature most vulnerable to negation in many instances seems to be a downgraded predication. Notice, for example, that it is only the modifying predication expressed by the adverb or adverbial phrase that seems to be affected by negation in the following:

(45) 'I haven't seen Bill *for three weeks*'.
(46) 'She hasn't polished the table *very nicely.*'
(47) 'I never eat Chinese food *with chopsticks.*'
(48) 'My father doesn't *often* go to the theatre.'

Normally interpreted, these sentences could be closely paraphrased as follows:

(45a) 'I have seen Bill [but not for three weeks].'
(46a) 'She has polished the table [but not very nicely].'
(47a) 'I (sometimes) eat Chinese food [but not with chopsticks].'
(48a) 'My father (sometimes) goes to the theatre [but not often].'

The actual expectations of (45) – (48) are the unnegated parts of (45a) – (48a), that is, those parts outside the square brackets.

My general feeling is, however, that it is not possible to predict absolutely, without reference to the individual context, which features will be effectively negated, and which will remain effectively positive. I feel that expectation relations are not to be found in the abstract logical system of language, but rather in the 'pragmatics' of communication, along with thematic ordering, information focus, etc. In support of this, note that expectation can vary not only according to scope of negation (itself, I have suggested earlier, a matter of surface syntax), but according to intonation focus. If we put a heavy stress and fall of intonation on *polished* in (46):

(46b) She hasn't POLISHED the table very nicely

the expectation shifts to the following: 'She has done something nicely to the table [but she hasn't polished it].'

Although, for the reason just given, there can be no hard and fast criterion for deriving expectation from semantic representations, one may attempt an approximate statement as follows:

Rule of Expectation: *If* X is a negative assertion
        and if F is the most communicatively
              significant feature within the
              scope of negation in X
        and if Y is an assertion identical to X
              except that it is positive and does
              not contain F
        then X expects Y

As with presupposition, there are other cases to which this rule does not seem to apply. In particular, what have been considered counterfactual presuppositions often fail the uncontradictability test, and therefore have to be considered counterfactual expectations instead:

(49) 'If we got married, we would be happy' expects 'We are not happy.'

It seems possible to add to the first sentence of (49) '. . . in fact we are happy already', and so to call this 'presupposition' is to represent the relation between the two sentences as stronger than it is. Similarly 'If you loved me, we could get married' does not seem to rule out the possibility of the marriage taking place, and furthermore even the counterfactual quality of the *if*-clause is weakened here, in so far as 'if you loved me . . .' can be interpreted as hypothetical only for the rhetorical purpose of inviting the hearer's denial.

Conclusions

The main conclusions of this chapter are:

1. There are at least three different relations of truth-dependence between predications: entailment, presupposition, and the weaker relation I have called expectation.

2. To a great extent at least, these relations of truth-dependence are regularly predictable by rule from the form of semantic representations as developed in previous chapters.

(a) Entailment is predictable from relations of hyponymy between arguments and predicates (as stated in Chapter 7), or more indirectly, from the relation between an embedded assertion and the assertion in which it is embedded.

(b) Presupposition in most cases has its source in the relation of downgrading between one predication and another.

(c) The relation of expectation seems to derive typically from the principle that when an assertion is negated, some of its content (even within the scope of negation) remains positive.

3. For a full account of these relations, however, it is necessary to suppose the existence of factuality features ('factual', 'non-factual', and 'counterfactual') which are attached to predications (both main and subordinate), and which act as conditions on rules of entailment, presupposition, and expectation. 'Factual' and 'counterfactual' features represent an assumption of truth and falsehood respectively; 'non-factual' features represent a lack of commitment either to truth or to falsehood.

4. A factuality feature can in many cases be predicted, by a type of selection restriction, from a higher predicate with which it is associated. On this basis, predicates can be classified as *factive*, *non-factive*, and *counterfactive*.

5. Factive predicates can be further subdivided into *pure factives* (which give rise to presuppositions) and *conditional factives* (which give rise to entailments).

14. Alternative Theories

The object of this book, as I declared in the Introduction, has been to follow through one approach to meaning, rather than to attempt a survey of different approaches. I believe this has been justified: such is the complexity of semantic issues and the variety of opinion on them that it is better to see the subject through the 'eyes' of a particular model (even if those eyes may be to some extent blinkered) rather than to receive a general and necessarily rather superficial survey of 'schools of thought' and the controversies in which they have engaged.

My hope is that the reader who has browsed, worked, or wrestled his way through this book will now have some firm bearings in the subject, which he can use in exploring other approaches, both theoretical and practical, on his own initiative. The *Background Reading* section following this chapter is intended to help him in this. But before we come to that point, I feel that I owe him some account, however inadequate, of the relation between the line of approach I have taken here, and other approaches which have been developing within contemporary linguistics. I have in mind especially the opposed 'generative' and 'interpretive' approaches to semantics, both of which have developed out of Transformational Grammar (see p. 326 below).

These two schools of thought (or rather, two variants of the same school) undoubtedly make up together the most influential and productive source of new ideas and insights into semantics at the present time. Also, within contemporary linguistics there has grown up an interest in the illocutionary approach to meaning, which originated in the writings of the Oxford philosopher J. L. Austin, and has since proved a fruitful avenue of inquiry both for philosophers and linguists. It is around these three trends in semantics – generative, interpretive, and illocutionary – that I shall concentrate the discussion of this chapter.

It goes without saying that my descriptions of alternative models, as well as my arguments in defence of the present model, will be grossly simplified and incomplete, if I am to confine them to a single chapter. In making this conventional apology, I feel less guilty than usual: such is the amazing speed at which linguistic semantics is evolving at present, that I could not hope, even if I expanded this chapter into a book, to recapitulate all the relevant arguments which have appeared in recently published literature. I hazard the guess that in linguistic semantics the amount of published research and scholarship has been greater during the four years that I have been planning and writing this book, than during the whole of the preceding years of the twentieth century. It is a measure of the rate of development in transformational grammar that the state of transformational theory reached in 1965 (with the publishing of Chomsky's influential *Aspects of the Theory of Syntax*) is now often referred to as 'classical'. In retrospect, it does indeed seem as if transformational grammar reached at that point a brief but blessed period of stable certainty which has evaporated in the *Sturm und Drang* of more recent developments.

'Generative' versus 'Interpretive' Semantics

The popular (though potentially misleading) labels *generative semantics* and *interpretive semantics* refer not so much to ways of studying semantics *per se*, as to ways of relating semantics to syntax. Both developed out of the 'classical' transformational grammar of 1965. Transformational grammar is the theory of language in which syntax is considered to have two kinds of rules: phrase-structure rules which specify the form of constituent-structure trees, and transformational rules, which in essence convert one kind of tree-structure into another (e.g. an active structure into a passive structure – see p. 200). In the earliest published version of transformational grammar – Chomsky's *Syntactic Structures*, (1957) – meaning was in effect ignored. It was assumed that syntactic rules operated in complete independence from meaning: their function was to 'generate' or specify by rule the grammatical sentences of a language, and to assign to these sentences their correct structure. In fact, many of the transformational rules, such as that which converted an active sentence structure into a passive sentence structure, happened in general to preserve the meaning of sentences unaltered (and therefore, in a sense, to be rules of paraphrase), but this was considered an irrelevant side-effect of such rules. Since that time, however, or more precisely, since a pioneering article on semantics by Katz and Fodor ('The Structure of a Semantic Theory', 1963), the history of transformational grammar has been broadly a matter of conceding to semantics a more and more important position in linguistic theory. But to my knowledge, no transformational grammarian of note, whether of generativist or interpretivist persuasion, has accorded to semantics the primacy that syntax was given in transformational theory up to 1965. Instead, in debating the relation between semantics and syntax, priority is still more frequently given to syntactic criteria (such as well-formedness of sentences) than to semantic criteria (such as logical entailment and inconsistency).

Whereas my own approach has been firmly based on semantic criteria, the approach to semantics in transformational grammar has always been *via* syntax. My own conclusions on the nature of semantic representation has in certain respects, however, been similar to those of the generative semanticists, and this convergence, considering the different points of departure, is an encouraging sign. In both generative semantics and the predicational analysis I have presented in this book, the semantic representation of a sentence can be seen roughly as the natural language equivalent of the formal symbolic logical representations of philosophy (see pp. 157–60).

Both interpretive semantics and generative semantics take as a point of departure the 'classical' theory of Chomsky (1965), in which a sentence was seen as organized syntactically on two chief levels: that of *deep structure* and that of *surface structure*. The surface structure of a sentence was derived from the deep structure by means of transformational rules involving such operations as the deletion of constituents, the movement of constituents from one part of a sentence to another, etc. The rules which specified the deep structure were phrase structure rules, which spelt out the basic constituency of sentences in terms of categories like Noun Phrases, Verbs, etc. These rules made up the *base* component of syntax, and had as their output (after the insertion of lexical items) deep structures; the transformational rules made up the *transformational* component of syntax, and had as their output surface structures. Apart from syntax, which was the central part of the total grammar, there were two 'interpretive' components: the phonological and the semantic. The phonetic interpretation of a sentence was derived from its surface structure by means of phonological rules, while the semantic interpretation of a sentence was derived from the deep structure through the operation of the so-called 'projection rules' of semantics. The whole theory, therefore, through the interaction of its various components, provided a matching of phonetic outputs with semantic outputs. It may be diagrammed as follows:

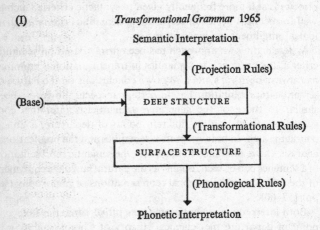

(I)   *Transformational Grammar* 1965

Semantic Interpretation

↑

(Projection Rules)

(Base) ⟶ DEEP STRUCTURE

(Transformational Rules)

↓

SURFACE STRUCTURE

(Phonological Rules)

↓

Phonetic Interpretation

Read from top to bottom, this diagram provides an account of the pairing of meanings with sounds which any complete linguistic theory must attempt. But the syntactic component, it is to be noted, has special status as the point from which the derivation of both sounds and meanings originates. Among the special claims of 'classical' theory are (a) that syntactic *surface* structure is the only level of syntax relevant to the specification of *phonetic interpretation*; and (b) that syntactic deep structure is the only level of syntax relevant to *semantic interpretation*. This second point brings with it the important principle that transformational rules are *meaning-*

preserving; that is, they do not in any way alter the meaning of the structures that they operate on. This means, in effect, that all sentences that have the same deep structures have the same meanings.

As we see, 'classical' theory provides for an *interpretive* semantic component; that is, the meaning of a sentence is specified by the application of semantic rules to a syntactic *base*. But since 1965, one important modification to the interpretivist position has been proposed. Chomsky (1970), Jackendoff (1968, 1972), and others have noticed that some aspects of meaning (mainly aspects involving negation, quantification, and information focus) appear to be more directly relatable to surface structure than to deep structure, and have therefore proposed that the 'projection rules' specifying meaning should operate on surface structures (and perhaps at intermediate points in a transformational derivation) rather than simply on deep structures. In other words, no longer does the interpretivist position involve a claim that all sentences with the same deep structures have the same meaning. The revised picture looks more like this:

(II)   *Revised 'Interpretive Semantics' Position*

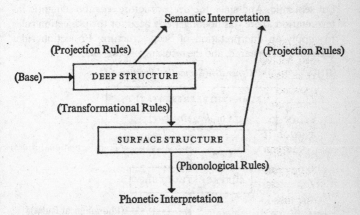

(The diagram does not represent the possibility of projection rules operating at intermediate points between deep and surface structure.)

Within this revised theory, deep structure reverts to being a level to be justified very largely on syntactic grounds alone. One can no longer argue (as one could with the 1965 model) that the synonymy of two lexically similar sentences is good *prima facie* grounds for supposing they have the same deep structure; instead, the argument has to be based on criteria such as syntactic well-formedness.

*

Generative semantics, like interpretive semantics, has arisen out of 'classical' theory, but it has developed along a quite different path. Arguments of the kind that gave rise to a deep structure level in the first place led, in the writings of Lakoff, McCawley, Ross, and others, to the 'deepening' of deep structure so as to make it closer to a representation of a sentence's meaning, and correspondingly to the lengthening of the transformational process of derivation from deep to surface structure. Syntax became more abstract. The logical terminus of this process was reached (in Ross and Lakoff 1967 and McCawley 1968a) when the deep structure of a sentence was declared to be so 'deep' as to be *identical* with its semantic representation. This now meant that the 'base' component, in the sense of Chomsky (1965), was no longer syntactic, but semantic. And since the deep structure *was* the semantic interpretation, there was no longer any need for the projection rules to supply an interpretation of deep structure. Projection rules therefore disappeared, and the resulting picture was:

(III)   *'Generative Semantics' Position*

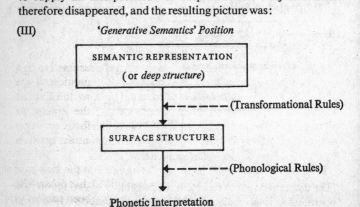

Because it eliminates the projectional rule component, the generativist model has the advantage of overall simplicity of design. But of course, this simplification is necessarily at the cost of expanding the transformational component, and making the chain of transformational derivation for each sentence considerably longer than was envisaged by Chomsky in 1965.

The labels 'generative' and 'interpretive' seem to have arisen because of a supposed distinction between base components of a grammar (which 'generate' sentences) and derived components (which 'interpret' the outputs of the base component). A simple way of defining interpretive and generative semantics on these lines is to say that in the one case the semantic representation of a sentence is derived from a syntactic base, whereas in the other, the (surface) syntactic representation is derived from a semantic base. These descriptions accord with the direction of the arrows on diagrams (II) and (III), which reinforces the idea that the direction of dependence is reversed. However, leading transformational grammarians of both generative and interpretive persuasions (Lakoff 1969, Chomsky 1971) deny that the question of direction of derivation has any substance. Although by mental habit linguists talk of 'X being derived from Y', 'X coming from Y', 'X being later in the derivation than Y', 'X being an output of Y', etc., it is difficult to refute the claim that any rule formulated in an 'X → Y' direction could equally well be formulated, if one wanted to, in a 'Y → X' direction.

The Generative-Interpretive Controversy

The question of 'directionality', then, is generally assumed to be a matter of no empirical consequence. It is not a question of the intrinsic properties of language, but rather of how the linguist chooses to formulate his rules. Consequently, the arguments between generativists and interpretivists tend to focus on some more substantial issues which are implicit in the contrast between diagrams (II) and (III).

The generativists, in the main, stay committed to the view that transformational rules do not change meaning. This has proved the most vulnerable principle in their model, and has been subject to the severest criticisms from interpretivists. As we have already seen, factors like scope of negation and scope of quantification are conditioned by surface syntactic ordering and surface constituent structure; and the same can be said (see Chomsky 1970; Fraser 1969, 1971) of other phenomena connected with scope, focus and emphasis (for example, the scope of the adverbs *only* and *even*). Another problem the generativists face in maintaining this principle is connected with their view that lexical items are inserted at various points *during* a transformational derivation, rather than at a single point, namely *before* the transformational derivation starts. Persuasive arguments (see, for example, Postal 1971b) have been put forward to show that at least some transformations must precede lexical insertion. This means that the lexical insertion rules (such as that which replaces 'COME+BECOME+NOT+ALIVE' by *die*) are simply a sub-class of transformations. But the difficulty with this is that these transformations often have the apparent effect of changing meaning, because of the influence of what, in an earlier chapter, I called 'petrification' (p. 226), and more generally, because of historical and idiosyncratic influences on the meanings of lexical items. If, for example, a rule is set up to derive 'John was tearful' from 'John was full of tears', and 'John was graceful' from 'John was full of grace' this will misrepresent the meanings of *helpful* ('full of help?'), *dreadful* ('full of dread?'), *hateful*, *pitiful*, *masterful*, etc. when we try to apply it to them.

The generativists, on the other hand, have concentrated their fire on the most vulnerable part of the interpretive position: namely, the claim that there is a valid level of linguistic abstraction corresponding to the deep syntactic structure of classical theory. Deep structure, according to the classical position, has a number of different functions, quite apart from that of being the level relevant to semantic interpretation:

(a) It is the level where lexical items are inserted into syntactic derivations.

(b) It is the level where relations of subcategorization are defined (e.g. classification of nouns in terms of 'countable' and 'mass'; classification of verbs according to selection restrictions).

(c) It is the starting point for the application of transformational rules.

(d) It is the level at which concepts such as 'Subject' and 'Object' are defined.

As Lakoff points out (1968), there is no particular reason to suppose that any single level has all these properties. On the contrary, there are good reasons for challenging its existence. McCawley (1968a) shows that selection restrictions are semantic (see p. 142), and so throws into doubt the 'subcategorization' function of deep structure. Further, generativists have argued (see especially Postal, 1971b) that the same rules are required to operate before lexical insertion as after it, and therefore that the interpretivist is compelled to deal with the same phenomenon in two different ways: in one case by projection rules, and in another by transformations. Thus, interpretive semantics, by insisting that there is a single level of lexical insertion prior to the operation of transformations, fails to recognize generalizations that can be made about transformational processes.

'Generative Semantics with Deep Syntactic Structure'

As I have suggested, the strongest arguments on both the interpretive and generative sides have been arguments against the rival position, rather than arguments positively in favour of one's own position. Accordingly, I feel there is nothing absurd about adopting a third position, which is neither strictly generative nor interpretive in the above senses, but in which some of the advantages of both sides are, I believe, to be gained. 'Generative semantics with deep structure' will seem like a contradiction, or at least like an inelegant hybrid, to those conditioned to the two-sided generative-interpretive debate. But I shall try, within severe limitations of space, to sketch one or two of the arguments for a model which meets this description.

It will be evident to anyone who has followed my remarks on the relation between semantics and syntax, both in Chapter 9 and elsewhere, that the position I have assumed does not accord in all respects with either the generative or the interpretive model. In Chapter 9, I put my money on a three-component model of language (semantics – syntax – phonology), and proposed *expression rules* which would have the function of translating (or 'recoding') semantic representations as syntactic representations, or vice versa (no directional precedence was assumed). But I distinguished such semantic-syntactic mapping rules from transformational rules, which I regarded as rules operating on syntactic representations only, mainly for thematic or stylistic arrangement. This distinction between semantic-syntactic mapping rules and transformations has no parallel in either of the dominant transformational grammar models: I am suggesting, more or less, that instead of the gradual transition from semantics to (surface) syntax that the generativists envisage, there is a definite break between the two. On the other hand, my proposal will not fit into the interpretive semantic model, because my view of a semantics with its own constituent structure accords with the generativist's concept of a semantic base, whereas for the interpretivist semantic representations are configurations of markers or features derived from syntactic constituent structures.

In Chapter 10 I put forward in some detail a model for the lexicon or dictionary, in which each lexical entry is composed of three specifications – morphological, syntactic, and semantic. I also proposed a separate morpheme index which would phonologically interpret the stems and affixes identified in the morphological specifications. These views again conflict with the transformational positions: in the classical transformational theory, lexical entries consist of semantic, syntactic, and *phonological* (not morphological) specifications; whereas from the generativist point of view, lexical rules are not a separate category at all, but rather a sub-class of transformations.

Then in Chapters 11 and 12 I developed the notion of rules of implication (in effect, rules of semantic equivalence), which have no formal equivalent in transformational grammar. I conjectured that such rules might fruitfully be formulated as semantic transformations relating 'deep semantics' to 'surface semantics' rather as syntactic deep structure, in classical transformational grammar, is related to syntactic surface structure by syntactic transformations.

The model which has been hinted at and discussed informally in various places in this book can now be formulated in a tidier manner:

(IV)   *Extralinguistic Reference*

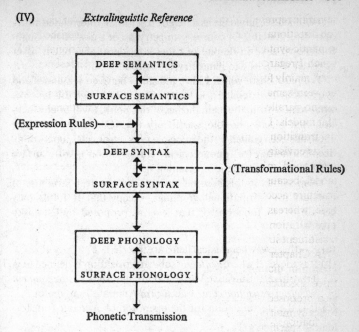

Phonetic Transmission

This model contains more specified levels of representation than those of (II) and (III), and so may give an appearance of greater complexity, but this is offset by the understanding that each stage of the diagram portrays a set of rules less complex than the analogous set of rules of the generativist or interpretivist models. For example, syntactic transformations in this model are restricted in the main to 'movement' transformations which shift elements around for thematic emphasis, etc. (this roughly corresponds to what has been called 'secondary topicalization'; see Fillmore 1968: pp. 57–8). Moreover, the diagram has the advantage of suggesting a symmetry in the overall structure of language which neither of the other models reflects. In this respect, it resembles some non-transformational models of language, such as the stratificational model of Lamb (1965), the tagmemic grammar of Pike (see Cook, 1969), and the system-structure model of Halliday (1961) –

all of which see language as a tiered structure of interrelated strata or coding systems. Of course, symmetry is not a goal to be sought for its own sake in despite of other considerations, but if other considerations lead to symmetry, all well and good.

The parallelism which I have indicated between semantics and syntax may be extended also to phonology. Although this is somewhat remote from the main themes of this book, I will briefly mention that recent phonological theory (e.g. Chomsky and Halle 1968) has been guided by the principle of a set of rules, connecting deep phonology (or 'phonological representation'), with surface phonology (or 'phonetic representation').

Deep syntax in this account is similar to the deep structure of classical transformational grammar, except that it fulfils only certain of the functions of that level as proposed by Chomsky (1965):

(a) It is the level where lexical items are inserted.
(b) It is the level where *syntactic* sub-categorization is defined (e.g. Transitive/Intransitive Verbs; Countable/Mass Nouns; *but not selection restriction categories such as* Animate/Inanimate).
(c) It is the starting-point for the operation of *syntactic* transformations.
(d) It is the level at which concepts such as 'Subject' and 'Object' are defined.

The italicized parts of these stipulations are those respects in which deep syntax is different from classical deep structure, as it was defined earlier (p. 332). None the less, the correspondence is considerable. At the same time, the semantic component of the model is 'generative' in that it has its own base, and structural conditions of well-formedness. Thus we have two separate bases, with syntax and semantics both having independent well-formedness conditions. In fact, various phonologists (see especially Sampson, 1970) have argued for a phonological base, and this view of phonology is the one I have assumed here. Hence the model differs from both the generative and interpretive moulds in containing more than one base component.

The remarks above may have helped to give this model some initial plausibility, but a fuller justification would obviously require detailed refutation of the objections of generativists and interpretivists from their respective positions. I can do no more than outline one or two of the arguments that play a part in the justification of the model.

In Justification of 'Generative Semantics with Deep Syntactic Structure'

To start with, it is necessary to clarify the main issues of such a debate.

(a) *From the interpretive point of view*, I have to defend adopting the generativist position that all conceptual meaning is specified in the semantic representation, and that there is no need to allow for the introduction of new factors of meaning by the rules mapping that representation on to surface syntax. The factors of meaning usually associated with surface syntax are those involving scope or focus. In particular, they include scope of negation and scope of quantifiers; also the semantic effect of intonation in determining information focus. I have already argued, however, that such factors of *thematic meaning* do not introduce further possibilities of interpretation in addition to those present in semantic representations, but rather filter out or suppress some of the possibilities inherent in the semantic interpretation (pp. 315–17). There appear to be no cases where additional features of meaning are added in surface syntax in such a way as to modify truth conditions positively. I therefore consider that through the distinction I have drawn between conceptual and thematic meaning (p. 22), this objection has already been answered.

(b) *From the generative point of view*, I have to justify the existence of a level of 'Deep Syntax' intermediate between (surface) semantic representations and surface syntactic representations. (I shall here, for convenience, adopt the transformationalist's conventional assumption that surface syntax is derived from deeper levels, rather than vice versa: that is, I shall discuss the mappings between levels in terms of a *speaker's model* (meaning-to-sound) rather than a *hearer's model* (sound-to-meaning).) The 'Deep Syntax' level has already been defined as a level (a) at which lexical insertion takes place; (b) at which syntactic subcategorization is introduced; (c) which is the input to syntactic transformations. I shall now put forward a number of arguments which can be used in support of a 'deep syntactic' level, and more generally, in support of the linguistic model diagrammed in Figure (IV).

(1) *Independent Well-formedness Conditions in Syntax*: In Chapter 9 (pp. 181–90) I pointed out a number of arguments, which I shall not recapitulate here, for the proposal of separate conditions of well-formedness in semantics and in syntax.

(2) *A Single Level of Lexical Insertion*: Generativists have argued that the insertion of lexical items into a sentence takes place during rather than before the operation of transformational rules on semantic representations. But their view that a lexical insertion rule is merely a type of syntactic transformation is, to my mind, a mistake. Such lexical insertion rules will fail in generality unless they try to capture the creative potentiality of the lexicon, as displayed in the discussion of lexical rules on pp. 210–28. Yet they will also fail unless they indicate the *limited* productivity of lexical rules, and the tendency for the semantic consequences of lexical rules to be modified, in the historical development of the lexicon, by the process I have called 'petrification' (p. 226). The combination of regularity and idiosyncracy in the lexicon can only be captured by a linguistic model which recognizes the separateness of lexical rules from syntactic rules. This difference is not recognized in the generative semantics model, but it is in the model I propose, where derived lexical definitions are not the output of transformations, but the product of lexical rules operating in the lexicon.

(3) '*Anaphoric Islands*': Postal (1969) has observed that certain linguistic units behave as 'islands' for purposes of anaphora or discourse reference (see p. 194), in that, for example, one cannot refer to elements inside them by means of a pronoun. In fact, these units correspond to the units we discussed in Chapter 10 as *lexical items*.

In support of his observation, Postal points out the unacceptability of the sentences marked (b) as paraphrases of the sentences marked (a) in such pairs as these:

(1a) Fred is a child whose *parents* are dead, but *yours* are still alive.

(1b) *Fred is an ORPHAN, but yours are still alive.

(2a) People who collect *stamps* sometimes pay vast sums for *them*.

(2b) *PHILATELISTS sometimes pay vast sums for them.

(3a) You can send your belongings by ship cheaper than you can by air.

(3b) *You can SHIP your belongings cheaper than you can by air.

(4a) A man who tames *lions* was mauled by *one* the other day.

(4b) *A LION-TAMER was mauled by one the other day.

(5a) The girl with red *hair* intends to dye *it*.

(5b) *The RED-HAIRED girl intends to dye it.

In the sentences marked (b), we notice that lexical items (such as those in capitals) are 'anaphoric islands' in that any constituent which is assumed to be in their underlying representation cannot be referred to by a pronoun, an ellipted ('understood') element, or any other anaphoric device. But when the meaning of the lexical item is spelled out more explicitly in terms of a syntactic construction, as in the (a) sentences, anaphora is possible. (The anaphoric item and its antecedent are signalled by italics in the (a) sentences, except in (3a), where anaphora is manifested in the ellipsis of *send their belongings*.)

The very notion of an 'anaphoric island' presupposes a framework in which lexical items such as *orphan* are presumed to arise transformationally, as substitutions for syntactic structures (in the case of *orphan* the syntactic element replaced would be a partial noun phrase containing a relative clause, something like *child whose parents are dead*). Such a substitution is necessary in the generative semantics model in order to account for the synonymy between pairs such as (1a) and (1b). Within the present model, on the other hand, *orphan* has no syntactic structure, only an underlying semantic structure. Thus the meaning of *orphan* is anatomized as a set of semantic features including a downgraded predication; the feature →PARENT occurs in that definition, but not the noun *parent*. Since anaphoric reference is a syntactic process, belonging to a different level of representation from the semantic representation, it follows naturally that no pronoun or other anaphoric device can refer to something within a lexical definition. Hence what

Postal discusses as an interesting phenomenon in need of explanation is automatically accounted for in a model which separates the semantic and syntactic representations of lexical items.

As is shown by examples (3a), (4a), and (5a), the same principle applies not only to morphologically simple items like *orphan*, but also to lexical entries derived by affixation, conversion, or compounding, from simpler lexical entries. Although *lion* in (4b) is a morphological base of the compound *lion-tamer*, it is not a syntactic constituent of the sentence, and therefore cannot be cross-referred to by a pronoun.

'Anaphoric islands', therefore, provide a second argument for the separation of lexical rules from syntactic transformational rules.

(4) *The Need for Distinct Semantic and Syntactic Categories*: In Chapter 9 (pp. 181–4) I assumed that syntactic categories (sentence, noun, verb, pronoun, etc.) are distinct from semantic categories (predication, argument, predicate), and it is interesting that this distinction is often informally assumed by generativists (e.g. McCawley 1968a, Lakoff 1970), who, when they start talking about semantics rather than syntax, replace syntactic labels by semantic ones. Obviously, if the vocabulary of categories in semantics is distinct from that in syntax, at some point in the specification of a sentence there must be a mapping of semantic categories onto syntactic categories, in a manner such as that sketched out on pp. 184–5. The generativists, so far as I know, do not discuss the possibilities of such as mapping, and assume simply that 'arguments' and 'predicates' are alternative names we might give to nouns and verbs on the deepest level of representation. But this leads to implausible efforts to reduce some syntactic categories to others: adjectives on the deepest level, are regarded as 'really verbs'; prepositional phrases are 'really noun phrases'; the quantifiers and the negative word *not* are also 'really verbs', and so on. It is often unclear, in such reductions, what are the criteria for deciding which category is derivative and which is fundamental – which the chicken, and which the egg. Could one not equally well argue, for instance, that verbs are adjectives rather than that adjectives are verbs? At the level where verbs are equated with predicates and nouns with arguments, all the properties which, in

grammatical tradition, have distinguished such grammatical categories (e.g. for verbs, modification for number, person, tense, aspect, non-finiteness, etc.) are absent.

Surely we are nearer the truth of the matter if we say that there are far fewer major categories of unit in semantics than there are in syntax, without insisting that the former have to make up a subset of the latter. The way this is handled in a multiple-base model is by the one-many mappings of expression rules (p. 184). By this means we are able to say that a verb phrase, a preposition, and a conjunction may all have *underlying* them a single semantic category, namely a predicate, without having to argue that such prepositions and conjunctions are 'really verbs'. The separation of syntactic from semantic categories is parallel to, and just as desirable as, the separation of syntactic categories (like 'word') from phonological categories (like 'syllable').

(5) *Semantic 'Transformations'*: Unlike the generative and interpretive models, the present model allows for a separate set of semantic transformations or rules of implication. The motivation for such rules, which was tentatively argued in Chapter 12, may also be considered a motivation for adopting a theory within which semantic transformations have an assigned function, analogous to the function of syntactic transformations in syntax. With semantic transformations it is sometimes possible to make generalizations beyond the power of syntactic transformations. For example, there is in most orthodox accounts of transformational grammar a 'Pseudo-cleft-sentence' transformation, which permits the formation of sentences such as (6b) and (7b) on the model of simpler sentence structures such as those of (6a) and (7a):

(6a) Bill likes cake.   (6b) What Bill likes is cake.
(7a) I had a fight with John.   (7b) John was who I had a fight with.

This, in the present account, is an unnecessary rule, because a paraphrase relation such as that between (6a) and (6b) is in any case generated by the semantic rule of identification, as we saw in Chapter 12 (p. 273). That is, the syntactic transformation can be dispensed with as dealing merely with a special case of the semantic transformation.

Two more arguments may be mentioned, finally, more generally in defence of a multiple-based model.

(6) *The Suspect Nature of Some Transformational Rules*: In the interpretive-generative debate, the interpretivists (see especially Chomsky,1972b) have criticised certain generativist rules (such as the rules of 'raising', 'predicate raising', and 'quantifier lowering' (see McCawley 1970b, Lakoff 1970)) which do not behave as other transformations, or else appear to lack syntactic motivation. These suspect rules would be dispensed with in a multiple-based model, their functions being assumed by expression rules and semantic transformations. Thus objections which have been made to generative semantics as a result of its extension of the function of transformational rules would not apply to the present model.

(7) *The Function of the Morpheme Index*: In Chapter 10 (p. 206) I proposed the separation of the lexicon (the list of lexical entries, in terms of semantic, syntactic, morphological specifications) from the morpheme index (a list of morphemes, i.e. stems and affixes, with their associated pronunciations). This separation is justified as a device of economy, which makes it unnecessary to repeat the phonological specification of a morpheme for each occurrence of that morpheme in a lexical item. Thus the pronunciation of the morpheme *book* in *book*, *bookish*, *handbook*, etc., only has to be given once – in the morpheme index. Such a separation of two traditional functions of the dictionary makes sense in a model where semantic, syntax and phonology are autonomous levels, since just as lexical insertion applies at the level of semantic-syntactic mapping, so the 'spelling out' of morpheme pronunciations must apply at the level of syntactic-phonological mapping. It is clear that the pronunciations of morphemes must be 'looked-up' at this point, because phonological information is irrelevant to the operation of syntactic transformations; on the other hand, the 'deep phonological' representation of *handbook* (let us say, as /hændbʊk/) can be modified by subsequent phonological rules (e.g. by the rule of assimilation which converts it to /hæmbbʊk/). Hence the two 'dictionary look-up' stages of a sentence's derivation fit neatly into the three-level model of Figure IV, by applying at the transitions between levels:

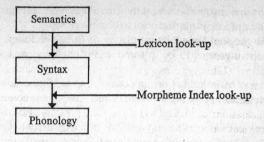

Illocutionary Force

We turn now from the interpretive-generative debate to another notable trend in modern semantics: this is the exploration of an approach to meaning engendered by the ideas of the philosopher J. L. Austin (*How to Do things with Words*, 1962). Austin was dissatisfied with the traditional concentration, in linguistic philosophy, on referential meaning and the truth and falsehood of statements. This led him away from the question of 'what do sentences mean' towards the question 'what sort of act do we perform when we utter a sentence'. This he called the *illocutionary* force of an utterance, distinguishing it from the *locutionary* force (roughly, the referential or cognitive meaning which had been the philosopher's traditional concern) and from the *perlocutionary* force (what sort of function or fulfilment of intention is accomplished by the sentence). The illocutionary purport of an utterance is to be expressed in terms of what Austin called 'happiness' or 'felicity' conditions, rather than in terms of truth and falsehood. One linguist who has been influenced by this approach, Charles J. Fillmore, gives, by way of illustration, the following conditions of 'happiness' or appropriateness for the simple imperative utterance *Please shut the door*:

 (i) The speaker and the addressee of this sentence are in some kind of relationship which allows the speaker to make requests of the addressee.

 (ii) The addressee is in a position where he is capable of shutting the door.

(iii) There is some particular door which the speaker has in mind and which he has reason to assume the addressee can identify without any further descriptive aid on the speaker's part.

(iv) The door in question, is, at the time of utterance, open.

 (v) The speaker wants that door to become closed.

We can see that the violation of any of these conditions would cause the utterance to be in some sense 'unhappy' or inappropriate.

One way of looking at presuppositions, as we found in the last chapter (p. 292), is to regard them as such 'happiness conditions'. In fact, conditions (iii) and (iv) above (and possibly also condition (ii)) are identifiable as presuppositions in the treatment of presupposition I have given. But conditions (i) and (v) are illocutionary in a narrower sense: they are circumstances which enter into the definition of what it is to perform a speech act of a particular sort, in this case a request. We may call such conditions *speech-act conditions*. One can imagine laying down similar conditions for other kinds of speech act, such as statements, questions, promises, warnings, apologies, etc. For a question to be 'felicitous' for instance, at least the following speech-act conditions must obtain:

(a) There is a piece of information (X) of which the questioner is ignorant.

(b) The questioner wants to know (X).

(c) The questioner believes that the addressee knows (X).

(d) The questioner is in a position to elicit (X) from the questioner.

Generally the illocutionary force of an utterance is not made explicit by the utterance itself; but a notable class of exceptions to this rule includes such sentences as:

> I do. (uttered at a marriage ceremony)
> I name this ship *Queen Elizabeth*. (said when smashing a bottle against the bows)
> I give and bequeath my watch to my brother. (in a will)
> I bet you sixpence it will rain tomorrow.

These sentences (Austin's own examples) illustrate the class of utterances Austin calls *performatives*; that is, they are utterances which themselves describe the speech act which they perform. Performatives look like statements syntactically, but as Austin points out, they differ from most statements semantically in that they cannot be declared false. Thus if speaker *A* says 'I declare that King Charles II was a coward' and speaker *B* replies 'That's false', he is denying not the performative utterance, but the statement that it contains, namely, 'That King Charles II was a coward'. In other words, 'That's false' in this context means 'Charles II was *not* a coward' rather than 'You do *not* declare that Charles II was a coward.'

The characteristic syntactic markers of a performative sentence are the following:

(I) The subject is in the first person. (*I* or *we*)
(II) The verb is in the simple present tense. (*state*, *ask*, *pardon*, etc.)
(III) The indirect object, if one is present, is *you*.
(IV) It is possible to insert the adverb *hereby*.
(V) The sentence is not negative.

All these characteristics are realized in:

I hereby declare to you my innocence.

But not all verbs referring to speech events can function as performative verbs, as we gather from the 'infelicity' of these sentences:

*I hereby remark that the weather is cloudy.
*I hereby persuade you to eat fish in Lent.
*I hereby denigrate your parents.

Performatives are problematic semantically because for every non-performative sentence it is possible to find one or more performative equivalents. Thus one can maintain, with Austin, that the only difference between *I order you to go*! and *Go*! is that the former is explicitly performative, while the latter is implicitly so. The problem is, how do we give an account of the quasi-equivalence of these utterances – a matter to which I shall return shortly.

Presuppositions and Context

In the preceding section, we saw that the 'happiness' conditions of an utterance could be regarded either as *presuppositions* (that is, as conditions which have to obtain in the context or more generally in the extra-linguistic universe if the utterance is to be considered appropriate), or as *speech-act conditions* which specify more narrowly the conventional social requirements for a given type of speech act. With these two aspects of linguistic communication can be associated two particular developments within generative semantics. The first, with which we dealt extensively in the last chapter, is the recognition of presuppositions as an important aspect of, or adjunct to, the meaning of utterances. What I have to add here is merely a footnote to the last chapter's treatment, explaining the connection between presuppositions and the illocutionary meaning, and attempting to combat what I consider a misleading tendency to separate presupposition from the logical content, or conceptual meaning of an utterance. This separation is partly encouraged by the characterization of a presupposition as a 'condition' of the speech situation:

> By the presuppositional aspects of a speech communication situation I mean those conditions which must be satisfied for a particular illocutionary act to be effectively performed in saying particular sentences. (Fillmore 1971: 276)

The danger of locating presuppositions in the extra-linguistic situation in this way is that it gives the illusion of explaining linguistic behaviour by reference to something outside language. I say 'illusion', because as I argued in Chapter 5 (p. 75), what lies outside language can only be formulated in terms of language: to relegate presuppositions to context is to fall foul of the linguistic 'bootstraps' fallacy, that one can somehow explain linguistic phenomena with reference to what is outside language. Thus presupposition, however we might *wish* to characterize it, can only in practice be explained as a relation between linguistic entities. This was the position I took in Chapter 13, where I defined presupposition as a relation between two predications.

The assumption that presuppositions are somehow outside language perhaps explains the separation that some linguists have made (see, e.g., McCawley 1968a: 141) between 'meaning' and 'presupposition', and the tendency (see Lakoff, 1970: 50–52) to treat presuppositions as extraneous to the logical structure, or main semantic representation, of a sentence. But this surely is an unnecessary if not harmful separation, since, as I showed in the last chapter, a large proportion of presuppositions can be directly predicted from the form of semantic representations. Thus, while recognizing the importance of presupposition, I see no reason for attempting to divorce it from the central conceptual meaning of an utterance. Another disadvantage of locating presuppositions in the extralinguistic situation is that the term 'situation' has its meaning stretched to include, potentially, any piece of information about the universe, past, present or future. For example, the question 'Did the murder of Julius Caesar take place in Rome?' carries the presupposition that 'Julius Caesar was murdered'; but to verify it as a happiness condition of that utterance, one would have to go outside the immediate context of utterance and search through two thousand years of history.

The Performative Analysis

The second recent trend relating to speech acts in generative semantics is the development of a so-called *performative analysis* of sentences. The gist of the performative analysis is that in its 'deepest structure' (which we may consider either its syntactic 'deep structure' or its semantic representation), every sentence is a performative; that is, every sentence contains as its main subject a first-person pronoun, and as its main verb a performative verb in the simple present tense. For example, the declarative sentence *Tomorrow will be rainy* has, in this view, a deep structure of a form such as *I state that [tomorrow will be rainy]* or *I predict that [tomorrow will be rainy]*, or *I warn you that [tomorrow will be rainy]*. Questions and commands are given a similar deep structure analysis:

Open the door. ← I command you [to open the door].
How much are those bananas? ← I request of you that [you tell me [how much those bananas are]].

The advantages of the performative analysis are argued persuasively by J. R. Ross in his article 'On Declarative Sentences' (1970). He points out that main clauses have many things in common with clauses which are indirect statements, indirect questions, etc. For example, the emphatic reflexive pronoun is acceptable in sentences (8) and (9) below, but not in sentence (10):

(8) Tom believed that the paper had been written by Ann and *himself*.

(9) The paper was written by Ann and *myself*.

(10) *The paper was written by Ann and *himself*.

If we accept the performative analysis, then all direct statements come to be seen as indirect statements, and therefore a single syntactic condition can explain two sets of circumstances which would otherwise require independent explanation for direct speech and indirect speech. In the case of (8) – (10) above, the main circumstances observed are that the coordinated emphatic reflexive pronoun either (a) must be in the first person if it occurs in the main clause; or (b) must agree with the noun phrase of the higher clause if it occurs in a subordinate clause. But by the performative analysis, (a) becomes a special case of (b), and so need not be stated as a separate condition. If we insert the performative clause *I state that . . .* in (9) and (10), condition (b) is fulfilled in (9) but not in (10); hence (10) is ungrammatical.

Ross adduces many other arguments of the same kind, and I shall only mention one more of them here. The phrase *As for . . . self* obeys the same sort of general rule as was illustrated above for coordinated emphatic reflexives: namely, that *myself* (or *ourselves*) occurs in main clauses, while in indirect speech, there occurs a pronoun in agreement with a noun phrase in the higher clause:

(11) Tom declared that as for *himself*, he was ravenous.

(12) As for *myself*, I am ravenous.

(13) *As for *himself*, Tom is ravenous.

Again, if we adopt the performative analysis and analyse (12) in depth as *I state that as for myself, I am ravenous*, the same rule that accounts for the acceptability of (11) accounts for the acceptability of (12) in contrast to (13).

Ross's analysis also explains the semantic equivalence, or virtual equivalence, between an ordinary statement like *Tomorrow will be rainy* and a corresponding performative like *I state to you that tomorrow will be rainy*. The difference between these, in the analysis, is simply that a transformational rule of *performative deletion* has applied to the former sentence, pruning away from the front of it the subject, performative verb, and indirect object.

Although it has not escaped criticism (see especially Matthews, 1972), the performative analysis has found widespread support among transformationalists. I confess that I number myself among the sceptics – and that my scepticism is founded initially on common-sense considerations. Performative sentences are so rare, that it seems highly unnatural to argue that every single direct statement is fundamentally an indirect statement, that every direct question is fundamentally an indirect question, etc. The unnaturalness grows distinctly suspicious when we consider that a discourse will generally have the same deep structure performative for each sentence it contains. So a newspaper report consisting of a hundred sentences will have 'I report that . . .' or some such performative clause repeated a hundred times. The objection becomes more substantial (as Ross himself points out) when we apply performative analysis to texts belonging to impersonal styles of discourse in which first and second pronouns are taboo (for example, in legal documents, regulations, bureaucratic instructions). Here the performative analysis forces us to allow first-person and second-person pronouns in the underlying structure of a sentence, but not to allow them in its surface structure.

There is an additional case, noted by Ross (1970:255), where the performative analysis gets into difficulties:

(14) As for myself, I promise you that I'll be there.

This sentence already contains an overt performative clause *I promise you . . .*, and yet the phrase *As for myself*, according to an argument mentioned in connection with examples (11) to (13), points to a higher performative clause within which *I promise you* is embedded. But this violates another rule which Ross finds it necessary to establish: that no performative can be embedded in another performative. In any case, to suppose that a double performative *I state to you that I promise you* underlies this sentence is to open the door to potential infinite regression of performatives, one within the other:

I state that X.
I state that I state that X.
I state that I state that I state that X . . .
(etc.)

If this sort of embedding is allowed, then every simple sentence can be derived from infinitely many deep structures.

Situation of utterance

Ross himself proposes an alternative to the performative analysis, which he calls the 'pragmatic' analysis. The outline of the 'pragmatic analysis' is that the subject and performative verb and indirect object are (in Ross's phrase) 'in the air' – that is, they belong to the extralinguistic context of the utterance rather than to its actual structure. Ross sees some advantage in the pragmatic analysis (notably that it resolves the difficulty of sentence (14) above), but sees no way of giving it formal status within transformational grammar.

Since for me the pragmatic analysis offers hope of an attractive common-sense alternative to the performative analysis, I shall now attempt to do what Ross declines to do – to give a reasonably precise characterization of what it means for elements of a speech act to be 'in the air' instead of being part of the underlying structural representation of a sentence. For this purpose, I shall propose that each speech act takes place in a *situation of utterance*, and that a situation of utterance includes:

(a) the utterance itself
(b) the speaker/writer of the utterance
(c) the hearer/reader of the utterance
(d) the speech act

(One might wish to extend the specification of a situation of utterance to include two further factors: (e) the place of utterance; (f) the time of utterance.) The utterance itself can refer to aspects of the situation of utterance by means of deictic items (p. 77) such as *this, now, here* (contrasting with *that, then, there* in terms of the binary taxonomy $\pm$THIS – see p. 168). In addition, first- and second-person pronouns are defined as referring to participants in the speech act. First-person pronouns are semantically distinguished from the others by the feature +EGO (signifying 'including reference to the speaker/writer'); second person pronouns are distinguished by the feature +YOU (signifying 'including reference to the hearer/reader, but not to the speaker/writer'). Third person pronouns are marked by the features —EGO and — YOU (i.e. 'not including reference to the speaker/writer or hearer/reader'). Other linguistic elements referring to the situation of utterance are performative verbs, which, when used in the present tense, refer to the speech act itself. Hence, if we wish to describe overtly a situation of utterance in which we have the role of speaker/writer, we may do so by means of a performative clause such as *I declare to you that X*, in which speaker/writer (*I*) speech act (*declare*), hearer/reader (*you*) and utterance (*X*) are named in that order.

It appears to be a general principle of conversation that a speaker/writer does not bother to describe aspects of the extralinguistic situation which are obvious to himself and the addressee. (This principle of least effort allows us to say simply *Butter, please* where the context makes it clear whether we mean 'Pass the butter, please', 'I want to buy some butter, please', etc. – for further examples see p. 77). The same principle of least effort explains why, in general, we do not specify the implicitly known features of an utterance situation by the use of a performative clause (see Grice (1968)).

A speaker can also, of course, refer to an utterance other than that in which he is engaged, either by direct quotation or by indirect report:

'Do you enjoy sailing?' John asked Mary.
John asked Mary whether she enjoyed sailing.

In such cases, the features of the utterance situation are explicit in the subject, verb, and (sometimes) indirect object of the main clause within which the reported utterance is included. This reporting clause denotes a *secondary situation of utterance* within the *primary* one.

A situation of utterance can therefore enter into the meaning of a sentence 'S' in three ways; it may be

(a) implicitly present as a primary situation of utterance of S ('in the air' in Ross's phrase)
(b) explicitly present as the primary situation of utterance of S denoted by a performative clause
(c) explicitly present as a secondary situation denoted by a reporting clause which introduces a sentence S′ embedded within S.

Metalinguistic Analysis

The performative analysis has generally been formulated in syntactic terms, as the postulation of an underlying subject, verb, etc., rather than in terms of semantic representation (where 'subject' and 'verb', for example, are reinterpreted as 'initial argument' and 'predicate'). But if, as generative semantics encourages us to do, we treat the underlying performative as belonging to semantic representation, then a new light is thrown on the relation between direct and indirect speech, and between primary and secondary situations of utterance. What we cannot overlook is that performative utterances are *metalinguistic* – and this, I believe, provides a clue to their correct analysis.

At this point, a digression on the metalinguistic function of language is necessary. Whereas in most instances the relation of *reference* holds between language and what is not language (e.g. the item 'hat' refers to an object which is a hat), there is apparently no restriction on the universe of things to which language may refer, and this means that it is possible for language to refer to language. Whenever we use language to talk or write about language, we use language in a *metalinguistic* function. Lexical items such as *word, syllable, sentence, question, negation,* etc., are examples of metalanguage: they are linguistic items which denote classes of linguistic items. It is worth noting that there are different *modes* of metalanguage, or ways of referring to objects identified at different levels of linguistic abstraction. For example, the word *word* is metalinguistic in a *syntactic mode* (because the word is a linguistic unit identified at the level of linguistic abstraction we call syntax); the word *syllable* is metalinguistic in a phonological mode; *statement* is metalinguistic in a *semantic mode*. It is also important to distinguish between elements referring to a class of linguistic entities, and those naming an individual entity. The chief device of metalinguistic naming is direct quotation or citation of the entity referred to, as illustrated in sentence (14) below:

(14) Mary asked '*What is the time*?'
(15) Mary asked a *question*.

While the noun *question* in (15) refers to a whole class of linguistic entities, 'What is the time?' in (14) actually refers to one member of that class: namely, the question which consists of the four words *what, is, the,* and *time,* in that order. Therefore, (15) differs in meaning from (14) only in being more general – or, in terms of basic statements, we may say that (14) entails (15).

A similar contrast obtains between (16) and (17):

(16) Jacob knows the meaning of *Fraülein* and *Bier*.

(17) Jacob knows the meaning of two German words.

(Here quotation is signalled by italics, instead of by quotation marks.) In such cases of direct quotation we may interpret the device of quotation as one of naming a referent by *demonstration*, in the same way as we may identify a referent by using the deictic word *this* accompanied by the physical gesture of pointing:

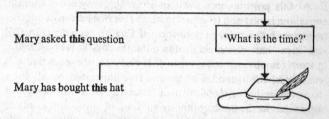

The only substantial difference between the two cases is that the reference for the metalinguistic utterance is structurally incorporated within the utterance itself, as in sentence (14) above.

The difference between direct quotation and indirect speech is a difference of mode: direct quotation is in the syntactic (or sometimes phonological) mode, identifying the form (and hence indirectly content as well) of the sentence quoted, while indirect speech is in the semantic mode, identifying its content without specifying its form. Hence the following sentences are not true paraphrases:

(18) Frank said 'I am enjoying my holiday.'

(19) Frank said that he was enjoying his holiday.

The difference between them is that in (18) the reporter commits himself to repeating the actual words spoken; but in (19) he does not. What Frank might actually have said was 'I'm really enjoying these two weeks in Zermatt' or simply 'I like it here', etc. In these

354 Semantics

cases, (19) would be a true report, while (18) would not. (18) entails (19), but (19) does not entail (18).

Apart from accounting for certain entailment relations such as that between (14) and (15) and that between (18) and (19), metalinguistic analysis is necessary for the explanation of a potentially infinite class of utterances which are acceptable although they contain deviations from normal linguistic usage:

(20) '*Mein Gott*!' muttered Hans.

(21) '*Me want for to be your amigo*' said the smiling stranger.

(22) In a fit of madness, Henry had complained that *his wristwatch was beating him with a bunch of curses*.

(23) Peter falsely claims that *rectangles have five sides*.

Each of these sentences is itself an acceptable sentence of English, even though part of it (the part in italics) for one reason or another transgresses the rules of well-formed English sentences. In (20) and (21) the utterance included in quotation marks is non-English in form for obvious reasons; in (22) and (23) the *that*-clause is semantically ill-formed. The general rule illustrated by all these examples is that a metalinguistic utterance in a language *L* is impervious to the unacceptability within *L* of a linguistic entity to which it refers. An English utterance can contain metalinguistically a German utterance without ceasing to be an English utterance; and a meaningful utterance can remain meaningful even though it contains absurd elements in indirect speech. This is not a difficult conclusion to accept, in the light of what was said earlier about metalinguistic utterances: the linguistic entity named in such an utterance is (in a sense) included within the utterance without being part of it; the unacceptable linguistic form or content is a property of the language reported, not of the language used.

This discussion has shown that no overall semantic description of a language can do without an account of metalanguage, if entailments, semantic anomalies, etc. are to be correctly specified. The metalinguistic functioning of language is not a device which has been called into being expressly in order to explain direct speech, indirect speech, and performatives. But once we accept that performatives and reporting utterances are metalinguistic in character, we have a simple (one might almost say trite) explanation of the parallel between indirect speech and direct speech on which Ross bases his performative analysis. The explanation is this: just as the extra-linguistic context defines the situation of utterance for a main predication, so a reporting utterance such as 'John told Harry . . .' defines the situation of utterance for a reported utterance. So the generalizations that Ross is able to make by reference to constituents of a 'higher clause' with a performative verb can be matched in the pragmatic analysis by generalizations about situations of utterance in relation to the utterances they contain.

How, in the pragmatic analysis, do we account for the equivalence between performative utterances and corresponding non-performative utterances (e.g. between 'I state to you that I am your friend' and 'I am your friend')? Informally, the equivalence is explicated by simply observing that a performative such as 'I state to you that X' overtly describes its own situation of utterance; and to the extent that this merely repeats information that is in any case deducible from the form and context of X, the addition of the performative adds nothing to the message. The equivalence may be stated more formally by means of a rule of implication (see pp. 263–79), in outline as follows:

PERFORMATIVE INTRODUCTION RULE

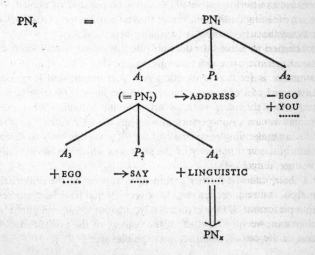

[*NOTES:* The vertical arrow under A_4 symbolizes the relation of reference whereby PN_x is marked as the referent of A_4. The feature +LINGUISTIC marks A_4 as denoting a linguistic entity. The four major factors of the situation of utterance are structurally included in the formula for the performative predication PN_1 as follows: A_4 denotes the utterance; A_3 denotes the speaker/writer; A_2 denotes the reader/hearer; P_2 denotes the speech act. The ellipsis dots (...) in A_2, A_3, P_2 and A_4 allow for the possibility that further features be specified.]

The performative introduction rule equates any predication PN_x with a more complex performative predication PN_1, which contains PN_x through metalinguistic incorporation. I shall not go into detail on the semantic specification of performatives, except to say that other features can be added to P_2 to indicate varieties of speech act ('promise', 'state', 'warm', 'bet', 'ask', etc.); also that features can be added to +LINGUISTIC in A_4 to indicate different metalinguistic modes and categories ('syntactic' versus 'semantic', 'statement' versus 'question', etc.). Some obvious selection restrictions between P_2 and A_4 have to be stipulated; these will forbid, for example, the 'asking' of a 'statement' or the 'stating' of a 'question'. As we have already incidentally noted, this rule does not make PN_x and PN_1 precisely equivalent in logical terms – because the performative PN_1 cannot be negated or denied. In terms of the factuality analysis of the last chapter (pp. 310–14), we may say that a performative has inalienable factuality.

The performative introduction rule just stated is analogous to Ross's performative deletion rule, except that it is formulated in semantic rather than syntactic terms, and except that it is conceived of as an optional expansion of a non-performative into a performative, rather than as an optional reduction of a performative into a non-performative. Thus the wastefulness of postulating underlying performatives for all sentences, only to delete them in the vast majority of the sentences which people actually produce, is avoided.

I shall note one further argument in support of the pragmatic analysis. This concerns a class of adverbials that have been studied under the name of *style disjuncts* (Greenbaum 1969), and might be more conveniently labelled, in the context of the present discussion, *speech-act adverbials*. Some examples are:

(24) *Frankly*, I was appalled.

      (i.e. 'I tell you frankly that I was appalled')

(25) *Briefly*, his domestic policy is a failure.

      (i.e. 'I tell you briefly that his domestic policy is a failure')

(26) *While I think of it*, get some more wine.

      (i.e. 'While I think of it, I request that you get some more wine')

(27) *In confidence*, he's a bully.

      (i.e. 'I tell you in confidence that he's a bully')

The paraphrases in parentheses may provoke some disagreements over detail, but the main principle is clear: that the adverbial expressions in italics are being used in these sentences to modify an unexpressed performative, rather than to modify the sentence to which they are overtly attached. Such examples, which are widespread in English, seem to support the performative analysis, and some examples have indeed been enlisted in that cause by Ross (1970) and Lakoff (1970). On the other hand, these speech-act adverbials are also compatible with the pragmatic analysis, if we treat the extension of (say) *frankly* from the function of an ordinary manner adverb to that of a speech-act adverb as an instance of a lexical rule of secondary conversion (see p. 216). So considered, the rule is no different in principle from one which converts mass nouns into countable nouns which denote a unit of some substance (as in *two coffees, two sugars, a cloth*, etc.). The rule for deriving speech-act adverbs will alter the definition of manner adverbs (here symbolized PN_3) as follows:

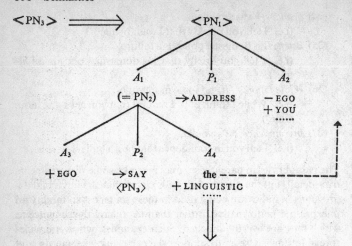

[*NOTES:* Both of the definitional formulae in this rule are shown as downgraded predications, in accordance with the normal convention for the semantic specifications of adverbials (see p. 151). ⟨PN₁⟩ is a downgraded equivalent (via the rule of sub-ordination, p. 265) of PN₁ in the performative introduction rule. The argument A_4 is coreferential to the main predication within which PN₁ occurs.]

The effect of this lexical rule is roughly to derive the meaning 'I tell you - - - ly' from the base meaning '- - - ly' (= 'in a - - - manner').

The reason why the relation between these two uses of adverbs is best dealt with by means of a lexical rule is that it exhibits the phenomenon of partial productivity which we have seen else-where (p. 211) to be characteristic of lexical rules. Not all seman-tically appropriate adverbs of manner can be used as *frankly* and *briefly* are used in (24) and (25); rather, there is a scale of accept-ability on which adverbs can be placed, as we placed adjectives in -*y* and metaphorical nouns in Chapter 10 (p. 213):

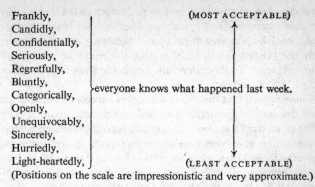

Frankly,
Candidly,
Confidentially,
Seriously,
Regretfully,
Bluntly,
Categorically,   everyone knows what happened last week.
Openly,
Unequivocably,
Sincerely,
Hurriedly,
Light-heartedly,

(MOST ACCEPTABLE)

(LEAST ACCEPTABLE)

(Positions on the scale are impressionistic and very approximate.)

It is possible to fit each one of these adverbs into the frame *I tell you . . . that X'* and to end up with an acceptable English sentence. But the ease with which the performative construction is omitted varies from adverb to adverb. It is not primarily a question of semantic appropriateness that is at issue, since *frankly* and *openly*, although from the same semantic grouping, differ markedly in acceptability as speech-act adverbs.

I have restricted myself here to the consideration of single adverbs acting as speech-act modifiers, but a similar scale of acceptability could be constructed for conjunctions used in a parallel way. Compare, for instance, the abnormality of (29) against the normality of (28):

    (28) What's the answer to this problem – *since* you're so clever.
    (29) What's the answer to this problem – *because* you're so clever.

To reconcile all these observations with the performative analysis, it would be necessary to attach to the performative deletion rule special conditions stating which adverbs resist the operation of the rule, and to what degree of acceptability. But with the pragmatic analysis this can be treated as an optional extension of meaning of the kind that is normally handled by lexical rules. My conclusion, then, is that the pragmatic analysis promises to do better than the performative analysis not only on grounds of economy (in avoiding the postulation of an extra stage of embedding in practically every sentence uttered), but also in being able to give an account more readily of certain facts, such as the limited and variable acceptability of speech-act adverbs. I say that 'the pragmatic analysis *promises* to do better' because I have here given only the briefest sketch of it, leaving the reader to take many things on trust. To this extent, the pragmatic analysis still suffers from a lack of clear formulation.

I have argued that the two illocutionary aspects of meaning we have discussed – presuppositions and speech acts – require very different kinds of treatment; that broadly, presuppositions belong to the content of an utterance, and speech acts to its extralinguistic context. These views seem to be the diametric opposite of prevailing opinion; they also seem to indicate an inconsistency of approach. But I hope to clarify my position in what follows.

The objection is this. I rejected the contextualist approach to presupposition on the grounds that it ran the danger of subscribing to the fallacy (the 'bootstraps fallacy') that linguistic phenomena can be explicated in terms of what is not language. But then why did I let explanation-by-context in again, in the shape of 'situation of utterance'? My answer is that appeal to context is only futile when one attempts to make analysis of extralinguistic context a substitute for the analysis of linguistic phenomena. This was the fault of the contextualism of the Bloomfield era (pp. 5, 75), and is potentially a fault of a presuppositional analysis (like Fillmore's) which identifies presuppositions with conditions of context. But the amount of contextual information introduced in the description of 'situation of utterance' is extremely limited; it may be limited, in fact, to the four factors of (a) utterance, (b) speaker/writer, (c) hearer/reader, and (d) speech act. Since the English language (and, presumably, all other languages) can make metalinguistic reference to speech acts, what we use for contextual description is only a small subset of the concepts which are present in language, and for which we are bound to provide a semantic description. Thus we use only a 'sub-language' of English for the description of situation of utterance, and there can be no question of falling into the trap of purportedly explaining linguistic phenomena in terms of non-linguistic phenomena. Rather it is the other way round: the categories of the contextual description are provided by the conceptual semantic analysis.

Conclusion

So much for this brief review of alternative theories. I have outlined the difference between the generative and interpretive views
on the relation between semantics and syntax, and have briefly
presented the case for an inbetween position. I have also given
attention to the 'illocutionary' idea, without conceding that this
approach threatens the validity of the approach which has provided the main orientation of this book: namely, the study of
conceptual meaning in terms of semantic representations and their
ability to account for 'basic statements'. I have argued, for instance, that the study of presupposition cannot be properly
separated from the semantic representations of an utterance.

   This last chapter will have left the reader with a clear impression
that basic issues are by no means decided in semantics. In spite of
rapid developments, we are still a very long way from turning the
discipline from a would-be science into a science. The theories that
have been constructed must be labelled with that cautionary term
'speculative'; but at least we have reached a point where relatively
clear and detailed formulations can be made about meaning in
natural language.

Background Reading

[This review of books and articles relating to semantics is organized on a chapter-by-chapter basis. Titles are frequently abridged and dates omitted to save space. The references are given in full in the Bibliography which follows.]

Introduction

Ullmann, *Words*, *Principles*, and *Semantics: an Introduction*, and Waldron, *Sense*, are all readable introductory books on semantics, taking a broad view of the subject which incorporates historical change of meaning. Ullmann's books largely reflect European traditions of semantic scholarship, also represented by Guiraud, *Sémantique*, and Koziol, *Grundzüge*. Older books in the European philological tradition are Bréal, *Semantics*, and Stern, *Meaning*.

Chs. 9 and 10 of Lyons, *Introduction* provide a broad perspective on the subject from a more theoretical point of view. Other useful introductory surveys are Lehrer, 'Semantics', and Ch. 1 of Ikegami, *Semological Structure*.

1. Meanings of Meaning

On the theoretical foundations of semantics as a branch of linguistics, consult Katz and Fodor, 'Structure', Lyons, *Structural Semantics*, Part I, Lyons, *Introduction*, Ch. 9, and Leech, *Semantic Description*, Chs. 1 and 5. (Also see Ch. 5 below.)

2. Seven Types of Meaning

The view (elaborated here) that total meaning can be separated out into various ingredients, of which conceptual or denotative meaning is the chief, has often been held by many writers on semantics (see, for example, Bloomfield, *Language*, Ch. 9, and Ullmann, *Semantics: an Introduction*, Ch. 5). The present breakdown into seven types is an elaboration of the five-fold classification of Bennett, 'English Prepositions'.

An opposite school of thought holds that meanings cannot

legitimately be anatomized in this way: that meaning is unitary. Chafe, *Meaning*, is a recent representative of this tradition.

With regard to stylistic meaning, Gregory, 'Aspects', and Crystal and Davy, *Investigating*, are studies of stylistic language variation.

The 'Semantic Differential' technique for quantifying associative meaning is the subject of Osgood, Suci, and Tannenbaum, *Measurement of Meaning*, and of Snider and Osgood, *Semantic Differential*. Linguistic implications of the technique are assessed by Weinreich, 'Travels'.

Thematic meaning has been handled by various scholars using varied terminologies ('theme'/'rheme', 'given'/'new', 'topic'/'comment', etc.). See especially Firbas, 'On Defining', Halliday, 'Transitivity and Theme' Parts II and III, and Quirk et al., *Grammar*, Ch. 14.

3. 'Bony-structured Concepts'

For classic relativistic views of conceptual structure, see Sapir, *Selected Writings*, and Whorf, *Language, Thought and Reality*. Fishman, 'Systematization', reinterprets Whorf. See also Lenneberg, 'The Relation'.

Semantic aspects of translation are dealt with in Nida, *Science of Translating*.

As background to the present chapter's discussion of concept-learning by children, read Brown 'How shall a Thing be Called?'. McNeill, *Acquisition*, and Dale, *Language Development*, are general books on acquisition of language each containing a chapter on semantics.

The recent revolution in linguistic thought that has brought universalism back into favour is best studied in the writings of its prime mover, Noam Chomsky (esp. *Cartesian Linguistics, Language and Mind*, and Ch. 1 of *Aspects*). Lyons, *Chomsky*, and Chomsky, *Selected Writings*, are convenient introductions to Chomsky's thought.

A universalist view on semantic structure is presented by Bierwisch in 'German Adjectivals' and 'Semantics'. (See further under Ch. 11.)

The 'counterlogical' or 'irrational' aspects of poetic language are explored in Wimsatt, 'Verbal Style' in *The Verbal Icon*, and in Leech, *Linguistic Guide*, Chs. 8 and 9.

4. *Semantics and Society*

Among the various classifications of the communicative and social functions of language that have been proposed, those of Bühler, *Sprachtheorie*, Jakobson, 'Linguistics and Poetics', and Halliday, 'Language Structure' are notable. The present account is a modified and simplified version of Jakobson's classification. The concept of 'phatic communion' (or the phatic function of language) originates with Malinowski, 'The Problem of Meaning'.

The influence of the popular intellectual movement of General Semantics founded by Korzybski (*Science and Sanity*) has been fostered by the International Society of General Semantics and its journal, *Etc.* Korzybski's ideas have been successfully popularized by Chase (*Tyranny of Words* and *Power of Words*) and Hayakawa (*Language in Thought and Action* and *Language, Meaning and Maturity*). The General Semantics movement has been criticized from various points of view by Black ('Korzybski's General Semantics'), Schaff (*Introduction*) and Youngren (*Linguistics*).

5. Is Semantics a Science?

The Malinowski-Firth approach to meaning via 'context of situation' can be traced through Malinowski 'The Problem of Meaning' and *Coral Gardens*, to Firth, *Tongues of Men* and *Papers* (esp. 'Technique of Semantics', 'Personality and Language', and 'Modes of Meaning'). An appraisal of Firth's semantics is given by Lyons, 'Firth's Theory'. One profitable by-product of the contextualism of Firth is the study of stylistic meaning which has flourished in Great Britain since the 1950s. Gregory, 'Aspects' documents this development.

Wittgenstein's *Investigations* provides an important philosophical backcloth to the contextualist era of semantic thought.

After Bloomfield, the tendency for American structuralists to ignore meaning, or else to redefine it in terms of the distribution of items within linguistic context, can be sampled in Harris, *Structural Linguistics*, esp. pp. 186–95.

In contrast, Katz, 'Mentalism in Linguistics' is a manifesto for the mentalism of linguists of the more recent Chomskyan era.

Experiments in semantic informant testing are reported and discussed in Bendix, *Componential Analysis*, Ariel, 'Semantic Tests', Leech, 'Semantic Testing', and Leech and Pepicello, 'Semantic versus Factual Knowledge'.

6. Components and Contrasts of Meaning

The structure of word meanings in terms of interrelations with other word meanings has been studied in a number of different ways in the literature of semantics. Two earlier European schools deserve mention for their contribution to structural semantics: that of the German 'Linguistic Field' (or 'Semantic Field') Theorists, and that of the Danish school of Glossematics, led by Louis Hjelmslev. On German

Field Theory, see Trier, *Deutsche Wortschatz*, and Weisgerber, *Vom Weltbild*, as well as articles in English by Öhman ('Theories'), Basilius ('Ethnolinguistics') and Spence ('Linguistic Fields'). On Glossematics, see Hjelmslev, *Prolegomena*.

Componential analysis proper originates with the work of Lounsbury and Goodenough on kinship terminology (see Bibliography). A brief appraisal of componential analysis is given by Lyons, *Introduction*, Ch. 10.

Other approaches which have much in common with componential analysis are Lyons's own study of meaning in terms of meaning relations such as hyponymy and incompatibility (*Structural Semantics* and *Introduction*, Ch. 10); also the theory of Katz and Fodor, 'Structure', involving the analysis of dictionary meanings into semantic 'markers' and 'distinguishers'. This theory, elaborated in further publications by Katz (esp. *Philosophy* and *Semantic Theory*), has been criticized by Bolinger ('Atomization') and Weinreich ('Explorations').

While Katz and Fodor, Lyons, and Weinreich, have been keen to formalize their approaches to meaning within the general linguistic model of Transformational Grammar (see under Ch. 14 below), other approaches, outside that model, have tended to have a more practical descriptive bias. Bendix ('Componential Analysis') studies verbs of 'having' in English and other languages; Leech (*Semantic Description*, Chs. 7 to 9) investigates the semantics of time, place, and modality in modern English; and Ikegami (*Semological Structure*) applies the 'stratificational' theory of Sydney Lamb to a fairly detailed analysis of English verbs of motion. Lehrer, 'Semantic Cuisine', is an application of componential analysis to English cookery terms.

On the nature of semantic oppositions in general, see Ogden, *Opposition*; on polar opposites in particular, see Sapir, 'Grading', and Bierwisch's excellent analysis of the German equivalents of spatial adjectives such as *high* and *low* ('German Adjectivals'). Teller, 'Some Discussion', modifies Bierwisch's analysis in applying it to English.

Folk-taxonomies are discussed in Conklin, 'Lexicological Treatment', and Frake, 'Ethnographic Study'.

With regard to 'fuzzy edges' and shifting definitions, see Lakoff, 'Hedges'. Waldron (*Sense*, Ch. 7) discusses under the heading of 'Shift' the type of semantic change exemplified by *holiday*.

7. The Semantic Structure of Sentences

The separability of semantic and syntactic levels of analysis is considered further in Chs. 9 and 14.

The term 'cluster' (p. 128) is borrowed from Weinreich, 'Explorations'; in *Semantic Description*, I used the expressions 'terminal cluster' and 'medial cluster' in place of 'argument' and 'predicate' respectively.

The semantic analysis of locative prepositions (p. 130) is a much simplified version of that in *Semantic Description*, Ch. 8. See also Bierwisch, 'German Adjectivals', and Teller, 'Some discussion'.

What are referred to here as 'predications', 'predicates' and 'arguments' are, in other accounts, often given the grammatical labels 'sentence', 'noun phrase' and 'verb' – for comment on this point, see Ch. 14, p. 340. Leaving aside this terminological difference, there are more substantial differences between the semantic structure of the sentence as proposed in this chapter and as proposed in other accounts. McCawley ('*VSO* Language') reasons that in English semantic representations, the predicate precedes the argument(s) (thus, in this widely-held view, a two-place predication has the structure Predicate + Argument + Argument, rather than Argument + Predicate + Argument). Fillmore ('Case for Case') allows for the possibility of more than two arguments per predicate. Chafe (*Meaning*), on the other hand, restricts the number of arguments per predicate to one, so that a structure like 'Roger kicked the door', which in the present system would be a two-place predication, is analysed in Chafe's system as one predication embedded inside another. (Here I use the term 'predication' even though it is not the term normally used by McCawley, Fillmore, or Chafe.) The relative advantages of these and other solutions are difficult to assess at the present time.

There have been marked changes in the analysis of selection restrictions over the past ten years. Chomsky in *Aspects* formalized some selection restrictions in terms of syntactic co-occurrence rules. McCawley, 'The Role of Semantics', challenged Chomsky's approach by arguing that selection restrictions are semantic rather than syntactic. Later still, in 'Noun Phrases', McCawley has claimed that selection restrictions are to a great extent a matter of extra-linguistic knowledge, and therefore outside the purview of linguistics altogether.

On the formulation of tautology and contradiction within linguistic theory, see Katz, 'Analyticity'. Philosophical perspectives on the same subject are conveniently assembled in the section on 'Analytic and Synthetic' in Olshewsky, *Philosophy of Language*.

There is an earlier treatment of downgraded predications in Leech, *Semantic Description*, Ch. 2. English tenses are semantically analysed in terms of downgrading in Ch. 7 of the same book.

8. Logic in Everyday Language

Quine, *Mathematical Logic*, Reichenbach, *Elements*, and Robbin, *Mathematical Logic*, are handbooks providing introductions to formal logic. Reichenbach's book is exceptional in containing an incisive analysis (Part VII) of the logic of everyday conversational language. On the other hand, Reichenbach clearly illustrates the normative tradition of philosophical logic in his critique of 'the deficiencies of conversational language', and also illustrates a mistaken tendency, among some logicians, to assume that grammarians are logicians *manqué*. Lakoff, 'Natural Logic', presents a more recent view of the relation between linguistics and logic, this time from the linguistic side of the fence.

An adaptation of symbolic logic to the complexities of natural language has been attempted by Weinreich ('Semantic Structure'), McCawley ('Role of Semantics'), and others. Weinreich's article also contains a section on formators and designators, and a section on deixis. The 'proximal'/'distal' distinction in deictic meaning is explored by Fillmore ('Deictic Categories'), with special reference to the verbs *come* and *go*.

The treatment of formators in this chapter is largely based on Ch. 3 of Leech, *Semantic Description* (except for differences of notation).

In contrast to the present device of indicating coreference by means of the definite formator, a method current in Transformational Grammar (see Ch. 14) is to use indices (variables such as x and y) such that identical indices signal identity of reference. See esp. McCawley, 'Noun Phrases'.

The treatment of the quantifiers 'all' and 'some' as predicates is justified in more detail in Leech, *Semantic Description*, Ch. 3. Quantifiers are also regarded as predicates by generative semanticists such as Lakoff ('Natural Logic'), who have proposed a somewhat different analysis to account for scope of quantifiers.

9. Semantics and Syntax

The syntactic categories sketched in this chapter closely resemble those of Quirk, et al., *Grammar*, Chs. 2 and 7.

This chapter's account of the relation between different linguistic levels may be compared with that of Chafe, *Meaning*, from which the particular notion of 'linearization' is derived. Fillmore, like Chafe, has advocated a semantic representation or 'deep structure' in which linear ordering is unspecified. 'Linearization' and 'thematization' in this chapter correspond approximately to Fillmore's 'primary' and 'secondary topicalization' (in 'Case for Case').

The technicalities of anaphoric relations are examined in Postal,

Cross-over Phenomena; a less technical account is that of Quirk et al., *Grammar*, Ch. 10. The distinction between coreference and anaphora drawn here partially corresponds to that between 'reference' and 'substitution' in Halliday, 'Transitivity and Theme', Part II, p. 206. Karlsen, *Connection of Clauses*, includes a detailed study of zero expression (ellipsis) as a form of anaphora in English.

Transformations are discussed further in Ch. 14, a chapter which also resumes the topic of semantics in relation to syntax.

10. Semantics and the Dictionary

On dictionary definitions, see Weinreich, 'Lexicographic Definition', and 'Webster's Third'.

On word formation, see Marchand, *Categories*, and Jespersen, *A Modern English Grammar*, Vol. VI.

In 'Explorations', Weinreich attempts to formalize processes of semantic transfer under the heading of 'the Construal Rule', and to set up a formal apparatus ('the semantic evaluator') for accounting for different degrees of productivity and comprehensibility.

Waldron, *Sense*, Chs. 8 and 9, deals with semantic transfer as a historical mechanism of meaning change.

Ch. 9 of Leech, *A Linguistic Guide*, is devoted to the operation of rules of transfer in the language of poetry.

11. Colour and Kinship: Two Case Studies in 'Universal Semantics'.

In addition to Berlin and Kay's *Basic Color Terms*, the following are useful readings in colour semantics: Brown and Lenneberg, 'Language and Cognition'; Lenneberg and Roberts, *Language of Experience*; Conklin, 'Hanunóo Color Categories'.

On kinship semantics, consult the publications of Lounsbury and Goodenough in the Bibliography. Lounsbury, 'Relativism and Kinship' has particular relevance to the theme of semantic universals.

The componential-predicational kinship analysis presented in this chapter is an elaboration of that in Leech, *Semantic Description*, Ch. 4. This method of analysis has affinities with that of Lamb ('The Sememic Approach'), as well as with Lounsbury's 'reduction-rule' method (see, for example, Lounsbury, 'Crow-Omaha').

Two useful collections of readings on anthropological semantics are Hammel, *Formal Semantic Analysis*, and Tyler, *Cognitive Anthropology*.

12. Semantic Equivalence and 'Deep Semantics'

The rules of implication in this chapter and in Chapter 11 are dealt with more technically, under the heading of 'rules of synonymy', in

Leech, *Semantic Description*, Ch. 4. The names of the rules have been changed to some extent, so that, for example, '1st rule of attribution' becomes 'rule of identification' in the present chapter.

13. Presuppositions and Factuality

From the mass of recent literature dealing with presuppositions, I select the following for mention: Fillmore, 'Lexical Information' and 'Verbs of Judging'; Fraser, 'Analysis of "Even"'; Garner, '"Presupposition"'; Horn, '*Only* and *Even*'; Keenan, 'Two Kinds of Presupposition', Lakoff, 'Natural Logic', Section V; Morgan, 'Treatment of Presuppositions'; Hajičová, 'Some Remarks'. (Hajičová's article relates presuppositions to thematic structure.)

On factuality and related topics, see Kiparsky and Kiparsky, '"Fact"', Karttunen, 'Implicative Verbs', and (at a less technical level) Leech, *English Verb*, Ch. 7.

On scope of negation, see Jackendoff, 'Negation' and (again at a less technical level) Quirk et al., *Grammar*, Ch. 7.

14. Alternative Theories

Key works in the development of Transformational Grammar are Chomsky, *Syntactic Structures*, Katz and Postal, *Integrated Theory*, and Chomsky, *Aspects*. Since 1965, no seminal books of this standing have been written: the speed with which ideas change is such that before a book is finished, it is almost inevitably out of date. Leading transformationalists therefore write not books, but working papers, which circulate in a pre-published form, with minimum delay, through the 'underground press' of linguistics department mailing lists. The working papers end up, as often as not, being published in one of the numerous collections of readings such as Kiefer, *Syntax and Semantics*, Fillmore and Langendoen, *Linguistic Semantics*, and Jacobs and Rosenbaum, *Readings*. But to keep up with the spearhead of linguistic thought, rather than wait for the collections of readings to appear, the devotee has to get his name on the right mailing lists, or to keep in touch with the Indiana University Linguistics Club, which circulates papers at cost. The strangeness of the situation is that by the time an article is properly published, it is already 'old hat' to its informed public.

The references given below are restricted to works in print, and are therefore necessarily somewhat behind the times.

The following publications from the point of view of Interpretive Semantics are to be noted: Chomsky, 'Deep Structure', Chomsky,

'Some Empirical Issues', Jackendoff, 'Quantifiers', Jackendoff, *Semantic Interpretation*, Katz, *Semantic Theory*.

From the Generative Semantics angle, the following are important: Lakoff, 'Instrumental Adverbs', 'On Generative Semantics', and 'Natural Logic'; McCawley, 'Role of Semantics', and 'Lexical Insertion'; Postal, ' "Remind" '.

On the question of directional precedence between levels, Chafe (*Meaning*, and 'Directionality') maintains, against prevailing opinion, that there is an intrinsic precedence between levels, in the direction of meaning-towards-sound rather than of sound-towards-meaning.

Philosophical perspectives on the theme of illocutionary force are provided by Alston in *Philosophy of Language*, and Searle in *Speech Acts*, as well as by Austin in *How to Do Things with Words*.

Bibliography

ALSTON, W.P. (1964), *Philosophy of Language*, Englewood Cliffs, N.J.: Prentice-Hall.

ARIEL, S. (1967), 'Semantic Tests', *Man* 2. 535–50.

AUSTIN, J. L. (1962), *How to Do Things with Words*, Cambridge, Mass.: Harvard University Press.

BACH, EMMON, and HARMS, R. T. (eds.) (1968), *Universals in Language*, New York: Holt, Rinehart.

BASILIUS, H. (1952), 'Neo-Humboldtian Ethnolinguistics', *Word*, 8. 95–105.

BENDIX, E. H. (1966), *Componential Analysis of General Vocabulary* (Part 2 of *International Journal of American Linguistics*, 32), Bloomington, Ind.: Indiana University Press; The Hague: Mouton.

BENNETT, D. C. (1968), 'English Prepositions: a Stratificational Approach', *Journal of Linguistics*, 4. 153–72.

BERLIN, B., and KAY, P. (1969), *Basic Color Terms*, Berkeley and Los Angeles: University of California Press.

BERNE, ERIC (1966), *Games People Play: the Psychology of Human Relationships*, London: Deutsch.

BIERWISCH, M. (1967), 'Some Semantic Universals of German Adjectivals', *Foundations of Language*, 3. 1–36.

BIERWISCH, M., (1970) 'Semantics'. In Lyons (1970b).

BIERWISCH, M., and HEIDOLPH, K. (1970), *Progress in Linguistics*, The Hague: Mouton.

BINNICK, R. I., DAVISON, A., GREEN, G. M., and MORGAN, J. L. (eds.) (1969), *Papers from the Fifth Regional Meeting of the Chicago Linguistic Society*, Chicago: Department of Linguistics, University of Chicago.

BLACK, MAX (1949), 'Korzybski's General Semantics'. In *Language and Philosophy*, Ithaca, N.Y.: Cornell University Press.

BLACK, MAX (1959), 'Linguistic Relativity: the Views of Benjamin Lee Whorf', *Philosophical Review*, 68. 228–38.

BLOOMFIELD, L. (1933/5), *Language*, New York: Holt, Rinehart, 1933; London: Allen & Unwin, 1935.

BOLINGER, D. L. (1965), 'The Atomization of Meaning', *Language*, 41. 555–73.

BRÉAL, MICHEL (1897), *Essai de Sémantique*, Paris: Hachette. Reprinted and translated as *Semantics: Studies in the Science of Meaning*, New York: Dover, 1964.

BROWN, ROGER (1958), 'How shall a Thing be Called?', *Psychological Review*, 65: 14–21. Reprinted in Oldfield, R.C., and Marshall, J. C. (1968), *Language: Selected Readings*, London: Penguin.

BROWN, ROGER, and LENNEBERG, E. H. (1954), 'A Study of Language and Cognition', *Journal of Abnormal and Social Psychology*, 49. 454–62.

BÜHLER, KARL (1934), *Sprachtheorie*, Jena.

CHAFE, WALLACE (1970), *Meaning and the Structure of Language*, Chicago: University of Chicago Press.

CHAFE, WALLACE (1971), 'Directionality and Paraphrase', *Language*, 47. 1–26.

CHASE, STUART (1937), *The Tyranny of Words*, New York: Harcourt, Brace.

CHASE, STUART (1954), *The Power of Words*, New York: Harcourt, Brace.

CHOMSKY, N. (1957), *Syntactic Structures*, The Hague: Mouton.

CHOMSKY, N. (1964), *Current Issues in Linguistic Theory*, The Hague: Mouton.

CHOMSKY, N. (1965), *Aspects of the Theory of Syntax*, Cambridge, Mass.: M.I.T. Press.

CHOMSKY, N. (1966), *Cartesian Linguistics*, New York & London: Harper & Row.

CHOMSKY, N. (1968), *Language and Mind*, New York: Harcourt, Brace.

CHOMSKY, N. (1970), 'Deep Structure, Surface Structure, and Semantic Interpretation'. In Jakobson, R., and Kawamoto, S. (eds.) (1970), *Studies in General and Oriental Linguistics*, Tokyo: T.E.C. Company. Repr. in Chomsky (1972a).

CHOMSKY, N. (1971), *Selected Writings*, edited by Allen, J. P. B., and Van Buren, Paul, London: Oxford University Press.

CHOMSKY, N. (1972a), *Studies on Semantics in Generative Grammar*, The Hague: Mouton.

CHOMSKY, N. (1972b), 'Some Empirical Issues in the Theory of Transformational Grammar'. In Chomsky (1972a).

CHOMSKY, N., and HALLE, M. (1968), *The Sound Pattern of English*, New York: Harper & Row.

CONKLIN, H. C. (1955), 'Hanunóo Color Categories', *Southwestern Journal of Anthropology*, 11. 339–44.

COOK, WALTER J. (1969), *Introduction to Tagmemic Analysis*, New York: Holt, Rinehart.

CRYSTAL, D., and DAVY, D. (1969), *Investigating English Style*, London: Longmans.

DALE, PHILIP S. (1972), *Language Development, Structure and Function*, Hinsdale, Ill.: Dryden Press.

FILLMORE, C. J. (1966), 'Deictic Categories and the Semantics of "Come"', *Foundations of Language*, 2. 219–27.

FILLMORE, C. J. (1968), 'The Case for Case'. In Bach and Harms (1968).

FILLMORE, C. J. (1969), 'Types of Lexical Information'. In Kiefer (1969).

FILLMORE, C. J. (1971), 'Verbs of Judging: an Exercise in Semantic Description'. In Fillmore and Langendoen (1971).

FILLMORE, C. J., and LANGENDOEN, D. T. (eds.) (1971), *Studies in Linguistic Semantics*, New York: Holt, Rinehart.

FIRBAS, J. (1964), 'On Defining the Theme in Functional Sentence Analysis', *Travaux Linguistiques de Prague*, 1. 267–80.

FIRTH, J. R. (1957), *Papers in Linguistics 1934–51*, London: Oxford University Press.

FIRTH, J. R. (1964), *Speech* and *The Tongues of Men*, London: Oxford University Press (*Language and Language Learning* 2). (First editions: *Speech*, 1930; *The Tongues of Men*, 1937.)

FISHMAN, J. A. (1960), 'Systematization of the Whorfian Hypothesis', *Behavioral Science*, 5.

FODOR, J. A. and KATZ, J. J. (eds.) (1964), *The Structure of Language: Readings in the Philosophy of Language*, Englewood Cliffs, N.J.: Prentice-Hall.

FRAKE, C. O. (1969), 'Ethnographic Study of Cognitive Systems', in Tyler (1969), 28–41.

FRASER, BRUCE (1969), 'An Analysis of Concessive Conditionals'. In Binnick et al. (1969), 66–75.

FRASER, BRUCE (1971), 'An Analysis of "Even" in English'. In Fillmore and Langendoen (1971), 151–80.

GARNER, RICHARD (1971), '"Presupposition" in Philosophy and Linguistics'. In Fillmore and Langendoen (1971), 23–44.

GOODENOUGH, W. H. (1956), 'Componential Analysis and the Study of Meaning', *Language*, 32. 195–216.

GOODENOUGH, W. H. (1965), 'Yankee Kinship Terminology: a Problem in Componential Analysis'. In Hammel (1965).

GOODENOUGH, W. H. (1970), *Description and Comparison in Cultural Anthropology*, Chicago: Aldine.

GREENBAUM, S. (1969), *Studies in English Adverbial Usage*, London: Longmans.

GREGORY, MICHAEL (1967), 'Aspects of Varieties Differentiation', *Journal of Linguistics*, 3. 177–98.

GRICE, H. P. (1968), 'The Logic of Conversation'. Unpublished mimeo, University of California, Berkeley.

GUIRAUD, PIERRE (1955), *La Sémantique*, Paris: Presses Universitaires.

HAJIČOVÁ, EVA (1972), 'Some Remarks on Presuppositions', *Prague Bulletin of Mathematical Linguistics*, 17. 11–22.

HALLIDAY, M. A. K. (1961), 'Categories of the Theory of Grammar', *Word*, 17. 241–92.

HALLIDAY, M. A. K. (1967/8), 'Notes on Transitivity and Theme in English', *Journal of Linguistics*, 3. 37–81; 3. 199–244; and 4. 179–215.

HALLIDAY, M. A. K. (1970), 'Language Structure and Language Function'. In Lyons (1970b), 140–65.

HAMMEL, E. A. (ed.) (1965), *Formal Semantic Analysis*. Special Publication of *American Anthropologist*, 67.

HARRIS, Z. S. (1951), *Methods in Structural Linguistics*, Chicago: University of Chicago Press. Reprinted as *Structural Linguistics*, 1961.

HAYAKAWA, S. I. (1964), *Language in Thought and Action*, 2nd edition, New York: Harcourt, Brace.

HAYAKAWA, S. I. (ed.) (1954), *Language, Meaning, and Maturity*, New York: Harper & Row.

HAYES, J. R. (1970), *Cognition and the Development of Language*, New York: Wiley.

HJELMSLEV, LOUIS (1953), *Prolegomena to a Theory of Language*, translated from the Danish (1943) by Francis J. Whitfield, Bloomington, Ind.: Indiana University Press.

HORN, LAURENCE R. (1969), 'A Presuppositional Analysis of *Only* and *Even*'. In Binnick et al. (eds.), 98–107.

HOUSEHOLDER, F. W., and SAPORTA, S. (1962), *Problems of Lexicography*, Bloomington, Ind.: Indiana University Press.

IKEGAMI, Y. (1969), *The Semological Structure of the English Verbs of Motion*, Tokyo: Sanseido.

JACKENDOFF, R. S. (1968), 'Quantifiers in English', *Foundations of Language*, 4. 422–42.

JACKENDOFF, R. S. (1969), 'An Interpretive Theory of Negation', *Foundations of Language*, 5. 218–41.

JACKENDOFF, R. S. (1972), *Semantic Interpretation in Generative Grammar*, Cambridge, Mass.: M.I.T. Press.

JACOBS, R. A., and ROSENBAUM, P. S. (eds.) (1970), *Readings in English Transformational Grammar*, Waltham, Mass.: Blaisdell.

JAKOBSON, R. (1960), 'Linguistics and Poetics'. In Sebeok, T.A. (ed.), *Style in Language*, Cambridge, Mass.: M.I.T. Press.

JESPERSEN, O. (1909–49), *A Modern English Grammar on Historical Principles*, 7 volumes, Copenhagen: Munksgaard, reprinted London: Allen & Unwin, 1954.

KARLSEN, ROLF (1959), *Studies in the Connection of Clauses in Current English: Zero, Ellipsis, and Explicit Form*, Bergen: Eides.

KARTTUNEN, L. (1971), 'Implicative Verbs', *Language*, 47. 340–58.

KATZ, J. J. (1964a), 'Mentalism in Linguistics', *Language*, 40. 124–37.

KATZ, J. J. (1964b), 'Analyticity and Contradiction in Natural Language'. In Fodor and Katz (1964), 519–43.

KATZ, J. J. (1966), *The Philosophy of Language*, New York and London: Harper & Row.

KATZ, J. J. (1970), 'Interpretative Semantics versus Generative Semantics', *Linguistic Inquiry*, 2. 313–32.

KATZ, J. J. (1972), *Semantic Theory*, New York: Harper & Row.

KATZ, J. J., and FODOR, J. A. (1963), 'The Structure of a Semantic Theory', *Language*, 39. 170–210.

KATZ, J. J., and POSTAL, P. M. (1964), *An Integrated Theory of Linguistic Descriptions*, Cambridge, Mass.: M.I.T. Press.

KEENAN, E. L. (1971), 'Two Kinds of Presupposition in Natural Language'. In Fillmore and Langendoen (1971), 45–54.

KIEFER, F. (ed.) (1969), *Studies in Syntax and Semantics*, Dordrecht: Reidel.

KIPARSKY, P., and KIPARSKY, C. (1970), ' "Fact" '. In Bierwisch and Heidolph (1970), 143–73.

KORZYBSKI, A. (1933), *Science and Sanity: An Introduction to Non-Aristotelian Systems and General Semantics*, Lancaster, Pa.: International Non-Aristotelian Library, 4th edition, 1958.

KOZIOL, H. (1969), *Grundzüge der Englischen Semantik*, Vienna: Braumüller.

LAKOFF, G. (1968), 'Instrumental Adverbs and the Concept of Deep Structure', *Foundations of Language*, 4. 4–29.

LAKOFF, G. (1969), 'On Derivational Constraints'. In Binnick et al. (1969), 117–39.

LAKOFF, G. (1970), *Linguistics and Natural Logic*, Ann Arbor: Phonetics Laboratory, University of Michigan. Revised version in *Synthese*, 22 (1971), 151–271.

LAKOFF, G. (1971), 'On Generative Semantics'. In Steinberg, D. D. and Jakobovits, L. A. (eds.) (1971), *Semantics, an Interdisciplinary*

Reader, Urbana, Ill.: University of Illinois Press; Cambridge: Cambridge University Press.

LAKOFF, G. (1973), 'Hedges and Meaning Criteria'. In McDavid, R. and Duckert, A. R. (eds.), *Lexicography in English*, New York: New York Academy of Sciences.

LAMB, SYDNEY, M. (1964), 'The Sememic Approach to Structural Semantics', *American Anthropologist*, 66.3 (Part 2). 37–64.

LAMB, SYDNEY M. (1965), 'Kinship Terminology and Linguistic Structure'. In Hammel (1965).

LEECH, G. N. (1969a), *A Linguistic Guide to English Poetry*, London: Longmans.

LEECH, G. N. (1969b), *Towards a Semantic Description of English*, London: Longmans.

LEECH, G. N. (1970), 'On the Theory and Practice of Semantic Testing', *Lingua*, 24. 343–64.

LEECH, G. N. (1971), *Meaning and the English Verb*, London: Longmans.

LEECH, G. N., and PEPICELLO, W. J. (1972), 'Semantic versus Factual Knowledge: an Experimental Approach'. Published in *Papers from the Symposium on Limiting the Domain of Linguistics*, 1972, Milwaukee: Linguistics Department, University of Wisconsin-Milwaukee.

LEHRER, ADRIENNE (1969), 'Semantic Cuisine', *Journal of Linguistics* 5, 39–55.

LEHRER, ADRIENNE (1971), 'Semantics: an Overview', *Linguistic Reporter*, 13 (Supplement 27). 13–23.

LENNEBERG, E. H. (1962), 'The Relation of Language to the Formation of Concepts', *Synthese*, 14. 103–9.

LENNEBERG, E. H., and ROBERTS, J. M. (1956), *The Language of Experience, a Study in Methodology*, Indiana Publications in Anthropology and Linguistics, 22. Bloomington, Ind.: Indiana University Press.

LOUNSBURY, F. G. (1956), 'A Semantic Analysis of Pawnee Kinship Usage', *Language*, 32. 158–94.

LOUNSBURY, F. G. (1964a), 'The Structural Analysis of Kinship Semantics'. In H. G. Lunt (ed.), *Proceedings of the IXth International Congress of Linguists*, Mouton: The Hague.

LOUNSBURY, F. G. (1964b), 'A Formal Account of Crow- and Omaha-type Kinship Terminologies'. In Goodenough, W. H. (ed.), *Explorations in Cultural Anthropology*, New York: McGraw Hill.

LOUNSBURY, F. G. (1965), 'Another View of Trobriand Kinship Categories'. In Hammel (1956).

LOUNSBURY, F. G. (1969), 'On Relativism and Kinship'. In Hook,

Sidney (ed.), *Language and Philosophy: a Symposium*, New York: New York University Press. Part I: 'Language and Culture', 3–29.

LYAS, COLIN (ed.) (1971), *Philosophy and Linguistics*, London: Macmillan.

LYONS, JOHN (1963), *Structural Semantics*, Oxford: Blackwell.

LYONS, JOHN (1966), 'Firth's Theory of "Meaning"'. In Bazell, C. E. et al. (ed.), *In Memory of J. R. Firth*.

LYONS, JOHN (1968), *Introduction to Theoretical Linguistics*, Cambridge University Press.

LYONS, JOHN (1970a), *Chomsky*, London: Fontana.

LYONS, JOHN (ed.) (1970b), *New Horizons in Linguistics*, London: Penguin.

MCCAWLEY, J. D. (1968a), 'The Role of Semantics in a Grammar'. In Bach and Harms (1968).

MCCAWLEY, J. D. (1968b), 'Lexical Insertion in a Transformational Grammar without Deep Structure'. In Darden, B. J., et al. (ed.) (1968), *Papers from the Fourth Regional Meeting of the Chicago Linguistic Society*, Linguistics Department, University of Chicago.

MCCAWLEY, J. D. (1970a), 'Where do Noun Phrases Come From?'. In Jacobs and Rosenbaum (1970).

MCCAWLEY, J. D. (1970b), 'English as a *VSO* Language', *Language*, 46. 286–99.

MCNEILL, D. (1970), *The Acquisition of Language: the Study of Developmental Psycholinguistics*, New York: Harper & Row.

MALINOWSKI, B. (1935), 'The Problem of Meaning in Primitive Languages'. Supplement I to Ogden and Richards.

MALINOWSKI, B. (1935), *Coral Gardens and their Magic*, Vol. II: 'The Language of Magic and Gardening', London: Allen.

MARCHAND, HANS (1969), *Categories and Types of English Word Formation*, 2nd edition, Munich: Beck.

MATTHEWS, P. H. (1972), Review of Jacobs and Rosenbaum (1970), *Journal of Linguistics*, 8. 125–36.

MORGAN, JERRY (1969), 'On the Treatment of Presupposition in Transformational Grammar'. In Binnick et al. (1969).

MORRIS, CHARLES W. (1955), *Signs, Language and Behavior*, Englewood Cliffs, N.J.: Prentice-Hall.

MORRIS, DESMOND (1967), *The Naked Ape*, London: Cape. (Reprinted as Corgi Book, 1969.)

NIDA, E. A. (1964), *Towards a Science of Translating*, Leiden: Brill.

OGDEN, C. K. (1932), *Opposition*, London: Kegan Paul.

OGDEN, C. K., and RICHARDS, I. A. (1923), *The Meaning of Meaning*, 8th edition, 1946, London: Routledge.

OLSHEWSKY, T. M. (ed.) (1969), *Problems in the Philosophy of Language*. New York: Holt, Rinehart.

ORWELL, GEORGE (1961), 'Politics and the English Language'. In *Collected Essays*, 2nd edition, London: Secker & Warburg. (First published 1946.)

OSGOOD, C. E., SUCI, G. J., and TANNENBAUM, P. H. (1957), *The Measurement of Meaning*, 2nd edition, Urbana: University of Illinois Press, 1967.

ÖHMAN, SUZANNE (1953), 'Theories of the "Linguistic Field" ', *Word*, 9. 123–34.

PETÖFI, J. S. (1971), '*Generativity' and Text-Grammar*, Gothenburg Papers in Theoretical Linguistics, 9.

POSTAL, P. M. (1969), 'Anaphoric Islands'. In Binnick et al. (1969).

POSTAL, P. M. (1971a), *Cross-Over Phenomena*, New York: Holt, Rinehart.

POSTAL, P. M. (1971b), 'On the Surface Verb "Remind" '. In Fillmore and Langendoen.

QUINE, W. V. (1951), *Mathematical Logic*, Revised edition, New York: Harper & Row.

QUINE, W. V. (1953), 'The Problem of Meaning in Linguistics'. In *From a Logical Point of View*, Cambridge, Mass.: Harvard University Press.

QUIRK, RANDOLPH, GREENBAUM, S., LEECH, G. N., and SVARTVIK, J. (1972), *A Grammar of Contemporary English*, London: Longman; New York: Seminar Press.

REICHENBACH, HANS (1966), *Elements of Symbolic Logic*, New York: The Free Press (First edition, 1947.)

ROBBIN, JOEL W. (1969), *Mathematical Logic: a First Course*, New York: Benjamin.

ROSS, J. R. (1970), 'On Declarative Sentences'. In Jacobs and Rosenbaum (1970).

ROSS, J. R., and LAKOFF, G. (1967), 'Is Deep Structure Necessary?', unpublished paper.

SAMPSON, GEOFFREY (1970), 'On the Need for a Phonological Base', *Language*, 46. 586–626.

SAPIR, E. (1944), 'Grading: a Study in Semantics', *Philosophy of Science*, 2. 93–116. (Reprinted in Sapir 1949.)

SAPIR, E. (1949), *Selected Writings in Language, Culture, and Personality* (edited by D. G. Mandelbaum), Berkeley: University of California Press.

SAUSSURE, F. DE (1916), *Cours de Linguistique Générale*, English translation by Wade Baskin, *Course in General Linguistics*, New York: Philosophical Library, 1959.

SCHAFF, ADAM (1962), *Introduction to Semantics*, English translation by Olgierd Wojtasiewicz, Warsaw: Państwowe Wydawnictwo Naukowe; New York: Pergamon.

SEARLE, JOHN R. (1969), *Speech Acts: An Essay in the Philosophy of Language*, Cambridge: Cambridge University Press.

SNIDER, J. G., and OSGOOD, C. E. (1969), *Semantic Differential Technique: a Sourcebook*, Chicago: Aldine.

SPENCE, N. C. W. (1961), 'Linguistic Fields, Conceptual Systems, and the Weltbild', *Transactions of the Philological Society*, 87–106.

STAATS, A. W. (1968), *Language, Learning and Cognition*, New York: Holt, Rinehart.

STEINER, GEORGE (1967), *Language and Silence: Essays, 1958–66*, London: Faber.

STERN, GUSTAV (1931), *Meaning and Change of Meaning*, reprinted by Indiana University Press, Bloomington, Ind. 1965.

TELLER, PAUL (1969), 'Some Discussion and Extension of Manfred Bierwisch's work on German Adjectivals', *Foundations of Language*, 5. 185–217.

TRIER, JOST (1931), *Der Deutsche Wortschatz im Sinnbezirk des Verstandes*, Heidelberg.

TYLER, STEPHEN A. (ed.) (1969), *Cognitive Anthropology*, New York: Holt, Rinehart.

ULLMANN, S. (1951), *Words and their Use*, London: Muller.

ULLMANN, S. (1957), *Principles of Semantics*, 2nd edition, Glasgow: Jackson; Oxford: Blackwell.

ULLMANN, S. (1962), *Semantics: an Introduction to the Science of Meaning*, Oxford: Blackwell.

WALDRON, R. (1967), *Sense and Sense Development*, London: Deutsch.

WEINREICH, U. (1958), 'Travels in Semantic Space', *Word*, 14. 346–66.

WEINREICH, U. (1962), 'Lexicographic Definition in Descriptive Semantics'. In Householder and Saporta (1962).

WEINREICH, U. (1963), 'On the Semantic Structure of Language'. In Greenberg, J. (ed.) (1963), *Universals of Language*, Cambridge, Mass.: M.I.T. Press.

WEINREICH, U. (1964), 'Webster's Third: a Critique of its Semantics', *International Journal of American Linguistics*, 30. 405–9.

WEINREICH, U. (1966), 'Explorations in Semantic Theory'. In Sebeok, T. A. (ed.) (1966), *Current Trends in Linguistics*, Vol. III., The Hague: Mouton.

WEISGERBER, J. L. (1953–4), *Vom Weltbild der Deutschen Sprache*, 2 vols., Düsseldorf: Schwann.

WHORF, B. L. (1956), *Language, Thought, and Reality* (edited by John B. Carroll) New York: Wiley.

WIMSATT, W. K. (1954), *The Verbal Icon*, Lexington, Ky.: University of Kentucky Press.

WITTGENSTEIN, L. (1953), *Philosophical Investigations*, Oxford: Blackwell; New York: Macmillan.

YOUNGREN, W. H. (1971), *Semantics, Linguistics, and Literary Criticism*, New York: Random House.

Index

(Major or defining page references are printed in **bold type**)

More about Penguins and Pelicans

Penguinews, which appears every month, contains details of all the new books issued by Penguins as they are published. From time to time it is supplemented by *Penguins in Print*, which is a complete list of all titles available. (There are some five thousand of these.)

A specimen copy of *Penguinews* will be sent to you free on request. For a year's issues (including the complete lists) please send 50p if you live in the British Isles, or 75p if you live elsewhere. Just write to Dept EP, Penguin Books Ltd, Harmondsworth, Middlesex, enclosing a cheque or postal order, and your name will be added to the mailing list.

In the U.S.A.: For a complete list of books available from Penguin in the United States write to Dept CS, Penguin Books Inc., 7110 Ambassador Road, Baltimore, Maryland 21207.

In Canada: For a complete list of books available from Penguin in Canada write to Penguin Books Canada Ltd, 41 Steelcase Road West, Markham, Ontario.

a Pelican Original

New Horizons in Linguistics

Edited by John Lyons

'The faculty of articulated speech', as Darwin once wrote, 'does not in itself offer any insuperable objection to the belief that man has developed from some lower form.' Perhaps not: but it makes a mighty big difference.

In recent years the scientific study of language has been pushed to a point where its findings necessarily interest philosophers, psychologists, sociologists, anthropologists and others concerned in any way with words and their meaning. This collection of essays by seventeen British, German, and American experts in various fields of linguistics forms a running report on the directions being pursued today in each branch of the discipline. These outlines of recent research and new theories in phonology, morphology, syntax, and semantics provide a highly authoritative introduction for first-year students and inhabitants of neighbouring intellectual worlds.

However, though Professor Lyons has not assembled a mere primer of linguistics, any reader who can regard such words as 'phonemic groups' or 'morphemic segments' as stimulants rather than narcotics will find this an intriguing study of a subject which is rightly attracting more and more interest.